Russia and the West from Alexander to Putin

Honor in International Relations

Since Russia has reemerged as a global power, its foreign policies have come under close scrutiny. In *Russia and the West from Alexander to Putin*, Andrei P. Tsygankov identifies honor as the key concept by which Russia's international relations are determined. He argues that Russia's interests in acquiring power, security, and welfare are filtered through this cultural belief and that different conceptions of honor provide an organizing framework that produces policies of cooperation, defensiveness, and assertiveness in relation to the West. Using ten case studies spanning a period from the early nineteenth century to the present day – including the Holy Alliance, the Triple Entente, and the Russia–Georgia war – Tsygankov's theory suggests that when Russia perceives its sense of honor to be recognized, it cooperates with the Western nations; without such a recognition it pursues independent policies either defensively or assertively.

ANDREI P. TSYGANKOV is Professor of International Relations and Political Science at San Francisco State University.

Russia and the West from Alexander to Putin

Honor in International Relations

Andrei P. Tsygankov

CAMBRIDGE
UNIVERSITY PRESS

University Printing House, Cambridge CB2 8BS, United Kingdom

Published in the United States of America by Cambridge University Press, New York

Cambridge University Press is part of the University of Cambridge.

It furthers the University's mission by disseminating knowledge in the pursuit of education, learning and research at the highest international levels of excellence.

www.cambridge.org
Information on this title: www.cambridge.org/9781107668034

© Andrei P. Tsygankov 2012

First published 2012
First paperback edition 2014

A catalogue record for this publication is available from the British Library

Library of Congress Cataloguing in Publication data

Tsygankov, Andrei P., 1964–
Russia and the West from Alexander to Putin : honor in international relations / Andrei P. Tsygankov.
    p.   cm.
Includes bibliographical references and index.
ISBN 978-1-107-02552-3 (hardback)
1. Russia – Foreign relations – Western countries.   2. Russia (Federation) – Foreign relations – Western countries.   3. Honor – Political aspects – Russia – History.   4. Honor – Political aspects – Russia (Federation) – History.   I. Title.
JZ1615.T77   2012
327.470182'1–dc23   2012000291

ISBN 978-1-107-02552-3 Hardback
ISBN 978-1-107-66803-4 Paperback

"In the life of states just as in that of private individuals there are moments when one must forget all but the defense of his honor."

Tsar Alexander II,
as cited in Wohlforth, "Honor as Interest"

Contents

List of Figures and Tables

Figures

Tables

Preface

This book grew out of my desire to develop the argument I introduced in the textbook *Russia's Foreign Policy: Change and Continuity in National Identity* (Rowman & Littlefield, 2006), which covers Russia's international behavior from Mikhail Gorbachev to Vladimir Putin. Encouraging reactions from colleagues, students, and members of the policy community, augmented by my own curiosity about Russian history, prompted me to refine my theory by testing it against a longer range of historical cases.

The result is a book with an explicitly developed theory of Russian-Western relations across two centuries and one that is centered on the concept of national honor. Rather than narrowly associating honor with international prestige or reputation, as some international relations theories do, I have tried to uncover what Russians themselves understand to be their honor and honorable foreign policy. I have found that Russia's idea of honor, although continuing to shape the country's foreign policy, reaches back to the premodern era and predates the system of nation-states. Because Russia's behavior originates from a culturally distinct source, its foreign policy has meaning that differs from that of other members of the international system. By studying such meaning, we have an opportunity to develop a rich understanding of a particular policy's source and future direction.

Through personal correspondence and conversations and through reading portions of this book, many friends and colleagues have contributed their support and ideas for improvement. Among them, I should like to especially mention Sanjoy Banerjee, David Foglesong, Pavel Tsygankov, and Matthew Tarver-Wahlquist. For financial support, I wish to thank IREX and San Francisco State University, which provided me with summer grants to conduct library-based research and interviews with Russian experts. Furthermore, I thank my students for their interest and feedback. I alone am responsible for the book's content and the remaining errors.

Parts of several chapters draw on my previously published book *Russia's Foreign Policy* and the article "Dueling Honors: Power, Identity and the Russia-Georgia Divide" (co-authored with Matthew Tarver-Wahlquist), *Foreign Policy Analysis*, vol. 5, no. 4 (2009). I thank the publishers for permission to use these materials in the book.

At Cambridge University Press, I am especially grateful to John Haslam for his steady support of the project and valuable editorial suggestions. Comments and constructive criticisms by anonymous reviewers have assisted me in improving the book, and I hope the final version will satisfy some of their expectations.

Finally, I owe a special debt to my family for their love and support. I dedicate this book to my son Pasha who at the age of eight is beginning to express interest in the country from which his family originates. Pasha wanted me to write a book "about good Russian tsars." Although this book will be only partly satisfactory on that account, I hope that it is a step in the right direction.

In transliterating names from Russian, I have used "y" to denote "ы"; "'" to denote "ь" and "ъ"; "yu" to denote "ю"; "ya" to denote "я"; "i" to denote "й" and "ий"; "iyi" to denote double "и"; "e" to denote "э"; "kh" to denote "х"; "zh" to denote "ж"; "ts" to denote "ц"; "ch" to denote "ч"; "sh" to denote "ш"; and "sch" to denote "щ." I have also used "Ye" to distinguish the sound of "e" (such as "Yevropa") in the beginning of a word from that in the middle of a word (such as "vneshnei"). Everywhere, I did not distinguish between "e" and "ë." Spelling is retained in quotations.

1 Introduction

"The student of politics who looks only at patterns of behavior but leaves out the meaning that actors give to their own and to each other's conduct turns into a specialist of shadows."

Robert Legvold[1]

The Question of Russia's International Motives

From a weak and inward-looking nation in the 1990s, Russia has emerged into a power that is increasingly capable of defending its international prestige using available economic and military means. Throughout the 2000s, it has exploited its energy clout to expand Russian business relations abroad and has cemented its military presence in the strategic area of the Caucasus by defeating Georgia's attack on South Ossetia. In a world that is increasingly post-American and post-Western,[2] Russia is likely to remain an influential power in the critically important Eurasian region. Even the unprecedented rise of China does not change the fact that Russia possesses a large arsenal of nuclear weapons, abundant supplies of natural resources, and the longest geographic border in the world. With a seat on the United Nations Security Council and membership in international organizations such as BRIC (Brazil, Russia, India, and China) and the Shanghai Cooperation Organization, Russia will continue to play a prominent role in world affairs. Even though the global financial meltdown in 2008 revealed Russia's economic vulnerability, it did not undermine its capability to export energy to both Europe and Asia.

In recognition of Russia's importance, the United States has attempted to "reset" relations with the Kremlin after years of estrangement under the George W. Bush administration. The European Union is also keenly interested in developing deeper economic and political ties with Moscow. Serious attempts made by the West to improve relations with Russia address a variety of issues, including the stabilization of Afghanistan and the Middle East, nuclear nonproliferation, NATO expansion, missile defense systems, the exploitation of energy reserves in the region, and the future of the former Soviet states.

However, the motives underlying Russia's international behavior remain puzzling to scholars and policy makers alike. Historically, Russia watchers have been divided between those who view its behavior as accommodationist and nonthreatening to the West[3] and those who perceive Russia as a state that is expansionist and does not abide by acceptable international rules.[4] The motives guiding Russia's foreign relations should determine which policy the Western nations advance toward the Eastern power. If Russia's interests and ambitions do not undermine existing international rules, the West is better off trying to engage Russia as an equal contributor in shaping the global system. If, however, Moscow harbors revisionist plans, it may represent a threat to Western interests and must be either contained or fundamentally transformed.

Overview of the Argument

In its systematic exploration of Russia's international behavior, this book takes a long-range perspective, studying the country's relations with Western nations since the early nineteenth century. During the last two centuries, Russia's relations with the West have followed three distinct patterns, which have endured social upheavals and rapidly changing historical circumstances.

The Three Patterns of Russia's Relations with the West

The first pattern – cooperation with Western nations – has its roots in Prince Vladimir's decision to accept Christianity in 988. Having survived two centuries of Mongol domination, Russia sought to strengthen its Christian roots by developing ties with the Holy Roman Empire and, later, joining the Holy League against the Ottoman Empire. Peter the Great tried to improve relations with Europe by sending ambassadors to important Western states and borrowing and adapting their technological achievements. Catherine the Great proclaimed Russia "a European power" and validated that status by continuing to restrain influences of the Ottoman Empire on the European continent. During the first half of the nineteenth century, Russia established the Holy Alliance and joined autocratic Europe in suppressing revolutionary activities on the continent. In the second half of the century, Russia participated in the Three Emperors League with Germany and Austro-Hungary, but then switched allegiances to the coalition of France and Britain – partly to preserve its connection to this increasingly influential part of the West.

The tradition of cooperating with the West continued even during the Soviet era. The Bolsheviks sought recognition by the Western states by championing ideas of peaceful coexistence and then collective security to deter Hitler's Germany. In the 1970s, the Soviet Union signed the Helsinki agreement of the Conference on Security and Cooperation in Europe. Mikhail Gorbachev then built on the agreement to promote human rights and "common human values" in his foreign policy of a "common European home." The dissolution of the Soviet state created conditions for an even stronger engagement with the West, with Russia seeking to capitalize on its similarity with the Western nations in terms of institutions and common threats. The most recent expression of such attempts was Dmitri Medvedev's policy of building "modernization alliances" with Western nations.

In addition to alliances and institution-building, Russia fought multiple wars alongside the West – most prominently, the First Northern War against Sweden (1655–60), the Seven Years War against Prussia (1756–63), the war against Napoleonic France, World Wars I and II, and, more recently, the global war on terror.

The second pattern of Russia's foreign policy is that of defensive reaction to the Western world. When Russian rulers were not successful in achieving their international objectives and did not receive sufficient support for their efforts from the West, they occasionally retreated into periods of relative isolation to gather domestic strength. In the early seventeenth century, after Moscow was defeated by Poland, it did not resume military engagements for another twenty years, when in 1654 Russia annexed Ukraine. In the eighteenth century, Russia used twenty years of neutrality from the war with Sweden to recover from financial and demographic losses. After being defeated in the Crimean War, Russia again pursued the policy of domestic reforms and flexible alliances to recover its lost position in Europe and the Black Sea. The Bolshevik slogan of "peaceful coexistence" contained elements of both cooperation and defensiveness, whereas Stalin's "socialism in one country" was a Soviet version of defensive foreign policy, engaged in to enable recovery from domestic weaknesses brought about by revolution and civil war. That Stalin later sided with Hitler in part reflected the Soviet leader's desire to shield the country against international disturbances and buy more time for internal reforms. After the end of the Cold War, Russia sought to recuperate from the Soviet collapse by maneuvering between the Western nations and China and India.

Finally, Russia is historically known for pursuing policies of assertiveness vis-à-vis the West. Acting from a position of perceived strength, Russia has asserted its interests unilaterally even after Western nations failed to support them. In the seventeenth century, Russia fought many wars with Poland and the Ottoman Empire, seeking control over national borders and to protect Balkan Slavs. In the early eighteenth century Peter the Great defeated Sweden, turning Russia into a great European power. Wars with Turkey continued up to the Crimean War, in which Russia fought against major European states. After recovering domestically, Russia returned to the Balkans and defeated the Turks in 1870s. During the Soviet era, the Bolsheviks initiated the doctrine of "world revolution," thereby challenging the very foundations of the system of states. They acted on this doctrine by launching an assault on Poland in 1920, which the Bolsheviks hoped would undermine European "capitalist" states. During the Cold War, Russia sought to establish its geopolitical presence in Eastern Europe, the Balkans, and northern Iran, acting in direct opposition to the Western nations. The Soviet Union also acted assertively during the Cuban missile crisis in 1962 and when it sent troops to Afghanistan in 1979. More recently, Russia intervened in the Georgia–South Ossetia military conflict despite the United States' and the European Union's warnings against the Kremlin's "bullish" and "revisionist" behavior.

Honor and the Formation of Russia's Foreign Policy

These patterns of international behavior can be understood in terms of Russia's established sense of honor, which can operate both on the individual and societal level. On the individual level, honor is associated with the readiness of the self to preserve its dignity and to fulfill its assumed moral commitments to its relevant social community.[5] Although scholars frequently view human actions as if they were designed to meet rationally determined objectives, beliefs and emotions may define the meaning of an action.[6] Honor constitutes a powerful emotional belief, and historians and theoreticians frequently credit it as important, even decisive, in determining the cause of human interactions.[7] On the societal level, honor may define a country's stake in the international system and its standards of appropriate behavior. Honor defines what is a "good" and "virtuous" course of action in the international society vis-à-vis the relevant other.

Russia's deep cultural connection to the West began when it became a student of Byzantium's faith in 988. Ever since that time Europe has played the role of Russia's "significant other," figuring prominently in domestic debates and creating the context in which Russia's rulers defended their core values.[8] Even when the tsarist system collapsed in the early twentieth century, the supposedly atheist Soviet state preserved – albeit in a sharply disfigured form – the desire to be recognized by the West.[9] Thus Russia's honor has been defined as the honor of being a part of the Western world and defending its core values.

At the same time, Russia's cultural lenses were, and are, different from those of Western nations – formed by distinct historical memory, ties with historic allies, and contemporary challenges.[10] Although Russia is culturally dependent on the West, its emotional and moral well-being has historically depended on relations with its own cultural communities, which are defined as Orthodox Christians, Slavs, ethnic Russians, or those who gravitate to Russia's institutions and share some of Russia's core values. Since the Schism of 1054 and the fall of Byzantium, Russia's rulers have positioned their country as one with its own special interests and cultural characteristics. Located in the middle of Eurasia, Russia has few natural boundaries and has been frequently attacked by outsiders from the Mongols to Napoleon and Hitler. A vast overland empire that follows the Eastern version of Christianity and has constant concerns over border security, Russia has always felt different from the rest of Europe. The fact that Europe's recognition of Russia as one of its own has always been problematic[11] has served to reinforce this identity of "difference" from the West.

The two essential dimensions of Russia's honor – European and local – help explain its relations with the Western nations. The two are dependent on each other, and the dialectics of their relationship is such that Russia may only act on its Europeanness when the West does not principally challenge the distinctive aspects of Russia's honor. Russian rulers have historically sought to be like the West and win its recognition by joining Western alliances or by trying to beat Western nations at their own power game. If the Western nations are great powers, Russia too aspires to such status. If the West demonstrates accomplishments in institution building, economic prosperity, and human rights protection, Russian rulers too are drawn to these accomplishments and attempt to replicate them at home. As long as it feels sufficient recognition and reciprocation from Western capitals, Moscow is prepared to act in concert with its significant other.

However, when the West challenges Russia's distinctiveness and internal sense of honor, Russia tends to adopt either defensive or assertive policy postures. For example, Russia could not act as a confident Western power when its actions were disruptive of its traditionally strong ties with Slavic and Orthodox allies. In the absence of external recognition of its international claims, Russia's pro-Western elites have historically run into opposition from advocates of a more independent foreign policy. Russia's internal confidence reflects both its material power and the perception of power by the ruling elite[12]; it is the degree of that internal confidence in its ability to pursue an independent foreign policy that determines whether Russia chooses a defensive or assertive direction.

If cooperation with Western nations has reflected Russia's sense of honor as loyalty to the West, then defensiveness and assertiveness have frequently been products of the nation's commitments to its historic allies and domestic subjects. Russian rulers have tried hard to pursue policies that would integrate both Western and local commitments. However, that integration has not always been possible, partly because the West has not always been supportive of Russia's aspirations to defend its cultural allies. For example, Nicholas I's assertiveness with regard to the Balkans and Crimea found little support among Western powers and resulted in the Crimean War.

Ethical Implications of the Argument

To argue that honor shapes foreign policy is not to characterize an international behavior as honorable. Rather, it is to draw scholarly attention to the moral and ethical implications a state action entails and to raise the question of responsibility for episodes of misunderstanding and failed cooperation in Russia–West relations.

Examples of such failures abound, and both sides bear responsibility for the clash in perceptions. What Moscow views as successful advancements of its honorable objectives – which have included security, welfare, and independence – Western nations occasionally perceive as unilateralist and revisionist behavior. In the Crimean War, for example, Nicholas I's aim was to force the Sultan to recognize the rights of the Orthodox Christians in Jerusalem and Palestine; however, the European powers interpreted Russia's ambitions as seeking to undermine the Ottoman Empire and, ultimately, to conquer Constantinople. Similarly, whereas the Kremlin assessed the outcome of the war with Georgia in August 2008 as a largely successful defense of ethnic Russians, South Ossetian civilians, and Russia's security objectives in the Caucasus, Western governments overwhelmingly condemned the war as an act of aggression against an independent state. Conversely, what the West sometimes viewed as honorable Russian policy, Moscow not infrequently considered something that compromised its national priorities. From the Holy Alliance to the New Thinking, Russians often have felt they made too many concessions for the purpose of gaining recognition by the Western powers.

It takes both sides to make the Russia–West relationship work. Acting on their perception of honor, Russia's leaders have often failed fully to consider the reaction from the West, as well as Russia's own capacity to initiate and implement a policy. As a result, some Russian policies have been successful and defensible, whereas others have not. The recipe for success in sustaining both Russia's internal and European honor claims is for Moscow to present its values and strategic vision in a way that does not principally contradict those of Western nations. The Western states too have historically demonstrated their dependence on unrealistic expectations and cultural stereotypes with regard to their Eastern neighbor. Their ability to engage Moscow will only be successful when they acknowledge Russia's distinctive values, interests, and right to develop in accordance with its internal perception of honor. To succeed, neither side should define its objectives in terms of superiority over the other.

Alternative Explanations

Theories of international relations based on the structure of the international system often discount the argument that honor serves as a motive of state behavior. Realists have been especially influential in advocating the notion of national interest and rationally defined action as defining factors in world politics. Realism draws our attention to considerations of state power, security, and prestige. Its basic insight that no policy can materialize without due consideration for the existing structure of the international system remains valid and impossible to ignore in understanding Russia's foreign policy. The problem with realism is not that it focuses on state power, security, and prestige, but that in so doing it underestimates the role of culture and ideas in international interactions. This book does not neglect realist theories, but argues for combining both realism and constructivism.

Admittedly, my way of combining realist and constructivist insights lies within the framework of social constructivism,[13] because a mutually satisfactory synthesis of the two theoretical schools would be impossible. I take factors of power and security seriously, but do not view their influence as decisive in determining foreign policy. For instance, the possession of extensive material resources may have the dangerous effect of reinforcing an assertive policy mood, but it does not have an independent causal effect. Rather, what determines Russia's foreign policy is the national ideal of honorable behavior augmented by its available material capabilities.

As a nation with a long-established sense of honor, Russia is a good case to demonstrate the limitations of international-system-based theories. Its honor myths reach back to Russia's premodern foundations – Orthodox Christianity and its Slavic cultural inheritance – which predate the very system of nation-states on which realists base their analysis. Russia's own cultural lenses are therefore at least as important in understanding its actions as the incentives coming from the international system. Even when Russia's actions seem similar to the behavior of other members of the system, they originate from a culturally distinct source and can have a different meaning. Moreover, Russia's traditional concept of honor has mutated in response to domestic and external developments, thereby gaining diverse and complex meanings.

The question then becomes whether an understanding of Russia's cultural foundations is necessary to analyze and predict its international policy. Whereas realists prefer to focus on behavioral patterns as driven by the structure of the international system, more socially sensitive accounts argue for the importance of understanding Russia's indigenous system of perception. As a leading scholar of Russia's foreign policy, Robert Legvold, wrote twenty years ago, "The student of politics who looks only at patterns of behavior but leaves out the meaning that actors give to their own and to each other's conduct turns into a specialist of shadows."[14]

Ignoring such internally shaped meanings comes at the price of misunderstanding Russia. For example, by assuming that states are risk averse, defensive realists[15] underestimate the cultural basis of Russia's assertive international behavior, such as that exemplified by the Soviet Union after World War II. In contrast, offensive and neoclassical realists[16] tend to overestimate Russia's propensity to engage in risky behavior for the purpose of maximizing international power and prestige. Presenting Russia as a potentially revisionist power without considering domestic ideas that guide its foreign policy may lead to a failure to understand the nation's innovations, such as Mikhail Gorbachev's New Thinking, or to anticipate Russia's attempts and gestures toward accommodation with Western nations. Ignoring domestic visions of honor may lead to misunderstandings about the sources and direction of Russia's foreign policy.

Case Selection and Organization

This book seeks to demonstrate change and continuity in Russia's foreign policy as shaped by considerations of state honor. To accomplish that aim, I select cases across historical eras and patterns of Russia's relations with the West. Cases of cooperation with the West include the Holy Alliance (1815–53) that was established soon after the defeat of Napoleon and lasted until the Crimean War; the Triple Entente (1907–17), the alliance of Russia with France and Britain against the rising threat of Germany; collective security (1933–39), Soviet efforts to respond to Hitler's growing international ambitions; and the war on terror (2001–5) that brought Russia and the West closer to each other in the post–9/11 world. Cases of defensiveness include the post-Crimean concentration or the recueillement (1856–71); Soviet peaceful coexistence (1921–39), the international corollary of Bolshevik efforts to "normalize" postrevolutionary politics; and the containment of NATO expansion after the Cold War (1995–2000). Finally, cases of assertiveness are the Crimean War (1853–6), the early Cold War (1946–9), and the Russia–Georgia War in August 2008.

These cases are sufficiently diverse to highlight both enduring components and dramatic changes within Russia's vision of honor and to provide a comprehensive and historically sensitive interpretation of Russia's relations with Western nations. They also serve as a basis for challenging realist accounts of state behavior and for formulating an alternative theory of foreign policy formation that incorporates insights from both realism and social constructivism. A good foreign policy theory should not only formulate a *cause–effect relationship* by identifying the most prominent social forces or variables that drive an international decision but also establish a *meaningful context* in which state leaders act and seek to achieve their objectives. Because I aim to develop a context-sensitive theory, I discuss realist explanations of Russia's international behavior as pertinent to individual state strategies in chapters relating to each of these cases.

The book is organized into four parts. Part I, Theory, accomplishes three aims. First, it reviews diverse interpretations of honor in international relations theory, from classical realism to social constructivism, and their application to foreign policy. Second, it reconstructs and analyzes Russia's complex notion of honor in both historical and contemporary settings. Third, it establishes the three patterns of Russia's relations with the West and proposes a framework for explaining and evaluating their change and continuity.

Parts II–IV analyze the cooperative, defensive, and assertive patterns in Russia–West relations, respectively. Beginning with the study of the Holy Alliance, each chapter reviews the record of Russia's foreign policy performance, proposes its interpretation from the honor perspective, considers contributions made by realist theories, and assesses the effectiveness of individual international strategies. The concluding chapter summarizes the main findings of the book. It also suggests some ways of employing the theory of honor-based constructivism for understanding the behavior of twenty-first-century powers outside Russia.

Notes

1 As quoted in Snyder, "Science and Sovietology: Bridging the Methods Gap in Soviet Foreign Policy Studies," 173.
2 Zakaria, *The Post-American World*; Barma, Ratner, and Weber, "The World without West"; Tsygankov, "Russia in the Post-Western World."

3 See, for example, Bowker, *Russia, America and the Islamic World*; Trenin, *Getting Russia Right*; Trenin, *Post-Imperium*; Mankoff, *Russian Foreign Policy*; Tsygankov, *Russia's Foreign Policy*; Larson and Shevchenko, "Status Seekers."

4 See, for example, Pipes, "Is Russia Still an Enemy?"; Ambrosio, *Challenging America's Global Preeminence*; Bugajski, *Expanding Russia*; Lucas, *The New Cold War*; Kanet, ed., *A Resurgent Russia and the West*.

5 Bowman, *Honor*, p. 4.

6 For scholarship on beliefs and emotions in international politics, see Klein, "The Humiliation Dynamic: An Overview"; Steinberg, "Shame and Humiliation in the Cuban Missile Crisis"; Crawford, "The Passion of World Politics"; Harkavy, "Defeat, National Humiliation, and the Revenge Motif in International Politics"; Haas, *The Ideological Origins of Great Power Politics*; Saurette, "You Dissin Me?"; Lebow, *A Cultural Theory of International Relations*; Löwenheim and Heimann, "Revenge in International Politics"; Fattah and Fierke, "A Clash of Emotions"; and Mercer, "Emotional Beliefs."

7 Offer, "Going to War in 1914"; Mercer, *Reputation and International Politics*; Wohlforth, "Honor as Interest in Russian Decisions for War, 1600–1995"; Lebow, *The Tragic Vision of Politics*; Kagan, *On the Origins of War and the Preservation of Peace*, p. 8; Donelan, *Honor in Foreign Policy*; Markey, "Prestige and the Origins of War"; Markey, "The Prestige Motive in International Relations"; Joshi, *Honor in International Relations*, pp. 2–3; Tsygankov and Tarver-Wahlquist, "Duelling Honors."

8 Neumann, *Russia and the Idea of Europe*.

9 English, *Russia and the Idea of the West*; Ringmar, "The Recognition Game."

10 The point about the significance of both international and domestic developments in the construction of Russia's system of perception is well made in Hopf, *Social Construction of International Politics*.

11 Neumann, *Uses of the Other*; Malia, *Russia under Western Eyes*.

12 For details of elites' calculations of Russia's power, see Wohlforth, "The Perception of Power" and Neumann, "Russia's Standing as a Great Power, 1494–1815."

13 International relations scholars have proposed to compensate for shortcomings of systemic rationalist theories by developing an approach that combines insights from realism with those of constructivism. The approach was formulated in debating the article by Samuel Barkin "Realist Constructivism," in which he proposed a new conceptualization of the relationship between power and ideas, referring to it as "constructivist realism." For additional efforts to bridge material and nonmaterial factors, see Jackson and Nelson, eds. "Constructivist Realism or Realist Constructivism? A Forum"; Jackson and Nelson, "Paradigmatic Faults in International Relations Theory"; Sorensen, "The Case for Combining Material Forces and Ideas in the Study of IR."

14 Snyder, "Science and Sovietology."

15 Jervis, "Cooperation under Security Dilemma"; Van Evera, *Causes of War*.

16 Kennedy, *The Rise and Fall of Great Powers*; Mearsheimer, *The Tragedy of Great Power Politics*; Wohlforth, "Unipolarity, Status Competition, and Great Power War."

Part I

Theory

Honor in International Relations

"As long as there are States, so there will be national pride, and nothing can be more warranted."

Emile Durkheim[1]

Although scholars frequently view human actions as if they were designed to meet rationally determined objectives, the world is full of examples of what can hardly be described as a rational behavior. Cognitive beliefs and human emotions expressing attachments, anger, and frustration are at least as significant in informing social interactions. Because humans are social beings, they can only be understood in relevant social settings and with the use of appropriate ethical categories. Beliefs and emotions define the meaning of actions that on the surface may seem rationally calculated.

Defining Honor

One powerful emotion underlying human interactions is honor. Honor is associated with the readiness of the self to preserve its dignity and its assumed commitments to the relevant social community.[2] Historians and theoreticians frequently credit honor as important, even decisive, in determining human interactions. If moral purpose is essential for a community's existence,[3] then an international community too must be shaped by moral considerations and obligations to honor them. The world's institutional arrangements, as well as alliances and power conquests, need to be understood in terms of their members' social commitments. As a student of conflict acknowledges, pursuing and satisfying honor may be more difficult than achieving material gains,[4] and "the reader may be surprised by how small a role . . . considerations of practical utility and material gain, and even ambition for power itself, play in bringing on wars, and how often some aspect of honor is decisive."[5]

Which aspect of honor may be decisive depends on the social situation. A commonly used typology includes the "inner" and the "outer" aspects of honor.[6] Inner honor refers to an individual's assessment – relating to notions of "integrity," "veracity," and "character" – of his or her obligation to a moral community. It pertains to children who learn to keep secrets "on their honor," as well as to soldiers, whose notion of military honor includes a commitment to defend one group (nation) from potential attacks by others. Over time, through service to the community, inner honor also gains qualities of pride and dignity.[7] Outer honor is linked more explicitly to assessment by others and is defined as "reputation" or "good name."[8] If one's reputation is besmirched, the pursuit of outer honor may lead its aspirants to competitive and even mutually destructive behavior. Outer honor then is viewed in exclusive and hierarchical terms: "when everyone attains equal honor, then there is no honor for anyone."[9] It is the honor that underlies great power competition and imperial rivalry.[10] In sum, "honor requires trueness to one's word when given on one's honor; readiness to defend one's home, and the right of oneself and one's group, and to avenge violations."[11]

Over time, honor has attained several distinctive meanings. The Athenians associated it with citizenship and civic obligations, but honor later became appropriated by the aristocracy, gaining hierarchical qualities. The Renaissance revived the notion of civil humanism, encouraging more egalitarian ties among individuals.[12] Capitalism broke down old particularistic barriers in Western societies and – accompanied by the rise of democratic nationalism – established the idea of national honor. Although it destroyed the medieval European hero,[13] the new capitalist era did not destroy a reformist zeal, but expanded its domestic boundaries.[14] As Geoffrey Best described the process,

Nationalism and democracy marched together through the nineteenth century to harden this creed and to broaden its base, so that what had previously been a precise code for noblemen became a popular code for patriots: "the nationalization of honor" having among its products the concept of "national honor," the importance of protecting or avenging it, the extension to the nation as a whole of the old personal preference of death to dishonor, and so on.[15]

It is during this transition to capitalism that honor became associated with defending nations, rather than dynastic political units, from external threats.

Honor in Realist Thought

Realist thinkers responded to this transition to capitalism and nation-state by putting forward the concepts of national interest and power as the ultimate justifications of international behavior. In their account, the notion of honor has become either indistinguishable from or secondary to that of rational interest.

Classical Realism

Realism is known for its sharp separation of rules guiding the domestic community from the realities of international politics. Thucydides was the first to defend domestic civic virtue from external interferences and to stress the absence of moral regulations in the world of nations that did not follow Greek ideals. He did not associate honor with power or profit, as some of his successors did, and was fearful of wartime's corrupting effects on the civic bonds within the Athenian community.[16] Nor did he support the position of Athenian imperialism as expressed in Melian dialogue: "whatever one is mighty, he rules. And we neither laid down this law nor are we the first to have used it as laid down ... if you become as powerful as we are, you would do the same."[17] Yet Thucydides clearly supported the position that war is permitted when a country is "forced to advance our dominion to what it is, out of the nature of the thing itself."[18]

This perspective on honor as in need of protection from external upheavals was alien to modern thinkers such as Niccolo Machiavelli and Thomas Hobbes. Living in the age of collapsing religious authority and the emergence of independent secular states, they both sought to subjugate the domestic community and its social virtues to the objectives of the state. Machiavelli did not hold civic community in high esteem, linking honor directly to the Prince and his expansionist activities. Unlike Thucydides, Machiavelli felt threatened by domestic rather than foreign developments. He was one of the first modern thinkers to associate honor with the glory of foreign conquests:

We are lovers of glory.... We seek to rule or at least to avoid being oppressed. In either case we want more for ourselves and our states than just material welfare. Because other states with similar aims thereby threaten us, we prepare ourselves for expansion. Because our fellow citizens threaten us if we do not allow them to satisfy their ambition or to release their political energies, we expand. In so doing, we create a state of war – insecurity abroad as a way of mitigating, but never successfully eliminating, insecurity at home.[19]

Hobbes too associated political order with the state only and viewed pride and "social passions" as forces of destruction.[20] "Before the names of Just and Unjust can have place, there must be some coercive Power."[21] He defined honor and morality in relation to state interests. As a scholar of realism commented, "good or bad was thus reduced to necessity and utility."[22]

Jean-Jacques Rousseau revived the notion of civic honor by introducing the ideas of constitutionalism and the just social contract.[23] The gradual consolidation of democratic institutions in the nineteenth century strengthened the thinking of those who, like Edward Carr, Hans Morgenthau, and Raymond Aron, sought to preserve political accomplishments at home in face of critical upheavals abroad, such as World War I, World War II, and the Cold War.[24] Like Thucydides, however, they did not associate honor with international politics, which they viewed as devoid of any moral rules. Instead, these thinkers viewed foreign relations in terms of rational interests in maximizing or preserving power among states. In the words of Morgenthau, "political realism refuses to identify the moral aspirations of a particular nation with the moral laws that govern the universe."[25] Power should be recognized for what it is, echoed Carr, even when it "goes far to create the morality convenient to itself."[26] Even Christian pacifists, such as Martin Wight, subscribed to the view that "hope is not a political virtue: it is a theological virtue."[27]

Neorealism

So-called structural realism or neorealism went further in denying significance to moral rules in international relations. By declaring the structure of the international system the key determining factor of state behavior, neorealists strengthened the classical realists' argument that survival and self-preservation were the ultimate social principles.[28] International politics was no longer about defending the social values of its participants – the argument occasionally advanced by some of neorealism's predecessors[29]; rather it was reduced to maximizing the "rational" interests of survival in the system. The triple classification of state motives in international politics advanced by classical realists – fear, interests, and honor[30] – was abandoned in favor of the single explanation of rational interests. The notion of honor was therefore fully replaced by that of rational interest, which was now understood in terms of material capabilities, rather than prestige or reputation.

Still, the new way of realist thinking did not eliminate the distinction between those who described states as oriented toward the international status quo and those who emphasized states' expansionist instincts. Both schools insisted on the "rationality" of such behavior, but could not agree on what constituted the correct response to pressures coming from the international system. Offensive realism expected states to maximize material power and, whenever possible, challenge existing political boundaries.[31] Defensive realism offered different explanations for state action in international politics. Rather than emphasizing the accumulation of power, defensive realists[32] focused on imperatives of security and survival and argued that states more commonly respond to security dilemmas by balancing or circling the bandwagons than with war or blackmail, as in offensive realism.[33] As primary motivating factors, defensive realists delineated misperceptions and institutional biases that stood in the way of a correct reading of signals coming from the anarchical international system.[34]

This disagreement among neorealists has called into question their ability to agree on a definition of rationality and rationally defined national interests, suggesting the possibility that rationality itself is a product of perception by scholars and policy makers. The problem with the offensive realist explanation of state behavior is that it lacks nuance and a sense of proportion: it presents all states as uniform power maximizers responding to the international anarchy-driven security dilemma with an equally relentless determination to achieve hegemony over all other states in the system.[35] The perspective from defensive realism is also not sufficiently sophisticated. Just as offensive realism assumes that the state's interest is to maximize power, defensive realism assumes without supportive evidence that the international system encourages security-seeking behavior. Even when defensive realism relies on explanatory factors other than power, such as misperceptions and institutional biases, it treats them as secondary to the role of the structure of the international system. In addition, neorealists occasionally apply in their analysis notions such as "will," "resolve," and "credibility" while continuing to claim the primacy of material factors.[36]

Neoclassical Realism

A new school of realist thinking – neoclassical realism – has developed these intangibles more explicitly.[37] Its advocates have restored the complexity of classical realism in perceiving state foreign policy preferences, no longer reducing them to either power or security. They have also added to their analysis several domestic factors such as perception, domestic politics, the degree of state strength, and ideology. Finally, neoclassical realists have revived the notion of honor as a key motive in state behavior. For example, William Wohlforth took issue with neorealists' materialist ontology by insisting that honor and prestige are critical for understanding state decisions to go to war, because leaders treat intangibles as vital interests.[38] Using the case of Russia, he argued that since 1601, "Russia's rulers have taken risks, spilled their subjects' blood, and emptied Kremlin coffers for the honor, prestige and reputation of the state."[39]

However, neoclassical realists remain in principal agreement with neo-realists about the primary significance of the structure of the international system to state behavior. Even when they employ factors other than power, such as perceptions and domestic politics, they assign them secondary roles relative to that attributed to the structure of the international system. From the neoclassical perspective, the structure of the international system itself determines the intangibles, and honor should be treated as an interest in preserving or enhancing the existing power position within the system, not as a locally shaped cultural concept with its own meaning. State ideas or visions of the world are therefore endogenous to the international power balance, not something that may have a potentially significant independent effect.[40] Therefore introducing intangibles and other variables does not change the overall thrust of the realist analysis, according to which the international environment is anarchic in nature and states are driven by security and power (national interest).

Among the casualties of such a reductionist perspective is the opportunity to understand the true sources of opportunities and threats in international politics. By ignoring the independent effects of ideas and emotions, realists employ a very narrow perspective on "change," limiting it to fluctuations of available power capabilities. As a result this perspective may miss opportunities in international politics. It is not that realism is necessarily wrong, but it is incomplete and therefore potentially wrong. For example, realists have overlooked or misinterpreted some far-reaching changes in Russia's foreign policy that were potent with potential for cooperation with Western nations; for example, Mikhail Gorbachev's New Thinking. In his polemic with two leading realists, Robert English pointed to the inaccuracy of presenting Gorbachev as the overseer of the Soviet strategic retreat. He argued that the origins of Gorbachev's New Thinking dated to the late 1950s and 1960s and had to do with domestic changes and the revival of cultural links to the West, not defense calculations and economic needs.[41] In addition, realism never fully answers this question, What drives the perception of threat in international politics? For instance, it does not fully explain why the United States and NATO are viewed as major threats to Russia's security in the Caucasus and where the origin of the threat lies. Is it individual, institutional, or perhaps cultural? How, and under what conditions, is the threat triggered and perpetuated? And if a rationality standard is of limited value in explaining state behavior, which emotions may drive it? What is the substance of participants' complains and frustrations? How and in response to which developments do these emotions consolidate to stand in the way of a "rational" calculation of interests?

Realism is not well equipped to answer these critical questions. Having assumed a constant drive for power and security in the international system, and being preoccupied with various *expressions* of power, it brackets its social and emotional *contexts*, treating them as secondary at best.[42] Why bother if the international system is a constant? As John Mearsheimer put it, the fact that anarchy has dominated the international relations discourse for centuries "strongly suggests that the basic structure of the international system . . . largely determines how states think and act toward each other."[43] Why should we care if participants have any feelings and what these feelings might be if, in the final analysis, they act as rational maximizers of their international objectives? This is the point at which we turn to social constructivism, which takes contexts and meanings of international actions seriously and does not treat them as predetermined by anarchy.

Honor and Social Constructivism

Honor and a Purpose of Social Action

Social constructivists view state behavior as shaped by both cognitive beliefs and emotions and by power. They are also united by the idea that power and the anarchical nature of the international system are by themselves not sufficient for defining state interests and policies. Power is a means, and not a purpose, of a social action. As Christian Reus-Smit argued, scholars ought to study normative fabrics of individual societies, especially their beliefs about the moral purpose of the state, because these beliefs are key to understanding state behavior and the resulting international system. These normative differences come before sovereignty, which is therefore only a secondary foundation of international society.[44] Even if anarchy is out there somewhere, constructivists say, we ought to focus on everyday interactions to understand what anarchy means and how social contexts of power are formed and unformed.[45] Without uncovering the meanings and emotions behind international relations, we are unlikely to adequately explain and predict state actions.

Although some classical realists acknowledge the importance of "differences in purpose for which power is sought," they are preoccupied with how such differences account for "variations in the scope and intensity of the quest for influence and power."[46] For example, Hans Morgenthau wrote about a "policy of prestige" that aims to demonstrate power.[47] Raymond Aron emphasized glory as "inseparable from the human dialogue" but "consecrated by victory and the enemy's submission."[48] Max

Weber too was thinking in power terms when he wrote, "A nation for-gives injury to its interests, but not injury to its honor."[49] Having sep-arated material interests from nonmaterial honor, Weber had in mind state prestige within the international system. Treating honor as a ratio-nal interest, realists focused on considerations of standing within the international system at the expense of attention to states' indigenous and culturally formed visions and worldviews.[50] Even when classical realists, such as Thucydides, Clausewitz, and Morgenthau, assumed that identi-ties of states and their societies were mutually constitutive, they did not explicitly acknowledge this assumption.[51] Their insights have yet to be systematically developed.

Constructivist theory places the notion of "meaning" at the center of understanding a social action; that is, state actions and interests are constructed by national and international environments. Constructivists argue that because particular social contexts define national interests, the formation of such interests should be carefully studied, rather than merely assumed to be rational or irrational. In the words of a promi-nent constructivist, "it is striking how little empirical research has been done investigating what kind of interests state actors actually have."[52] Although the international system assists states in their socialization and understanding of interests in world politics, one must not privilege inter-national social practices at the expense of those of local origins. Local conditions, such as historical memory, the state of the military and the economy, relations among different social groups, or the type of political regime, are just as important in shaping national perceptions and for-mulating ideas of national self.[53] Because each nation operates within a distinct social condition, each has distinct concerns and therefore views the world in its own way. For instance, perceptions of reality by rich nations will differ from those of poor countries. Some local concerns are more stable and are formed across a long time span, whereas others are more immediate and emerge in response to short-term developments. Yet in both cases, they serve as cultural lenses through which each nation views the outside world.

The concept of honor is often at the heart of how a nation expresses its historical experience and formulates a moral purpose in world poli-tics. Honor defines what is a "good" and "virtuous" course of action for a state vis-à-vis other members of international society. Some interna-tional interactions are constructed to facilitate loyalty and commitment to allies, whereas others create the context in which an honorable action requires noncooperative behavior. The former tends to promote a defini-tion of honor as a subjective *duty*, whereas the latter demands that honor be recognized as a *right*. In both cases, there is a clear expectation of reciprocity on the part of the self, which requires that we consider honor as a relational and interactive process, rather than something given.

The Self and Other in Honor-Based Interactions

More than some other virtues, "honor obliges its possessor to show others that he possesses honor."[54] We honor others, said Aristotle in the *Nicomachean Ethics*, in virtue of something that they are or have done to merit the honor.[55] As with other intangibles, nations define what they view as honorable behavior by interacting with other members of international society. Before they figure out how best to defend their interests with available material and diplomatic means, they first seek to understand what these interests in the international society are. Through social interactions, nations develop affiliations, attachments, and – ultimately – their own identities. Over time, some nations or cultural communities emerge as more significant in certain contexts, and it is through these significant others that national selves define their appropriate character and types of actions.[56] The very existence of the self becomes difficult without recognition from the other. As a cultural phenomenon, honor assists the self in expressing its emotional and evaluative orientations toward its significant other. The significant other establishes the meaningful context for the self's existence and development and therefore exerts a decisive influence on the self.

The self is not a passive learner, and its emotional assessment of the other may be subject to variation, depending on the other's willingness to accept the self's influence. Scholars with constructivist sensitivities have advanced a series of arguments suggesting that in cross-cultural interactions the self and the other are different but morally equal, and for that reason, both are sources of potential learning. Critics of modernization theory have revealed its unilinear and progressive pro-Western bias.[57] Postcolonial scholars have insisted that through modernization theory the Western other historically justified its colonial practices – offering no reciprocal engagement with the non-Western self, treating it as a dependent subject ("subaltern"), and expecting it to merely follow the other's lead.[58] "Non-Western" feminists have scrutinized ethnocentric assumptions common in Western feminist scholarship.[59] Scholars of world order and critical geopolitics have analyzed cultures and civilizations, viewing them as complex visualizations of the self and other's relationships across the globe, with a diversity of ideas and social visions coexisting, engaging in dialogue, and competing for influence.[60]

In their own way, each of these research circles has demonstrated that no matter how much the other may be willing to promote its vision of "virtue" and "good" to the outside world, the self is unlikely to fully accept a vision that undermines its own system of cultural meanings. Through its actions, the other then may reinforce or erode the earlier established meaning of honor. Depending on whether these influences are read by the self as extending or denying it recognition, they may generate either *hope* or *resentment* toward the other,[61] thereby encouraging or discouraging the self to act cooperatively. A resentful attitude is typically accompanied by the self's insistence on independence in forming its own judgment vis-à-vis other members of the international community. Consider, for example, Bismarck's public statement made in the wake of the Franco-Prussian War of 1870, conveying Prussia's resentment toward any potential criticisms of its actions: "Gentlemen, my honor lies in no-one's hand but my own, and it is not something that others can lavish on me . . . no-one is judge of it and able to decide whether I have it."[62]

Honor and Foreign Policy

In state-to-state interactions, both local conditions and international influences affect the formation of honor and are critical in understanding the process of foreign policy formation and change. Although international influences contribute to creating the meaningful context in which the national self evolves and shapes foreign policy, local conditions and the national memory of past interactions with its external environment are no less important in establishing a social purpose, or a system of meanings in which to act.[63] A national self then has relative autonomy in influencing foreign policy, and that autonomy is historically established. Such autonomy is confirmed by diverse economic, cultural, and political conditions in which nations act and that have long been a subject of foreign policy analysis. These conditions are critically important, and the constructivism that was initially oriented toward the international is now moving toward incorporating domestic-level variables.[64] Foreign policy begins when the state manages to transcend the dichotomy of internal/external pressures and develops multiple strategies of responding to world challenges.[65]

A nation is not a homogeneous entity and rarely speaks with a unified voice. Different traditions or schools of thinking about the world develop in response to international and local conditions, and these schools compete for political influence. They hold different conceptions of a nation's identity, the nature of the external world, and the appropriate policy response. In a relatively open society, they compete openly for dominance and are supported by various social groups/coalitions. Constructivists do not view foreign policy as a product of a unitary state that advances its power, as in realism, or as a particular group pursuing modernization interests, as in liberalism. Rather, the role of a coalition is to put forward a particular image of national identity/honor that will speak to existing local conditions and be recognized by the significant other. Identity coalitions are broader and more fundamental than interest coalitions, and they seek to achieve social recognition, rather than to maximize wealth or power.

National honor is therefore a complex and contested concept that may become a product of discursive competition among different groups/coalitions drawing on different actions of the other and interpreting contemporary international and local influences in a way that suits their perceptions and interests. The process that links international and local conditions, national honor, and foreign policy is a complex one, and it includes vigorous debates over the nature of national honor and interests. Because international society contains multiple norms and influences, some of them may conflict in influencing the self. For instance, Western realists emphasize the need to be strong, whereas Western liberals insist that the world revolves around values of a free economy and society. Both strength and liberty can serve as powerful normative messages that the modern West sends to the outside world. However, just as realists and liberals disagree, the norms of strength and liberty can come into conflict in shaping an identity of the self and its perceptions of appropriate/honorable behavior.

Ultimately, "rationalist" theories are inadequate in identifying the nature and origins of various concepts of national honor that guide states' international behavior. In particular, they ignore the fact that nations do not view power or modernization as their ultimate objectives. Rather, nations contextualize economic and political imperatives, viewing them as means of satisfying broader social ideas and purposes. Depending on a nation's internal self-confidence, external pressures may generate varying emotions at home and be viewed by political elites as either opportunities or threats to national development. When viewed as opportunities, external influences are likely to generate positive emotions of hope or camaraderie, strengthening those aspects of honor that favor international cooperation. However, when viewed as threats, foreign pressures tend to bring to life emotions of fear, resentment, anger, and righteousness, leading to a more nationalistic and exclusive definition of honor that frequently underlies competitive and conflictual behavior in international relations.[66]

During times of uncertainty, perceptions of honorable behavior may become highly contested with different honor coalitions being formed to promote their visions. Promoted in both public and private spaces, honor contestation is especially intense until one of the visions becomes

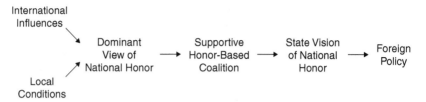

Figure 2.1. An Honor-Based Explanation of Foreign Policy

predominant. The activities of political entrepreneurs, appropriate material and ideational resources, conducive institutional arrangements, and historical practices can considerably influence this process of persuading the general public and elites. When the persuasion part of the process is complete, the state appropriates the dominant vision of nationally honorable behavior as a guide in policy making. That vision may then be publicly presented as the national interest. Other things being equal, one can expect a reasonable degree of foreign policy consistency based on the adopted image of national honor (Figure 2.1 describes the causal influences on foreign policy as viewed from a honor-based perspective).

Notes

1 Durkheim, *Professional Ethics and Civic Morals*, p. 75.
2 Bowman, *Honor*, p. 4.
3 Reus-Smit, *The Moral Purpose of the State*.
4 Kagan, *On the Origins of War and the Preservation of Peace*, p. 569.
5 Ibid., p. 8.
6 Stewart, *Honor*.
7 Freyberg-Inan, *What Moves Man*, p. 25.
8 Stewart, *Honor*, pp. 11–12.
9 Lebow, *The Tragic Vision of Politics*, pp. 271–3.
10 Kagan, *On the Origins of War*, pp. 38, 8.
11 O'Neill, *Honor, Symbols, and War*, p. 87.
12 Reus-Smit, *The Moral Purpose of the State*, p. 72.
13 Hirschmann, *The Passions and the Interests*, p. 11.
14 For different interpretations of honor's disappearance, see Bowman, *Honor* and MacIntyre, *After Virtue*.
15 Best, *Honor among Men and Nations*, xii.
16 Freyberg-Inan, *What Moves Man*, pp. 25–30.
17 Pangle and Ahrensdorf, *Justice among Nations*, pp. 17–18.
18 Freyberg-Inan, *What Moves Man*, p. 9.
19 Doyle, *Ways of War and Peace*, p. 105.
20 Freyberg-Inan, *What Moves Man*, p. 51.

21 Wight, *International Theory*, p. 103.
22 Haslam, *No Virtue like Necessity*, p. 31.
23 Doyle, *Ways of War and Peace*, pp. 137–48.
24 For recent reconstructions of classical realism as an ethical tradition, see Williams, *The Realist Tradition and the Limits of International Relations* and Lieven and Hulsman, *Ethical Realism*.
25 Morgenthau, *Politics among Nations*, p. 12.
26 Freyberg-Inan, *What Moves Man*, p. 51.
27 Ibid.
28 For example, see Morgenthau's references to state self-preservation as a "moral principle" and a "duty" (Pangle and Ahrensdorf, *Justice among Nations*, p. 227).
29 Ibid, p. 226.
30 Lebow, *The Tragic Vision of Politics*. Aron wrote of security, glory, and honor (Aron, *Peace and War*).
31 Mearsheimer, *The Tragedy of Great Powers*.
32 See, for example, Jervis, "Cooperation under Security Dilemma"; Waltz, *Theory of International Politics*; Snyder, *Myths of Empire*.
33 Mearsheimer, *The Tragedy of Great Powers*, p. 138.
34 Jervis, "Cooperation under Security Dilemma"; Walt, *Origins of Alliances*; Snyder *Myths of Empire*.
35 Mearsheimer, *The Tragedy of Great Powers*, p. 40.
36 As one scholar wrote, today "honor" is seldom mentioned by its own name, but it has survived under different names (O'Neill, *Honor, Symbols, and War*, p. 245).
37 For overviews, see Rose, "Neoclassical Realism and Theories of Foreign Policy"; Lobell, Ripsman, and Taliaferro, eds., *Neoclassical Realism, the State, and Foreign Policy*.
38 Wohlforth, "Honor as Interest in Russian Decisions for War, 1600–1995." For a similar argument, see Wohlforth, "Unipolarity, Status Competition, and Great Power War."
39 Wohlforth, "Honor as Interest," 22.
40 In a similar fashion, two realists analyzed the role played by Mikhail Gorbachev's New Thinking in changing Soviet behavior and ending the Cold War (Brooks and Wohlforth, "Power, Globalization and the End of the Cold War"). Rather than viewing Gorbachev as a conceptual innovator with a new vision for the world, Brooks and Wohlforth presented him as the overseer of the Soviet strategic retreat. For a constructivist response, see English, "Power, Ideas, and New Evidence on the Cold War's End."
41 English, "Power, Ideas, and New Evidence."
42 Classical realism too was mainly interested in expressions of power, although it paid greater attention to the context, origins, and formation of that power.
43 Mearsheimer, *The Tragedy of Great Powers*, p. 369.
44 Reus-Smit, *The Moral Purpose of the State*.
45 Guzzini, *Realism in International Relations and International Political Economy*; Wendt, *Social Theory of International Politics*; Hopf, *Social Construction of International Politics*.

46 Wolfers, *Discord and Collaboration*, p. 106.

47 Donnelly, *Realism and International Relations*, p. 46.

48 Aron, *Peace and War*, p. 73.

49 Donelan, *Honor in Foreign Policy*, p. 117.

50 Realists normally do not separate inner and outer aspects of honor and view them as interchangeable with prestige, glory, and status. For realist treatments of honor, see also Joshi, *Honor in International Relations*.

51 Lebow, *The Tragic Vision of Politics*, p. 268.

52 Wendt, *Social Theory of International Politics*, p. 133.

53 The literature on ideas and their role in shaping cultural identities is large. See, for instance, Mannheim, *Ideology and Utopia*; Habermas, *Theory and Practice*; Huntington, *The Clash of Civilizations and the Remaking of World Order*; Wolfe, *Whose Keeper?*; Said, *Culture and Imperialism*; Suny and Kennedy, eds., *Intellectuals and the Articulation of the Nation*; Chakrabarty, *Provincializing Europe*; English, *Russia and the Idea of the West*; Mandelbaum, *The Ideas That Conquered the World;* Oren, *Our Enemy and US*; Helleiner and Pickel, eds., *Economic Nationalism in a Globalizing World*.

54 O'Neill, *Honor, Symbols, and War*, p. 244.

55 MacIntyre, *After Virtue*, p. 116.

56 Neumann, *Russia and the Idea of Europe*; Neumann, *Uses of the Other*; Ringman, "The Recognition Game"; Oren, *Our Enemy and US*.

57 Wiarda, "The Ethnocentrism of the Social Science; Oren, "Is Culture Independent of National Security?"

58 Vitalis, "The Graceful and Generous Liberal Gesture"; Inayatullah and Blaney, *International Relations and the Problem of Difference*; Jones, ed., *Decolonizing International Relations*.

59 Oyewumi, *The Invention of Women*; Mohanty, "Under Western Eyes."

60 Cox, "Civilizations: Encounters and Transformations"; Alker, Amin, Biersteker, and Inoguchi, "How Should We Theorize Contemporary Macro-Encounters"; O'Hagan, *Conceptualizing the West in International Relations*; Tsygankov, *Whose World Order*; Tsygankov, "Self and Other in International Relations Theory."

61 Suny, *Why We Hate You*.

62 Bowman, *Honor*, p. 89.

63 Katzenstein, *Cultural Norms and National Security*; Lieven, *America Right or Wrong*; Legro, *Rethinking the World*; Haas, *The Ideological Origins of Great Power Politics*.

64 As one scholar suggests, "identity explanations are likely to become 'foreign policy-ized' by connecting identity to other factors and theories that have long been part of the FPA agenda" (Kaarbo, "Foreign Policy Analysis in the Twenty-First Century," 160). International relations scholars have recognized the internal/external bind by referring to it as a "two level game" (Putnam, "Diplomacy and Domestic Politics").

65 For additional hypotheses about international influences and their interaction with local conditions, see Snyder, "International Leverage on Soviet Domestic Change"; Richter, *Khrushchev's Double Bind*.

66 Henry Kissinger wrote in his memoirs as if honor had prevented the United States from withdrawing from the Vietnam War. Similarly, some prominent American officials favored nuclear retaliation in case of potential Soviet attack on the West even if such retaliation meant incineration of American cities (O'Neill, *Honor, Symbols, and War*, pp. 85–6). In the latter case, honor was equal to the reputation of power to be feared, rather than trusted.

3   The Russian State and Its Honor

"The task of our internal history has been to enlighten the people's community with the community of the Church. . . . The task of our external history has been to defend political independence of the same ideal not only for Russia, but for all Slavs, and to do so by establishing a strong state that neither replaces, nor constrains the communal ideal."

Yuri Samarin[1]

The Russian myth of honor has been established over the course of millennia. Rooted in Eastern Christianity, it came to include a distinctive concept of spiritual freedom and the ideal of a strong and socially protective state capable of defending its own subjects from abuses at home and threats from abroad. Over time, this notion of honor has also incorporated a component of state loyalty to those who shared the Russian idea of honor but lived outside its borders. It is this combination of domestic institutions and commitments to cultural allies that has constituted the myth of honor, providing the state's international policy with a sense of purpose.

The Honor of the Russian State: Origins and Content of the Myth

International politics is not and should not be viewed as primarily a struggle for power. What on the surface often appears to be a political competition among states for power and the preservation of sovereignty may have the deeper purpose of protecting and advancing moral values. As Christian Reus-Smit wrote, the states of ancient Greece, Renaissance Italy, and absolutist Europe all "faced the problem of stabilizing territorial property rights, yet they each constructed different fundamental institutions to serve this task."[2] Fundamental institutions captured these states' moral purpose. The ancient Greeks were believers in informed political involvement and the exercise of discursive justice within the community of the polis. The Italian city-states cultivated a moral purpose defined as civic glory, designed to spur the city on to greatness and to prevent the development of factionalism by enacting norms of procedural justice. The European states that emerged out of the Peace of Westphalia in 1648 established Christian and dynastic values as their fundamental principles, guiding the exercise of hierarchical and authoritative justice by their monarchs. Finally, modern states' moral purpose centers around the notion of individual freedom and potentiality and of legislative justice.[3]

This thinking can be helpful in reconstructing institutions and values shared by other political communities. For example China, with its social hierarchy, is close to the European absolutist states, albeit without their Christian beliefs. In contrast, Russia is a species of European Christian absolutism but with its own characteristics, the most important being Orthodox or Eastern Christianity as a moral basis of Russian statehood. Prince Vladimir, in selecting Christianity for the Russians in 988, was not only making a religious choice but was also deciding on the long-term basis for social consensus, national honor, and external recognition of his country.[4] To Russians, Eastern Christianity became a critically important part of their identity for centuries to follow.[5] Internally, the Church promoted a new type of social relations, arguing against blood revenge and advocating stable marriage and humane treatment of the lower classes. In Sergei Platonov's words, "the Church provided the secular society with an example of a better and more humane life, in which both rich and poor could be defended. . . . The Church influenced all sides of [the] social system including political deeds of Princes and [the] private life of each family."[6] Another prominent Russian historian, Vasili Kluchevski, believed that the search for justice reflected in the principles of *Russkaya pravda* (the Russian truth) of the twelfth century had its roots in Eastern Christianity.[7]

It was also within the Eastern Christian tradition that the Russians established the state's duty to provide, to the extent possible, its citizens with decent living conditions. Before Russia embarked on territorial expansion in the fifteenth century, Russian princes had been guided by detailed community-based and religious welfare principles. Rooted in Orthodox Christianity, these principles included a foremost respect for the land [*zemlya*], support for a community of free peasants [*mir*] with the power to decide critical issues and choose a prince [*veche*],[8] and mutual responsibility, which meant that if one household was unable to contribute the required dues and taxes, the others were expected to make up the difference. Introduced in the Kievan Rus', the principle of mutual responsibility was codified in 1649.[9] The voice of the people was viewed, in the words of Patriarch Job (1589–1605), as the "voice of God."[10] Later, when serfdom emerged in the mid-nineteenth century in response to the peasants' accumulated debt to the nobles and the state ban on free migration,[11] many in Russia viewed the system as an emergency, rather than normal or natural condition.[12]

Similarly, the principle of autocracy was first introduced not to support the absolute control of Russia's political rights and economic wealth, but rather to provide ordinary Russians with the stability required to improve their living conditions and protect them from possible abuses by local authorities and nobles.[13] The Church and the existing self-governing institutions were not established to interfere with the monarch's duties, but to facilitate them by developing specific locally sensitive responses. The autocrat, in turn, had no plans to control the entire social life of Russia, but only to serve as the ultimate guarantor of citizens' rights. As Nicholas Petro argued, "In contrast to the prevailing view that nationality and religion served only to prop up the autocracy . . . they constrained the autocracy by emphasizing the monarch's accountability to the popular will and to the Church."[14] Such a perspective governed Muscovy and only changed after the Time of Troubles, especially under Patriarch Nikon's reforms[15] and the absolutist rule of Peter the Great. Before then, as another scholar wrote, "The Russian tsar was not the master of slaves . . . for the Muscovites the language of servitude implied mutual obligations: the 'master' protected the 'slave' and the latter served the former."[16] The vision of a socially responsible state survived Peter's rule and was later revived in the writings of nineteenth- and twentieth-century thinkers, such as Ivan Ilyin, Sergei Gessen, Pavel Novgorodtsev, and Pyetr Struve.

Eastern Christianity also became the basis for unifying the Russian lands while enabling coexistence with culturally diverse groups. Although there were tensions between the Russians and other nationalities in the Russian empire, these tensions were not as pronounced as in overseas empires. As Geoffrey Hosking wrote, "annexed territories became full components of the empire as soon as practicable."[17] The relationships between Christians and Muslims were the most difficult, yet over time the state learned to coexist with Islam. Beginning with Catherine the Great, the Russian empire developed special ties with Islam by supporting those Muslim authorities who were willing to submit to the empire's general authority, and it even served as an arbitrator in disputes between Muslims from the Volga River to Central Asia.[18]

Finally, Vladimir's choice to accept Christianity in 988 was critical from the perspective of foreign relations and security. No longer an isolated and provincial land, Russia found itself in the orbit of the great Byzantine civilization, which was then at the center of the world's cultural development. Having adopted Orthodox Christianity in 988, before the Schism of 1054, Russia became a student of Byzantium's spirituality and high culture.[19] The acculturation process continued until the fall of Byzantium to the Ottomans in 1453, even throughout the years of the Mongol Yoke from submission to Khan Batyi in 1237 to the victorious Battle of Kulikovo in 1380. In addition to assisting the Russians in unifying their lands and building a common identity, Christianity gave Russia greater visibility in the world and a connection to the West's cultural center.[20]

Russia's Security Imperatives and State Honor

As the geopolitically insecure state became preoccupied with defending its borders since the fifteenth century, political independence and the international reputation of a great power figured prominently in Russia's idea of honor. The country was often in an uncertain and volatile external environment and could only survive by constantly defending its unstable borders from the expansionist ambitions of its neighbors. Located in the middle of Eurasia, Russia had few natural boundaries and was frequently attacked by outsiders, from the Mongols to Napoleon and Hitler. In addition, the rules of European great power politics since the days of Louis XIV often encouraged, rather than constrained, territorial expansion and war.[21] As Dominic Lieven wrote, "In the European system all great powers were bent on increasing their strength in order to secure their interests in an extremely ruthless and competitive world."[22]

Such security predicaments dictated Russia's constant preoccupation with territorial self-sufficiency and secure borders. In addition to insisting on its cultural autonomy after declining the offer to join the Holy Roman Empire in the fifteenth century,[23] Russia demanded political independence. Since then political independence has remained one of Russia's important objectives,[24] inspiring much of Russian geopolitical writing. Influenced partly by local realities and partly by the works of European geographers,[25] Russian thinkers believed in the "inevitable logic of geography,"[26] which prescribed that their country expand in several directions by obtaining "natural boundaries." According to the same logic of geography Russia needed to become a great power to sustain itself amid strong outside pressures. Vladimir Putin reflected the beliefs of the overwhelming majority of Russian leaders when he said, "Russia can only survive and develop within the existing borders if it stays as a great power" and that "during all of its times of weakness . . . Russia was invariably confronted with the threat of disintegration."[27]

Threatened from several directions, Russia had to fight multiple wars, many of which were defensive. Immediately following the defeat of

the Mongols, Russia expanded to establish its influence on the Volga
river and forestall possible future attacks from the south. During the
modern era, Russia shared a long border with hostile European powers
and "was invaded more often and with more force than any other early
modern empire."[28] The invasions included those by the Poles, Ottomans,
and Swedes in the seventeenth century; by the Swedes, Austrians, and
Ottomans in the eighteenth century; the French, British, and Ottomans
in the nineteenth century; and the Germans (twice) and the Allies in the
twentieth century.[29] It was this logic of competition with the most powerful European nations that often drove Russia's decisions to wage war and
expand its territory. From the beginning of Europe's world domination
in the seventeenth century, the economically backward Russians strove
to become a great power and accept the realities of militarism. Avoiding wars was not an option, because the very rules of inclusion in the
great power club "were simple and brutal: to belong, you had to defeat
a current member in war."[30] As Prince Baryatinsky, the viceroy of the
Caucasus, noted in the second half of the nineteenth century, "England
displays its power with gold. Russia which is poor in gold has to compete with force of arms."[31] Expansion in Asia was especially aggressive –
partly because the region was more vulnerable than Europe and partly
because the Russians too believed that they were performing a European
mission to civilize Asia.[32]

In addition to increasing the importance of political independence, the
grim reality of insecurity made it difficult for Russia to act on domestic
components of its myth of honor. In the early seventeenth century, Russia's political and economic system was not much different from those
of the Western European states.[33] Since that time, however, Russia's
state-building institutions moved toward centralization at the expense of
spiritual freedom and strong social welfare policies. After liberating itself
from Mongol occupation, Muscovy was in a generally favorable strategic
situation until an arms revolution took place in Europe. Gunpowder and
drill provided European armies with better armed and more disciplined
troops, and Russia had to rise to the challenge.[34] The state could no
longer afford to share the clerical authorities' position on gunpowder as
spiritually harmful.[35] Autocracy too had to be transformed to comply
with the imperatives of military modernization, because the likely alternative was the colonization of Russia by Western powers, following the
fate of China and India.[36]

Russia's traditional institutions were transformed in response to the
new strategic situation. The Church and other autonomous centers of
social life yielded gradually to state centralization. Soon after being re-
created from below following the Time of Troubles, the state displayed

new tendencies to suppress potential checks and balances of its power. In the era of increasingly secular sovereign statehood in Europe, Peter the Great imposed a new ideology of state patriotism, or loyalty to the state[37] – a sharp break with the religious Russia that had emerged after 200 years of rule by the Mongols. European politics was centered around the accumulation of national power, and religion was increasingly subjugated to the considerations of the state. Relative to Europe, however, the Russian state possessed a much greater capacity to undermine sources of autonomous political power. By the time of European secularization, Russia had legalized serfdom, which simplified the collection of taxes and military mobilization. Poverty and relative economic backwardness proved an asset in at least two respects – the state was able to defeat opposition from the nobles[38] and to impose the command system of long-service conscription. From a military standpoint, it was precisely "because Russia was so 'backward', according to European standards, that it was so powerful."[39]

The price of becoming competitive in military terms was the degradation of important aspects of Russia's honor. As the state was taking on burdens of external defense, the autocracy was increasingly neglecting its traditional responsibility to protect social freedoms from abuses at home. In George Vernadsky's words, "Autocracy and serfdom were the price the Russian people had to pay for national survival."[40] Many observers, especially in the West, became convinced that Russia had no honor except the honor of power and strength. "The role of Orthodoxy, and of moral principles in general, in the formulation of a grand strategy is very difficult to assess.... Their [Russians'] only interest was to impose the empire's supremacy in Europe and Asia,"[41] wrote one historian recently. "When Russian statesmen debated among themselves, when they quarreled with each other about the sort of policies Russia ought to pursue, they generally employed the cold-blooded language of strategy and analysis ... they justified their policies in terms of the benefits they anticipated for Russian power and security,"[42] echoed another. Military superiority was being gradually turned from a means of people's welfare into an end of state policies. With increasingly weak checks on autocracy, it was up to the monarch and the royal court to articulate and sustain the objectives of social honor.

Russia and Its Cultural Allies

In addition to spiritual freedom, a strong state, and great power status, the Russian myth of state honor included the reputational aspect of protecting cultural allies (see Table 3.1). Having established the Orthodox

Table 3.1. *Content of Russia's Honor Myth*

Spiritual freedom
Strong state: political domination and social justice
Great power
Protector of cultural allies

foundations of its statehood, Russia felt responsible for the livelihood of those co-religionists who resided outside the Russian state. After the fall of Byzantium to the Ottomans in the mid-fifteenth century, Russia proclaimed itself to be the Third Rome, or the center of Orthodox Christianity worldwide. Throughout the eighteenth and nineteenth centuries, Russia fought multiple wars with Turkey in part to protect the rights of the millions of Christians living within the Turkish empire – more than a third of its population. A complex system of treaties between St. Petersburg and Constantinople had to be developed before the Russian Empire could feel satisfied that its reputation as a protector of cultural allies was secure.

The definition of cultural allies changed over time. In the twentieth century, the ideologically transformed Soviet Russia was no longer committed to defending Christians or Slavs as it had been a century earlier. Instead, the state's international assistance was geared to support the honor of socialism and egalitarian ideology. The Soviet rulers provided financial assistance and political support for communist parties across the world. The Kremlin also intervened abroad to suppress influences of the alternative "capitalist" system; the best known interventions were Hungary in 1956, Czechoslovakia in 1968, Afghanistan in 1979, and Poland in 1981. The Cold War was as much about ideology and propaganda as it was about power and geopolitics.[43] The Soviet Union was in the business of defending and promoting an alternative idea of freedom, an idea that resonated with many outside the West partly because it was defined as freedom from the expansionist ambitions of Western powers.

After the disintegration of the communist system in 1989, Russia has proposed a different definition of its cultural allies. Although still a work in progress, the new ideological project includes the Kremlin's commitment to ethnic Russians and to those who have historically gravitated toward Russia. In the mid-1990s, the state began to advocate for dual citizenship in the former Soviet region, responding in part to pressure from those living outside Russia who continued to identify with the country. High-profile state officials, such as Foreign Minister Yevgeni Primakov, also supported the idea of Eurasia as a multicultural, multiethnic, and multireligious community in place of the former Soviet Union.[44] In August 2008, Russia intervened in the Georgian-South Ossetian conflict; fearing a humanitarian catastrophe in South Ossetia, the Kremlin justified this intervention by the need to protect Russian citizens in the region. Acting on this definition of its cultural allies, Russia then recognized South Ossetia and Abkhazia's independence from Georgia.

Russia and the West: Similarity versus Distinctiveness

Russia's idea of honor has developed in tension with that of Western nations. Historically a part of Western civilization, Russia has also been unmistakably different.

As a Christian power, Russia has had a distinct religious tradition to defend in the world. By adopting Christianity as the state religion, Russia established its belongingness with Western, at the time Byzantine, civilization. Less than a century later the Russian rulers had to take a side in the schism between Orthodoxy and the Catholic West. Two centuries of Mongol domination added to Russia's traumatic experience. When in 1453 the Ottomans conquered Byzantium, Russia found itself standing alone between Islam and Catholic Europe. To indicate to the Holy Roman Empire its cultural autonomy, Grand Duke of Muscovy Ivan III refused to accept the Catholic empire's superiority and famously signed his written answer to the emperor with the title, "Great Ruler of all of Rus' by God's grace."[45] He later married Sophia Paleologue, a niece of the last Byzantine Emperor Constantine IX to claim a blood relation to the fallen Eastern Roman Empire. Forty years later, the idea of cultural autonomy crystallized in the notion of Muscovy as the Third Rome.[46]

Russia's communist system too had its similarities and differences from the political systems of the Western European states. Communism and social democracy had emerged from the same egalitarian roots of the French Revolution. Many Soviet policies were socially and economically egalitarian and therefore compatible with European practices. However, the Soviet objective was to stimulate a revolutionary new order, at the expense of liberal political reforms pursued by advanced European states. For some seventy years until the end of the Cold War, Soviet Russia avoided integrating European liberal and democratic values and traditions.

Table 3.2. *Russia as Both Part of and Distinct from
the West*

Russia as Part of the West	Russia as Distinct from the West
Christianity	Orthodox Christianity
Absolutism	Autocracy
Europe's system of alliances	Special relations with the east
Social democracy	Communism

Table 3.2 summarizes some of Russia's values in comparison with those of the West.

The Historical Evolution of Russian Honor

Aspects of the Russian myth of honor – Eastern Christianity, the strong state, and loyalty to cultural allies – functioned differently throughout Russia's long history. The nineteenth-century construction of honor included the triad of Orthodox Christianity, autocracy, and support for Orthodox and Slav people abroad. In the early twentieth century, in response to what some historians have called the European "civil war"[47] between liberalism and autocracy, the Russian state underwent a major mutation. The new vision rested on communist ideology, the practice of a single-party state, and commitment to communist parties and social-ist states across the world. An aberration, rather than a natural phase of Russia's historic statehood,[48] the Soviet system reproduced parts of the old honor myth in a sharply disfigured form. Religion was replaced with communist ideology, the autocratic state with the rule of the sin-gle party, and the commitment to co-religionists with that to ideolog-ical allies. Yet, no matter the absolutist and centralized nature of the Soviet state, it provided citizens with important social and economic rights, and many of them had reasons to honor the new system and be proud of it. Finally, Russia's post-Soviet state is in the process of designing a new ideological construction that incorporates the notions of Russian civilization, revived state strength, and support for Russian and pro-Russian communities abroad. These days the Kremlin ideolo-gists argue that, although Russia is a part of the West, it is a culturally distinct "sovereign democracy" with important obligations at home and abroad.[49]

Table 3.3 summarizes the three distinct constructions of Russian honor.

Table 3.3. *Historical Constructions of Russian Honor*

	Nineteenth Century	Soviet	Contemporary
Spiritual Freedom	Orthodox Christianity	Communism	Russian civilization
Strong State	Autocracy	Single-party state	Sovereign democracy
Cultural Allies	Orthodox and Slav peoples	Communist parties and socialist states	Russian and pro-Russian communities

Notes

1 As cited in Zhaba, *Russkiye mysliteli o Rossiyi i chelovechestve*, p. 59.

2 Reus-Smit, *The Moral Purpose of the State*, p. 5.

3 Ibid., pp. 7–9.

4 On individual honor and the role of litigation practices in defending honor in Muscovite Russia, see Kollmann, *By Honor Bound*.

5 Berdyayev, *Russkaya ideya*; Billington, *The Icon and the Axe*; Duncan, *Russian Messianism*.

6 Platonov, *Polnyi kurs lektsii po russkoi istoriyi*, pp. 96–7. On the Church's social influence, see Riasanovsky, *A History of Russia*, p. 54; Hosking, *Russia*, p. 225; Bushkovitch, *Religion and Society in Russia*.

7 Platonov, *Polnyi kurs*, p. 111.

8 Petro, *The Rebirth of Russian Democracy*, p. 31; Pushkarev, *Obzor russkoi istoriyi*, pp. 49–60.

9 Hosking, *Russia*, p. 198.

10 Petro, *The Rebirth of Russian Democracy*, p. 33.

11 Kovalevskii, "The Growth of Serfdom," pp. 105–9.

12 As Nicholas I said in the State Council in 1842, "There is no doubt that serfdom, in its present form, is an evil obvious to all; but to touch it now would of course be an even more ruinous evil" (Hosking, *Russia*, p. 148).

13 Platonov, *Polnyi kurs*, p. 204; Solonevich, *Narodnaya monarkhiya*, p. 421.

14 Petro, *The Rebirth of Russian Democracy*, p. 33.

15 Nikon introduced changes in religious rituals in 1652 to achieve uniformity between the Russian and Greek Orthodox practices, but he also had political ambitions. Tsar Alexei I thwarted Nikon's political ambitions, but supported the changes within the Church, one of which was that "the parishers, formerly democratic in structure, were deprived of independence. The election of the priests replaced by their nomination by the bishops" (Zenkovsky, "The Russian Church Schism," 145).

16 Poe, *"A People Born to Slavery,"* p. 226.

17 Hosking, *Russia: People and Empire*, p. 40.

18 Crews, *For Prophet and Tsar*. The Ottoman Empire developed similar relations with its Jewish and Christian minorities (Lieven, *Empire*, p. 149). For

reviews of Russia's historical experience with Muslims, see Lieven, *Chechnya*; Gadzhiyev, *Geopolitika Kavkaza*; Yemelyanova, "Islam in Russia: An Historical Perspective"; Sakwa, *Chechnya*.

19 Averintsev, *Kresheniye Rusi i put' russkoi kul'tury*; Florovski, *Puti russkogo bogosloviya*, chapter 1.

20 Lieven, *Empire*, pp. 236–7; Utkin, *Vyzov Zapada i otvet Rossiyi*, pp. 45–6.

21 Holsti, *Peace and War*, p. 151. This is also the argument of John Mearsheimer's *The Tragedy of Great Power Politics*, which views such a state of affairs as natural for international politics in general.

22 Lieven, *Empire*, p. 267.

23 In response to Emperor Frederick III's offer to confer on him the title of king, Ivan III answered, "By God's grace, we are the ruler of our land from the beginning, from the first of our ancestors, it has been given us by God, and as it was for ancestors, so it is for us" (Neumann, "Russia's Standing as a Great Power, 1494–1815," 15).

24 On continuity in Russia's international objectives, see especially Black, "The Pattern of Russian Objectives"; Rieber, "Persistent Factors in Russian Foreign Policy; Legvold, ed. *Russian Foreign Policy in the Twenty-First Century and the Shadow of the Past.*

25 Bassin and Aksenov, "Mackinder and the Heartland Theory in Post-Soviet Geopolitical Discourse"; Wohlforth, "Heartland Dreams."

26 Vernadsky, *A History of Russia*, pp. 4–5.

27 Putin, "Poslaniye Federal'nomu Sobraniyu Rossiyskoy Federatsii," May 16, 2003, http://president.kremlin.ru/mainpage.shtmle.

28 Poe, *The Russian Moment in World History*, p. 50.

29 Ibid., p. 66; Wohlforth, "Honor as Interest in Russian Decisions for War," 38.

30 Wohlforth, "Honor as Interest," 27.

31 Lieven, *Empire*, p. 267. For development of this argument, see especially Fuller, *Strategy and Power in Russia.*

32 On Russian thinking about Asia, see Hauner, *What Is Asia to Us?*; Bassin, *Imperial Visions*; Schimmelpenninck Van Der Oye, *Toward the Rising Sun*; Laruelle, *Russian Eurasianism.*

33 Lynch, *How Russia Is Not Ruled*, p. 23.

34 Poe, *The Russian Moment*, pp. 44–5.

35 Ibid., p. 45.

36 Lynch, *How Russia Is Not Ruled*, p. 25.

37 Tolz, *Russia*, p. 27. See also Chernaya, "Ot ideyi 'sluzheniya gosudaryu' k ideye 'sluzheniya otechestvu' v russkoi obschestvennoi mysli."

38 In Europe, state centralization was not as pervasive partly because it required negotiating complex deals among kings, merchants, and feudal lords (Spruyt, *Sovereign State and Its Competitors*).

39 Fuller, *Strategy and Power in Russia*, p. 455.

40 Lynch, *How Russia Is Not Ruled*, p. 18.

41 LeDunne, *The Grand Strategy of the Russian Empire*, p. 141.

42 Fuller, *Strategy and Power in Russia*, p. 132.

43 See, for example, Oren, *Our Enemy and US*; Foglesong, *The American Mission and the "Evil Empire."*

44 The issue was also related to preserving cultural balance inside Russia, which included by far the largest number of ethnic groups (some 140), with only five of its twenty-one ethnic republics having a clear majority of its titular nation: Chechnya, Chuvashia, Ingushetia, Tuva, and North Ossetia (Zevelev, *Russia and Its New Diaspora*, p. 175).

45 Neumann, "Russia's Standing as a Great Power," 15.

46 Duncan, *Russian Messianism*, p. 11.

47 Roberts, *A History of Europe*.

48 McDaniel, *The Agony of the Russian Idea*. What Western Sovietologists viewed as a norm was dictated in Russia's historical development by harsh imperatives of survival under external emergency conditions. The initial argument about continuity between the old and new Russia was formulated by Berdyayev, *Istoki i smysl russkogo kommunizma*.

49 For analysis of Russia's still emerging state ideology, see Chadayev, *Putin i yego ideologiya*; Tsygankov, "Finding a Civilizational Idea"; Feklyunina, "Battle for Perceptions"; Evans, *Power and Ideology*; Laruelle, *In the Name of the Nation*.

4   Russia's Relations with the West

"[T]he West is not necessarily most alarmed when Russia is in reality most alarming, nor most reassured when Russia is in fact most reassuring."

Martin Malia[1]

Historical Traditions

Russia's Foreign Policy Traditions

Russia's political establishment has rarely acted uniformly when interpreting challenges to the nation's honor and security or proposing strategies for responding to them.[2] At different times, different groups within the political class, depending on their social position and historical memory, have proposed different concepts of honorable international behavior. These concepts have generally complied with traditional Russian meanings of honor, defined as *chestnost'* (commitment, reputation), *dostoinstvo* (dignity, pride), or *slava* (glory, achievement).[3] Guided by these meanings, Russia's leaders at various times have advanced policies of cooperation, defensiveness, or assertiveness in relation to the West. These policies differed in (1) their methods of advancing Russia's preferences, (2) their degree of commitment to relationships with Western nations, and (3) the opposition such policies elicited at home (see Table 4.1).

The tradition of cooperating with Western nations places the emphasis on Russia's similarity with them and advocates the notion of honorable behavior as loyalty to and cooperation with the West as a historic and cultural ally. Those defending a definition of honor that differentiates Russia from the West view Russia as an independent power free to choose international allies that best suit its vision and national interests. This group feels less committed to relationships with Western nations, especially when their actions are perceived as inconsiderate to Russia's identity and interests. Supporters of assertiveness in foreign policy also

Table 4.1. *Russia's Concepts of Honorable Behavior toward the West*

	Cooperation	Defensiveness	Assertiveness
Methods	Pro-Western alliances	Flexible alliances & internal concentration	Unilateralism
Commitment to the West	High	Low	Low
Opposing Camps at Home	Defensiveness & assertiveness	Cooperation & assertiveness	Cooperation & defensiveness

believe in Russia's special role in the world and are bound more by the nationalistic sense of honor and social obligations than by loyalty to Western nations. However, unlike those on the defensive side, assertiveness advocates argue for a more aggressive and unilateral defense of Russia's international position that goes beyond flexible alliances and soft balancing tactics. Each of these traditions has been brought to life by different historical developments and political conditions.

Cooperative Enhancement of Honor

Russia's tradition of cooperating with Western nations has its roots in Prince Vladimir's decision to accept Christianity. Throughout the long years of Mongol domination, Russians preserved their cultural affiliation with the West, which was reinforced by the sense of threat from culturally alien or non-Christian people of the South. Attempts by Muscovy's rulers to gain recognition by the Holy Roman Empire in the late sixteenth to early seventeenth century, including opening a permanent mission in Rome and obtaining the Holy Emperor's support in a war against Lithuania, continued the tradition of cooperation with the West as an important spiritual authority. The Romanov dynasty followed this tradition by participating in the First Northern War against Sweden (1655–60) as a member of the Western coalition that included the Polish-Lithuanian Commonwealth, Prussia, Rome, and Norway. Although the war was not irrelevant to Russia's geopolitical interests, the decision to participate also reflected Russia's cultural values. Also of importance was Russia's decision to join the Holy League (Austria–Poland–Venice) against the Ottoman Empire after signing the Eternal Peace with the Polish-Lithuanian Commonwealth (1686), Russia's key rival.

Importantly, Peter the Great's foreign policy also began with an attempt to establish cooperative relations with Europe by assembling a strong coalition against Sweden during his Grand Embassy trip. Although the trip was not successful, Peter continued to move his country closer to the European system by strengthening contacts and sending Russia's ambassadors and representatives to the Netherlands, Sweden, Vienna, and other states.[4] Peter's subsequent defeat of Sweden, which turned Russia into a great power and a critically important member of the European system of states, would have been impossible without his insistence on using Western technology to overcome Russia's backwardness. Russian Westernizers – those who emphasize Russia's similarity with the West and view the West as the most viable and progressive civilization in the world – often trace their intellectual roots to Peter,[5] who admired the West for its technological superiority.

Peter's successors sought to build on his accomplishments and went even further in establishing cooperative arrangements with European states. Russia joined the Seven Years War (1756–63) against Prussia, and in 1766 Catherine the Great proclaimed that "Russia is a European power." As part of the system of European great powers, Russia sought to present itself as a loyal member of the family of Western monarchies while not neglecting its geopolitical interests. For example, it participated in all of the late-eighteenth-century divisions of Poland among Austria, Prussia, and Russia to check the influence of the Ottoman Empire on the European continent. An even more prominent example was the early-nineteenth-century "Holy Alliance" with Germany and Austria to suppress revolutionary activities on the continent. After the defeat of Napoleon, Alexander I championed the so-called legitimist policies, seeing himself as a consistent European in defending the values of autocratic Europe and vigorously opposing the spread of French egalitarian ideas.[6] As Europe was becoming an arena for balance-of-power politics, Russia was holding to its "holy" principles longer than other powers.

Even when caught between two Europes – the liberal one associated with the French Revolution and the autocratic one – Russia tried to make its international choices not unilaterally, but in coalitions with other Western states. After the Holy Alliance, it participated in the Three Emperors League with Germany and Austro-Hungary, which came into existence in 1872–3 and which served to maintain Russia's cultural ties with its Orthodox allies in the Balkans.[7] In the early twentieth century, Russia joined an entirely different coalition of France and Britain, the Triple Alliance – partly to prevent the dominance of Germany and partly to ally itself with the new European ideas of freedom and equality. Some rulers – most prominently Alexander II – attempted to redefine the country's identity in line with these new European ideas. Although Alexander III continued policies of repression at home and siding with European autocracies abroad, the strengthening European pressures of enlightenment, constitutionalism, and capitalism were increasingly difficult to ignore.

After the era of the Great Reforms when Russia shifted its alliance from Germany to France and Britain, the tsarist government seemed more willing to be open to the new European influences. Russia's decision to participate in World War I in part reflected its membership in the Triple Alliance and its cultural commitment to Europe. Pavel Milyukov, once a foreign minister and a leader of Russian liberals, took the most active pro-European position by insisting that Russia must stay in the war as an active member of the anti-German coalition. To Milyukov, support for the European allies – despite all the devastations that the war had brought to Russia – was a matter of principle and reflected the country's orientation.

Even the Soviet rulers, despite their fundamental conflict with the West, did not see the USSR as a non-European state. Soon after the first failures of the revolution, Bolshevik leaders began to seek recognition by the Western states and to advocate some accommodations with the "capitalist" West.[8] Maxim Litvinov, for instance, supported a "collective security" system in Europe to prevent the rise of Fascism. Nikita Khrushchev wanted to break the taboos of isolationism and to bring Soviet Russia closer to Europe. He called for a return to Vladimir Lenin's principles of coexistence with the capitalist world, although he later engaged in several confrontations with the West. Both Litvinov and Khrushchev saw themselves as supporters of Lenin's later course, which abandoned the idea of world revolution in favor of learning to live and trade with the potentially dangerous capitalist world. The Soviet Union also cooperated with Western nations by participating in the grand alliance against Nazi Germany during World War II.

In 1975, the Soviets took part in the Helsinki Conference on Security and Cooperation in Europe and signed its Final Act, thereby pledging to respect human rights and fundamental freedoms. Signing this document indicated that prominent groups within the Soviet system saw Russia as standing not too far apart from European social-democratic ideas. For instance, one of Mikhail Gorbachev's favorite lines of thinking was that Soviet Union had to "purify" itself of Stalinist "distortions" and become a democratic, or "human," version of socialism (*gumannyi sotsializm*). In his foreign policy, Gorbachev pursued the notion of mutual security with the West, presiding over a series of revolutionary arms control agreements with the United States and Soviet military withdrawals from Europe and the Third World. By introducing the idea of a "common European home" Gorbachev meant to achieve Russian-European integration based on the principles of European social democracy.

Russia's cooperative engagement with the West has continued after the breakup of the Soviet Union. Boris Yeltsin and his first foreign minister Andrei Kozyrev argued for the "natural" affinity of their country with the West based on such shared values as democracy, human rights, and a free market. They insisted that only by building Western liberal institutions and joining the coalition of what was frequently referred to as the community of "Western civilized nations" would Russia be able to preserve its true cultural identity and respond to key threats. Yeltsin's successor Vladimir Putin too sought to frame his country's international choices as pro-Western ones. In the context of growing terrorist threats in the world after 9/11, Putin worked hard to establish a partnership with the United States; his initial statements emphasized the common strategic threats of terrorism and political instability. It was only later when Russia departed from its initial definition of honorable behavior, and it did so in response to perceived humiliation by Western powers.[9]

Defensive Honor

If cooperation with Western nations reflected Russia's sense of honor as loyalty to the West, then defensiveness and assertiveness were frequently products of the nation's commitments to its Slavic and Orthodox allies. Russian rulers tried hard to pursue policies that would integrate both Western and Slavic/Orthodox commitments. However, doing so was not always possible, partly because the West was not always supportive of Russia's aspirations to defend its historic allies. For example, Nicholas I's assertiveness with regard to the Balkans and the Crimea found little support among Western powers. Indeed, his own foreign minister, Count Nesselrode, wrote to his master after the Crimean War had begun that "honor does not oblige us to hurl ourselves into a bottomless abyss."[10] Russia therefore did not always have the luxury of honoring commitments to its historic allies. Even when it opted in favor of the Slavic/Orthodox notion of honor, Russia had to seriously consider the balance-of-power imperatives. Such calculations of power often determined the choice whether to retreat into a period of defensiveness or pursue a more active policy.

Following its attempt to consolidate its statehood after the period of Mongol domination, Russia entered a period of anarchy, or *Smuta*, and could no longer continue with the "gathering of Russian lands" policy. Soon after recovery, however, Russia was determined to secure territories populated by Russians in Smolensk, Kiev, and other areas, and that meant confronting the Polish-Lithuanian Commonwealth. These skirmishes were not always successful, and Russia on occasion retreated into periods of defensiveness. In 1634, for example, Russia lost the Smolensk war to Warsaw, and Moscow did not resume military offensives for twenty years until 1654 when it subjugated Ukraine. Success in the Ukrainian war temporarily reconciled Russia with Poland, which considered Moscow a key ally because of its decision to join with the Polish-Lithuaniain Commonwealth in the First Northern War against Sweden.

In the eighteenth century, Catherine the Great exercised a defensive policy when she took a neutral stance and withdrew Russia from the Seven Years War against Prussia. Although it fought a successful war against Turkey, Russia did not engage in another major military campaign against Sweden until 1887. One of Catherine's key advisors, Nikita Panin, believed that Russia needed time after the Seven Years War to deal with financial and demographic issues, and he recommended minimizing the risk of a major war by avoiding foreign adventures that might catalyze coalitions of powerful enemies against Russia.[11] A similar but even more pronounced defensive policy took place in the nineteenth century after Russia's defeat in the Crimean War. The Count Alexander Gorchakov, Alexander II's foreign minister, devised the policy of recueillement – developing a system of flexible alliances and limiting Russia's involvement in European affairs. The idea too was to recover Russia's lost honor.

The Soviet rulers acted in a similar fashion when they were in no position to act on their sense of obligation to spread their vision and values abroad and strengthen ties with cultural allies. Josef Stalin's doctrine of "socialism is one country" may be viewed as an example of consolidation in the face of security challenges by the "imperialist" West. Stalin sought to peacefully coexist with Western nations while pursuing an ambitious program of domestic recovery. When justifying the need for rapid industrialization, Stalin famously framed his argument in terms of responding to powerful external threats:

The history of the old Russia was the continual beating she suffered because of her backwardness. She was beaten by the Mongol khans. She was beaten by the Turkish beys. She was beaten by the Swedish feudal lords. She was beaten by the Polish and Lithuanian gentry. She was beaten by the English and French capitalists. She was beaten by the Japanese barons. All beat her – for her backwardness. . . . We are fifty or a hundred years behind the advanced countries. We must make good this distance in ten years. Either we do it, or we shall be crushed.[12]

Stalin's pact with Hitler, as well as Brezhnev's "correlation of forces" strategy, also reflected the will to defend Soviet honor against perceived dangerous influences from the outside world. By signing the treaty of friendship with Nazi Germany, Stalin hoped to isolate Russia from World War II or at least to buy enough time to prepare for it. His successors operated on a world scale, and with the "correlation for forces" doctrine, they intended to respond to the perceived growing global influence of the West. Both strategies meant to preserve Russia's independence in world affairs and had some elements of Gorchakov's strategy of consolidation.

Yevgeni Primakov's opposition to NATO expansion after the Soviet disintegration also resembled defensive policies of the past. He directly referred to Gorchakov as his inspiration, and he viewed Russia's honor in terms of its strength and ability to pursue historic obligations, including in the former Soviet region and the Balkans, without veto from the United States.[13] In domestic policies, Primakov wanted to bring more order and control to social and political life by restoring state domination and controlling big business. He was also trying to rebuild the former Soviet Union and contain the United States through a strategic alliance with China and India.[14] Primakov and his supporters agreed on the importance of developing ties with the West by building a market economy and political democracy. However, they were not prepared to sacrifice historically tested traditional allies and the notion of a strong state to these new values.

Assertive Enhancement of Honor

Russia has been assertive whenever it has acted from a position of perceived strength while differing from the West in its assessment of an international situation. Russia's assertive enhancement of honor may be traced to Muscovy's "gathering of Russian lands" policy in efforts to wrest control over Russian Orthodox subjects from the Mongols and from Poland. First bringing Smolensk into Moscow's orbit in 1514, Russia expanded to conquer Kazan, Astrakhan, and Siberia. In the seventeenth century, following its recovery from the Time of Troubles, Russia returned to policies of assertiveness and fought multiple wars with the Catholic Polish-Lithuanian Commonwealth; the Kremlin was not satisfied until it had added eastern Ukraine to Russia's area of domination. Moscow then signed the Eternal Peace with Warsaw in 1686 to challenge another cultural enemy of the Orthodox Christians – the Turks.

Competition with the Ottoman Empire became especially intense in the eighteenth century, as Peter and his successors attempted to protect Balkan Slavs and secure control over the Black Sea. In 1739, Russia defeated Turkey and gained part of the Black Sea coast through the Treaty of Belgrade. Catherine the Great then fought two more successful wars with Turkey and gained additional control over the areas of Azov, the Crimea, and Odessa. The empress wanted to "drive the Turks from Europe," and some in her court urged her to go further by partitioning the Ottoman Empire.[15] The policy of protecting Slav-Orthodox "brothers" continued in the nineteenth century when Russia fought Turkey over Greece's independence and even achieved a protectorate over the Orthodox Christians in the Danubian provinces of Moldova and Walachia.[16] As far as Russia was concerned, the policy of protecting the Orthodox Christians was not inconsistent with the Holy Alliance's objectives of preserving Christian unity in Europe.

However, acting without explicit support from Western alliances had its costs, of which the Crimean War may be the prime example. Nicholas I started the war in part because he was convinced of Russia's military superiority over the declining Ottoman Empire and in part because he could not persuade Britain to join forces with Russia. He did not anticipate that Britain, as well as France, would join forces with the Sultan. Having recovered from the defeat, Russia returned to a foreign policy of assertiveness in the Balkans and Asia. In the Balkans, Russia mobilized its forces in response to Christian revolts in Bosnia-Herzegovina in 1875–6.[17] Facing another Crimean War-esque explicit denial of support from Western allies, Russia restrained the indignant Serbs when they revolted against Austro-Hungary's annexation of Bosnia-Herzegovina in 1908.[18] However, the preoccupation with pan-Slavism and great power prestige contributed to Russia's involvement in World War I. Influential supporters of moderate views, such as Sergei Witte, Pyotr Stolypin, and Vladimir Kokovtsev, were sidelined and replaced by ardent supporters of the culturally nationalist sense of honor. Russia also continued to pursue provocative policies in Asia, which resulted in defeat by Japan in 1905 and growing social unrest at home.

Other illustrations of Russia's assertiveness can be found in the Soviet era. The initial policy pursued by the Bolsheviks was not to be bound by any obligations to maintain relations with the West, which was a radically different attitude from the one held by the tsarist government. No matter how assertive, the tsars always attempted to achieve an understanding with influential European nations, and they were often involved in simultaneous multilateral arrangements with the West. The Bolsheviks were the first to challenge the core foundations of the West's system of values, insisting on the cultural superiority of Soviet Russia. The Lenin-Trotski doctrine of world revolution was an example of this thinking. In the early part of 1920, Bolshevik leaders expected that their offensive in

Poland would result in social revolutions throughout the rest of Europe.[19] Although this doctrine died as an official philosophy with Lenin's commitment to coexistence with capitalism in 1921, many members of the official and social circles remained convinced of the virtues of this thinking.

The emergence of the Cold War era saw a different example of Soviet assertiveness. Soviet leaders had readily participated in creating the United Nations, but they also felt they were owed a bigger role in shaping European security. They felt that the Soviet Union had single-handedly won the most important battles against the Nazis, including the battles for Moscow, Kursk, and Stalingrad, and had contributed a disproportionally greater share of resources to overall victory. To Josef Stalin, victory meant a demonstration of his nation's social advantages: "our victory means . . . that our Soviet social system has won, that the Soviet social system has successfully withstood the trial in the flames of war and proved its perfect viability."[20] The West, however, was mistrustful of the Soviet Union, and the United States felt it had to play an active role in shaping world affairs – the belief in internationalism had predated the Pearl Harbor attack by Japan and emerged in response to the Nazi invasions of France and the Soviet Union.[21] Other examples of assertive Soviet behavior include decisions to place nuclear missiles in Cuba in 1962 and send troops to Afghanistan in 1979.

Russia's more recent assertiveness stems from its determination to recover some of its lost international position. Around 2005, Russia signaled that it sought greater stakes in the international system and would no longer accept the status of junior partner to the West that it had during the 1990s. In addition to its desire to capitalize on its energy competitiveness and break into Western economic markets, Russia no longer viewed the old methods of preserving stability and security as sufficient. In August 2008, in response to Georgia's use of force against one of its autonomous areas, Russia cemented its military presence in the Caucasus by defeating Georgia and recognizing South Ossetia's independence. Putin's speech at the Munich Conference on Security Policy, which was extremely critical of U.S. "unilateralism," became a high point in Russia's new assertiveness. Russia's president then accused the United States of "disdain for the basic principles of international law" and having "overstepped its national borders in . . . the economic, political, cultural and educational policies it imposes on other nations."[22] Through its actions in the Caucasus, Russia has demonstrated that, while maintaining an essentially defensive security posture, it believes in a more assertive strategy in defense of national interests and is ready to use force in the areas that it views of critical importance.

Table 4.2 summarizes Russia's foreign policy traditions throughout its history.

Evaluating Russia's Foreign Policy

Russia's foreign policy decisions can be evaluated by whether they achieved their objectives, which include both the enhancement of honor and meeting the country's security, welfare, and autonomy interests. The security interest is met when there are no military threats to the nation, particularly (but not limited to) from the outside. The welfare interest is met when foreign policy choices create external conditions favorable for improvements to the standards of living, defined as economic growth, new jobs, and social services. Autonomy has to do with the state's ability to make decisions and withstand pressures from special interests inside and outside of the country.

Judged by these objectives, some of Russia's policies were successful and defensible, whereas others were not. Except for the Holy Alliance, Russia's attempts to cooperate with the West – whether by joining allies in World War I, entering the League of Nations in an attempt to stop Hitler, or seeking to rejoin the West after the Cold War – were not effective. In all three instances, Russia's engagement with the West neither prevented instability nor halted economic decline at home, and they all ultimately failed to enhance Russia's honor. The defensive foreign policy has had a mixed record of success. For example, Gorchakov's strategy of "concentration" provided the country with the necessary time to build up its resources and recover its lost international position. Stalin's doctrine of "socialism in one country" and his pact with Hitler won some time for Russia to prepare for the war, albeit not as much as Stalin had hoped. However, Primakov's policy of preventing NATO expansion proved to be a failure. Russia did not improve its international standing or its ability to protect its historic allies nor did it achieve greater security or prosperity. Russia's assertiveness has also brought mixed results. The Crimean War was a failure, and the Cold War was a success only in the sense that the Soviet Union was able to preserve its presence in the areas of perceived strategic importance for as long as did. It remains to be seen what will be the record of Putin/Medvedev's international assertiveness.

Russia's foreign policy has been successful when its leaders were accurate in their calculations of their own resources and the West's reaction to their policies. The historical record suggests that Russia is only successful in defending its perceived interests when its assessment of an international situation – and threats and opportunities that stem from it – is more similar to than different from that of Western nations. All

Table 4.2. *Foreign Policy Traditions throughout Russian History*

	Cooperation	Defensiveness	Assertiveness
16th cent.	Rapprochement with Rome, 1495–1514	Moscow as the Third Rome, 1511	Post-Smolensk expansion, 1514–83
17th cent.			War with Poland, 1632
	Northern War, 1655–60	Between wars with Poland, 1634–54	War with Poland, 1654
	Holy Alliance with Austria and Poland, 1686		
	Peter's Grand Embassy trip, 1697–8		
18th cent.			War with Sweden, 1700–21
			War with Turkey, 1738–9
	Seven Years War, 1757–62		
		Neutrality, 1762–87	War with Turkey, 1768–74
	Poland's divisions, 1772, 1793, 1795		War with Turkey, 1787–92
19th cent.	Holy Alliance, 1814–53		War with Turkey, 1828
			Crimean War, 1853–6
		Gorchakov's Concentration, 1856–71	
	Three Emperors Alliance, 1873–91		War with Turkey, 1878
20th cent.	Triple Alliance, 1907–17		War with Japan, 1904–5
			World Revolution, 1920
	Collective Security, 1933–8	Peaceful Coexistence, 1921–41	
	World War II, 1941–5		
	New Soviet Initiatives, 1958	Correlation of Forces, 1964–85	Warsaw Pact, 1955–88
			Cuban Missiles, 1962
	OSCE Helsinki Treaty, 1975		
			Afghanistan's Invasion, 1979
	New Thinking, 1987–90		
	Integration with the West, 1991–3		
		Opposing NATO Expansion, 1995–9	
21st cent.	War on Terror, 2001–45		
			Putin's Assertiveness, 2005–8

too often, widely varying assessments, as well as Russia's internal weakness, prevented the country from defending its international position and making the necessary adjustments to enable economic modernization. Even when Russia's leaders were confident of success, it failed to achieve its objectives because of the West's concerted interference. During the Crimean War, Russia miscalculated both its own resources and the Western reaction. In the Cold War not only poor diplomacy and an inability to read the West's intentions but also Russia's confrontational ideological vision – accompanied by excessive military expenditures – made it practically impossible to arrive at an accurate assessment of an international situation. To succeed Moscow has to formulate its strategic vision in such a way that it does not principally contradict those of Western nations. It should strive to present to the world a clear perspective on its values and interests that is distinct and yet not incompatible with those of the West.

Honor and the Formation of Russia's Foreign Policy

Cultural Formation of Russia's Foreign Policy

Both external and local developments have contributed to validating or undermining Russia's sense of honor in international interactions.[23] Externally, Europe in particular and the West in general have played the role of the significant other and prominently figured in Russia's debates about national identity. Europe and the West created the meaningful environment in which Russia's rulers defended their visions of national honor and interests.[24] Even though the West rarely recognized Russia's claims to be a part of the Western world, those claims reflected a domestically strong motivating force in Russia's foreign policy. Throughout its history Russia has sought to be recognized by the Western other and to modernize in like manner. The strength of identification with Western civilization explains why Russia has sought to achieve its objectives in cooperation with Western, especially European, nations. Whether internally weak or strong, Russia has always been responsive to the behavior of the West and – when progressive leaders have wielded power in the Kremlin – prepared to mend fences and pursue cooperation, rather than confrontation.

However, honor is a relational concept, and its meaning may change in response to externally significant developments. Each time Russia began its movement toward its significant other, Moscow could only continue for as long as it felt a sufficiently progressive recognition of and reciprocation from Western capitals. Russia's cultural lenses are different

Table 4.3. *Cultural Explanation of Russia's Foreign Policy*

		Internal Confidence	
		Weak	Strong
West's recognition	Strong	Cooperation	Cooperation
	Weak	Defensiveness	Assertiveness

from those of Western nations and have been formed by locally distinct historical memory, ties with historic allies, and contemporary challenges. For example, Russia has had traditionally strong ties with Slavic and Orthodox allies and could only act as a confident power when its actions were not disruptive to these historical ties. In the absence of external recognition of Russia's cooperative honor claims, the reform-minded leadership in the Kremlin would run into opposition from advocates of more defensive and assertive definitions of honor. As the previous chapter explains, the nation is not a homogeneous entity, and in times of relative openness, different concepts of honor compete for a dominant position within the ruling establishment and are supported by various political and social groups. Depending on how internally confident Russia felt to pursue an independent foreign policy,[25] it could choose either a defensive or assertive direction. Table 4.3 summarizes the hypothesized effects of the West's recognition and the local sense of confidence on Russia's foreign policy.

Therefore the dynamics of honor in Russia's foreign policy are more complex than as seen in classical and neoclassical realism. Where realists emphasize the honor of a great power and its ability to shape the international system, a culturally sensitive account identifies three distinct meanings of honor, with great power prestige being only one of them. Constructivism views that prestige as merely an expression of a more general aspiration to be "like the West." If the Western nations are great powers, Russia too aspires to such status. If, however, the West demonstrates accomplishments in institution building, economic prosperity, and human rights protection, Russian rulers are equally drawn to these accomplishments and attempt to replicate them at home. In addition to great power status and ability to shape the international system, Russia has a historically developed sense of internal honor that stems from its special religious (Orthodox Christian), ethnic (Slavic), and geographic background.

To illustrate the effects of external recognition and internal confidence, let us briefly consider Russia's far-reaching cooperation with the West immediately following the Cold War. Moscow's efforts to aggressively integrate with Western economic and political institutions soon stumbled over a relatively sanguine reaction from the Western nations. The new Russian leaders were decisively breaking with the Soviet past and were hoping for rapid and massive assistance from the West. In the words of Russia's first foreign minister, Andrei Kozyrev, the country's very system of values was to be changed,[26] and the expectation was that such change would assist greatly in bringing Russia to the front-rank status of countries, such as France, Germany, and the United States, within ten to twelve years. Russia was presented as a "naturally" pro-Western nation, and its success was predicated on support and recognition from the West.

No matter Russia's efforts, the West's response was either excessively cautious or insensitive.[27] The decision made by the Western nations to expand NATO eastward, excluding Russia from the process, is a case in point. It came as a major blow to the reformers, dashing Moscow's hopes to transform the alliance into a nonmilitary one or to admit Russia as a full member. The exclusion of Russia strengthened the sense that Russia was not being accepted by Western civilization, and it provided critics of cooperating with the West with the required ammunition for questioning the objectives of the new government. In addition, the growing interference of Western nations in Yugoslavia without consulting Russia exacerbated its sense of failure to fulfill its obligations to Slavic/Orthodox allies.[28] Joining the West was no longer viewed as honorable, because honor was increasingly associated with preserving Russia's autonomy and independence in international affairs.

In response to the sense of growing humiliation by the West, the Kremlin moved from cooperative to increasingly defensive policy actions. Because of a lack of internal confidence, assertiveness was not an option. The disintegration of the Soviet state led to a growing sense of national anxiety, creating a whole series of new conflicts in the Russian periphery and exacerbating the sense of identity crisis experienced by Russians.[29] In addition, the domestic context of rising disorder, corruption, and poverty that had resulted from Yeltsin's reforms was not conducive to changing state policy in an assertive direction.

Realism and Its Limitations

As the dominant international relations theory, realism concentrates on considerations of state power, security and prestige. By emphasizing the notion of national interests, realists insist on the objectivity of their analysis and view moral principles as largely irrelevant to the conduct of foreign policy. Although classical realists recognize the power of moral principles, they dismiss them as too dangerous to rely on. In Hans Morgenthau's memorable formulation, a "foreign policy founded upon moral principles rather than the national-interest issues, by its inner logic," tends to evolve "into the tribalism or religious wars and of nationalistic crusades."[30] Other schools within realism – defensive, offensive, and neoclassical – go even further in excluding from the list of state motives national memory, emotions, beliefs, and other factors not defined by the structure of the international system.

Defensive realists focus on imperatives of security and survival, and they argue that states more commonly respond to security dilemmas with balancing or bandwagoning than with war or blackmail, as in offensive realism.[31] To defensive realists, states are risk-averse entities, and they go to war or get involved in other types of aggressive behavior only when they incorrectly read signals coming from the international system. Specifically, this group of scholars delineates misperceptions and institutional biases as motivating factors for aggressive foreign policy actions.[32] For example, defensive realists explained that World War I was caused by inaccurate perceptions of the security dilemma by key powers, including Russia. Rather than being rational, such perceptions or biases stemmed from parochial interests of the military that found their reflection in offensive war plans.[33] Similarly, Jack Snyder explained Soviet security expansionism by the role played by imperial myths. The early Cold War, Khrushchev's missile diplomacy, and Brezhnev's assertiveness in the Third World occurred because leaders in the Kremlin held offensive beliefs and had the power to shape state policy.[34]

Scholars influenced by these perspectives may see Russia's policies as serving objectives of security consistent with the country's military capabilities. If psychological and institutional biases do not stand in the way of assessing its military capabilities, Russia should be expected to engage in cooperative behavior or bandwagoning with Western nations when it feels vulnerable. However, a more strong and confident Russia is more likely to pursue policies of balancing against the Western power. What I have described as defensiveness may be viewed by defensive realists as typical of a strong Russia. Assertiveness is a risky type of behavior that may result from internal bias or misperception, but is not commonly engaged in by a rational power coping with a security dilemma.

Offensive and neoclassical realists would expect states to engage in more aggressive behavior in attempting to maximize power or status in the international system. Russia then should be expected to pursue an assertive policy when it is strong and a defensive policy when it is weak.[35] Cooperation, or bandwagoning, as offensive realism makes clear,[36] does

Table 4.4. *Russia's Relations with the West: Realist and Constructivist Expectations*

	Cooperation	Defensiveness	Assertiveness
Defensive Realism	Common for a weak state	Common for a strong state	Not common and irrational
Offensive and Neoclassical Realism	Not common	Common for a weak state	Common for a strong state
Constructivism	Common for a recognized state	Common for a nonrecognized and weak state	Common for a nonrecognized and strong state

not commonly occur in a system that encourages aggression and power maximization. A number of studies have explained Russia's assertive or expansionist behavior using insights from offensive and neoclassical realism.[37] Russian studies scholars, whether consciously or not, have reasoned about the motives of Russia's foreign policy using the offensive realist logic. They frequently advocate viewing Russia as a state that is expansionist and does not abide by acceptable rules of international behavior.[38] As a revisionist state, Russia is expected to use available opportunities to upset the West's international policies.

Overall, realism views as typical some aspects of international behavior, but not others. Just like offensive realism assumes that the state interest is to maximize power, defensive realism assumes without testing that the international system encourages security-seeking behavior. As a result, as Table 4.4 shows, defensive and offensive realists tend to offer contradictory predictions of some examples of Russia's behavior, which casts doubt on their overall power to interpret the whole range of cases as summarized in Table 4.2. In addition, even when realists accurately predict the general direction of Russia's foreign policy, they are not always clear about the sources of such policy. Because of their emphasis on the role of the international system in determining foreign policy, realists tend to miss other important sources of state strategy, such as local historical memory and ideas of national honor. It is not that realism is necessarily wrong, but it is incomplete and therefore potentially wrong.

The approach taken in this book incorporates domestic ideas of honor, power, and recognition, and there is no expectation that an anarchical environment will necessarily determine the nature of foreign policy. Rather, I expect that both ideas and material capabilities will figure prominently in shaping Russia's international behavior. The most dangerous combination is its growing sense of humiliation by Western powers accompanied by Russia's rising material capabilities.

First Look at the Historical Cases

A first look at the cases in this book suggests the increased significance of the constructivist explanation in comparison to its likely rivals (see Table 4.4 for a summary of realist and constructivist expectations about Russia's relations with the West).

Both defensive and offensive realists have difficulties explaining Russia's cases of cooperative foreign policy. The Holy Alliance, for example, may seem like an engagement with the Western nations that is too far reaching for a nation that emerged victorious and potentially hegemonic after defeating Napoleon. Instead, realists would expect Russia to pursue a revisionist or back-passing strategy.[39] The Triple Alliance with France and Britain that Russia entered in 1907 is also difficult for realists to explain. After the lost war with Japan and a revolution at home, Russia joined the alliance from a position of weakness, and at that point it was still unnecessary to balance against Germany. In addition, based on calculations of material power, it is not clear why Russia allied with the cumulatively stronger France and Britain, rather than Germany. It is similarly unclear why the weak Soviet Union engaged in the process of collective security in Europe, warning about the dangers of potential German revisionism, instead of letting France and Britain take the initiative. In addition, Putin's choice to build a strategic partnership with the United States after the terrorist attacks on September 11, 2001, is puzzling in light of Russia's relative weakness and potential availability of alternative alliance options (China).

Although realist theories fare better at explaining Russia's defensive choices, their explanations are still not entirely satisfactory. Defensive realism would expect a weak Russia to bandwagon with stronger powers, yet the cases of the country's post–Crimean War recueillement, the postrevolutionary peaceful coexistence, and the post–Cold War containment of NATO expansion indicate a different strategy. Offensive and neoclassical realists may find Russia's behavior compelling, viewing it as an approximation of balancing against a potential hegemon. This interpretation is incomplete, however, and does not take into consideration Russia's damaged sense of honor and obligations to cultural allies. In the cases of recueillement and containment of NATO expansion, Russia acted on its perceived obligations to Slavic/Orthodox allies in the Balkans and the former Soviet region. Recovering lost honor was critical for a self-respected power, and Russia could not rest until it had recovered its lost

Table 4.5. *A First Look at the Cases*

		Internal Confidence	
		Weak	Strong
West's recognition	Strong	Triple Alliance Collective security War on Terror	Holy Alliance
	Weak	Recueillement Peaceful coexistence Containment of NATO	Crimean War Cold War Russo-Georgian War

strategic positions, as it did when it regained the right to have fleets in the Black Sea under Gorchakov. Similarly, a self-respecting Soviet power would have pursued a more assertive policy to maintain and extend a sphere of socialist influence if it were not for its weakness and the need, in Vladimir Lenin's expression, to "catch a breath."

Finally, Russia's decisions to use an assertive strategy are also difficult to understand without considering its obligations to its cultural allies, on the one hand, and the lack of recognition from the Western nations, on the other. Defensive realists may find Russia's decision to enter the Crimean War, the Cold War, or the military conflict with Georgia as exemplars of irrationality, yet these choices made sense in terms of Russia's self-perceived honor. In each of these cases, the Kremlin acted consistently with its perceived historic obligations, using available material resources that it deemed sufficient for achieving its objectives. Offensive and neoclassical realists are better than their defensive counterparts in predicting the direction of Russia's international actions from a position of strength, but they misinterpret the sources of Russia's behavior. These sources have more to do with an honor-based purpose than a blind drive to maximize power or status. Realists sometimes correctly predict the foreign policy direction and arrive at what on the surface resembles a plausible interpretation of facts, but tend to miss important contextual factors and internal justifications of international actions. In policy terms, neglect of these contextual factors may translate into missed opportunities to cooperate with Russia whenever possible and avoid confrontation where unnecessary. The first look at the ten cases shows that they fit comfortably within the proposed honor-based theory of Russia's foreign policy (see Table 4.5). The following chapters explore the cases in greater detail and develop the proposed constructivist explanation.

Notes

1 Malia, *Russia under Western Eyes*, p. 8.
2 For classifications of Russia's foreign policy preferences and debates, see Hopf, *Social Construction of International Politics*; Zimmerman, *The Russian People and Foreign Policy*; Tsygankov, *Russia's Foreign Policy*; Clunan, *The Social Construction of Russia's Resurgence*.
3 For example, these meanings are identified in the popular Russian dictionnary by Ozhegov, *Slovar' russkogo yazyka*, pp. 880–1.
4 Neumann, "Russia's Standing as a Great Power," 21.
5 For an overview of Peter's reception by Russian intellectual currents, see especially Riasanovsky, *The Image of Peter the Great in Russian History and Thought*.
6 In the eyes of European monarchs, Napoleon was "the embodiment of revolutionary objectives" (Orlik, *Rossiya v mezhdunarodnykh otnosheniyakh*, p. 19).
7 Holborn, "Russia and the European Political System," 393–4.
8 Ringman, "The Recognition Game: Soviet Russia against the West."
9 Tsygankov, "Russia's International Assertiveness."
10 Fuller, *Strategy and Power in Russia*, p. 248.
11 Ibid., p. 134.
12 As cited in: Sakwa, *The Rise and Fall of the Soviet Union, 1917–199*, pp. 187–8.
13 See Primakov, "Rossiya v mirovoi politike"; Ivanov, *Vneshnyaya politika Rossiyi v epokhu globalizatsiyi*, pp. 313–30; *Strategiya dlia Rossiyi*. Russian supporters of cooperation with the West, in contrast, are often critical of Gorchakov's diplomacy. See, for example, Fyodorov, "Krizis vneshnei politiki Rossiyi."
14 For details, see Tsygankov, *Russia's Foreign Policy*, chapter 4.
15 Ragsdale, "Russian Projects of Conquest in the Eighteenth Century," 100; Fuller, *Strategy and Power in Russia*, p. 142; Schroeder, *The Transformation of European Politics, 1763–1848*, p. 20.
16 Donaldson and Nogee, *The Foreign Policy of Russia*, p. 9; Headley, *Russia and the Balkans*, pp. 14–16.
17 For details, see Tuminez, *Russian Nationalism since 1856*, pp. 90–113.
18 Headley, *Russia and the Balkans*, p. 18.
19 Mlechin, *Ministry inostrannykh del*, pp. 44–45.
20 Quoted in Banerjee, "Attribution, Identity, and Emotion in the Early Cold War," 30.
21 In January 1941, only 39 percent of the public felt that U.S. intervention in World War I was a mistake, compared to 68 percent in October 1939 (Legro, *Rethinking the World*, p. 67).
22 Putin, "Speech at the Munich Conference on Security Policy."
23 For discussion of international and domestic developments in the construction of Russia's identity, see especially Hopf, *Social Construction of International Politics*; Clunan, *The Social Construction of Russia's Resurgence*; Larson and Shevchenko, "Status Seekers."
24 For a development of this argument, see Neumann, *Russia and the Idea of Europe*; English, *Russia and the Idea of the West*.

25 Internal confidence is partly a product of material power and partly of perception of power by the ruling elite. For details of complex calculations of Russia's power, see Wohlforth, "The Perception of Power" and Neumann, "Russia's Standing as a Great Power."

26 See, for example, Kozyrev, "Rossiya v novom mire" and Kozyrev, "Russia and Human Rights."

27 See, for example, Rutland, "Mission Impossible?"; Gould-Davies and Woods, "Russia and the IMF"; Black, *Russia Faces NATO Expansion*.

28 Headley, *Russia and the Balkans*, p. 483.

29 For greater details, see Sperling, Kay, and Papacosma, eds. *Limiting Institutions?*

30 Pangle and Ahrensdorf, *Justice among Nations*, p. 221.

31 Mearsheimer, *The Tragedy of Great Power Politics*, p. 138.

32 Jervis, "Cooperation under Security Dilemma"; Jervis and Snyder, eds. *Dominous and Bandwagoning*; Snyder, *Myths of Empire*.

33 Snyder, *The Ideology of the Offensive*; Van Evera, *Causes of War*.

34 Snyder, *Myths of Empire*, chapter 6, "Soviet Politics and Strategic Learning."

35 For example, some realists have explained Russia's liberal momentum of the late 1980s–early 1990s and the searches for active accommodation with the West by the Soviet defeat in the Cold War and the need to respond to the emergence of the American-centered global unipolar system. In this perspective, Russia's hegemonic policy in the former Soviet area and a nonconfrontational engagement with the West were the only rational strategies given the fundamental weakness of Russia's post–Cold War capabilities (Neil MacFarlane, "Realism and Russian Strategy after the Collapse of the USSR"; Lynch, "Realism of Russian Foreign Policy").

36 Mearsheimer, *The Tragedy of Great Power Politics*, p. 139.

37 In addition to Mearsheimer's *The Tragedy of Great Power Politics*, see Wohlforth, "Honor as Interest" and Wohlforth, "A Test of Neorealism." See also Kennedy, *The Rise and Fall of Great Powers*; Fuller, *Strategy and Power in Russia*.

38 Luttwack, *The Grand Strategy of the Soviet Union*; Pipes, "Is Russia Still an Enemy?"; Brzezinski, *The Grand Chessboard*; Tuminez, *Russian Nationalism since 1856*; LeDonne, *The Grand Strategy of the Russian Empire, 1650–1830*.

39 On revisionist and back-passing strategies, see Mearsheimer, *The Tragedy*, pp. 267–333.

Part II

Honor and Cooperation

"I am not here for war, but to consolidate the tranquility of Europe."

Alexander I[1]

The Era of the Holy Alliance

The Holy Alliance

The Holy Alliance came into existence at about the same time the Vienna system was established, and it lasted for about as long (see the timeline).[2] After the European countries failed to restrain France's hegemonic ambitions and one after another submitted to Napoleon,[3] Russia dealt a decisive blow to French efforts to dominate the continent. Before doing so, Russia had been part of the third anti-French coalition and had suffered serious defeats in Austerlitz. After Austria withdrew from the coalition and it suffered another defeat in Freiland, Russia signed a treaty of peace and friendship with France in Tilsit on June 22, 1807, which was followed by a secret agreement to form an alliance.[4] These agreements, however, did not last, and in June 1812 Napoleon moved on Russia to eliminate the last obstacle to his control of Europe. Appealing to nobles, the Church, and the peasants to "carry the cross in your hearts and the sword in your hands,"[5] Alexander called on them to take up arms against France. Due to a combination of reasons, including severe climate, Russian heroism, good logistics, and effective military strategy, the French army of 600,000 men could not last until the autumn and had largely disintegrated even before Napoleon ordered a retreat.[6] Assisted by Prussia, Russia then chased the emperor's army all the way to Paris.

Having emerged victorious, Russia presided at the Vienna Congress, leading the effort to design a new territorial settlement for Europe. Determined to prevent a future threat arising from central Europe, Alexander wanted to dominate Poland and was ultimately able to control most of it. Russia reconciled with Austria and formed a quadruple alliance, with England and Prussia as additional members. France, despite Talleyrand's efforts, was isolated and did not join the alliance until a few years later at the Aachen conference in 1818.[7] It was in this context that Alexander proposed the establishment of the Holy Alliance to guarantee a peace in Europe based on principles of Christian ethics.[8] Signed on September 26, 1815, by Russia, Austria, and Prussia, the declaration establishing the Holy Alliance was anything but a diplomatic document. It contained only three articles, the first of which pledged,

Comfortably to the words of Holy Scripture which commands all men to look upon each other as brothers, the three contracting monarchs will continue united by the bonds of a true and indissoluble fraternity, and, regarding themselves as compatriots, they shall lend aid and assistance to each other on all occasions and in all places, viewing themselves, in their relations to their subjects and to their armies, as fathers of families; they shall direct them in the same spirit of fraternity by which they are animated for the protection of religion, peace and justice.[9]

Although most European states eventually joined the Alliance, they had difficulty understanding or sharing Alexander's perspective or commitment.[10] Alexander was a firm believer in the arrangement and, along with his contribution to the quadruple and the quintuple alliances, did "more than any other European leader ... to develop co-operation and unity in Europe."[11] His vision included proposals to disarm national armies and to form a permanent international army.[12]

At the Aachen conference Alexander proposed to create a universal league of sovereigns to guarantee not only each others' frontiers but also their political systems, which ideally would be based on constitutions granted by their monarchs.[13] By that time, Alexander had already granted a constitution to Poland while continuing to deny one to the rest of the Russian Empire. Although Austrian Chancellor Klemens von Metternich and the British Foreign Secretary Viscount Castlereagh supported the Holy Alliance, they both objected to Alexander's proposal. The former rejected the notion of constitution, and the latter did not approve of intervention as a principle of international relations.[14] In general, the Vienna participants did not think much of the Alliance. Metternich referred to it as a "high sounding nothing," Talleyrand called it a "ludicrous contract," and Castlereagh said it was no more than a "piece of sublime mysticism and nonsense."[15] Recognizing the role of Alexander in establishing the Vienna system, they realized they needed to be a part of the Alliance, but they each hoped to mold it into something that fit their own worldviews.

At another conference in Troppau, Russia, Austria, and Prussia finally agreed on some principles when they signed, on November 19, 1820, a Preliminary Protocol; they committed themselves to not recognize a regime brought to power by a revolution and to take necessary actions, including force, against it.[16] Despite the protests of England, this agreement was put into effect, thereby serving as an important precondition of the Alliance's existence. Despite Alexander's initial vision, the arrangement was beginning to resemble what A. J. P. Taylor called the system of Metternich, which was "conservative in a double sense" – being opposed to both changes of frontiers and constitutional concessions within states.[17] The system fully matured by 1833 when Russia and Austria signed the treaty of Munchengratz, binding them to maintain the status quo in Turkey, preserve control over their parts of Poland, and help suppress liberalism in other European states.[18] Alexander's Foreign Minister Count Nesselrode described the Alliance's essentially conservative position in his letter to Metternich: "The old Europe has not existed for more than forty years; let us take it as it is today and try to preserve it lest it becomes something much worse."[19]

Russia's evolving policy on the Polish question reflected this conservative position. After granting Poland a constitution in 1815, Russia withdrew it in 1832 after Polish demands for independence spurred the uprising of 1830–1. Russian came to see political liberalism as a threat, and Alexander's old idea of using Poland as a testing ground to guide the launch of similar reforms in Russia[20] was abandoned. Poland was made "an indivisible part" of the Russian Empire, as Nicholas demonstrated even greater loyalty to the new conservative thrust of the Holy Alliance than his younger brother Alexander.[21] By suppressing the Polish revolt, Russia merely did what the system of Metternich expected it to, yet it was Nicholas who was labeled the "Gendarme of Europe." To European liberals, Poland became a symbol of progressive values, whereas Russia was associated with imperialism and repression. It was deemed too "barbaric" and "Asiatic" by nature to absorb European civilization.[22]

The Greek Question

The Greek revolt against the Turkish Sultan became an important test of Alexander's commitment to the Alliance. Not fully recognized by Europe as one of its own, Russia had historically sought to pursue policies consistent with the European political mainstream. In addition to perceiving themselves as European and Christian by culture, Russian rulers also viewed their country as the Third Rome, or the legitimate heir of the Byzantine Empire and protector of the Orthodox people. They felt a special responsibility to the millions of Balkan Christians residing in the Ottoman Empire, whose loyalty could also facilitate the attainment of Russia's geopolitical objectives in the East. Not surprisingly, at

the Vienna Congress Russian officials, such as Nesselrode and Count
Andrei Razumovski, saw the Balkan Christians as a "moral force which
has always worked in favor of Russia and paralyzed the hostile designs
of the Ottoman Empire" and Russia as "the natural protector of the
Christians of the Greek Oriental rite."[23] Although Russia did not see its
European and Balkan commitments as in conflict, its ability to meet both
of them partly depended on the perception of Russia's actions by both
the East and the West.

When Greece revolted, Alexander was tempted to go to war with the
Sultan to support Greek independence. From a military standpoint, Russia was in a favorable position, because outside the country "everyone
believed that a Russo-Turkish war would destroy the Ottoman Empire
in Europe."[24] Inside Russia, many in Alexander's court argued that the
Christian principles of the Holy Alliance did not extend to the sovereignty
of the infidel Turkey.[25] The pressure to act was great, because the Sultan
ordered the Greek patriarch to be hanged in front of his palace and Russia severed diplomatic relations with Turkey by recalling its ambassador
Baron Grigori Stroganov from Constantinople.

Alexander ultimately sided with supporters of a more moderate course,
such as Nesselrode and Grand Prince Constantine, and decided to
pursue nonmilitary actions. By 1821, he had been convinced that
supporting the Greek revolt would violate the Alliance's principle of
opposing revolutions, and he shared Metternich's view that the rebellion was part of a worldwide revolutionary conspiracy centered in
Paris.[26] Alexander's commitment to preserving common ground with
the Allies was formidable. In 1822, he told the French diplomat Vicomte
Chateaubriand, "I first have to show loyalty to the principles upon which
I have founded the Alliance."[27] Russia pursued largely ineffective diplomatic policies, and as the Greek revolt continued, in 1824 Alexander
proposed the creation of three separate Greek principalities under Turkish sovereignty. Indeed, when at the St. Petersburg conference in 1825
Metternich surprised everyone by proposing the creation of a small independent Greek state, Alexander found it unacceptable.[28]

Nicholas I then fought a successful war with Turkey in 1828–9, but he
perceived that the war was fought over long-standing conflicts of interests
between the two empires, and not to support the Greeks: "I detest, I
abhor the Greeks, I consider them as revolted subjects and I do not
desire their independence. My grievance is against the Turks' conduct
to Russia."[29] Even while unintentionally assisting Greek independence
by fighting Turkey, Russian officials never wanted to topple the Ottoman
Empire and were explicit that they had much more limited objectives.[30]

Support for Conservative Powers

Consistent with their views, both Alexander and Nicholas extended support to leading conservative powers to suppress revolutionary activities in Europe. In 1820–1, Alexander urged military intervention by the Alliance against the constitutionalist revolutions in Spain, Portugal, Piedmont, and Naples. In particular, Russia supported Austria's suppression of revolutionary movements in Italy against possible French counter-intervention in the 1820s.[31] In 1830, Russia acted to support Dutch rulers in their attempts to quell a revolt in Belgium. Although Russia lacked sufficient funds and suffered a cholera epidemic, it mobilized troops and would have likely intervened militarily in the Netherlands, were it not for a revolt in Poland that required Nicholas's full attention.[32] As Europe was becoming more divided, resembling what British Foreign Minister Lord Palmerston called a Europe of "the Two and the Three"[33] – with England and France on one side, and Russia, Austria, and Prussia on the other – Russia was taking steps to establish "the closest union of the three states, which is the only guarantee of universal peace."[34] In 1833, Nicholas even supported the Turkish Sultan in suppressing the Egyptian revolt.[35]

Russia's role in assisting its European allies was especially prominent during the 1840s nationalist revolutions. In 1846, Russia led the way in suppressing a Polish uprising in Krakow, which was part of the Hapsburg state under the Vienna Convention. In July 1848, Nicholas suppressed revolutions in the Danubian Principalities of Moldavia and Walachia – partly to assist Turkey in defeating the Rumanian nationalist movement.[36] In 1849, Russia provided Austria with financial and diplomatic assistance to strengthen its position in Italy, and Nicholas committed almost 200,000 troops to help the Hapsburgs suppress the revolt in Hungary.[37] As it did everywhere in Europe, Russia acted in a multilateral spirit and had no hegemonic ambitions of its own. The Hungarian war, for example, was costly and unpopular at home,[38] and it generated fears among allies of Russia's overwhelming military presence. Prussia too wanted to help Austria but as a means of dominating Germany,[39] whereas Russia had no such conditions and was assisting Austria to fulfill its Holy Alliance obligations. Nicholas did not want to be viewed as acting against the Alliance and was "prepared to accept anything on which Austria and Prussia agreed."[40] Nesselrode described Russia's stance this way: "let the other countries manage as they can, we shall let them alone as long as they do not touch us."[41]

The Holy Alliance and the Concert of Europe, 1814–53: Timeline

1812–4	Russia defeats Napoleon in a "war of liberation"
1815	Vienna Congress; Alexander proposes the Holy Alliance Russia grants limited autonomy to Poland
1820	A "Preliminary Protocol"
1821	Revolt in Greece
1824	Alexander proposes a conference about Greece
1829	Russia defeats Turkey and demands Greek independence
1830	Revolt in Belgium; Russia mobilizes troops
1832	Revolt in Poland; Nicholas suppresses revolt and takes away Polish autonomy
1833	Revolt in Hungary; Russia sends troops
1848–9	European revolutions; Russia sends troops to Romania and Hungary
1853	Crimean War

Explaining the Holy Alliance

The Tsars' Sense of Honor

Alexander and Nicholas's commitment to the Holy Alliance was firmly within the tradition of enhancing Russia's honor by cooperating with European nations. Russia had seen itself as a protector of the Christian world since the Ottoman Turks had conquered Byzantium, and the idea of a united Europe had a strong religious component. Before the second half of the nineteenth century, international politics was centered on managing interreligious relations, and European monarchs – from the Protestant rulers of Britain to the Orthodox tsars of Russia – were expected to be defenders of the faith. As Barbara Jelavich wrote, each tsar inherited a moral code of honor and duty that was "typical not only of Russia, but of the general outlook of most European monarchs."[42] In terms of foreign policy, this outlook implied the concept of cultural allies and cultural adversaries, associated with European states and Turkey, respectively.

Alexander I had a strong commitment to European values and came to power as a European liberal, whose political views had been shaped by his teacher, the Swiss philosopher Frederic-Cesar La Harpe. Alexander's plan for internal reforms was far reaching and included liberation of the serfs, changes in the administrative and educational systems, and creation of the constitution.[43] Indeed, according to his close friend Prince Adam

Czartoryski, Alexander expressed some "extreme opinions," being very enthusiastic about the republican principles of the French Revolution and viewing hereditary monarchy as an "unjust and absurd institution."[44] The Tsar's vision of a liberal European order could be found in his instructions issued in 1804 to the Russian envoy in Great Britain. He expected Russia to play an important role in European affairs outside its traditional interests in Poland and the Balkans.[45] In particular, on completion of the Napoleonic wars Alexander wanted a new peace treaty to be concluded that would serve "as a basis for the reciprocal relations of the European states," binding the participating powers not to begin a war without exhausting all means of mediation and empowering members of the treaty to turn against its offender.[46]

Alexander's war experience challenged and transformed his secular liberal outlook. In September 1812, when Napoleon occupied Moscow and the Tsar's popularity was at its lowest point, Alexander turned to religion and "commended the fate of Russia to the Almighty."[47] His evolving views of the objectives of the Holy Alliance were most likely shaped by this transformative experience. The Tsar's initial proposals for the Alliance in Vienna (1815) and Aachen (1818) were liberal and republican, but no longer secular. By the time of the conference in Troppau (1820) Alexander had emerged as a committed believer in suppressing revolutionary regimes, viewing them, along with Metternich of Austria and Frederick William of Prussia, as the principal threat to Europe. He grew increasingly fearful of French revolutionary ideas, no longer separating them from Napoleon's imperialism.[48] Still a believer in liberal and republican ideals,[49] Alexander nonetheless did not want these ideals to come from below in the form of a revolution. He therefore supported military interventions in Spain, Portugal, and Italy. Choosing between Russia's moral commitment to fellow Orthodox believers in the Balkans and the broader commitment to keep the order in Europe, the Tsar refused to go to war with the Ottoman Empire over Greek independence.

Nicholas underwent nothing of Alexander's complex evolution and was a committed European autocrat from the beginning of his rule. Not having the luxury of Alexander's sophisticated education, Nicholas was more traditional and "excessively literal-minded," including in his definition of national honor.[50] He held an essentially Christian dynastic vision of European order and at one point even tried to convert the Sultan to Christianity.[51] Nicholas insisted that "good morality" was "the best theory of law," and he "disliked organically all theories and abstractions" as having no practical application.[52] He cared little for economic reforms and instead introduced the concept of official nationality, which he also understood in the dynastic sense. Rather than emphasizing popular sovereignty, the concept promoted loyalty to the tsar.[53] A firm believer in the Holy Alliance, Nicholas justified it on moral and dynastic grounds. He was in full agreement with Baron Brunnow's memorandum written to him in 1838 that the alliance was "solidly founded on principles analogous to our own" and was necessary as a "moral barrier" between Russia and France.[54] Until the Crimean War, Nicholas never challenged the Alliance's principles, and it was only during that war that he began to feel that Russia's interests were different from those of European monarchies.[55]

Social and Political Support

Russia's rulers envisioned the Holy Alliance as a means of unifying the European and Russian people through religion. They presented the defeat of Napoleon as the victory of a truly Christian society over an atheist one. Alexander sought to make the scriptures available to all people, and he encouraged the creation of a synthesis of the Christian faith across the entire continent by bringing together members of Orthodox, Roman Catholic, and Lutheran churches.[56] The text of the declaration establishing the Holy Alliance was published and read from every Russian pulpit.[57]

Despite these state efforts, the Russian public's reception of the Alliance was not uniformly positive; three factors worked against this religion-based idea of cooperation with Europe. First, Russia had absorbed some secular European ideas of Freemasonry and republicanism, partly because of Alexander's initial convictions and partly because of the country's exposure to European intellectual influences during the war with Napoleon. Later, these ideas became the basis for various pro-Western movements, from the Decembrists to the Westernizers. However, at the time Russia was still too isolated and commercially weak for republican ideas to take hold, and they attracted "only a tiny section of Russian society."[58] Alexander's evolution in a religious direction further undermined the influence of secular liberalism.

Second, the Holy Alliance was opposed by those in Alexander's court who supported Russia's hegemony on the European continent. Alexander felt sufficiently confident to decide unilaterally the territorial settlement after the Napoleonic wars and, if necessary, by force – "as did *Napoleon*."[59] Soon, however, the Tsar indicated that he favored a multilateral arrangement and had no ambition to become the new continent's dictator. During the Greek revolution, Alexander also felt pressure to use force against the Sultan. Balkan independence movements generated strong support inside Russia from liberal republicans and advocates of Slav/Orthodox unity.[60] Still, their pressure was not strong enough to convince Alexander to go to war against the Ottoman Empire or to push Nicholas toward seizing Constantinople or establishing a permanent military presence on Turkish territory.

The third factor that reduced popular support of the Holy Alliance was Russia's isolationism. Soon after defeating Napoleon, some members of the court and military commanders, such as Marshal Mikhail Kutuzov, argued that pursuing and destroying the French army would only benefit England.[61] In addition, a number of Russian statesmen, such as Nesselrode himself, favored the principles of balance-of-power politics, rather than those of the Holy Alliance. The Russian Church fiercely resisted the idea of "universal" Christianity.[62] Russia's rulers, however, remained loyal to the Alliance.

Despite these factors, the public's opinion of the Holy Alliance was, on the whole, favorable. Within the elite, support came from advocates of European messianism and defenders of state autocracy at home. The former included adherents to movements such as Vladimir Odoevsky's Society of Wisdom-Lovers, which was inspired by German idealism[63] and later gave birth to another prominent movement, the Slavophiles. In addition, many conservative nobles and members of the court supported the state's international policy as a way to consolidate the Russian autocratic system. Their leader, historian Nikolai Karamzin, argued that the Alliance was needed to preserve Russia's traditional institutions and to keep liberal European developments at a distance. The historian took issues with the reformist ideas of Alexander's advisor, Mikhail Speranski, which Karamzin regarded as a mere imitation of those of the French Revolution.[64] Other conservative intellectuals, such as Professor Mikhail Pogodin and Count Sergei Uvarov, later contributed to Nicholas's notion of the official nationality,[65] thereby solidifying the domestic pillar of the Holy Alliance.

Alternative Explanations

The case of the Holy Alliance is especially problematic for offensive realism, which assumes the state's aggressive posture and continual readiness to increase its power in the international system. In general, offensive realists avoid discussing the Alliance and concentrate, as John Mearsheimer does, on long-term historical developments.[66] In particular, Mearsheimer predicts that states attempt, whenever possible, to achieve the position of a regional hegemon.[67] Russians then should have been expected to pursue a policy of dominating Europe by all means available and to exercise restraint only when its military capabilities were limited. Some geopolitically minded scholars of Russia have indeed insisted that it has demonstrated expansionist or offensive behavior throughout its entire history. For example, John LeDonne made a case for Russia's "expansionist urge" that remained "unabated until 1917,"[68] and he argued that during the 1830s and 1840s, the Russians were "dangerously close to the establishment of their hegemony in the Heartland."[69] According to this view, the only reason why Nicholas I did not seek to establish European hegemony was because he was contained by Britain and other leading powers: "There is no greater misreading of Nicholas I's foreign policy than to see it dominated by the pursuit of 'honor', by respect for treaties and the determination to maintain the status quo."[70]

However, the Russia of Alexander and Nicholas never wanted to dominate in Europe, and there is hardly any reason to question the sincerity of its efforts to establish a multilateral system of great powers based on shared values and honor. As Martin Malia wrote, "The first half of the 19th century was an age when politics was exalted and ideological," and "states fought not merely for power, but for a triumph of good over evil."[71] Russia was no exception: it used the Vienna settlement to promote its religious-colored perspective of international relations because Alexander had faith in his vision of the Alliance, not because he had ulterior power motives. More than anything else he acted on moral grounds even though realist-minded politicians of his age had difficulty understanding him. Immediately following the defeat of Napoleon, Russia emerged as so powerful that Alexander briefly considered the hegemonic option, but soon ruled it out in favor of a cooperative approach, which he pursued even at the expense of Russia's traditionally strong ties with Greece. The same point applies to Nicholas, who passed up a number of opportunities to dominate in the Balkans and Europe after suppressing revolutionary movements there during the 1830s–1840s. On several important occasions, Russia abstained from using force actively or preventively, thereby exercising both restraint and self-restraint.[72] As scholars have recognized, Russia was the strongest nation in the system, but it exploited its strength to design and maintain the Concert of Europe,[73] not to impose a unilateral settlement.[74]

Defensive realists tend to view the Holy Alliance as a balancing coalition against powerful competitors, such as Britain and France. Although some offensive realists, such as LeDonne, agree with this view, they differ from defensive realists in their assessment of Russia's position of power. Offensive realists see Russia as contained and therefore insufficiently strong to impose its hegemony, whereas defensive realists find the case of Russia very puzzling precisely because St. Petersburg was so powerful and yet refrained from engaging in hegemonic behavior. The answer that defensive realists provide has to do with constraints of the international system and Russia's attitude of self-restraint.[75] This answer does not specify, however, why Russia took on the burden of leadership in the European system when it could have adopted a more isolationist approach, recommended by Kutuzov, or simply joined a balancing coalition against Napoleon, as it did before 1812. The behavior that St. Petersburg demonstrated can hardly be described as balancing. Rather, as Paul Schroeder described it, Russia followed the strategy of *transcending*: "attempting to surmount international anarchy and go beyond the normal limits of conflictual politics: to solve the problem, end the threat, and prevent its recurrence through some institutional arrangement involving an international consensus or formal agreement on norms, rules, and procedures for these purposes."[76]

The important role played by ideas and morality in the Holy Alliance is therefore undeniable. Indeed, it is so powerful that historically sensitive realists usually acknowledge it.[77] One even proposed a revision of the defensive realist outlook by explicitly recognizing that "defensive 'realism' is a *synthesis* of realist and non-realist theories."[78]

Assessment of the Holy Alliance

Overall, the Holy Alliance should be judged as successful in meeting Russia's foreign policy objectives. Alexander's original idea of European-wide constitutionalism imposed from above failed to materialize, but even the conservative version of the Alliance favored by Metternich assisted Russia in preserving international peace, political prestige, and stability at home. If peace is defined as the absence of a general war among major powers, then it existed in Europe for almost forty years.[79] As a critically important part of the Vienna system, the Alliance provided the continent with "the longest period of peace it had ever known."[80] During this period, Russia was generally satisfied with the safety of its borders,[81] and neither Alexander nor Nicholas were interested in exploiting opportunities to challenge the status quo. Until the Crimean War, Russia also acted consistently with the reputation of an honorable European power by maintaining a difficult balance between its commitments to Western nations and its Orthodox allies in the Balkans. Although Alexander refused to challenge the Ottomans over Greece, a few years later Nicholas defeated the Sultan, restoring Russia's previously undermined position as the leader of the Orthodox world. Finally, Russia maintained stability at home, albeit at the price of delaying liberal political changes.

The relatively smooth functioning of the Alliance was made possible by Russia's self-restrained vision and willingness to devote its formidable power to a multilateral agenda. The former helped forge a sense of shared values across major European nations, whereas the latter provided the necessary material resources. Russia's internal confidence did not result in policies of challenging other powers, and until this was the case, the system continued to function.

Over time, however, important flaws were revealed in the Vienna system, and the Holy Alliance became increasingly responsible for the system's shortcomings. Austria, Britain, and Prussia frequently sought to exploit the system to their narrowly defined advantages. That the Ottoman Empire was not covered by the Alliance increased tensions between Russia, with its Orthodox commitments, and other countries such as Britain that were growing critical of St. Petersburg's eastern policy. No less importantly, Russia and the European powers were moving apart in terms of their internal political developments, with the former doing its utmost to consolidate its autocratic institutions and the latter challenging such institutions. Nicholas's "Orthodoxy, Autocracy, and Nationality" at home and brutal suppression of the Polish revolt in 1832 united European liberals against Russia, making it ever more difficult to preserve the Alliance. Russia was becoming a social/political anachronism, as even its most conservative allies had abolished serfdom – Prussia after its defeat by Napoleon in 1806 and Austria after the revolution of 1848.[82] Once shared values became widely divergent, and Russia's international legitimacy was rapidly eroding. The combined challenge to Russia's vision and power made the Vienna system and the Holy Alliance hostage to time.

Notes

1 As quoted in Rendall, "Defensive Realism and the Concert of Europe," 529.
2 Historians, such as A. J. P. Taylor, view the alliance as lasting until the Crimean War (Taylor, *The Struggle for Mastery in Europe, 1848–1918*).
3 For analyses of how Napoleon achieved his goals by organizing most of Europe against a single isolated foe, see Schroeder, *The Transformation of European Politics, 1763–1848*, especially pp. 100–287 and Tarle, *1812 god*, pp. 145–93.
4 For texts of the agreements, see Dmytryshyn, ed., *Imperial Russia*, pp. 142–52.
5 "Alexander's Proclamation to the Nation," 159.
6 For a detailed account of the war and Russia's military strategy, see especially Fuller, *Strategy and Power in Russia, 1600–1914*, chapter 5, "The Baleful Consequences of Victory: Russian Strategy and the War of 1812"; Tarle, *1812 god*, pp. 729–800; Troitskiy, *Aleksandr I protiv Napoleona*; Lieven, *Russia against Napoleon*.
7 Riasanovsky, *A History of Russia*, pp. 314–15; Schroeder, *The Transformation of European Politics*, pp. 523–38.

8 As he later explained to his ambassador in London, Count Lieven, the idea behind the Alliance was "to apply more efficaciously to the civil and political relations between states the principles of peace, concord and love which are the fruit of religion and Christian morality" (Hosking, *Russia: People and Empire*, pp. 138–9).

9 "The Holy Alliance," in Oliva, ed., *Russia and the West from Peter to Khrushchev*, 66.

10 Schroeder, *The Transformation*, p. 559. For a more detailed description of beliefs of key European states, see Holsti, *Peace and War*, pp. 116–26.

11 Riasanovsky, *A History of Russia*, p. 317.

12 Ibid., pp. 317–18.

13 Seton-Watson, *The Russian Empire*, p. 175.

14 Ibid.; Orlik, *Rossiya v mezhdunarodnykh otnosheniyakh*, p. 31.

15 Holsti, *Peace and War*, pp. 121–2.

16 Seton-Watson, *The Russian Empire*, p. 177.

17 Taylor, *The Struggle for Mastery*, p. 2.

18 Ibid.

19 Fuller, *Strategy and Power*, pp. 226–7.

20 Holborn, "Russia and the European Political System," 383.

21 Riazanovsky, *Nicholas I and Official Nationality in Russia*, p. 187.

22 Malia, *Russia under Western Eyes*, p. 99.

23 Jelavich, *Russia's Balkan Entenglements*, p. 40.

24 Schroeder, *The Transformation*, p. 617.

25 Malia, *Russia*, 92; Orlik, *Rossiya v mezhdunarodnykh otnosheniyakh*, p. 85.

26 Schroeder, *The Transformation*, p. 618.

27 Orlik, *Rossiya*, p. 90. In early 1826, an internal report prepared for Tsar Nicholas I also noted that Alexander had abstained from using force due to "the fear of altering the nature of his relations with the leading European powers, the danger of thus weakening the guarantees of the general peace" (Rendall, "Defensive Realism and the Concert of Europe," 531).

28 Seton-Watson, *The Russian Empire*, p. 182.

29 Riasanovsky, *Nicholas I and Official Nationality in Russia*, p. 239.

30 As stated by Nesselrode, "We do not want Constantinopole. This would be the most dangerous conquest we could undertake" (Orlik, *Rossiya*, p. 112). In 1829, a special committee appointed by Nicholas I and composed of six leading assistants of the Tsar concluded, "The advantages offered by the preservation of the Ottoman Empire in Europe exceed the inconveniences which it presents; therefore, its fall would be contrary to the true interests of Russia; consequently, it would be wise to try to prevent this fall by utilizing all the possibilities that might yet occur for the conclusion of an honorable peace" (Riasanovsky, *Nicholas I*, pp. 239–40).

31 MacFarlane, "Russian Perspectives on Order and Justice," 184.

32 Rendall, "Defensive Realism," 534–5.

33 Malia, *Russia*, p. 96.

34 Fuller, *Strategy*, p. 230.

35 Ibid., p. 222.

36 Riasanovsky, *Nicholas I*, p. 248.

37 Ibid.
38 Ibid., p. 249.
39 Taylor, *The Struggle for Mastery*, p. 30.
40 Ibid, p. 43.
41 Fuller, *Strategy*, p. 232.
42 Jelavich, *Russia's Balkan Entanglements*, p. 33.
43 Platonov, *Polnyi kurs lektsii po russkoi istoriyi*, pp. 731–43. Riasanovsky, *A History*, pp. 302–7; Natan Eidel'man, *"Revolutsiya sverkhu" v Rossiyi*, pp. 78–93.
44 "Czartoryski on the Education of Alexander I," 60.
45 Seton-Watson, *The Russian Empire*, p. 174.
46 "Alexander's Vision of the Future," 65.
47 Seton-Watson, *The Russian Empire*, p. 136.
48 In the eyes of European monarchs, Napoleon was "the embodiment of revolutionary objectives" (Orlik, *Rossiya v mezhdunarodnykh otnosheniyakh*, p. 19).
49 In 1818, he returned to the idea of a Russian constitution and asked his advisor Count Nikolai Novosiltsev to draft it. In 1819, Alexander still intended to implement a constitution but complained to Prince Vyazemsky about a shortage of money and the prejudices of the court (Seton-Watson, *The Russian Empire*, p. 157).
50 Fuller, *Strategy*, pp. 233, 245–8. For a similar assessment, see Lincoln, *Nicholas I*, p. 109.
51 Riasanovsky, *Nicholas I*, p. 265.
52 Ibid., p. 189.
53 Ibid., pp. 235–7, 255.
54 Holborn, "Russia and the European Political System," 385.
55 For example, he appointed Alexander Gorchakov to replace the Baltic German Baron Friedrich Meyendorff in order to strengthen Russia's interests even at the risk of aiding European revolutions. For the first time during his rule, the Tsar felt surrounded by too many Europeans and – acting over Nesselrode's objections – Nicholas appointed someone who was both Russian and Orthodox (Taylor, *The Struggle for Mastery*, p. 78).
56 Hosking, *Russia*, p. 139.
57 Neumann, *Russia and the Idea of Europe*, p. 18.
58 Seton-Watson, *The Russian Empire*, p. 197.
59 Such were Alexander's words to his Russian companions (Rendall, "Defensive Realism," 529).
60 Alexander's foreign policy advisor John Capodistria, a native Greek, advocated Russia's intervention and was opposed by another key advisor, Count Nesselrode (Riasanovsky, *Nicholas I*, p. 46). Capodistria was later elected as president by the Greek assembly, but was murdered in 1831 by a personal enemy (Seton-Watson, *The Russian Empire*, p. 301).
61 Holborn, "Russia," 382. Foreign Minister Rumiantsev also opposed crossing the Russian frontier (Ragsdale, "Russian Foreign Policy, 1763–1815," 150).
62 In 1824, the abbot of the Yur'ev Monastery in Moscow, Arkhimandrit Fotii, presented his memorandum to the Tsar asking him to abandon the idea of

universal Christianity and restore the Holy Synod's traditional role: "God defeated the visible Napoleon, invader of Russia: let Him now in Your Person defeat the invisible Napoleon" (Hosking, *Russia*, pp. 140–1).

63 Neumann, *Russia and the Idea of Europe*, p. 20.
64 Hosking, *Russia*, p. 132.
65 Riasanovsky, *Nicholas I*, pp. 51–60; Tolz, *Russia*, pp. 78–9.
66 Mearsheimer, *The Tragedy of Great Power Politics*.
67 Ibid., chap. 7 "The Offshore Balancers."
68 LeDonne, *The Russian Empire and the World, 1700–1917*, p. 348.
69 Ibid., p. 314.
70 Ibid., p. 357.
71 Malia, *Russia under Western Eyes*, p. 97.
72 Rendall, "Russia, the Concert of Europe, and Greece, 1821–1829"; Rendall, "Defensive Realism."
73 Ibid.; Hagan, "Domestic Political Sources of Stable Peace," 44–5; Schroeder, *The Transformation*, p. 559; Slantchev, "Territory and Commitment," 601.
74 Indeed, as Russian historians have acknowledged (Platonov, *Polnyi kurs*, p. 752; Orlik, *Rossiya*, p. 249) Russia did not always act in its best interests and became too involved on behalf of Austria and others.
75 See, for example, Rendall, "Defensive Realism."
76 Schroeder, "Historical Reality vs. Neo-realist Theory," 430.
77 For example, Henry Kissinger wrote that the most important reason for the Vienna system's success "was that the Continental countries were knit together by a sense of shared values" (Kissinger, *Diplomacy*, p. 79).
78 Rendall, "Defensive Realism," 524.
79 Kissinger, *Diplomacy*, p. 79; Kupchan and Kupchan, "Concerts, Collective Security, and the Future of Europe," 123; Vasquez, "The Vienna System," 236.
80 Kissinger, *Diplomacy*, p. 79.
81 Jelavich, *A Century of Russian Foreign Policy*, p. 291.
82 Malia, *Russia*, pp. 146–9.

"[T]o protect the honor, dignity and safety of Russia and its position among the Great Powers."

Nicholas II's manifesto before World War I, 1914[1]

The Policy of Realignment with the West

Russia's decision to go to war in 1914 should be viewed in the context of its growing ties with Western nations, especially France and Britain, and its preoccupation with protecting traditional Balkan allies. Step by step, the Tsar ruled out the equivalent of the moderate policy of recueillement and the preservation of even-handed relations with Germany – the policy that was advocated by diplomats of the old school and Russia's top ministers. Ever since signing a treaty of cooperation with France in the early 1890s, Russia's international policy was becoming increasingly pro-Western and anti-German.

The policy evolved in several stages, each reflecting Russia's increasingly deep engagement with France, Britain, and the Balkans. Russia's new political and military agreements with France of 1891 and 1892 heralded the first stage. The second stage began after defeat in the 1905 war with Japan, which resulted in Russia's dependence on Western economic assistance. In April 1906, Russia agreed with France that the defeat of Germany would be the central objective of a major war should such a war take place. In 1907 St. Petersburg broadened relations with Britain by formally dropping anti-British elements of previous agreements with France. The final stage followed a breakdown of the status quo in the Balkans and Austria's annexation of Bosnia and Herzegovina. In response to a German ultimatum to accept the annexation, the Tsar – supported by his allies and his own military – devised an offensive military plan that put the country on a path to a European war.

The Russo-French Alliance

The initial decision to develop closer relations with France was consistent with the policy of maintaining even-handed ties with important European powers pursued by Chancellor Alexander Gorchakov. The unification of Germany after Russia's denunciation of the Black Sea clauses in 1870 demanded new attention to the rising giant. The dismissal of Chancellor Bismarck in 1890 and the subsequent refusal of Germany to renew the existing Reinsurance Treaty between the two countries indicated the possible emergence of a new policy line for the German emperor. Soon, St. Petersburg's diplomats came to believe, as Foreign Minister Count Vladimir Lamsdorff stated, that "to be generally on good terms with Germany the alliance with France is necessary."[2] The Russo-French alliance was also important to French ruling circles that wanted guarantees of their security in the event of a conflict with Germany.[3] Such was the context in which the two nations concluded a political agreement in August 1891.

A military agreement concluded a year later was more controversial. Supported by Tsar Alexander III and the military, it was opposed by the Foreign Ministry and those in Russia who were worried about altering the balance in relations between France and Germany. According to Lamsdorff, "if our military needs to have an agreement in anticipation of some future possibilities, then at least they must do it without compromising us by some written document and by preserving our full freedom of action."[4] He believed that "the object of French attention is precisely our freedom of action and desire to control us by a formal agreement."[5] Acting on such beliefs, Russia's foreign minister Nikolai de Giers did what was in his power to delay ratification of the agreement; it did not take effect until January 1894 – a year before his retirement. If it was not for a trade war between Russia and Germany,[6] the ratification might have been delayed even longer.[7]

Alexander III, however, believed that Germany was bent on war with Russia and that an alliance with France was a necessary defensive precaution.[8] The emperor staked his policy on France in the hope that it might ultimately lead to the dissolution of Germany. When Giers reportedly asked him "what would we gain by helping the French to destroy Germany?" Alexander replied, "What we would gain would be that Germany, as such, would disappear. It would break up into a number of small, weak states, the way it used to be."[9] According to the secret agreement signed by Russia, it was obligated to provide military assistance to France in the event of a German attack.[10]

Political and economic considerations further consolidated Russia's ties with France. In March 1902, the two signed an agreement on the Far East, which, however, did not prevent an attack on Russia by Japan in February 1904. St. Petersburg also signed a commercial treaty with Germany, ending the protectionist rivalry between the two countries, but declined a defensive pact proposed by the German emperor. On Lamsdorff's advice, Nicholas urged Emperor Wilhelm to include France in the coalition – a proposal that Germany found unacceptable. Eventually, the two powers signed an agreement that Nicholas hoped could be amended to include France.[11]

The defeat in the war with Japan made Russia dependent on French financial assistance. A loan of 2,250 million francs in April 1906 provided Nicholas II with the funds needed to suppress the growing Russian revolution and in reality "saved the Tsarism from the inevitable collapse."[12] The revolution of 1905 followed Russia's external defeat, revealing the regime's internal weakness. The Tsar eventually yielded to workers' demands by promising a constitution and new political freedoms. So dependent was Russia on French financial assistance that its finance minister at one point informed a prominent French banker of Russia's tentative budget before making it public in Russia.[13] It was in this context that Russia agreed with the French assessment that defeat of Germany was the main aim of a European war.

Russia–Britain Relations

It was also largely through French efforts that Russia's traditionally difficult relations with Britain evolved toward closer cooperation. In addition to agreeing with France on the threat assessment, Russia dropped the anti-British element of the military agreement signed in 1892. Meanwhile, relations with Germany remained at the previous level of commercial ties, but did not develop in the direction of military cooperation. A meeting between the Russian and German emperors in August 1907 did not change the situation. However, during the same year Russia concluded a convention with Britain that effectively transformed the Russo-French bilateral alliance and the French–British entente into the Triple Entente – a new force on the European continent. Russia's new foreign minister, Alexandr Izvol'sky, took office in 1906 and was instrumental in forging a new consensus that Russia's internal weakness required an accommodation with Britain. Although members of the cabinet held different views of Britain – from Izvol'sky's Anglophilia to Stolypin's German sympathies – they accepted the agreement with Britain as a way of limiting Russia's engagement in Asia.[14] The emergent triple alliance then assisted Russia in reaching a settlement with Japan, thereby strengthening the new relationship.[15]

Russia and Balkan Politics

The year 1908 heralded the final stage of Russia's realignment with the West. In February, Izvol'sky warned of the probable breakdown of the status quo in the Balkans, sensing the growing ambitions of Austria. In October of the same year Austria indeed occupied Bosnia and Herzegovina, demanding Russia's acceptance of the annexation. Russia refused, seeking to confirm its position as the protector of a sizable Orthodox Christian population residing in the peninsula and to protect its vital interest in controlling the Mediterranean Straits through which Russia exported most of its grain to Europe. In response Germany, acting as Austria's benefactor, issued an ultimatum to Russia to accept annexation in March 1909. Internally weak, Nicholas felt he had to accept the ultimatum even though the humiliation, as the Tsar later admitted in a private correspondence, "sickened" his "feelings."[16]

Nicholas then engaged Germany in earnest yet again in an attempt to devise a mutually acceptable arrangement for the Balkans. In November 1910, he and Sergei Sazonov, the new foreign minister, visited Potsdam and reached an agreement that Germany would not support Austria's Balkan ambitions.[17] In addition, Russia introduced a new Turkey policy, working to undermine Austria by encouraging rapprochement between Turkey and the individual Balkan states.[18] However, the two Balkan wars in 1912 and 1913 upset existing arrangements and demonstrated the inability of Russia and other great powers to ensure peace on the peninsula. Russia's relations with Austria continued to worsen, with the former backing Serbia and Greece and the latter supporting Albania while both powers competed for influence in Bulgaria.[19] Meanwhile, Germany, although not supporting Austria formally, was calculating its chances to become stronger at Russia's expense.[20]

These developments convinced Nicholas of the need for additional military preparations. As early as July 1910 he supported a new Russian plan for war in Europe – a clear sign of preparation for the failure of diplomacy. In May 1912, the Tsar endorsed an even more offensive war plan devised by the military and opposed by several of his ministers.[21] After the Balkan wars, a military confrontation among great powers was only waiting to be ignited by an additional provocation.

The assassination of Archduke Francis Ferdinand by Serbian nationalist Gavrilo Princip provided that provocation. By the time Austria declared war on Serbia, Nicholas had already decided – on the advice of

Foreign Minister Sazonov – to support the Balkan nation.[22] ~~From that point, events quickly progressed to war.~~ Russia and Austria declared mass mobilizations. Germany first issued an ultimatum to Russia and then – after the latter refused to comply – declared war on Russia and France in August 1914. During the same month, Britain entered the war on the side of the Triple Entente. As in 1905, the war had a devastating effect on Russia's fragile political system. Repeated military defeats[23] resulted in the abdication of Nicholas and, ultimately, another Russian revolution. In October 1917, the Bolsheviks ended the agony of transition by exploiting the situation of social and political instability in the country and taking power.

The Triple Entente, 1907–1917: Timeline

1891 August	Russo-French political agreement
1892 August	Russo-French military agreement
1894 January	Russo-French military alliance ratified
1902 March	Russo-French agreement on the Far East
1904 February	Japan attacks Russia
April	Anglo-French entente
July	Russo-German commercial treaty
October	Germany proposes defensive alliance to Russia; Russia declines
1905 January	Fall of Port Arthur
	"Bloody Sunday"
October	Tsar's manifesto promising a constitution
December	Moscow uprising
1906 April	2,250 million franc loan from France to Russia
	Russia and France agree on defeat of Germany as the main aim in a European war. Anti-British element of previous agreement is dropped
1907 August	Meeting of Russian and German emperors
	Russo-British convention
1908 February	Izvol'sky's warning of probable breakdown of status quo in the Balkans
October	Austria annexes Bosnia and Herzegovina
1909 March	German ultimatum to Russia to accept annexation
1910 July	New Russian plan for war in Europe
1912 May	Revised, more offensive Russia's war plan
July	Nicholas II and William II meet
October	First Balkan war begins; Russia and Austria begin military preparations

1913 June	Second Balkan war begins
November	Nicholas II approves "Great Military Program"
1914 June	Assassination of Archduke Francis Ferdinand
July	Nicholas II decides to support Serbia
	Austria declares war on Serbia
	Russia's and Austria's mobilization
	German ultimatum to Russia
August	Germany declares war on Russia and France
	Britain declares war on Germany
1917 March	Nicholas II abdicates
October	Revolution and Bolsheviks

Source: Lieven, *Russia and the Origins of the First World War*, pp. 155–62.

Explaining Russia's Realignment with the West

The Triple Entente further isolated Russia from Germany, its former continental ally, while the Balkans became the lightning rod of the war of great power ambitions. Nicholas's commitment to his Western allies served to strengthen his determination to defy Germany, thereby protecting the honor of Russia as a power that would not tolerate the humiliation of its co-religionists. As it had been predicted by Bismarck, the war began with one foolish mistake in the Balkans.

Nicholas's Sense of Honor

Nicholas's manifesto expressed his understanding of state honor, which included protecting the "dignity and safety of Russia and its position among the Great Powers."[24] Having the prestige of a great power implied the need for Russia to be true to its traditional obligations in the Balkans and to inspire respect among other European powers.

Nicholas's notion of honor also meant that, weak or strong, Russia had to demonstrate loyalty to its European allies and be part of the effort to contain the increasing strength of Germany. Already in 1902 – years before the revolution and the French loan needed to suppress it – Nicholas commanded that all war planning be based on the assumption of a massive German attack.[25] After 1906, the Tsar moved to a belief in deterring, rather than engaging Germany, to preserve the European peace. He therefore abandoned the older vision of the continental alliance of Russia, France, and Germany. Nicholas also supported all military and rearmament programs even when his top ministers opposed them. Eager to modernize Russia, Nicholas II was just as loyal to the traditional ideal of autocratic honor and just as inflexible in acting on it as was his predecessor Nicholas I.

Alternative visions of honorable behavior, including those similar to Gorchakov's defensive view of the continental alliance, were also known within the state and were shared by many outside the military. However, these visions failed to prevail partly because of Nicholas's reliance on "favorites" and informal advisors who worked to perpetuate his traditionalist beliefs about the Tsar's complete unity with the people. Notoriously indecisive, he never became comfortable with the enormous power bestowed on him and was especially dependent on his advisors' recommendations.[26] In his memoirs, Prime Minister Vladimir Kokovtsev, dismissed by Nicholas before the war, identified those who were especially influential with the Tsar. For example, the publisher of the periodical *Grazhdanin*, Prince Pyort Meshcherski, was actively working to perpetuate the public image of Nicholas as the only one who truly cared about Russia.[27] Nicholas was heavily influenced by the Empress Alexandra, whose views on autocracy were "much more radical than those of the Emperor," despite the reforms he introduced in response to the revolution of 1905.[28]

Nicholas's increasingly anti-German views affected policy formation and the process of selecting government officials. Within the foreign policy establishment, moderates such as Giers and Lamsdorff were gradually replaced by the more pro-Western Izvol'sky and Sazonov. The latter were known for their Anglophile views, which they combined with a strong Russian nationalism and militarism – an attitude that made the clash with Germany all the more probable. For example, Izvol'sky believed that "basic political reform will bring us closer to Europe, and ease the foreign minister's task abroad"[29]; yet he also supported the Tsar's expensive military and rearmament programs as a means "to remain among the great powers."[30] Because of the growing popularity of such beliefs, the Russo-French alliance, which was initially viewed as a necessity, began to be viewed as a triumph of Russian diplomacy.

The other prominent supporters of Nicholas's vision served on the General Staff. At the time when Giers was expressing his doubts about the binding nature of the military agreement with France, Chief of Staff General Nikolai Obruchev emerged as its principal advocate. As Dietrich Geyer wrote, "[t]he military was in fact the driving force behind the Franco-Russian Alliance."[31] In 1906, the military initiated the Rearmament Program, with the secret objective to revise the Straits convention. The military fought a hard battle with the finance minister, Vladimir Kokovtsev, who argued against the new program of rearmament, which he viewed as undermining the economy and national finance. However, while Kokovtsev insisted that "Russia cannot be a great power with an economy in ruins," his chief opponent and Obruchev's successor, Chief of Staff General Palitsyn, was arguing that even the largest military budget costs less than a lost war.[32] It was the military that devised offensive plans in 1910 and 1912,[33] and it was the military that was quick to propose mobilization in response to the Balkan wars.[34]

Although the Tsar's vision was similar to that of the War Ministry, it had less to do with military capabilities than diplomacy, as evident from the spending choices he made. However weak and indecisive, Nicholas nevertheless always supported military requests for additional expenditures, defying his prime ministers and ministers of finance. For example, Sergei Witte, who served as finance minister before the war with Japan, complained that he always had to keep cash on hand out of fear of his budget being undermined by notorious war hawks, such as Alexandr Bezobrazov and Vyacheslav von Pleve.[35] Kokovtsev, who succeeded Stolypin as prime minister, recalled how Nicholas justified his support of minister of war V. A. Sukhomlinov's requests as a means to solve the conflict in the Balkans:

In your arguments with Sukhomlinov, the truth is on your side, but I want you to understand that I support Sukhomlinov not because I don't trust you, but because I cannot say No to military expenditures. With God's help, we may be able to extinguish the fire in the Balkans. I will never forgive myself if I refuse credits to the military even for one Ruble.[36]

Russia's Domestic Conditions and Support

The increasingly pro-Western and anti-German feelings within Russian society and the political class supported the Tsar's vision of state honor. Both the liberal and nationalist strata came to be largely sympathetic to Nicholas's views, partly because of Russia's domestic condition as a modernizing state. Domestic weakness called for moderation in international relations, and a growing reliance on foreign assistance led to a more dependent and less balanced foreign policy.

As a modernizing state, Russia struggled to improve ties with the wealthiest countries in Europe, France and Britain – partly out of the necessity to maintain a high level of defense expenditures worthy of a great power. From 1885–1913, such expenditures were 25 percent of the overall state budget (see Fig. 6.1).[37] Despite these high expenditures, during the entire period of 1856–1914, "Russia's performance . . . was bad enough to show most of her political leaders the wisdom of moderation in foreign policy."[38] Meanwhile the economy was following a pattern of highly uneven development, indicating serious structural imbalances.[39]

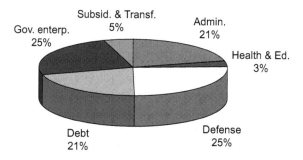

Figure 6.1. Average Annual Distribution of Central Government Expenditures, 1885–1913 (as a percentage of the total). *Source*: Khromov, *Economicheskoye razvitiye Rossii*, p. 284.

It grew rapidly during the 1890s and 1910s, but sank into depression during the 1880s and 1900s. In addition, the government did little to improve working conditions and health care, which led to a increase in the number of economic and political strikes.[40]

Russia's weakness and economic need increased its dependence on the allies. The large loans and other assistance received to settle relations with Japan raised expectations for Russia's successful modernization and Westernization. Domestic support for France and Britain was growing, partly because the public and political class were unaware of the Tsar's secret treaties and military commitments made to the Western nations. Only six people in the Russian Empire were informed of the alliance with France in 1894.[41]

In addition to the Tsar and the increasingly pro-Western foreign policy establishment, support for Westernization came from the expanding liberal part of the political spectrum, the intellectual and commercial classes. After Nicholas's 1905 manifesto and creation of the State Duma, the Constitutional Democrats (*Kadets*) gained political prominence and did not hide their sympathies for the British and French models of development. Some of the party's leaders, such as Pavel Milyukov, advocated for the ideas of British Prime Minister Gladstone and showed little interest in foreign policy.[42] The rising capitalist class also favored the West, as Russia was increasing its grain exports to Britain, and French and British capital were playing an increasing role in the Russian stock market.[43] The national discourse was that of modernization and catching up with liberal Europe, rather than the preservation of state sovereignty and autonomy in international affairs.[44] The Slavophiles were becoming increasingly unpopular, and few public figures warned against the dangers of unbalanced Westernization.[45] Even the Slavophiles' spiritual leader, the philosopher Vladimir Solovyev, was attacking the new voices of cultural nationalism, such as Konstantin Leontyev and Nikolai Danilevskiy, as advocating dangerous attempts to create a Slav future on the ruins of European culture.[46]

Simultaneously, Russian society in general and its political class in particular were developing strong anti-German attitudes. Soon after the 1905 revolution, it was no longer just the Tsar and the military that believed in the virtues of becoming stronger for the purpose of confronting Germany. Pan-Slavism, which had emerged in response to the national humiliation of the Crimean War, advocated a forceful policy of liberating Balkan Slavs and was especially critical of Germany and the "Romano-Germanic cultural type" – to use the nationalist vocabulary – it represented. In the mid-nineteenth century, pan-Slavists had attacked Gorchakov's foreign policy as excessively pro-German, and they grew stronger in the context of the Bosnia crisis and the two Balkan wars. These developments politicized society, and the majority of the media was both pro-Western and pan-Slavist. By the end of the nineteenth century, Russia's German commercial interests also became weaker, which explains the government's often protectionist policies toward Germany.

In political circles, many Kadets sympathized with pan-Slavist ideas.[47] Milyukov, who initially had pacifist leanings, defended the idea of war with Austria after the Bosnian crisis and showed an ever stronger militarist attitude after assuming the duties of foreign minister.[48] During World War I, he famously insisted on not signing a peace agreement.[49] Yevgeniy Trubetskoi was an even more extreme example of the merger of Westernist and pan-Slavist ideas. After his appointment to the Foreign Ministry, Trubetskoi soon became close to Sazonov and in 1907 argued against the moderates who favored Russia's alliance with both France and Germany: "To seek a middle way is equivalent to wanting to sit between two stools. This is scarcely either a profitable or an honorable position."[50] A champion of the national Slavic idea, Trubetskoi explained Russia's defeat in the war with Japan as due to the absence of such a concept, and he welcomed the war with Germany as inspired by pan-Slavism.[51]

After the Balkan wars, only a small minority of politicians on the extreme right and extreme left displayed pro-German attitudes.[52] Although Minister of Internal Affairs Pyotr Durnovo and conservative landowners wanted to restore the old Holy Alliance-like system of autocratic states, the radical leftist Bolsheviks worked to accelerate the collapse of the tsarist system, advocating the defeat of their own government in the war with Germany.

Table 6.1 summarizes the political currents in Russia before the war.

Table 6.1 *Political Currents in Russia before World War I*

	Pro-Western and Anti-German	Moderate	Pro-German and Anti-Western
1891–1905	Tsar Obruchev (Army)	Giers (F. Ministry) Witte (Finance)	
1905–8	Tsar Palitsyn (Army) Kadets (Duma) Izvol'sky (F. Ministry) Public opinion	Stolypin (Prime Minister) Kokovtsev (Finance)	

1908–14	Tsar and advisors
	Sazonov (F. Ministry)
	Sukhomlinov (Army)
	Kadets (Duma)
	Public opinion
		Kokovstev (Prime
		  Minister)
			Durnovo (Internal
			  Affairs)
			Lenin (Bolsheviks)

The Allies

France and Britain played a critical role in developing the Triple Entente with Russia. Without their financial assistance and political nudging, Russia's threat assessment might have not been as focused on Germany and could have even stayed at the level of Gorchakov and Gier's diplomacy; that is, the idea of a continental alliance with Germany as a member could have survived well after 1906. By recognizing Russia's aspiration to become a part of the West commercially, Paris and London shaped St. Petersburg's identity as a Westernizing state, strengthening the conditions for a security entente. In 1906 Germany posed no military threat to others, yet the Western coalition had already recognized it as such.

After suffering the devastating war with Japan and the revolution of 1905, Russia's economy was in no position to survive without large foreign loans and investments provided by France and Britain. Neither country was shy to exploit this leverage. For example, France only provided its 2,250 million franc loan in April 1906, more than a year after the Tsar had experienced serious political difficulties because of his brutal suppression of public demonstrations in St. Petersburg on January 5, 1905 ("Bloody Sunday"). Paris took advantage of Nicholas's weakness by orchestrating a campaign against "tsarist despotism" at home and pressuring him to revise his threat assessment. The loan had restrictions and was granted only after the Tsar had agreed that defeat of Germany was the main aim in a European war.[53] Franco-British investments too were growing, and by 1914 their share of foreign investment in the Russian economy reached 54.6 percent, in contrast to Germany's share of 19.7 percent.[54]

As characterized by a German scholar, Russia's financial and politico-economic ties with France had become "entangled," and the established dependence was "prone to work more to the disadvantage of the Russians."[55] Russia's 1907 settlement with Japan was reached with British political assistance, in the interests of Anglo-French entente, and soon after Russia revised its threat assessment and dropped the anti-British element from its previous military agreement.[56] Having engaged Russia as a dependent member of the coalition, the two Western states then exploited the "entanglement"; for example, in 1913 France encouraged Nicholas to take a harder line toward Austria.[57]

In contrast, Russia's ties with Germany had been weakening since the 1890s. Germany was a source of massive credit for Russia's war with Turkey in 1877–8, and in 1881 Russia, Germany, and Austria signed the Three Emperors League agreement.[58] However, during the 1890s Russia and Germany, both with mercantilist leanings, became involved in a bitter trade war,[59] which marked the beginning of the decline of their bilateral relations. Although Russia managed to secure a substantial loan from Germany in 1902, Germany continued to weaken its ties with the former ally in response to its rapprochement with France. For example, it forbade Berlin banks to participate in the 1906 loan to Russia because of St. Petersburg's behavior during the Moroccan crisis.[60]

Alternative Explanations

Realists' explanations for Russia's foreign policy and decision to go to war in 1914 are either flawed or insufficient.

According to those realist thinkers who believe in relative power as the payoff of international politics, St. Petersburg made a logical choice by joining the Triple Entente and then going to war with Germany because Russia was too weak to fight against the rising threat alone. As historian A. J. P. Taylor wrote, "There had been a real European Balance in the first decade of the Franco-Russian alliance; and peace had followed from it."[61] Yet this argument does not fully explain why Russia had to side with France and Britain against Germany and Austria, and not vice versa. Power considerations alone, especially under conditions of multipolarity, do not dictate which allies to chose nor why they are chosen.[62] As a number of scholars have argued, a military clash with Germany was not inevitable.[63] Rather, a long sequence of actions taken by different sides, especially before 1912, constructed the clash. The Triple Entente did not emerge overnight and was not merely a defense pact; it was also an organization of states with increasingly similar economic interests and cultural identities. Over time, its members developed a similar assessment of threats and of appropriate actions in response to it.

In addition to balancing options, the weak Russia had a choice of back-passing, at least before the Balkan wars. From the standpoint of power alone, competition with Germany hardly made sense: Russia was weakened after taking part in several wars and was only beginning to catch up economically. It went to war even though until 1912 it viewed itself as weaker than even material calculations of power suggested[64] and despite many prominent statesmen's recommendations for moderation in foreign policy.

To defensive realists, Russia's policy and the decision to go to war resulted from an incorrect perception of the international balance of power. Despite inadequate resources to go to war, the military supported an offensive strategy and convinced the Tsar to act accordingly.[65] An incorrect assessment of international conditions was responsible for other policy errors, such as Sazonov's defiance of Stolypin's moderate policy in the Balkans.[66] However, Russia's threat assessment was similar to those of France and Britain, and it had sufficiently broad support at home. If Russia acted on a policy bias, then it was a bias largely shared by allies and domestic subjects alike. It is therefore more likely that a nationally supported system of perception with roots in a particular idea of honor was at work.

Neoclassical realists come closer to adequately explaining Russia's behavior, because they emphasize the importance of great power prestige to Nicholas.[67] The historian Hugh Seton-Watson provided this interpretation consistent with neoclassical realism:

[I]t is hard to see how Russian and Austrian aims – or if Austria had dissolved, Russian and German aims – could have been reconciled. Nor does it help to suggest that both Powers should simply have refrained from imperialism, should have left the Balkans alone. The Balkans would not leave them alone. . . . If Russia had yielded in 1914 as she had yielded in 1912 and 1909 there would have been peace. Both nothing would have remained of Russia's status as a Great Power. She would have become a vassal of Germany, and France would have been delivered into German hands.[68]

The explanation is valid, yet by highlighting only the external aspects of Russia's cultural obligations in the Balkans, it underestimates the domestic origins of Russia's threat assessment. Just as Christian beliefs defined Nicholas I's decision to pressure the Ottoman Empire over the Holy Lands, the same beliefs played a critical role in determining Nicholas II's choices. The Tsar's choices played into widely held perceptions of the international situation, and they also reflected the West's reading of German intentions.

Finally, some scholars have argued for the primacy of Russia's nationalism or "pan-Slavist imperialism" in determining the Tsar's policy

decisions in the early twentieth century.[69] The approach provides a useful corrective to the inadequate neoclassical explanation. However, the
nationalism of the Russian public was only partially constructed by the
country's historically developed honor commitments. Just as neoclassical realism downplays the domestic and cultural source of Russia's
great power claims, the nationalist approach underestimates its external
sources. Russia's "imperialism," to a large extent, was also shaped by the
international system and expectations of the allies. The West encouraged
Nicholas to adopt the cooperative vision of honor and did not discourage him from taking a hard line on Russia's cultural commitments in
the Balkans. Both domestic and external aspects of Russia's honor were
important, interacting with and reinforcing one another.

Assessment

Considerations of honor figured prominently in Russia's decision to go
to war in 1914. Nicholas's notion of state honor encompassed both the
obligation to protect the Balkans from possible encroachment by Austria,
Germany, and Turkey and a commitment to Western allies to confront
Germany in case of a major European war. Although various parts of the
political class offered divergent visions of state honor, the Tsar prevailed
over those who questioned the wisdom of isolating Germany and acting
on pan-Slavist feelings in Russian society. Nicholas's beliefs are therefore
partially responsible for involving the country in a war that led to the
collapse of the entire system of government.

However, alternative belief systems were present in the national discourse. Their advocates included late-nineteenth-century diplomats and
members of the Tsar's government. Among the diplomats, Giers and
Lamsdorff sought to buy years of domestic and international tranquility and develop "a beneficial balance of forces," not a military alliance
that would offend Germany.[70] Gorchakov, whose policy of recueillement
made German unification possible, wanted to have strong and balanced
ties with both France and Germany as a way of preventing hegemonic
ambitions of either one. Thus when Germany came close to attacking
France in 1875, the chancellor made known his support for the latter.[71]
His successor Giers followed Gorchakov's policy and even helped devise
a new version of the Holy Alliance, the Three Emperors League, which
was negotiated and signed in 1881.

Among other statesmen, Sergei Witte and his successor Vyshnegrad-
skiy understood the importance of maintaining strong and balanced ties
with Germany for the sake of preserving peace and continuing necessary
modernization at home. Unlike the more pro-Western elites who came
to shape policy attitudes after 1906, Witte understood that even Russia's

political sovereignty, let alone great power status, was not assured under conditions of economic dependence:

Russia's economic relations with western Europe are still very similar to the relations between colonies and their mother countries.... However, there is one essential difference in comparison with the situation of colonies: Russia is a powerful, political independent state. It has the right and the might not to remain eternally in debt to the economically more advanced states.[72]

As a solution, Witte defended a flexible borrowing policy, and he too supported a broad continental alliance with Germany and France despite the two countries' growing tensions over Morocco.[73]

After Witte's resignation, Stolypin and Kokovtsev advocated his position of moderation. The former was successful in restraining radical pan-Slavist instincts until the Bosnian crisis of September 1908.[74] After Stolypin's assassination in the fall of 1911, Kokovtsev became prime minister and also favored a moderate foreign policy. However, he was not favored by the Tsar and was dismissed in January 1914, after the positions on war in the Balkans of the war minister Sukhomlinov and the foreign minister Sazonov won out.[75] Before Sazonov became responsible for Russia's foreign policy in 1912, Izvol'sky also had tried to follow a policy of balancing among different powers. His objective was to avoid "entangling alliances" by concluding separate issue-specific agreements with different powers – with Britain and Japan in Asia, and Germany and Austria in Europe. The policy failed because the level of hostility between the two blocs was already too high.[76]

Having rejected the moderate course of action, the Tsar presented Russia with a false dichotomy of honorable versus dishonorable behavior during the July 1914 crisis. By aligning himself with France and Britain, he jeopardized Russia's traditionally strong ties with Germany and the fragile peace in the Balkans. Rather than concentrating on domestic modernization – as prescribed by the recueillement policy – Nicholas engaged in provocative behavior in the Far East, which resulted in the devastating military defeat by Japan and the revolution at home. Russia's dependence on Western political mediation and economic assistance grew stronger, making it ever more difficult to preserve its freedom of action in international affairs. After Russia's humiliating acceptance of the German ultimatum to recognize the Austrian annexation of Bosnia-Herzegovina in 1909, the larger war became exceedingly difficult to prevent. The problem, as described by William Fuller, was that "the tsarist regime was reluctant to display any signs of weakness in its dealings abroad and was therefore reluctant to accept any diminution in Russia's international standing and prestige."[77] St. Petersburg acted on a great power nationalism, an inflexible pro-Western agenda, and anti-German paranoia.

Although William II was no Hitler, Russia failed to engage Germany by designing deterrence and then offensive war plans. Rather than staying focused on modernization and economic reform, it turned to an adventurous foreign policy. The vision of honor that was cooperative and inclusive vis-à-vis the Western nations turned out to be hostile and exclusive toward Germany. In October 1917, Russia paid dearly for the mistakes of its leadership.

Of course, Russia was not solely responsible for the failure to prevent World War I. Other powers played a part as well. France and Britain largely understood peace in Europe as the deterrence and humiliation of Germany[78] – an exclusive and assertive definition of honor that was common among great powers.[79] Germany too developed offensive plans because it had not renewed the Reinsurance treaty with Russia.[80] Despite the need for moderation and even-handedness, European powers developed expansionist nationalist beliefs and became locked in a tight security dilemma.

Notes

1 Lieven, *Russia and the Origins of the First World War*, p. 5.
2 Ibid., p. 30.
3 Bovykin, *Ocherki istoriyi vneshnei politiki Rossiyi*, p. 15.
4 Lamsdorf, *Dnevnik. 1891–1892*, p. 39.
5 Ibid.
6 Geyer, *Russian Imperialism*, pp. 159–60.
7 Bovykin, *Ocherki istoriyi vneshnei politiki Rossiyi*, p. 16.
8 Fuller, *Strategy and Power in Russia*, p. 360.
9 Kennan, *The Fateful Alliance*, pp. 153–4.
10 For the text of the agreement, see Dmytryshyn, ed. *Imperial Russia*, pp. 358–9.
11 McDonald, *United Government and Foreign Policy in Russia*, pp. 78–9.
12 Bovykin, *Ocherki istoriyi vneshnei politiki Rossiyi*, p. 53; Kagarlitski, *Periferiy-naya imperiya*, p. 400.
13 Bovykin, *Ocherki istoriyi vneshnei politiki Rossiyi*, p. 59.
14 McDonald, *United Government and Foreign Policy in Russia*, pp. 110–11.
15 Geyer, *Russian Imperialism*, p. 250.
16 Lieven, *Russia and the Origins of the First World War*.
17 Fuller, *Strategy and Power in Russia*, p. 422.
18 McDonald, *United Government*, p. 159.
19 Khvostov, "Bor'ba Antanty i Avstro-germanskogo bloka," 612–16; Seton-Watson, *The Decline of Imperial Russia*, pp. 354–6.
20 Van Evera, *Causes of War*, pp. 195, 238; Khvostov, "Bor'ba Antanty," 624–5; Kissinger, *Diplomacy*, pp. 204–5.

21 Snyder, *The Ideology of the Offensive*, p. 179.

22 McDonald, *United Government*, pp. 169, 207.

23 On Russia's strategy during the war, see Utkin, *Zabytaya tragediya*.

24 Lieven, *Russia and the Origins of the First World War*, p. 5.

25 Fuller, *Strategy and Power in Russia*, p. 384.

26 As one Russian diarist wrote, Nicholas "agrees with each of his ministers in spite of the fact that they report the opposite of one another" (McDonald, *United Government*, p. 16). For characterizations of the Tsar as too inexperienced to rule, see also views by Lamsdorff and Sergei Witte, as quoted in Geyer, *Russian Imperialism*, p. 143.

27 Kokovtsev, *Iz moyego proshlogo*, vol. 2, p. 263.

28 Ibid., pp. 290–1.

29 Neumann, *Russia and the Idea of Europe*, p. 82.

30 Geyer, *Russian Imperialism*, p. 278. On Sazonov's views, see especially McDonald, *United Government*, pp. 180–5 and 203–7.

31 Geyer, *Russian Imperialism*, p. 175.

32 Ibid., pp. 251, 256.

33 Snyder, *The Ideology of the Offensive*, chap. 7.

34 On disagreement between minister of war V. A. Sukhomlinov and Kokovtsev over mobilization on the Austrian border in 1913, see McDonald, *United Government*, pp. 181, 184–6.

35 Witte, *Izbrannyye vospominaniya*, p. 415.

36 Kokovtsev, *Iz moyego proshlogo*, p. 96.

37 Some sources indicate that the rate of defense expenditures was closer to 30% of the budget (Gartell, *The Tsarist Economy*, p. 221).

38 Lieven, *Russia and the Origins of the First World War*, p. 21.

39 Geyer, *Russian Imperialism*, pp. 125–7.

40 The average length of the work day was 13–14 hours, salaries were very low, and living conditions were poor. As a result, the rate of accidents at work was very high (Khromov, *Economicheskoye razvitiye Rossiyi*, pp. 316–17).

41 Ragsdale, "Introduction: the Traditions of Imperial Russian Foreign Policy," 11.

42 Following Gladstonian liberalism, Milyukov and a number of other Kadets merely opposed all wars and were against war with Germany (Lieven, *Russia and the Origins*, pp. 124–25; McDonald, *United Government*, p. 107). Others, like Pyotr Struve, advocated that Russia should follow the strong foreign policy of a great power. On foreign policy differences between different factions of Kadets, see also Stockdale, *Paul Miliukov and the Quest for a Liberal Russia*, pp. 208–12 and Uribes-Sanches, "Rossiyskoiye obschestvo i vneshnyaya politika," 375. At a later stage, both factions supported a war with Germany.

43 Bovykin, *Ocherki istoriyi vneshnei politiki Rossiyi*, pp. 57–8.

44 Lieven, *Russia and the Origins*, p. 17; Neumann, *Russia and the Idea of Europe*, p. 82.

45 An exception was the collective volume *Vekhi* (Landmarks) published in the early twentieth century in response to the revolution of 1905. The volume called for the Russian intelligentsia to be constructive, rather than "nihilist," in its social criticism and held the Russian radical intelligentsia responsible for the revolutionary violence.

46 Tsygankov, "Self and Other in International Relations Theory."

47 Stockdale, *Paul Miliukov and the Quest for a Liberal Russia*, p. 210.

48 Tuminez, *Russian Nationalism since 1856*, p. 143.

49 Uribes-Sanches, "Rossiyskoiye obschestvo i vneshnyaya politika," 378.

50 Lieven, *Russia and the Origins*, p. 98.

51 Trubetskoi, *Iz proshlogo*, p. 275.

52 Kerenskiy, *Istoriya Rossiyi*, p. 159; Uribes-Sanches, "Rossiyskoiye obschestvo," 396.

53 Geyer, *Russian Imperialism*, pp. 233, 243–4.

54 Utkin, *Vyzov Zapada i otvet Rossiyi*, p. 167.

55 Geyer, *Russian Imperialism*, pp. 176–7.

56 Ibid., p. 250; McDonald, *United Government*, p. 105.

57 "[I]n December 1912 the French government was actually chiding the Russians for not taking a stronger stance in response to Austrian military preparations" (Lieven, *Russia and the Origins*, p. 48).

58 Fuller, *Strategy and Power in Russia*, p. 331.

59 Geyer, *Russian Imperialism*, pp. 150–1.

60 Ibid., p. 245.

61 Taylor, *The Struggle for Mastery in Europe, 1848–1918*, p. 528.

62 In 1939, for example, Russia made a different choice by ultimately aligning with Germany. See Chapter 7 for details.

63 See for example, Kennan, *The Fateful Alliance*; Fuller, *Strategy and Power*, pp. 377–93; Utkin, *Vyzov Zapada*, pp. 158–9, 171.

64 For a discussion of Russia's weakness, see especially Kennedy, *The Rise and Fall of Great Powers*, pp. 232–43 and Wohlforth, "The Perception of Power."

65 The misperception argument in application to World War I is developed in Snyder, *The Ideology of the Offensive;* Trachtenberg, *History and Strategy*, chap. 2; Van Evera, *Causes of War*.

66 McDonald, *United Government*, p. 180.

67 William C. Wohlforth, "Honor as Interest in Russian Decisions for War."

68 Seton-Watson, *The Decline of Imperial Russia*, pp. 378–9. For a similar argument, see Copeland, *The Origins of Major War*, p. 82.

69 Geyer, *Russian Imperialism*; Tuminez, *Russian Nationalism since 1856*.

70 Fuller, *Strategy and Power in Russia*, p. 332.

71 Ibid., p. 294.

72 Quoted in Geyer, *Russian Imperialism*, p. 145.

73 McDonald, *United Government*, p. 80. Before the war with Japan, Witte had advocated a program of *expansion pacifique* in Asia, which was thwarted when Russia provoked Japan to war by seizing Port Arthur in 1898. For details on Witte's perspective, see Schimmelpenninck, *Toward the Rising Sun*, pp. 61–81.

74 After the crisis Nicholas begun to withdraw his support for Stolypin (McDonald, *United Government*, pp. 150, 160–2).

75 Ibid., pp. 197, 216–17; Kokovtsev, *Iz moyego proshlogo*, pp. 280–90.

76 Lieven, *Russia and the Origins*, pp. 33, 38.

77 Fuller, *Strategy and Power in Russia*, p. 462.

78 Historians disagree over whether Britain was too hard or too soft on Germany. The latter view is advanced by Ferguson (*The Pity of War: Explaining World War I*). Others argue, instead, that Britain pursued a semi-appeasement policy

with Germany, failing to unequivocally side with France and Russia (Lieven, *Russia and the Origins*, pp. 4, 26). Such was also the view of Russia's Foreign Minister Sazonov (Sazonov, *Vospominaniya*, p. 201).

79 Kagan, *On the Origins of War and the Preservation of Peace*, pp. 203–5.

80 On German offensive beliefs, see Lieven, *Russia and the Origins*, p. 153; Snyder, *The Ideology of the Offensive*, pp. 125–56; Holsti, *Peace and War*, pp. 160–3; Copeland, *The Origins of Major War*, pp. 79–117. For an alternative perspective, see Ferguson, *The Pity of War*.

7   The Collective Security, 1933–1939

"We have expressly announced our readiness to take part in collective action to rebuff the aggressor jointly with other great states, and small states too. But there is no collective for the rebuff yet."

Maxim Litvinov[1]

The Soviet Struggle for Collective Security

The appointment of Hitler as Germany's chancellor general, as well as the rising threat from Japan, led to important changes in Soviet foreign policy. Oriented toward Germany since the treaty of Locarno (1925) and the treaty of Special Relations with Berlin (1926), the Kremlin now moved in the opposite direction by trying to establish closer ties with France and Britain to isolate the growing Nazi threat. This policy became known as "collective security" and was associated with Maxim Litvinov, the Soviet foreign minister at the time. The pursuit of collective security lasted approximately as long as he held that position. Japan's war with China took some pressure off of Russia by allowing it to focus its diplomatic efforts on relations with Europe.

Joining the League of Nations

The Soviet decision to join the League of Nations in 1934 marked a clear departure from the old Locarno line in Bolshevik diplomacy. The Kremlin never supported the conditions imposed on Germany by the Versailles Treaty, and after World War I Russia's relationship with Germany strengthened in economic and military areas.[2] The new policy of collective security was about to place important political limitations on their deepening relations. Collective security was also a blow to leftist ideas of world revolution and worker solidarity across the globe. It reflected the Kremlin's new view of the Comintern, an extension of the world revolution, as ineffective in solving pressing international problems.

In December 1933 – the year Hitler was appointed chancellor of Germany – the Politburo passed a resolution in support of collective security and approved Litvinov's proposals for action. In addition to joining the League of Nations, the proposals included signing nonaggression treaties with all members of the League and negotiating a regional security pact with European nations including Poland, Czechoslovakia, the Baltics, Finland, Belgium, and France.[3] Russia viewed the participation of France and Poland as especially important in enabling the pact to be an effective constraint on Germany's actions.[4]

That the League of Nations formally invited Russia to become a part emboldened Litvinov and gave hope to Stalin that an anti-German coalition could be assembled. It also immediately raised the status of Soviet Russia as a responsible and peace-oriented power. The foreign minister had been initially reluctant to formally apply for membership in the organization out of fear of being rejected.[5] Litvinov viewed such a possibility as a potentially serious blow to the Soviet Union's prestige and waited until the League itself invited the USSR to join. It then entered the organization on its own conditions.[6]

The USSR now had an important platform from which to engage other nations. The Soviet political class viewed membership in the League as opening new diplomatic horizons and signifying that "we have gained equal rights with the largest *bourgeois* countries that had so far refused to recognize us."[7]

Litvinov's Crusade

The key to understanding Litvinov's security strategy lies in understanding his conception of aggressive action in international politics. The foreign minister had articulated this approach only a week after Hitler came to power, but it took ten months for the Politburo to support him by passing the collective security resolution. At the Disarmament Conference on February 6, 1933, Litvinov proposed a new definition of an "aggressor" as any state that declares war on another state; invades the territory of another state without declaration of war; bombards the territory of another state by its land, naval, or air forces; or imposes a naval blockade. He further insisted, "No considerations whatsoever of a political, strategic or economic nature, including the desire to exploit natural riches or to obtain any sort of advantages or privileges on the territory of another state . . . shall be accepted as justification of aggression."[8]

Later that year, in December 1933, in one of his most important speeches delivered to the Central Executive Committee of the Supreme Soviet, Litvinov challenged not only the old Boshevik line of the "inevitable war" with capitalism[9] but also the notion of peaceful coexistence with all states as well. "If it is possible to speak of diplomatic eras, then we are now without doubt standing at the junction of two eras," he said.[10] He further argued that "even hostilities which do not begin directly on the frontiers of our Union may threaten security" and that "the ensuring of peace cannot depend on our efforts alone; it requires the collaboration and co-operation of other States."[11] The minister divided Europe into revisionist and status quo powers, and quoting from *Mein Kampf*, he pointed to Hitler's ambitions to "enslave the Soviet people."[12] Both the language of revisionism and the reference to racist ideology aimed to persuade the West to perceive a common assessment of threat.

Outside the country, Litvinov showed sympathy for the French position and indicated his readiness to move in a post-Rappalo direction in early 1933, at the World Disarmament Conference in Geneva. Breaking with the peaceful coexistence line, Litvinov had already launched a series of diplomatic initiatives, such as signing nonaggression pacts with leading countries, reversing the old line toward the moderate socialists in Europe, and pressuring the League of Nations to act against Germany. In his conversation with Konstantin von Neurath, the new German foreign minister, Litvinov warned, "We certainly cannot look kindly upon the prospect of an anti-Soviet bloc involving Germany and France."[13] The Germans clearly understood the new policy direction. In March 1933, after speaking with Litvinov, von Neurath wrote to Berlin that the Soviet minister was "thinking of developing relations with France further" and was unusually hostile during their meeting.[14]

In fact, the Soviet Union had already signed nonaggression treaties with Finland, Estonia, Latvia, Poland, and France in 1932.[15] Soviet diplomacy was now working to unite the signatories into an "eastern Locarno," or a broad multilateral pact, in which France and the Soviet Union would serve as guarantors of the smaller states' security. A critical part of this effort was an attempt to negotiate a separate Franco-Soviet treaty, which would not only strengthen the general pact but also obligate the two nations to provide direct mutual assistance in the case of war.[16] In June 1934, Litvinov and Louis Barthou, the French foreign minister, reached agreement on supporting a multilateral eastern pact of mutual assistance with participation of Eastern European countries. In May 1935, the Soviet Union and France also reached a bilateral agreement on mutual assistance, although they could not agree on the magnitude of the assistance.[17]

The collective security policy also transformed Comintern. At its Seventh World Congress in July–August 1935, Stalin legitimized the new Soviet policy by reversing his hostility toward the social democratic parties in Europe and calling on communists and socialists to form a united front against the rise of Fascism.[18] Thus the organization abandoned its agenda of overthrowing capitalist governments in favor of endorsing Soviet mutual assistance pacts with France and Czechoslovakia.[19] From a narrow-based organization with an "anti-bourgeois" agenda, it evolved into a broad movement that pledged a popular front of support for collective security.

Finally, Litvinov emerged as a tireless critic of the League of Nations' lack of enforcement capabilities. Any collective security system, he argued, would not be effective if it failed to muster a sufficient force to respond to an aggressor.[20] He further insisted that the League must become an organization dedicated to collective assistance and collective defense.[21] The minister was especially critical of the League's lack of response to Italy's invasion of Abyssinia, Ethiopia, in October 1935 and to Germany's reoccupation of the Rhineland in March 1936: "we don't need a League that is safe for aggressors . . . for such a League will turn from a peace defender into the opposite of it."[22]

For its part, the Soviet Union indicated its firm intention to act in support of collective security despite its own limited resources. In Geoffrey Roberts' words,

When Mussolini invaded Abyssinia in 1935 the USSR was the strongest proponent of League of Nations sanctions against Italy. When the civil war in Spain erupted in 1936 it was the Soviet Union that supplied arms to the Republican forces. When Japan invaded North China in 1937 it was from Moscow that Chiang Kai-shek received vital military aid. When Czechoslovakia was threatened by Germany in 1938 it was the Soviet Union that lent the greatest moral and political support the embattled Czechs.[23]

Recent research has found that the USSR was prepared to provide military assistance to Czechoslovakia and would have done so had not its prime minister decided to capitulate.[24]

Setbacks

Soviet efforts notwithstanding, collective security suffered increasing setbacks in the mid-1930s. After formally withdrawing from the League of Nations, Germany restored compulsory military service in March 1935 and engaged in a massive rearmament program.[25] During 1935–6, Germany's ally Italy invaded Abyssinia (Ethiopia), and Germany reoccupied the Rhineland. In 1936, Germany also signed an anti-Comintern pact with Japan. Around this time, Litvinov declared that Germany had shifted from the original plan to attack France to the plan of invading Russia.[26] Stalin too was convinced that a major war was approaching and abandoned his attempt to mobilize the League to the Soviet defense.[27]

Indeed the League failed to respond to Germany and Italy's acts of aggression. It stood by passively as Hitler acted in defiance of the Versailles Treaty and could not overcome France and Britain's blocking of sanctions against Italy. Litvinov anticipated the consequences of the Italian aggression in Ethiopia and the German occupation of the Rhineland, but could not convince France and Britain to support any meaningful sanctions against the aggressors.[28] His insistence that "peace is indivisible" had no effect, and his warnings to the League that it would become "a laughing-stock" or even "harmful"[29] if it failed to act on the Rhineland issue were proving increasingly prophetic.

The Soviet Union was also unable to obtain a commitment to collective security from the two major countries it had designated as absolutely necessary for success – France and Poland. The new French foreign minister, Pierre Laval, was much more skeptical of the Soviet Union than his predecessor and announced before the French Senate that "the French government will never do anything which justifies Germany in thinking that we intend to practice a policy of isolation toward her."[30] Worried about French attempts to secure a separate agreement with Germany and trying to push Laval into an agreement with the Soviet Union, Litvinov even offered Germany a bilateral nonaggression pact on May 8, 1935.[31] France signed the pact but did not ratify it until February 1936, and it consistently resisted including any military obligations in collective security. Poland too indicated its mistrust of both Russia and France. Rather than cooperating with them, Warsaw signed a nonaggression treaty with Berlin in January 1934. Between the Germans and the Russians, the Poles preferred the former.[32]

At home, Litvinov was devastated by Stalin's purges in 1937, directed at Communist Party leaders, high-ranking military commanders, and diplomats. On fabricated charges of treason, the NKVD arrested and shot not only the best Red Army generals – Tukhachevski, Yakir, Uborevich, Kork, Eidman, Fel'dman, Primakov and Putna – but also the best of the diplomatic corps. Litvinov's colleagues and comrades, such as his first deputies Karakhan, Krestinski, Sokol'nikov, and Stomonyakov, were purged, and the commissar of foreign affairs himself was waiting to be arrested any day. The purges had a severely negative impact on the policy of collective security. The terror emboldened Hitler, who was happy to see the "catastrophic weakening" of Soviet military power,[33] and it reinforced potential allies' already significant mistrust of the Soviet system.

Munich and After

During 1938–9, the collective security policy suffered additional blows from which it could not recover. In March 1938, Hitler invaded Austria and then called for Czechoslovakia's secession of its ethnically German Sudetland. Disappointed with the Anglo-French unwillingness to strengthen collective security, the Soviet Union blamed the two countries for their inaction, yet failed officially to condemn Germany's annexation of Austria. France only partially mobilized in response to the German threat to Czechoslovakia and was looking for a diplomatic solution to the crisis.[34] As the Czechoslovaks were getting ready to fight, the Soviet government made it clear it would act on its obligations to defend the country if France agreed to do so as well.[35] However, on September 29, 1938, France and Britain met with Germany and Italy in Munich and agreed to partition Czechoslovakia without consulting the Soviets. Czech Prime Minister Benes accepted the results.

After the Munich Conference, Litvinov expressed his disgust with Czechoslovakia's dismemberment and predicted – again correctly – a similar outcome for Poland. During his meeting with the French ambassador, Litvinov said, "I merely note that the Western powers deliberately kept the USSR out of negotiations. My poor friend, what have you done? As for us, I do not see any other outcome than a fourth partition of Poland."[36]

In the meantime, domestic support for special relations with Germany grew stronger. Stalin too was distancing himself from Litvinov and his policy. In March 1939, Germany invaded Czechoslovakia. Stalin responded by saying that a "new imperialist war has become a fact,"[37] thereby indicating that he was returning to the traditional line of balancing between Western powers and Germany and that Litvinov's policy of mustering a collective resolve was now alien to him. In April, Litvinov made one last attempt to engage France in a security arrangement to guarantee the independence of the Baltic states, receiving what he described a "humiliating" response.[38] In May 1939, Stalin replaced him with the leading advocate of the pro-German line, Vyacheslav Molotov.

Yet Stalin was not yet prepared to enter an alliance with Germany and did not reach a final decision to do so until mid-August 1939.[39] By replacing Litvinov, he meant to signal to France and Britain that he had other options, were they to continue harboring hopes of their own special deal with Hitler. As one historian wrote, "There is a good reason to believe that Litvinov may have been sacked because he was skeptical about the Soviet triple alliance initiative."[40] However, negotiations over the "grand alliance" were proceeding slowly, and Stalin began to signal – through lower-level contacts – his interest in signing a separate agreement with Berlin.[41] In early August, in response to his urgent invitation to hold a military convention, Western powers sent only low-level delegations to Moscow that were unable to offer any commitments. Then, on August 24, Stalin made the decisive step of authorizing Molotov to sign a nonaggression treaty with his German counterpart, Joachim von Ribbentrop.[42] Once again, as in the early twentieth century, the grand alliance failed to materialize, and this time Russia found itself on the other side.

The Collective Security, 1933–1939: Timeline

1933 January	Hitler appointed Chancellor of Germany
	Mutual assistance treaties with Finland, Poland, and the Baltic states
October	Germany withdraws from the League of Nations
December	Communist Party leadership proposal on collective security
1934 June	Russia–France agreement on the "eastern Locarno"
September	Russia joins the League of Nations
	Polish–German nonaggression pact
1935 March	Hitler restores compulsory military draft
May	Mutual assistance pacts with France and Czechoslovakia
July	Seventh Congress of the Comintern in Moscow
October	Italy invades Abyssinia
1936 March	Germany reoccupies Rhineland
July	Spanish civil war starts
November	Anti-Comintern pact between Germany and Japan
1937 June	Purges against Tukhachevski and seven other generals
August	Soviet–Chinese nonaggression treaty
1938 March	Germany occupies Austria
September	France, Britain, Germany, and Italy meet at Munich
	French–German nonaggression declaration
December	British–German nonaggression declaration
1939 March	Germany invades Czechoslovakia
	Britain guarantees the independence of Poland
April	USSR proposes triple alliance to Britain and France
May	Litvinov dismissed and replaced by Molotov
August	Soviet–British–French military negotiations in Moscow
	Soviet–German pact signed in Moscow

Explaining Soviet Cooperation

Stalin's and Litvinov's Worldviews

Both Stalin and Litvinov were proud advocates of the Soviet concept of honor as derived from ideology, Communist Party membership, and state employment. Soon after its emergence, the Soviet system established the notions of *chest'* ("debt of honor") and *pochet* ("honorary title") for the purpose of expanding its legitimizing reach within society.[43] Diplomatic imperatives of peaceful coexistence with capitalism notwithstanding, the Soviet Union was not about to surrender its ideological mission in the world.[44] Indeed, the Soviet state viewed its ideological commitments as essential for preserving world peace. As Litvinov stated in one of his international speeches,

The Soviet State . . . perceives its State duties to lie not in conquest, not in expansion of territory; it considers that the honor of the nation demands that it should be educated not in the spirit of militarism and a thirst for blood, but in the fulfillment of the ideal for which the Soviet State was brought in existence and in which it perceives the whole meaning of its existence, namely, the building of a Socialist society.[45]

Stalin and Litvinov therefore had a strong basis for a shared understanding of how to organize relations with Western nations. They shared communist ideological values and their Leninist interpretation. That interpretation ended the brief Soviet commitment to the idea of world revolution in favor of the doctrine of peaceful coexistence with capitalism.[46] Both politicians were also pragmatic in projecting Soviet power abroad. It was Stalin's desire to practice moderate state-centered diplomacy by moving away from the early Bolshevik ideological fervor that led to his decision to replace Georgi Chicherin as commissar for foreign affairs with Litvinov.[47]

However, although they shared commitments to an ideologically inspired yet pragmatic foreign policy, the two statesmen differed in their interpretations of pragmatism and collective security. To Stalin, collective security was merely a defensive alliance to restrain Hitler, whereas Litvinov advocated a more expansive and institutionalized vision for establishing a lasting peace in international relations. Whereas Stalin's perspective on honor was defensive and isolationist, Litvinov's was more cooperative and internationalist.

With its concentration on domestic priorities and tactics of flexible alliances between Germany and France, Stalin's statesmanship was a Soviet, perhaps more isolationist, version of the Russian recueillement policy. Like his tsarist predecessors Gorchakov and Stolypin, Stalin was preoccupied with domestic modernization and stability. His state-building priorities became especially clear in the mid-1930s. By that time, Stalin's "socialism in one country" had obtained a clear nationalist dimension, and the term *rodina* (motherland) was reintroduced to strengthen the Soviet notion of patriotism.[48] At the Seventeenth Communist Party Congress in January 1934, Stalin stressed that the Soviet Union was not interested in either a pro-Polish or pro-French policy, but instead "oriented itself in past and present to the USSR, and only the USSR."[49]

Externally, Stalin showed himself to be a shrewd practitioner of flexible alliance tactics by waiting until the last moment to conclude the nonaggression pact with Hitler.[50] That Stalin was not in favor of an alliance with Germany is evident from his initial support for collective security diplomacy and efforts to engage Britain and France even after dismissing Litvinov. Yet it is equally true that Stalin never fully trusted Litvinov's efforts and continued to keep lines of communication with Germany open. Stalin's attitude toward collective security was similar to that toward the disarmament efforts of the late 1920s, which he dismissed as "imperialist pacifism":

There are naïve people who think that since there is imperialist pacifism, there will be no war. That is quite untrue. On the contrary, whoever wishes to get at the truth must reverse this proposition and say: since imperialist pacifism and the League of Nations are flourishing, new imperialist war and intervention are certain.[51]

Stalin too believed in state honor, but saw it achieved not in cooperation with Western powers, but with whoever assisted the Soviet Union in better achieving its objectives. Such was the meaning of Stalin's words to Ribbentrop as he was leaving Moscow on August 23, 1939: "The Soviet Government... could guarantee on his word of honor that the Soviet Union would not betray its partners."[52]

In contrast, Litvinov was a practitioner of cooperative and internationalist collective security. His background – as a Jew who spent ten years of his life in Britain and was married to a British woman – lent his policy beliefs a Westernizing, anglophile leaning. Whereas Stalin viewed peace as temporary and resulting from international power balancing and imperialist wars, Litvinov assumed peace to be "indivisible," requiring international cooperation. As if he was arguing with his boss, the minister stated on one occasion, "What other guarantees of security are there – military alliance and the policy of balance of power? Pre-war history has shown that this policy not only does not get rid of war, but on the contrary unleashes it."[53]

Without becoming a liberal internationalist, Litvinov went beyond Stalin's realist thinking and embraced a cautiously cooperative vision of honor. Whereas Stalin favored flexible alliances, Litvinov openly advocated "entangling alliances" that would require the commitment of military and other resources to the cause of preventing international aggression and making "war itself impossible."[54] In addition, the minister felt a personal animosity toward Hitler and rarely missed an opportunity to emphasize his "mad ideas"[55] – points that Stalin and his realist-minded supporters did not necessarily find relevant.

Yet his commitment to a cooperative vision of honor did not make Litvinov a radical Westernizer or a foreign policy dove. As a diplomat and a politician, he exercised his power cautiously. No enthusiast for Rappalo, the minister nevertheless wanted to preserve good relations with Germany while it was still possible.[56] In addition, Litvinov did not exclude pressure from his policy arsenal and applied it to allies to persuade them to act more decisively. In December 1937, for example, he suggested to the French ambassador Robert Colander that a German-Soviet rapprochement was "perfectly" possible, as a warning against the West's appeasement of Hitler regarding Czechoslovakia.[57]

Despite Litvinov's differences with Stalin, the foreign minister's views and policy were significant in executing collective security. He was ultimately Stalin's choice over Chicherin, and Stalin viewed him as a professional, rather than a party apparatchik, at a time when Stalin's own views on international matters were not fully formed. The fact that the foreign minister was excluded from the party's inner core[58] suited Stalin well. Apparently, he also had personal respect for the man, sparing Litvinov during the purges while arresting his many comrades and colleagues.

Domestic Conditions and Support

Judging by domestic conditions, the Soviet Union was hardly in a position to pursue an assertive foreign policy. During most of the 1920s, Russia was recovering from the recent war with Germany, a civil war, and a mass famine. The 1930s brought the real fear of a Japanese threat after the Kwantung Army's invasion of Manchuria in 1931, followed by the threat of another war with Germany. Thus the Soviet Union was far from ready to respond adequately to the new dangers. Short of revenue, it also lacked the industrial and military capabilities required for meeting external challengers. As one historian wrote, "Never had the regime been less prepared to withstand the shock of war, and yet never had war seemed to be more likely."[59] It was then, in the early 1930s, that Stalin put his emphasis on accelerating "the tempo" of industrial development, justifying it in terms of responding to powerful external threats:

> To slacken the tempo would mean falling behind. And those who fall behind get beaten... the history of the old Russia was the continual beating she suffered because of her backwardness. She was beaten by the Mongol khans. She was beaten by the Turkish beys. She was beaten by the Swedish feudal lords. She was beaten by the Polish and Lithuanian gentry. She was beaten by the British and French capitalists. She was beaten by the Japanese barons. All beat her – because of her backwardness.... We are fifty or a hundred years behind the advanced countries. We must make good this distance in ten years. Either we do it, or we shall go under.[60]

It was the constant fear of an external attack that drove the paranoid Stalin to conduct, at enormous human cost, mass collectivization and purges. There was also a massive increase in Soviet defense spending, from 5 percent of the overall budget in the 1920s to 26 percent in the 1930s and 43 percent in 1941.[61] Although at the Seventeenth and Eighteenth Communist Party Congresses in January 1934 and March 1939, Stalin cited indicators of the absolute increase in Soviet industrial production[62] relative to the stagnating and depressed "countries of capitalism," he did not fail to note that the USSR remained behind much of the world in terms of per capita production.[63]

Given the external and domestic conditions, some within the Soviet political class favored the Litvinov-advocated policy of collective security as the appropriate response to the rising German threat. Litvinov and his supporters within the Narkomindel also opposed increasing trade with Germany as advocated by David Kandelaki, the Soviet trade representative in Berlin from 1935–7.[64] In addition to the Narkomindel, collective security in its increasingly anti-German version found support within the party and military circles. For example, the leading party ideologist Nikolai Bukharin strongly shared Litvinov's conviction that Hitler's ideology "had cast a dark and bloody shadow over the world," representing a danger to all humanity.[65] Among the military, the influential Marshal Tukhachevski supported the anti-Fascist front, which German intelligence even tried to counter by disseminating disinformation about him and forwarding it to the Soviet authorities.[66] However, both Bukharin and Tukhachevski were soon purged, thereby weakening internal support for collective security.

Stalin's own attitude was flexible. He authorized Litvinov to go ahead with collective security, but grew skeptical of it over time. A member of the flexible alliances school, he was uncomfortable with the idea of "entangling alliances" and was reluctant to support sanctions against

Germany and its allies. For example, when in September 1935 Litvinov insisted on implementing "serious sanctions" over Italy's aggression in Abyssinia as "a formidable warning for Germany as well," Stalin did not authorize them.[67] Still, until about 1937, he largely abstained from interfering with the domestic dispute between advocates and critics of the anti-Fascist front. That year signs of Soviet leaders' increasing support for Germany included purges of the Jewish ambassador in Berlin – to the liking of the Germans – and of anti-German military commanders, such as Tukhachevski.[68]

Litvinov was never a full-fledged member of the Soviet political establishment. More influential were Vyacheslav Molotov, Andrei Zhdanov, and Lazar' Kaganovich – all members of Stalin's inner circle and supporters of continuing with the Rappalo line. Molotov, the leading critic of Litvinov who was to be his successor, either publicly advocated for including Germany in the collective security system or avoided mentioning the system at all.[69] Despite his caution, he nevertheless clearly asserted, as he did in this interview with *Le Temps* in March 1936, that although "there is a tendency among certain sections of the Soviet public toward an attitude of thoroughgoing irreconcilability to the present rulers of Germany . . . the chief tendency, and one determining the Soviet Government's policy, thinks that an improvement in Soviet-German relations is possible."[70]

Western Allies

The Western partners provided quite limited support to the Soviet Union. Although both Litvinov and Stalin understood the importance of involving France and Britain in a coalition,[71] those countries acted from their own strategic calculations. In the 1930s, France was no longer capable of catching up with Germany economically, but built defensive land fortifications, expecting the Maginot Line to provide sufficient protection from external attack. Britain played for time and was even more in favor of appeasing Hitler than was France.[72] Neither power trusted the USSR enough to enter into a binding coalition with it, and each, at times, harbored hopes to channel Germany's aggression to the East.

France had difficulty accepting Litvinov's definition of international aggression from the start.[73] Although it became more cooperative under Foreign Minister Louis Barthou, his tragic assassination in October 1934 returned the French course to its traditional skepticism of the USSR's motives. Having concluded the agreement on mutual assistance with the Soviet Union in May 1935, France never specified its scope nor did it ever pledge any military assistance. As late as 1937 – and despite an important decline in France's material capabilities relative to those of Germany[74] – the French leadership was against any form of military cooperation with the Soviet leaders.[75] Laval was also categorically opposed to any sanctions against Italy and Germany in response to their occupations of Ethiopia and the Rhineland, respectively. While delaying any meaningful cooperation with the Russians, the French hoped to strengthen their ties with Germany. Litvinov was alarmed by the increasing frequency of the French ambassador's meetings with Nazi leaders in Berlin and by Laval's perception of the French-Soviet pact as an "obstacle" to any improvement in France's relations with Germany.[76] In March 1938, the Soviet foreign commissar felt compelled to remark to U.S. ambassador Joseph Davies that "France has no confidence in the Soviet Union and the Soviet Union has no confidence in France."[77]

Britain was even less cooperative, signaling its desire to strengthen ties with the USSR only after the Munich Conference. In March 1939, responding to the German invasion of Czechoslovakia, the British government sent notes to Greece, Yugoslavia, France, Turkey, Poland, and the Soviet Union, inviting a collective response to possible aggression against Romania.[78] However, just as Poland refused to be a part of a coalition with the Soviets, Neville Chamberlain too confessed to his "profound distrust of Russia":

I have no belief whatsoever in her ability to maintain an effective offensive even if she wanted to. And I distrust her motives which seem to me to have little connection with our ideas of liberty and to be concerned only with getting every one else by the ears.[79]

The architect of appeasement, Chamberlain not only had a poor understanding of Hitler's intentions but also acted on his Russophobic instincts.[80] The British prime minister's real objective was to exclude the Soviet Union from European affairs.[81] As A. J. P. Taylor suggested, "the British government . . . merely wanted to chalk a Red bogey on the wall, in the hope this would keep Hitler quiet."[82]

The United States, as significant a power as it was, had not recognized the Soviet Union until November 1933. Litvinov saw that event as securing yet more recognition of Soviet Russia as a great power and as the "fall of the last position, the last front of the capitalist world's offensive against us which after the October [revolution] took the form of non-recognition and sabotage."[83] However, in the 1930s the U.S. government took a largely isolationist position toward European and Asian affairs[84] and, despite the generally favorable attitude toward Litvinov, failed to provide any form of the support he requested. President Franklin Delano Roosevelt showed no interest in signing a nonaggression pact in the Pacific, or sending a warship to Vladivostok or Leningrad, or giving the Soviet Union a loan.[85]

Poland, which the Soviets perceived as another important power, was never interested in cooperating with the USSR and never took collective security seriously. Instead, it signed a nonaggression treaty with Hitler and was quietly preparing to take advantage of growing German strength. In particular, the Polish foreign minister Colonel Josef Beck expressed his readiness to cooperate with the Germans and the Hungarians in partitioning Czechoslovakia: the Sudetens for Germany, Slovakia for Hungary, and Teschen for Poland.[86] As the Soviets were preparing to defend Czechoslovakia, the Poles were planning to take over a piece of it.[87] They were among the first to recognize Hitler's invasion of Austria, and the Soviet leaders suspected the Poles of fomenting unrest inside the USSR for the same expansionist purposes.[88]

Alternative Explanations

One common perception of collective security among scholars is that Stalin was never serious about this policy, placing his hopes instead on an imperialist war. Fully aware of Russia's weakness, he wanted to exploit Germany and the Western powers' contradictions, thereby winning time to strengthen his country's military capabilities. From this perspective, collective security was an insignificant episode in Stalin's larger strategic design.[89]

For example, in Henry Kissinger's assessment, Stalin by nature was a realist – indeed "the supreme realist . . . patient, shrewd, and implacable, the Richelieu of his period."[90] Furthermore, "Stalin, the great ideologue, was in fact putting his ideology in the service of *Realpolitik* . . . . In due course, Stalin did move into the anti-Hitler camp, but only very reluctantly and after his overtures to Nazi Germany had been rebuffed."[91] Kissinger does not make much of Litvinov and describes Soviet policy during the 1930s as Stalin's "bazaar for bids on a Soviet pact – one which the democracies had no hope of winning if Hitler was prepared to make a serious offer."[92]

Such an interpretation does not explain why the ideologically flexible Stalin chose to ally with authoritarian Germany over Western democracies. If indeed he was thinking strictly in security terms, it would have made more sense to side with the West, given that France and Britain were together stronger than Germany.[93] Even more problematic is the assumption that Litvinov's beliefs and policy were insignificant. Stalin indeed did think like a realist, saying in 1927 that "a great deal . . . depends on whether we shall succeed in deferring the inevitable war with the capitalist world... until the time... when the capitalists start fighting each other."[94] Still, during the 1930s, he proved flexible enough to entertain the possibility of cooperation with the West and empowered Litvinov to exploit it. While remaining deeply mistrustful of France and Britain's intentions, the Soviet Union nevertheless worked hard to implement collective security and was even prepared to fight for it in the case of aggression against Czechoslovakia. The opportunity for building an anti-Hitler coalition existed, and the West also bears responsibility for letting it slip away.

Even less convincing is the argument that the Soviet Union always sought an alliance with Germany and that it did so for offensive, rather than defensive, purposes. In this interpretation, Litvinov is not merely insignificant; he is viewed as in "unreserved agreement with Stalin and with the Rappalo line" and as merely playing a "double game"[95] of pretending to be anti-German for the West's benefit, while in fact working to strengthen Soviet relations with Berlin. Some scholars go so far as to claim that Stalin wanted a European war as much as Germany did and even deliberately aided Hitler's rise by undermining the Comintern and German communists.[96] They claim that Stalin's hidden objective from the start, or at least since 1939, was to increase Soviet territorial gains in Europe, which was ultimately achieved by signing the secret protocols.[97]

This perspective too downplays the Western powers' contribution to the failure of collective security, and it ignores evidence of the Soviet Union's relative openness to the possibility of an anti-Fascist pact and of Litvinov's fierce struggle to see it come to fruition. By presenting Stalin as consistently supportive of the Rappalo line, it attributes to him the superhuman ability to foresee the pact with Germany some ten tumultuous and complicated European years earlier. A more realistic view is that "Stalin always exploited opportunities as they appeared at a given moment"[98] and that he wanted to give collective security a chance. During the mid-1930s, another historian contends that it was quite natural to hope for the policy's success and share Litvinov's view about the importance of restraining Hitler's ambitions. Indeed it is only "from the perspective of 1939 and the Nazi-Soviet pact" that "such warnings appear Machiavellian."[99]

Assessment of Collective Security

The Soviet case of collective security can be well interpreted according to the honor perspective. Communist ideology modified but did not principally change the state's motivations and strategy of achieving its international objectives. Litvinov's thinking about state honor was similar to that underlying Nicholas II's decision to commit Russia's resources to restraining the power ambitions of Wilhelmian Germany. Both statesmen stressed the importance of a strong international coalition for preserving peace, and both demonstrated their commitment to a more cooperative vision of honor than the one favored by Gorchakov, Stolypin, and Stalin. Although the latter statesmen also interpreted international politics in terms of honor, they understood it as loyalty to the narrowly defined interests of modernization and stability at home. The opposing side, Nazi Germany, also based its foreign policy on concepts of honor and prestige and did not hesitate to accuse Litvinov of conducting "a dishonorable policy (*unherliche Politik*)" when it caught him departing from the Rappalo line.[100]

Overall, the policy of collective security failed to achieve the key Soviet objectives of assembling a sufficiently strong anti-Hitler coalition; it succeeded only in delaying the emergence of a pro-German government in France.[101] Much of the responsibility for this failure lies with Stalin and his deep mistrust of Western allies and of his own comrades at home. Although he gave collective security a chance by providing Litvinov with considerable freedom to pursue the policy until 1938, Stalin occasionally blocked the actions of his commissar for foreign affairs; for example, by not supporting sanctions against Italy in 1935. By isolating European social democratic parties from the Comintern until 1935, Stalin also inadvertently contributed to the rise of Hitler. One of Hitler's first actions after he came to power in 1933 was to ban the Communist Party and arrest its leaders. Finally, Stalin's horrendous internal purges severely undermined Soviet credibility in the eyes of potential allies, and "the credit accumulated by Litvinov's diplomacy and by Russia's industrialization was largely dissipated."[102]

However, the West's contribution to the failure of Litvinov was important as well. A key difference between collective security and the Triple Alliance was the degree of support by the Western allies, which at Litvinov's time were noncommittal at best, despite that fact that the danger of Hitler's regime was incomparably more serious than that posed by Wilhelm's Germany. France and Britain did not merely have little confidence in the Soviet Union's ability and willingness to fight. They suspected the Russians of plotting behind their backs to destroy the West by Hitler's hands, and they addressed these suspicions by attempting to channel the Nazi expansionist ambitions to the East. According to one historian, Western powers viewed Fascism as "a lesser evil when compared with the contagion of communism."[103] Another historian agrees that "anti-Communism . . . was all the more powerful as an unstated, instinctive and rooted aversion, tending to reinforce decisions made at Soviet expense for other and seemingly more exalted reasons."[104] The West began to understand the danger of not establishing a coalition with the USSR only after Hitler's invasion of Czechoslovakia – too late to reverse its initial course.

As a result, Stalin's only remaining choice after Munich seems to have been to try to delay the war, rather than establish peace. By concluding the pact with Hitler, the Soviet government – through a Molotov statement – publicly acknowledged that "the negotiations with France and England had run into insuperable differences and ended in failure."[105] The pact was an achievement on the part of Stalin, but no more than a second-best solution.[106] The Soviet Union only managed to reverse the priorities of Nazi Germany temporarily, for Hitler never deviated from his key objective, which he stated to the high commissioner of Danzig on August 11, 1939:

Everything I undertake is directed against Russia. If the West is too stupid and too blind to comprehend that, I will be forced to come to an understanding with the Russians, to smash the West, and then after its defeat, to turn against the Soviet Union, with my assembled forces.[107]

Notes

1 Roberts, *The Unholy Alliance*, p. 53.
2 For details of cooperation between the Red Army and the Reichswehr, see Hochman, *The Soviet Union and the Failure of Collective Security*, pp. 18–22.
3 Haslam, *The Soviet Union and the Struggle for Collective Security in Europe*, p. 29; Mlechin, *Ministry inostrannykh del*, p. 134.
4 See the text of the proposals "Iz predlozheni Soyuza SSR po sozdaniyu v Yevrope sistemy kollektivnoi bezopasnosti, odobrennykh TsK VKP(b) 19 dekabrya 1933 g."
5 Sheinis, *Maksim Maksimovich Litvinov*, p. 322.
6 Russia did not recognized articles 12 and 15, which it viewed as legalizing the use of force, and article 23, which it viewed as too restrictive of racial and national equality. Ibid.
7 Mikoyan, "Diplomat leninskoi shkoly," 7.
8 The text of the Soviet "Draft Declaration Regarding a Definition of Aggression" is available in Oliva, ed. *Russia and the West from Peter to Khrushchev*, pp. 198–9.
9 The line comes from Vladimir Lenin's classic work *Imperialism, the Highest Stage of Capitalism*, which was written in 1916 and argued the predatory nature of capitalism at its imperialist stage (Lenin, *Selected Works*, vol. 1).
10 Roberts, *The Soviet Union and the Origins of the Second World War*, p. 14.
11 Ibid.
12 Kennedy-Pipe, *Russia and the World*, p. 39.
13 Haslam, *The Soviet Union and the Struggle for Collective Security*, p. 7.

14 Phillips, *Between the Revolution and the West*, p. 129.
15 Ulam, *Expansion and Coexistence*, p. 209.
16 Phillips, *Between the Revolution and the West*, p. 145.
17 Ibid., p. 151.
18 Kennan, *Russia and the West under Lenin and Stalin*, p. 276; Zagladin, *Istoriya uspekhov i neudach sovetskoi diplomatiyi*, p. 100.
19 Nation, *Black Earth, Red Star*, p. 86.
20 For a similar argument in contemporary scholarship, see for example Kupchan and Kupchan "Concerts, Collective Security, and the Future of Europe" and "The Promise of Collective Security."
21 Sipols, *Sovetski Soyuz v bor'be za mir i bezopasnost'*, p. 113.
22 Sheinis, *Maksim Maksimovich Litvinov*, p. 337.
23 Roberts, *The Unholy Alliance*, p. 44.
24 Hugh Ragsdale shows in his book that the Red Army mobilized before Munich and, not having a common border with Czechoslovakia, made arrangements with the Romanian General Staff for transit through Romanian territory. Ragsdale, *The Soviets, the Munich Crisis, and the Coming of World War II*.
25 See especially, Overy, *War and Economy in the Third Reich*.
26 Hochman, *The Soviet Union and the Failure of Collective Security*, p. 50.
27 Ulam, *Expansion and Coexistence*, p. 222.
28 Phillips, *Between the Revolution and the West*, pp. 155–7.
29 Ulam, *Expansion and Coexistence*, p. 236.
30 Phillips, *Between the Revolution and the West*, p. 149.
31 Ibid., p. 154.
32 Ragsdale, *The Soviets, the Munich Crisis, and the Coming of World War II*, p. 9.
33 Phillips, *Between the Revolution*, p. 162.
34 Suny, *The Soviet Experiment*, p. 299.
35 The Red Army was making the necessary preparations by mobilizing and deploying tanks and infantry in the regions of Volochinsk and Kamenets-Podol'ski and moving cavalry to the Polish border. Ragsdale, *The Soviets, the Munich Crisis*, p. 113. Litvinov too indicated in a private conversation that "[I]f they [the Czechs] fight, we'll fight alongside them." Roberts, *The Unholy Alliance*, p. 90.
36 Suny, *The Soviet Experiment*, p. 300.
37 Nekrich, *Pariahs, Partners, Predators*, p. 107.
38 Nation, *Black Earth, Red Star*, p. 98.
39 Roberts, *The Unholy Alliance*, p. 5.
40 Roberts, *The Soviet Union and the Origins of the Second World War*, p. 72.
41 Donaldson and Nogee, *The Foreign Policy of Russia*, p. 49.
42 Nation, *Black Earth, Red Star*, p. 99.
43 For elaboration on the internal Soviet concept of honor and prestige, see Brooks, *Thank You, Comrade Stalin!*, pp. 126–77.
44 The doctrine of peaceful coexistence included, in addition to interstate normalization and replacement of war with diplomacy, "continuation of a sharp ideological struggle and support for the revolutionary movement." Nadzhafov, "Bor'ba za ukrepleniye Versal'skogo perioda i vosstanovleniye yevropeiskogo ravnovesiya (1921–1926)," 157–8.
45 Litvinov, *Against Aggression*, p. 17.

46 For various analyses of how the Soviet state adjusted to international realities, see Ulam, *Expansion and Coexistence*; Nation, *Black Earth, Red Star*; and Jacobson, *When the Soviet Union Entered World Politics*.

47 Gorodetsky, *Grand Delusion*, p. 2.

48 Haslam, *The Soviet Union and the Struggle for Collective Security*, p. 5; Timasheff, "World Revolution or Russia."

49 Stalin, *Voprosy leninizma*, p. 435.

50 Kissinger, *Diplomacy*, p. 337; Kennan, *Russia and the West*, p. 268.

51 Hochman, *The Soviet Union and the Failure of Collective Security*, p. 29.

52 Roberts, *The Soviet Union and the Origins*, p. 91.

53 Ulam, *Expansion and Coexistence*, p. 218.

54 Nation, *Black Earth, Red Star*, pp. 77–78.

55 Mlechin, *Ministry inostrannykh del*, pp. 141, 144.

56 Roberts, *The Unholy Alliance*, p. 48; Sheinis, *Maksim Maksimovich Litvinov*, p. 374.

57 Ragsdale, *The Soviets, the Munich Crisis, and the Coming of World War II*, pp. 30–1.

58 Roberts, *The Unholy Alliance*, p. 49.

59 Nation, *Black Earth, Red Star*, p. 74.

60 Stalin, "On the Tasks of Workers in the Economy," 294–5.

61 The figures are from the Soviet historian A. M. Nekrich as quoted in Nation, *Black Earth, Red Star*, p. 87. Alec Nove provides more modest yet impressive rises in military expenditures, from 3.4% in 1933 to 16.1% in 1936, 25.6% in 1939, and 32.6% in 1940. Nove, *An Economic History of the USSR*, pp. 228–9. Some of these expenditures, other historians argue, were completely unnecessary. Zagladin, *Istoriya uspekhov i neudach sovetskoi diplomatiyi*, pp. 102–3.

62 Stalin, *Voprosy leninizma*, pp. 427–9.

63 Ibid., p. 577. For more data of the Soviet relative weakness, see Kennedy, *The Rise and Fall of Great Powers*, pp. 330, 332.

64 Roberts, *The Soviet Union and the Origins*, pp. 24–5. As Litvinov wrote to the Soviet ambassador in Berlin Jacob Suritz in December 1935, "There is no point in strengthening present-day Germany too much. It is enough, in my view, to maintain economic relations with Germany only at a level necessary to avoid a complete split between the two countries." Ibid., p. 33.

65 Bukharin contrasted his principles of "socialist humanism" to those of "fascist bestiality." Cohen, *Bukharin and the Bolshevik Revolution*, pp. 360–1.

66 Nation, *Black Earth, Red Star*, p. 93.

67 Haslam, *The Soviet Union and the Struggle*, pp. 67, 64.

68 Hochman, *The Soviet Union and the Failure*, p. 116; Nation, *Black Earth, Red Star*, p. 93.

69 Nation, *Black Earth, Red Star*, p. 85; Haslam, *The Soviet Union and the Struggle*, p. 95; Phillips, *Between the Revolution and the West*, p. 160; Uldricks, "Debating the Role of Russia in the origins of the Second World War," 143–4.

70 Roberts, *The Soviet Union and the Origins*, p. 39.

71 Sipols, *Sovetski Soyuz v bor'be za mir i bezopasnost'*, p. 113.

72 Browley, "Neoclassical Realism and Strategic Calculations," 95.

73 Haslam, *The Soviet Union and the Struggle*, p. 24.
74 Kennedy, *The Rise and Fall of Great Powers*, p. 337.
75 Kissinger, *Diplomacy*, p. 296.
76 Haslam, *The Soviet Union and the Struggle*, pp. 89–90.
77 Ragsdale, *The Soviets, the Munich Crisis*, p. 37.
78 Kissinger, *Diplomacy*, p. 340.
79 Haslam, *The Soviet Union and the Struggle*, pp. 206–7. For a more detailed analysis of Chamberlain's foreign policy views and perception of Russia, see Neilson, *Britain, Soviet Russia and the Collapse of the Versailles Order*, pp. 254–317, especially pp. 275–7, 285, 294, 316.
80 Churchill, of course, saw things differently by advocating an alliance with the Soviet Union and France. Ibid., pp. 166, 169.
81 Uldricks, "Debating the Role of Russia," 136.
82 Ibid, 137.
83 Sheinis, *Maksim Maksimovich Litvinov*, p. 314. Stalin saw it similarly and even gave Litvinov a summer house ("*dacha*") as a gift of appreciation for his work. Mlechin, *Ministry inostrannykh del*, p. 140.
84 Polls too show the isolationist mood of the public. As late as October 1939, 68% felt that U.S. intervention in World War I was a mistake – the feeling that only declined by early 1941. Legro, *Rethinking the World*, p. 67.
85 Phillips, *Between the Revolution and the West*, pp. 132–3.
86 Ragsdale, *The Soviets, the Munich Crisis*, p. 9.
87 Ibid., p. 119.
88 Mlechin, *Ministry inostrannykh del*, p. 135.
89 In his overview of Soviet international thinking before the war, William Wohlforth focuses on the hostility and the correlation-of-forces approaches without ever mentioning the collective security policy. Wohlforth, *The Elusive Balance*, pp. 32–58.
90 Kissinger, *Diplomacy*, p. 333.
91 Ibid., p. 335.
92 Ibid., p. 337.
93 Ulam writes that the Soviet statesmen were "not entirely immune to the illusions that ruled Europe's minds in 1935: the democracies were sluggish, but they represented tremendous power, dwarfing Germany's." Ulam, *Expansion and Coexistence*, p. 227.
94 Kissinger, *Diplomacy*, p. 334.
95 Hochman, *The Soviet Union and the Failure*, pp. 32, 45
96 Raack, *Stalin's Drive to the West, 1938–1945* and Tucker, "The Emergence of Stalin's foreign policy." For various overviews of the "German" school, see Roberts, *The Soviet Union and the Origins*, pp. 1–8 and Uldricks, "Debating the Role of Russia," pp. 140–9.
97 The latter view is advanced in Suvorov, *Icebreaker* and Nekrich, *Pariahs, Partners, Predators*, p. 110. Kissinger too seems to support the expansionism since 1939 interpretation: "Hitler alone was in a position to offer him the territorial gain in Eastern Europe that he was after, and for this he was quite willing to pay the price of a European war which spared the Soviet Union." *Diplomacy*, p. 344.

98 Gorodetsky, *Grand Delusion*, p. 7.

99 Ulam, *Expansion and Coexistence*, p. 236.

100 Haslam, *The Soviet Union and the Struggle*, p. 31.

101 Ulam, *Expansion and Coexistence*, p. 254.

102 Ibid., p. 241.

103 Nation, *Black Earth, Red Star*, p. 101.

104 Haslam, *The Soviet Union and the Struggle*, p. 231.

105 Suny, *The Soviet Experiment*, p. 302. For a review of Soviet historical accounts of the decision, see Roberts, *The Holy Alliance*, pp. 11–22.

106 For similar assessments, see Kissinger, *Diplomacy*, p. 346 and Haslam, *The Soviet Union and the Struggle*, p. 232. For the most favorable assessment of Soviet actions by Western historians, see Taylor, *The Origins of the Second World War*.

107 Kissinger, *Diplomacy*, p. 346.

"Russia and the United States bear a special responsibility for strengthening the global stability.... [T]he trustworthy partnership of Russia and the United States is not only in the interests of our nations. It has a positive impact on the entire system of international relations and therefore remains our unconditional priority."

Vladimir Putin[1]

Vladimir Putin's Choice

Engaging the United States in Counterterrorist Cooperation

The 9/11 tragedy took place on American soil, but was seen as an equally tragic and dangerous development by Russia as well. By 2001, Russia had already experienced multiple terrorist attacks, and many Russians felt instinctively sympathetic to the American people and government (see Table 8.1). President Vladimir Putin was among the first to call President George Bush to express his support and pledge important resources to help America in its fight against terror. Despite the reservations of the political class and other areas of society, Putin offered America broad support for its operations in Afghanistan, including sharing intelligence, opening Russian airspace to relief missions, taking part in search-and-rescue operations, rallying Central Asian countries to the American cause, and arming anti-Taliban forces inside Afghanistan.

However, Putin's efforts to engage the United States predated September 11. The new leader had wanted to start fresh after the NATO military campaign against Serbia that had considerably soured Russia–West relations, and he had began to cultivate ties with the American administration soon after he came to office. Washington's initial reaction was cold. The new George W. Bush administration in the United States made it clear that it did not foresee any breakthroughs in relations with Russia. It made public the arrest of FBI agent Robert Hanssen, who had spied for the

Russians, and it subsequently expelled fifty Russian diplomats. It threatened to end any economic aid except for nonproliferation projects and – through Secretary of Defense Donald Rumsfeld – accused Russia of aiding in the proliferation of nuclear materials and weapons technologies. As late as February 2001, Bush's National Security Advisor Condoleezza Rice insisted that Russia was a threat to America and its European allies. Putin, however, persisted in his efforts to strengthen ties with the United States and finally had a breakthrough in a meeting with the American president in Ljubljana, Slovenia, in the summer of 2001. The relationship began to thaw, largely thanks to personal chemistry between the two leaders. It was after that summit meeting that Bush made his famous remark about their relationship: "I was able to get a sense of his soul."[2]

Determined to overcome skepticism at home and abroad, Putin pressed forward by stressing the broad positive potential of the new Russian-U.S. relationship. In particular, beginning with his interview in the *Wall Street Journal* in February 2002, he emphasized Russia as a reliable alternative to traditional Middle Eastern sources of oil and natural gas. At that time Russia was the world's single largest non-OPEC oil exporter, with 10 percent of known oil reserves and 9 percent of world output. Yet it only accounted for 1 percent of American imports in 2001.[3] Putin projected that Russia would increase production of crude oil at an annual rate of 9 percent, with much of this increase intended for export, and a considerable part of that for the United States. In May of 2002 the U.S. and Russian presidents signed a joint declaration on energy cooperation at their summit in Moscow. Then followed the Houston "energy summit" in October, at which Russian officials said that they could export as much as a million barrels a day to the United States within five years. *The Economist* summed up these efforts at the time: "America's relations with Russia are now better than at any time since the end of the Second World War and are improving."[4]

U.S.-Russian relations also improved in the area of military security. Putin moved to organize security relationships with Western countries on the common basis of counterterrorism. After initially supporting Milosevic, he opted to minimize Russian involvement in the affairs of the post-Kosovo Balkans. In August 2003, Moscow withdrew its peacekeeping mission from Bosnia and Kosovo. Putin's efforts to focus the security agenda on issues of counterterrorism resonated with the White House. In addition to supporting the U.S. anti-Taliban operation in Afghanistan, Putin sought to develop a new framework of strategic interaction with the United States. He saw the decision by Bush to withdraw from the ABM treaty as potentially threatening, but at a time of relative Russian weakness and emerging trust between the two countries Putin decided to swallow hard in the interests of pursuing other Russian objectives. Despite formidable domestic resistance, he expressed little opposition to the U.S. decision to build nuclear missile defense systems unilaterally, and he accepted Bush's conclusion that "the ABM treaty hinders our government's ability to develop ways to protect our people from future terrorist or rogue state missile attacks."[5] Although Putin viewed the U.S. decision to withdraw from the treaty as a "mistake," his reaction was nonthreatening, despite some expectations of a confrontational response.

At one point the Russian leader even expressed interest in joining NATO, and some NATO leaders indicated their support of Russia's membership in the alliance. In late 2001, NATO secretary general Lord Robertson, supported by President Bush and Prime Minister Tony Blair, advocated giving Russia a status equal to the alliance's nineteen permanent members, including veto power over certain decisions. In the assessment of the *New York Times*, the plan promised a "fundamental shift in behavior for the 52-year-old organization, which was founded after World War II specifically to contain the military power of the Soviet Union" and would result in Russia's "full partnership with Western democracies."[6] An important step in that direction was the establishment at the May 28, 2002, summit in Rome of a new NATO-Russia Council for consulting on principles and actions against common threats. The U.S.-Russian joint declaration at the summit became the high point in their fast developing relationship. It stated the two nations' "belief that new global challenges and threats require a qualitatively new foundation for our relationship" and that "we are achieving a new strategic relationship. The era, in which the United States and Russia saw each other as an enemy or strategic threat has ended. We are partners and we will cooperate to advance stability, security, and economic integration, and to jointly counter global challenges and to help resolve regional conflicts."[7]

Supporting the United States in Afghanistan, but Not Iraq

Despite Putin's active support of America after 9/11, he chose to oppose the U.S. military intervention in Iraq. With France and Germany, Russia decided to join the coalition of those opposing the unilateral American war.

Supporting the U.S. war against the Taliban regime in Afghanistan was quite simple – for a long time, Russia had supported the Northern Alliance and was happy to have its long-time rival that sponsored terrorism in Chechnya removed from power without a single Russian shot fired. While offering his support to the Northern Alliance, Putin made it clear that he would operate within the framework of the United Nations, based on support of the UN Security Council. His support for the United States was therefore strong yet conditional.

The war in Iraq was a different matter. Along with Russia's foreign policy officials, Putin was opposed to proceeding without UN authorization for the use of force. As in Afghanistan, his objective was to reduce terrorist threats to Russia, and he wanted to provide his country with better conditions for economic modernization. Unconvinced by claims about the existence of a nuclear program in Iraq and the putative links between Saddam Hussein's regime and the Al Qaida terrorist network – the key arguments advanced by the Bush administration for the war – he saw it as a deviation from the global war on terror. With many others in Russia's political circles, Putin believed that terrorism, as a stateless phenomenon, was a challenge to the very system of nation-states. In his view, terrorism could only be defeated through the coordination of state efforts, and not by taking on relatively established states, such as Iraq.

Putin's decision to side with Europe, and not the United States, partly reflected pragmatic considerations. First, Russian ties with Europe were strong and becoming stronger. Russia's energy markets were primarily in Europe, which accounted for 40 percent of Russia's foreign trade against a mere 5 percent with the United States.[8] In June 2003, Putin also sealed a joint venture with British Petroleum worth more than six billion dollars. Second, there was the issue of Iraq's sizable debt to Russia – $7–8 billion, by different calculations – and Russia's worries that it would never see the money if the war was waged. Russian experts also forecasted a drastic fall in world oil prices in the event of war – another nightmare for a country in which a considerable portion of revenue came from exporting natural resources. In addition, the war was not popular at home, with the public skeptical about supporting the United States. In April 2003, only 2 percent approved of the U.S. military action, whereas 83 percent were opposed.[9] Finally, the world outside Russia – as the Pew Global Attitudes survey demonstrated – overwhelmingly denied the legitimacy of the American decision.[10] Table 8.1 shows the degree to which different nations, including Russia, held decreasingly favorable views of the United States over time.

Putin's opposition was also shaped by the compatibility of his vision with that of Western European nations and the discrepancy between the Kremlin's perception and that of the United States. To Russia, it

Table 8.1. *Declining Percentage of Citizens Who Held a Favorable View of the United States*

	1999/2000	March 2002	March 2003
Britain	83	75	48
France	62	63	31
Germany	78	61	25
Poland	86	79	50
Russia	37	61	28
Turkey	52	30	12

Sources: What the World Thinks in 2002; America's Image Further Erodes.

remained critically important not to recognize the use of force against established states and to rely on the United Nations as the only legitimate body to make such a decision.

The U.S.-Russian Partnership, Unraveled

The U.S.-Russian partnership was not to last. As the immediacy of the post-9/11 threat subsided, Washington backed away from its initial commitment to take its relationship with Moscow to a new level of cooperation and returned to expecting Russia to follow America's foreign policy agenda.

In late 2002–3, the United States perceived Russia's efforts to secure its borders and territorial integrity as a reflection of Russia's revisionist and expansionist agenda. The United States insisted on Russia providing a "political solution" to the Chechnya problem, by which Washington meant holding talks with those whom the Kremlin considered terrorists. The United States also downplayed links between Chechen terrorists and al Qaida, which made it possible for it to grant political asylum and media exposure to those closely affiliated with Chechen terrorists.[11] In addition, in line with its new regime change strategy, the United States applied pressure on the entire former Soviet region to transform its political institutions,[12] which the Kremlin viewed as largely destabilizing and unhelpful in fighting the war on terror. The U.S.-Russian relationship further suffered in the area of military security. In addition to withdrawing from the ABM treaty, the United States took steps to move its military infrastructure closer to Russia's borders, raising further suspicions in Moscow. Finally, there was little left of the two nations' efforts to establish an energy partnership. Washington no longer looked for ways to work with Russia as a partner and instead routinely denounced Russia's leaders for using energy as "political leverage" to influence its neighbors' policies. The initially ambitious global counterterrorist agenda was largely abandoned.

The War on Terror, 2001–2005: Timetable

1999 August	Chechen terrorists invade Dagestan
	Two bombs exploded in Moscow's residential buildings
September	Russia launches a counterterrorist operation in Chechnya
2000 March	Vladimir Putin is elected president of Russia
2001 Summer	The United States and Russia hold summit in Ljubljana, Slovenia
September	Terrorists attack the United States
	Putin announces support for the United States and pledges intelligence assistance
November	The United States launches a counterterrorist operation in Afghanistan
December	The United States leaves the ABM treaty. Russia shows no serious opposition
2002 February	Putin begins to position Russia as an energy alternative to Middle East
May	New NATO-Russia Council is established
	The United States and Russia declare their ties a "strategic relationship"
June	President Bush formulates his preemption strategy
2003 January	Russia argues for the UN role in sanctioning the use of force in Iraq
March	Terrorist attacks take place in Spain
April	United States invades Iraq
May	Russia and five other ex-Soviet states form the Collective Security Treaty Organization for fighting terrorism
2004 March	Putin reelected as president
September	Chechen terrorists' attack in Beslan, Northern Ossetia
November	Orange Revolution takes place in Ukraine

Explaining Putin's Policy Choices

Putin's Sense of Honor

Much like his tsarist predecessors, Putin viewed the honor of the state as being realized by advancing Russia's status as a European great power – a power with Christian roots able to defend itself against external threats and obligated to champion the larger international objectives of the Western world. The Kremlin therefore saw Russia's participation in a global struggle with terrorism as fully consistent with its Westernness and as an affirmation of its great power status.

Putin's commitment to European identity as he understood it is obvious in his many speeches and public interviews. He came to power as a believer in Peter the Great's philosophy of catching up with Europe and did not seem to have much faith that developing relations with the East would benefit Russia. For example, he shared the concern that, if Moscow failed to improve its economic situation, Asian neighbors could exploit Russia. In one of his speeches, the president issued this explicit warning: "I do not want to dramatize the situation, but if we do not make every real effort, even the indigenous Russian population will soon speak mostly Japanese, Chinese, and Korean."[13] In addition, some of his statements regarding the Chechens further revealed his ethnocentric bias. The insistence on Russia's belonging to Western European culture reflected his beliefs more accurately than his attempts to cast himself as a supporter of strengthening ties with the East, as seen in the following passage:

Above all else Russia was, is and will, of course, be a major European power. Achieved through much suffering by European culture, the ideals of freedom, human rights, justice and democracy have for many centuries been our society's determining values.[14]

When the Orange Revolution in Ukraine challenged Russia's influence in the former Soviet region, Putin sought to reaffirm his commitments to European values and in 2007 declared that he saw Russia moving toward the same "ideals of freedom, human rights, justice and democracy," albeit at its own pace and given its own conditions.[15]

While revealing his bias toward Europe, Putin saw his task as strengthening Russia domestically, which was essential if the nation was to act on its European commitments. He envisioned Russia becoming a "normal" great power,[16] pursuing the objective of becoming a full-fledged member of the Western community. Yet he also recognized that Russia could not join the Western community at the expense of its sovereignty, material and human capabilities, territorial size, and political reputation among cultural allies outside the West. Referring to the threat of terrorism and territorial disintegration, Putin perceived that remaining a great power was a security necessity for Russia, claiming that "Russia can only survive and develop within the existing borders if it stays as a great power" and reminding his audience that "during all of its times of weakness . . . Russia was invariably confronted with the threat of disintegration."[17] Great power status was therefore not a goal in itself for Putin, but rather a necessary condition for Russia's more advanced engagement with the world.

In addition to security imperatives, the president emphasized Russia's need to modernize by warning of the danger of its turning into a Third World country. Ridiculing overdone great power rhetoric – "let us not recollect our national interests on those occasions when we have to make some loud statements" – Russia's new leader compared Russia to Portugal, the EU's poorest member.[18] Despite Russia's economic recovery after the 1998 financial crisis, the size of its economy at purchasing power parity was less than one-fourth of the economies of China and Japan and less than one-tenth of the economies of the United States and the European Union.[19]

Putin therefore sought to engage the West in honorable joint projects, such as fighting a global war on terror. After 9/11, his foreign policy was pragmatic, focused on improving Russia's domestic conditions and cooperation with Western nations. Despite the presence of anti-Western sentiments among some of the members of Russia's political class, the president showed little support for the previously popular concept of building a multipolar world, and – until 2005 – he was more active in promoting Russia's relationship with the United States and Europe than with the East.

Domestic Support

Putin's vision of honor and his decision to support the United States in the post-September 11 struggle against terrorism found sufficient domestic support, but were also met with criticism from some members of the political class.

Among elites, a coalition of commercial and security interests embraced Putin's vision.[20] Liberal and commercially oriented elites had strongly supported him and his election as president. Especially important were Russia's oligarchs, super-wealthy businesspeople who had emerged as a powerful political force in 1996. At that time they were able to overcome their differences and pull together the financial resources to reelect the unpopular Yeltsin. After the August 1998 financial crisis, the recovery of the economy provided commercial elites with new opportunities for development. Russia's foreign trade had been enjoying a structural surplus, and the economy was wide open for commercial operations. Foreign trade's share of the GDP was around 50 percent, making the Russian economy about as open as Germany's. Although the stock of foreign direct investment accumulated since 1989 remained low,[21] rising world oil prices provided Russia with new growth opportunities.

At the same time, many members of the security elite also felt compelled to embrace the new president because of his background in the security service and his beliefs in strengthening the state and social order. Initially, even people such as Aleksandr Prokhanov, the editor of the hardline newspaper *Zavtra*, were writing favorably about him, although a year later he returned to his typical "irreconcilable" opposition to the Kremlin. The intensification of terrorist activities in the Caucasus and worldwide strengthened the positions of the security elites. In August 1999, Chechen rebels led by Shamil Basayev and the Arab fighter Khattab occupied parts of the neighboring republic of Dagestan, in response to which the Kremlin resumed military operations in the region. In that same month, two bombs exploded in Moscow residential buildings, killing hundreds of civilians. The sheer magnitude of violence was unprecedented. Russians united behind Putin, who was running for president on the platform of "eradicating extremism" in Chechnya and reestablishing a "strong state" throughout the entire Russian territory.[22]

Although the liberal commercial elite and the security elite held fundamentally different worldviews, at the time they agreed on Putin's vision of state honor as a Westernizing great power and hoped to win his support to their respective viewpoints. Commercial elites were hopeful that the president would come to accept an even more pro-American worldview after September 11, whereas members of the security class expected him to become less supportive of the United States, which they believed had the potential to damage Russia's own interests and special relations with China and the Muslim countries.

The Russian general public, too, showed signs of increasing concern over America's actions in the world. According to data from the Russian Center for the Study of Public Opinion, 63 percent of all Russians felt that 9/11 was a form of "retribution for American foreign policy," and another 64 percent perceived Washington's military activities in Afghanistan as dangerous for Russia.[23] In November 2001 – immediately after the terrorist attacks on the United States, when Russians felt a strong sympathy toward Americans – only 30 percent agreed with the statement that cooperation with the West was the main prerequisite for Russia's economic

prosperity.[24] At the same time, Russians continued to show strong support for Putin's decision to side with the West in general.[25]

Western Recognition

The cooperative vision of honor became possible in the context of a growing convergence of economic interests and security concerns between
Russia and the West, and it lasted for as long as that convergence
remained in place. Russia's economic recovery again made it attractive
to foreign investors, reinforcing the Kremlin's desire to further integrate
with the Western world.

On the security front, both Russia and the West, especially the United
States, had been subject to terrorist attacks and had to find an appropriate
international response to the new global threat. The September 11 terrorist attacks on the United States in 2001 and subsequent attacks on Spain
in 2003 strengthened the sense of solidarity among all those fighting terrorism across the world. President George W. Bush proclaimed terrorism
to be "pure evil" directed at freedom-loving people throughout the world
and argued the need to launch the strategy of preemption.[26] Several leading intellectuals called on the West to capture or kill Osama bin Laden
and linked the terrorist attacks to Islam and the Middle Eastern region.[27]
In Russia, these developments provided Putin with a formidable opportunity to bolster his domestic and international posture and to vindicate
his conception of security threats.

The subsequent development of closer ties between Russia and the
United States strengthened the ground for the cooperative, rather than
unilateral, vision of honor. President Bush's conviction that "old suspicions are giving way to new understanding and respect" and that the
two countries are "allies in the war on terror" moving "to a new level
of partnership,"[28] along with practical steps toward integrating Russia
into NATO and deepening energy relations, provided the Kremlin with
additional assurances about its foreign policy direction. Russia's relative
weakness, on the one hand, and the emerging trust between Russian and
Western leaders, on the other, explain why Putin initially did not object
to several unilateral moves on the part of the United States, such as
withdrawal from the ABM treaty and the drive to nuclear primacy. From
2001–3, the Kremlin was hoping that strong counterterrorist cooperation between Russia and the West would develop, and it was willing to
overlook policies that gave a unilateral advantage to the United States.
It was only later – in response to a new wave of NATO expansion, criticisms of Russia's role in Chechnya, promotion of democracy among the
former Soviet states, and renewed energy competition in Eurasia – that

Putin revised his vision of honor from a cooperative one into one that was more assertive and unilateral.

Alternative Explanations

Although offensive realism is hardly applicable in explaining Putin's war on terror – Russia was not strong enough to challenge the United States and did not engage in balancing behavior – defensive realists may feel compelled to argue their case. According to them, Russia's eagerness to establish closer ties with Western nations after 9/11 should be viewed as an example of rational accommodation or bandwagoning with the strongest states in the international system. Similarly, scholars of American "unipolarity" and hegemony have long noted the overwhelming power that the United States has in the international system,[29] and they have constructed an intellectual tradition that cherishes America's dominance in the world above all other imperatives.[30] Many neoconservative pundits supported this thinking.[31] They argued that Russia was simply in no position to complain about U.S. policies or to demand a greater role in the world. A proper assessment of the international balance of power or unipolarity required that Moscow become dependent on Washington, and if Russia did not accept this role, it had to be made to follow the U.S. lead.[32]

This argument focusing on the structure of the international system is compelling because the United States is by far the most powerful nation on earth and therefore is in a position to shape the policies of other nations. However, power by itself does not dictate imperial or hegemonic policies and does not require that other nations agree to accept such policies. Indeed Russia had sufficient power to assume important responsibilities for maintaining peace and stability in Eurasia. More importantly, however, Russia acts based on the perception of its ties with the West, rather than on rational interests. Although Russia was unable to challenge significantly the position of the United States in the world, many within the Russian political class recommended that the Kremlin do so by strengthening relations with China, the Shanghai Cooperation Organization, and the Muslim world.[33] Much like President Bush, the hard-liners viewed the post–September 11 world in terms of a struggle between "good" and "evil," except they found America on the wrong side of the barricade.

Another alternative explanation places emphasis on Moscow's expansionist beliefs and anti-Western political culture, arguing that the Kremlin was never sincere about its cooperative strategy.[34] Proponents of this view are even more skeptical that Russia would enter into cooperative arrangements with Western nations voluntarily. As a revisionist state,

Russia is expected to use every available opportunity to upset American plans to remain the dominant world power. Russia therefore represents a threat to American interests and must be either contained or fundamentally transformed. To dictate terms to Russia is not only possible; it is indeed necessary because it is the only language Russia can understand.[35] If this reasoning is correct, the post-9/11 partnership was doomed from the beginning, and American policy makers would be wise to abandon any search for common solutions and stay firm in resisting Russia's power aspirations.

This explanation is inaccurate in its portrayal of Russia and unrealistic in its recommendations to contain or punish Moscow. Rather than presenting Russia as an expansionist state, it is important to point out that, at least since Peter the Great, Russia's behavior has been formed by interactions with Europe and, after World War II, the West in general. Western civilization played an especially prominent role in creating the system of meanings in which to defend Russia's international choices.[36] Russia therefore has always been responsive to the behavior of Western nations and – with progressive leaders in the Kremlin – prepared to mend fences and pursue cooperation, rather than confrontation. This chapter's analysis indicates that after 9/11 Putin went far to establish a working partnership with the United States. His initial vision of honor and assessment of strategic threats had little to do with the anti-Americanism for which Putin is frequently blamed. Russia's president emphasized threats coming from economic backwardness and terrorism, and like many Western leaders, he saw terrorism as a threat to the very system of modern international relations.

The correction of Russia's course toward a greater assertiveness and criticism of the United States' role in the world took place after the so-called colored revolutions and a new wave of NATO expansion. The new language of the Kremlin began to form in 2004–5 and found its full expression in Putin's speech at the Munich Conference on Security Policy in January 2007. By then the Kremlin was highly critical of the United States, but the development was to a great extent a product of America's own policies that ignored Russia's concerns and security interests. The U.S. methods in the war on terror and its efforts to undermine Russia's geopolitical position in Eurasia compelled the Kremlin to reevaluate its initially pro-American policy.

Assessment

As with other cases of Russia's cooperation with the West, Putin's counterterrorism policy demonstrates that Russia may act on perceived honor to cooperate with Western nations to preserve peace and stability within the self-defined cultural community (the West). Put differently, the belief in honorable behavior emerges and matures under conditions of recipro- cal behavior on the part of Western nations. By extending strong support to the United States after 9/11, Putin was clearly intending to address a number of domestic issues, such as the affirmation of Russia's territo- rial integrity. However, his offer of cooperation with the West was also shaped by the belief in Russia's Europeanness and Westernness. Putin came to power as a conditional Westernizer, willing to give cooperation a chance even after the 1990s, which many around Putin viewed as a decade of Russia's failed attempts to engage the Western nations. This explains why in attempting to reengage the West, he was willing to invest considerable political capital and take considerable risks at home. For example, only 15 percent of the membership of the Russian Duma sup- ported the direction of Putin's policy, and it was equally controversial among the military.[37]

Putin's risks, however, did not pay off – certainly not according to him. Although some elements of cooperation with the West survived – sharing counterterrorist intelligence information and coordinating poli- cies against nuclear proliferation – the United States and other West- ern nations backed away from their initial commitment to take rela- tions with Moscow to a new level of cooperation. Instead of developing a partnership in economic and security relations, Russia had to suffer through a new round of NATO expansion, the U.S. withdrawal from the ABM treaty, U.S. military presence in Central Asia, the invasion of Iraq, plans to deploy elements of a nuclear missile defense in Eastern Europe, and a media war implicating Russia as a potential enemy.[38] In addition, Moscow had to live with Washington's strategy of global regime change, which in the post-Soviet context meant instability and which the Krem- lin viewed as directed against its own power and security. The colored revolutions in Georgia, Ukraine, and Kyrgyzstan from 2003–5 not only failed to bring greater stability and prosperity but also greatly politicized the regional environment.

Russia's shift from a cooperative to an assertive concept of honor was therefore driven in part by policies of the Western nations, and it would be misleading to ignore the interactive nature of Russia–West relations or to present Russia as an essentialist entity with once-and-forever formed values. After the West's post–Cold War encroachment into what Rus- sia perceived as the sphere of its geopolitical interests, and the West's efforts to achieve nuclear superiority, Moscow developed a strong con- viction that the United States was preparing to isolate Russia econom- ically, politically, and morally. Humiliated by the West's unwillingness to accept Russia as an equal partner – first by breaking the promise given to Mikhail Gorbachev not to expand NATO, second by denying a greater integration into Western institutions under Boris Yeltsin, and then by not developing the post–9/11 coalition – the Kremlin revised its worldview. Although Russia was well prepared to improve its ties with the United States and Europe during Putin's first term, the Russian leadership could not sacrifice Russia's interests and great power status, and its attitude soon toughened. As Max Weber said, "A nation forgives injury to its interests, but not injury to its honor."[39]

Notes

1 Putin, "Vystupleniye na rasshirennom soveschaniyi s uchastiyem poslov Rossiyskoi Federatsiyi v MID Rosiyi."
2 As cited in Herspring and Rutland, "Putin and Russian Foreign Policy," 237.
3 Aron, "Russian Oil and U.S. Security."
4 "Bush's Russian Romance."
5 Perez-Rivas, "U.S. Quits ABM Treaty."
6 Wines, "NATO Plan Offers Russia Equal Voice on Some Policies."
7 Text of Joint Declaration.
8 In fact, if Europe is understood in the wider sense – as an entity that includes the EU, Central and Eastern Europe, Norway, and Switzerland – then the share of Russia's trade with Europe increased to 55 percent (Hanson, "Joining but Not Signing Up?")
9 A poll taken in April by the All-Russian Center for Public Opinion Studies (VTsIOM) as quoted in Petrov, "The War in Iraq and the Myth of Putin."
10 The surveys were conducted among 38,000 respondents of forty-four nations. They found that "despite an initial outpouring of public sympathy for America following the September 11, 2001 terrorist attacks . . . images of the U.S. have been tarnished in all types of nations: among longtime NATO allies, in developing countries, in Eastern Europe, and most dramatically, in Muslim societies."
11 For example, in May 2004, political asylum was granted to Ilyas Akhmadov, the foreign minister of the separatist Chechen government that was viewed by the Russian government as responsible for terrorist violence.
12 For details and background, see, for example, MacKinnon, *The New Cold War*.
13 Putin, "Vystupleniye na soveschaniyi 'O perspektivakh razvitiya Dal'nego Vostoka i Zabaikalya.'"
14 Putin, "Poslaniye Federal'nomu Sobraniyu Rossiyskoy Federatsiyi," April 25, 2005.
15 The theme of non-interference in Russia's domestic developments from outside only became stronger over time, and in his addresses to the Federation Council in May 2006 and April 2007, Putin put an even greater emphasis on values of sovereignty and strong national defense. Putin, "Poslaniye Federal'nomu Sobraniyu Rossiyskoy Federatsiyi," May 10, 2006, April 26, 2007.

16 Tsygankov, "Vladimir Putin's Vision of Russia as a Normal Great Power."

17 Putin, "Poslaniye Federal'nomu Sobraniyu Rossiyskoy Federatsiyi," May 16, 2003.

18 Putin, "Rossiya na rubezhe tysyacheletiy."

19 Wohlforth, "Russia," 199.

20 Because commercial elites often defended Russia's Westernist identity, whereas military and security elites promoted the identity of a strong independent state, the new coalition was sometimes referred to as the alliance of oligarchs and *siloviks*, or *chekists* (from the Russian *CheKa*, the original name of the Bolshevik security service).

21 Hanson, "Joining but Not Signing Up?"; Vercuil, "Opening Russia?"

22 Initially, the popularity of then-Prime Minister Putin was only 2 percent, but in two months it jumped to 26 percent, and as the war in Chechnya progressed, it reached the unprecedented 58 percent mark in January 2000. Rose, "How Floating Parties Frustrate Democratic Accountability," 221–2.

23 Oslon, ed., *Amerika*, pp. 27, 124.

24 Kolossov and Borodullina, "Rossiya i Zapad."

25 Oslon, ed., *Amerika*, pp. 34, 124; "Rossiyani podderzhivayut sozdaniye soyuza RF i SshA v bor'be s mezhdunarodnym terrorizmom."

26 This was the heart of George Bush's strategy: "The war on terror will not be won on the defensive. We must take the battle to the enemy, disrupt his plans, and confront the worst threats before they emerge. In the world we have entered, the only path to safety is the path of action.... our security will require all Americans to be forward-looking and resolute, to be ready for preemptive action when necessary to defend our liberty and to defend our lives." Bush, "Graduation Speech at West Point."

27 On September 20, 2001, Francis Fukuyama, William Kristol, Jeane Kirkpatrick, Richard Perle, Martin Peretz, Norman Podhoretz, Charles Krauthammer, and others signed an "Open Letter to the President." The letter urged Bush to "capture or kill Osama bin Laden" and warned that failure to invade Iraq and topple Saddam Hussein would "constitute an early and perhaps decisive surrender in the war on international terrorism." This should be done "even if evidence does not link Iraq directly to the attack." Cited in Ali, *The Clash of Fundamentalisms*, p. 272.

28 Bush's statement after his meeting with Putin in Camp David on September 27, 2003. *Remarks by the President and Russian President Putin.*

29 For some key statements see Krauthammer, "The Unipolar Moment"; Krauthammer, "The Unipolar Moment Revisted,"; Brooks and Wohlforth, *World out of Balance.*

30 Madsen, *American Exceptionalism*; Mead, *Special Providence*; Callahan, *Logics of American Foreign Policy*; Lieven, *America Right or Wrong*; Mickethwait and Wooldridge, *The Right Nation.*

31 See, for example, Boot, "The Case for American Empire"; Kaplan, "The Hard Edge of American Values"; Ferguson, "Our Imperial Imperative"; Kagan, *Of Paradise and Power.*

32 For example, the leading advocate of U.S. unipolarity, Charles Krauthammer insisted during the 2004 U.S.-Russian conflict over election outcomes

in Ukraine that "this is about Russia first, democracy only second. This Ukrainian episode is a brief, almost nostalgic throwback to the Cold War.... The West wants to finish the job begun with the fall of the Berlin Wall and continue Europe's march to the east." Krauthammer, "Why Only in Ukraine?"

33 See, for example, Kortunov, "Rossiysko-Amerikanskoye partnerstvo?" 69; Prokhanov, "Ameriku potseloval angel smerti"; Dugin, "Terakty 11 Sentyabrya."

34 See, for example, *Russia's Wrong Direction*; Lapidus, "Between Assertiveness and Insecurity"; Legvold, "Russian Foreign Policy during State Transformation," 98.

35 As Winston Churchill put it in his famous "Iron Curtain" speech, "there is nothing they [Russians] admire so much as strength, and there is nothing for which they have less respect than for military weakness." Cited in Sakwa, *The Rise and Fall of the Soviet Union*, p. 295.

36 For a development of this argument, see Neumann, *Russia and the Idea of Europe*; English, *Russia and the Idea of the West*; Tsygankov, *Russia's Foreign Policy*.

37 "Putin policy shift is bold but risky."

38 For details and examples, see Tsygankov, *Russophobia;* English and Svyatets, "A Presumption of Guilt?"

39 As quoted in Donelan, *Honor in Foreign Policy*, p. 117.

Part III

Honor and Defensiveness

"The alliance of those who, together with us, have defended principles that preserved peace in Europe for more than a quarter century no longer exists. . . .

The circumstances have given us back a full freedom of action. The Emperor has decided to devote himself to well-being of his subjects and concentrate on development of internal resources and look outward only when Russia's interests categorically require it."

Alexander Gorchakov[1]

The Policy of Recueillement

Gorchakov's Note

Nicholas I had understood the tensions between his commitment to the Holy Alliance and Russia's own interests but still chose to focus on the Holy Alliance. By appointing Prince Alexander Gorchakov to lead the Foreign Ministry, the new emperor Alexander II sought to redirect policy to concentrate on internal affairs. However, this was not a popular appointment. Gorchakov's predecessor, Count Karl Nesselrode, was a long-term supporter of the Holy Alliance and was not pleased by this appointment. Nesselrode did not think much of Gorchakov's abilities and had recommended someone else for the position.[2] In addition, Gorchakov himself first declined the offer, citing health reasons, to which Nesselrode reportedly remarked semi-sarcastically, "Prince, you shouldn't decline the position of the minister. Now that the Paris peace is concluded there will be practically no work to do."[3] Even though he recognized that attention needed to be paid to Russia's domestic needs after defeat in the Crimean War,[4] Nesselrode favored a revival of the Holy Alliance in some form.[5]

Gorchakov, who took over foreign affairs in May 1856, soon demonstrated that he was of a different opinion. He did not think Russia had to be passive in foreign policy and did not feel that an alliance with Austria and Prussia would be effective in helping Russia meet its objectives. The chancellor viewed the restoration of Russia's influence in the Balkans and access to the Black Sea as critically important objectives without which state honor could not be preserved. He therefore saw his task as ensuring a diplomatic return to the pre-Paris conditions. Gorchakov formulated his policy to Russia's ambassador in Paris this way: "I am looking for a man who will annul the clauses of the treaty of Paris, concerning the Black Sea question and the Bessarabian frontier; I am looking for him and I shall find him."[6] A believer in Russia's "return" to European politics, the chancellor liked to quote the words of Catherine the Great: "time will tell that we are not following anyone's tale."[7]

Often posing as a passive executor of the Tsar's plans,[8] Gorchakov in practice exercised a major influence on Alexander and played an active role in foreign policy formulation.[9] In August, only a few months after accepting his new position, Gorchakov sent to European governments a note in which he formulated the new course of action and its justification. The two key principles of his foreign policy were relative isolation from European affairs and no commitment to coalitions with other states. The former principle was deemed necessary for implementing domestic reforms after defeat in the war, and the latter was designed to provide the international calm required for domestic recovery.[10] "The circumstances have given us back a full freedom of action," wrote Gorchakov,[11] referring to the collapsed Holy Alliance and the perceived betrayal of Austria. To the outside world, the chancellor sought to clarify that Russia had adopted a new policy because of its domestic needs, and not because it was angry at the European powers: "La Russie ne boude pas – elle se recueille."[12] Scholars characterized the recueillement as a moderate and defensive policy that yet aimed to revise the status quo established by the Paris treaty.[13]

Rapprochement with France

However, Russia could not be entirely isolated from European affairs and needed to build some international ties to buy time for domestic reforms. Gorchakov's preference was to cultivate relations with France, rather than with Austria and Prussia, as recommended by Nesselrode. Eager to implement his policy of flexible alliances, the chancellor wanted to explore whether Russia's state interests could be better served by pursuing ties with Napoleon.

The rapprochement with France brought Russia some policy dividends by strengthening its role in the Balkans and helping neutralize potentially damaging British influences. Together with France, Russia provided

strong support to Montenegro and Serbia by weakening the Austrian role
in the region. Russia also protested the Sultan's military interference in
Montenegro and supported an anti-Turkish rebellion in Herzegovina
financially and diplomatically.[14] In Gorchakov's words, Serbia "became
the center and point of support for other areas of Turkey," and Russia's
assistance helped it establish greater independence and enhance Russia's
own military standing.[15]

Meanwhile Napoleon was hoping to obtain Alexander's support for
French plans to annex Italy's provinces, whereas Russia needed France's
assistance in revising the Paris conditions. In March 1859, the two nations
signed a bilateral Treaty of Neutrality and Cooperation, in which Russia pledged a "political and military position of benevolent neutrality"
toward France in case of the latter's war with Austria.[16] Austria tried
to weaken Russo-French ties by offering support for Russia's interests
in the Black Sea, based on principles of "conservative solidarity," but
Alexander no longer trusted Austria and refused to negotiate with it.[17]
When a Polish revolt broke out in 1863, the French position was also
more moderate than that of Britain.[18]

However, Alexander and Gorchakov were also disappointed by the
French. On issues that were most important to Russia, such as the
Paris conditions and the status of Poland, the French position proved
to be either vague or critical of Russia. When Alexander tried to link his
support for territorial changes in Italy to abolition of the Paris clauses,
Napoleon and his foreign minister Walewski offered a vague assurance
that "the modification of existing treaties" may be addressed after the
coming war with Austria.[19] By that point Gorchakov had little faith
in France, although Alexander remained hopeful that Napoleon would
prove helpful in the future.[20] St. Petersburg also viewed as insufficient
French support for Russia's actions in the Balkans during the series
of revolts after 1860. For example, although the two cooperated on
resisting Turkish military intervention in Chernogoria in 1862, France
was wary of Russia's growing influence and not eager to pressure the
Sultan.[21]

Increasingly, Russia was becoming convinced that French objectives
had more to do with the politics of revolution than those of a traditional
great power[22] and therefore were hardly compatible with those of St.
Petersburg. For this reason the two could not cooperate on preventing the
rise of Germany, in addition to other issues. The Polish revolt confirmed
this tension, and the two nations began to drift apart, with the French
foreign minister declaring in 1863 that "France too resumed full freedom
of judgment and action."[23] Soon after, Alexander wrote to William I of
Austria and offered to revive their old ties.[24]

The Polish Revolt and Russia's Diplomacy

The Polish revolt further demonstrated the limitations of Russia's ties with the European powers. In early 1863 nationalist groups prevailed within the Polish political elite and led an uprising, demanding secession from Russia. Yielding to nationalist pressures was out of the question. In Alexander's perception doing so would have opened a Pandora's box of similar secessionist claims by Lithuania, Belorussia, and parts of Ukraine.[25] However, the Polish issue had to be handled in a delicate manner, given that Europe supported Poland and that Russia could not afford to go to war over the issue. Another serious complication was that Russian public opinion was united in opposition to Polish nationalism, demanding a tough response that would further worsen Russia's standing in Europe. According to Mikhail Katkov, a leading spokesman for Russian nationalism, the issue was no longer whether Russia or Poland "will become mightier," but "which one of them will exist."[26] Alexander decided to suppress the revolt, but also introduce administrative and land reforms to undermine both the domestic and foreign appeal of Russian nationalists.[27]

However, the European powers made it more difficult for Alexander to manage the issue by pressuring him to accept the demands of Polish nationalists. Believing that Alexander was weak and seeking to further undermine him, Britain exerted especially strong pressure on Russia. The British foreign minister Earl Russell argued for a restoration of the Polish constitution of 1815 and claimed that by not granting it Russia would exclude itself from the civilized world.[28] Napoleon too requested the restoration of Polish self-government,[29] although not in the tough language used by the British. Instead, France proposed to deal with the issue in a multilateral way by addressing it at a European congress.[30] Prussia refrained from exerting diplomatic pressure, yet Count Otto Bismarck, the Prussian chancellor, was hoping to exploit the issue geopolitically by "Germanizing" an independent Poland within three years.[31] Finally, Austria again joined what looked like the new "Crimean coalition." In April 1863, Britain, France, and Austria each sent similar notes to the Russia government asking that Poland be independent and include Lithuania and Ruthenia.[32]

In addition, Russia could not count on strong support from the Balkan nations, where the new generation of politicians were more Western and nationalist and the Orthodox appeal had weakened.[33] Even Serbia, a stronghold of Russia's influence, was helping the Polish uprising by attempting to instigate a larger movement to dissolve the Ottoman Empire.[34]

As before the Crimean War, Russia was threatened with isolation and had to find a flexible response to the crisis. Although the Poland insurrection was considered an internal matter, Gorchakov played an important role in resolving the crisis and providing Alexander with the confidence necessary for carrying out the Great Reforms at home.[35] Generally pro-reform and moderate on Poland,[36] Gorchakov nevertheless firmly deflected European pressures by pointing out that the Polish issue was "exclusively the matter of Russia, and not Europe."[37] Seeking to weaken the unity of the European governments, the chancellor then conceded that Austria and Prussia might legitimately discuss the issue as co-participants in Poland's partition.[38] Gorchakov also wrote individually to each European power and promised various concessions, reforms, and amnesty in exchange for the rebels' surrender.[39] To Britain, he even promised a constitutional order for Poland similar to the British, although not in the near future.[40] Simultaneously, Russia accelerated its efforts to suppress the Polish revolt.

The approach worked, gradually reducing tensions and diffusing the power of the European coalition. As Seton-Watson wrote, "defeat of the rebellion increased Russian prestige in Europe: the Russians were no more loved than they had been, but they were more respected."[41] In tacit acknowledgment of this increased respect, Prussia expressed its readiness to assist the Russian government by offering to fight the Polish rebels on Prussian territory.[42] Most importantly, Gorchakov isolated Britain, which was the only power ready to fight Russia over Poland. The British government was the most important of the chancellor's concerns because of his conviction that "in the Black Sea and in the Baltics, on the coasts of the Caspian Sea and in the Pacific – everywhere Britain is the unwavering enemy of our interests, everywhere she opposes us in the most aggressive fashion."[43]

Rapprochement with Prussia and Repudiation of the Paris Terms

The Polish revolt served as a critical test of Gorchakov's flexible coalition approach. Disillusioned with rapprochement with France and sensing an opportunity to strengthen its relationship with Prussia, Russia began to cultivate ties with the Prussian leadership. Alexander and Gorchakov came to believe that the support of the rapidly rising European power might prove sufficient to bring about revision of the Paris conditions. Prussia indicated its willingness to support Russia in exchange for Russia's not opposing Bismarck's drive to unify the German lands around Prussia – which could only come at the expense of Prussia's neighbors including Austria, France, and the Netherlands. Both

Alexander and Gorchakov opposed the unification,[44] but Bismarck threatened the prospect of building an alliance with France and raising the Polish question anew.[45] As Russia and Prussia were moving closer, Napoleon III failed to notice the similarity of Alexander and Gorchakov's anti-unification position to his own and to exploit the opportunity for the purpose of restraining Prussia.

That Russia decided to use Prussia for the purposes of revising the Paris conditions became clear in 1866, when Alexander did not respond to Austria's offer of cooperation and did nothing to prevent the Prussia-Austria war. Russia's growing support of Balkan independence from the Ottoman Empire also put St. Petersburg at odds with Paris and Vienna. As the possibility of Prussia's war with France was becoming real, Alexander and Gorchakov visited Paris in April 1867 to clarify their relationship as foreign policy partners. The meeting with Napoleon was not successful,[46] solidifying Russia's position of benevolent neutrality in the case of a Prussian-French war. In 1868, in exchange for Bismarck's assurance of support, Russia pledged to neutralize Austria by sending 100,000 troops to the Austrian border.[47] The pledge provided Prussia with the necessary political room to fight, and in 1870, the powerful Prussian army defeated France, even taking the French emperor prisoner. Although Russia was disappointed by Bismarck's claims to the French territories of Alsace and Lorraine, Alexander and Gorchakov remained faithful to the agreement with Prussia.

This was the opportune time for Russia to neutralize the Paris Treaty by announcing to the European powers its denunciation of the Black Sea clauses. In his note to Russian ambassadors on October 31, 1870, Gorchakov explained that Russia could no longer be bound by the treaty, given that it constrained Russia's sovereign rights and that other European powers had already violated the agreement.[48] France and Austria were too weak to resist the move by Russia. Prussia was acting on the promise of support from Russia, which it still needed because it had not yet signed a peace treaty with France.[49] Great Britain was the only power that indicated its willingness to fight Russia, but it was marginalized by the lack of international support. Indeed, diplomatic historians view the British position as merely an attempt to signal to Prussia its desire to have it as a member of a new anti-Russian coalition.[50] In the meantime, the unified Germany had no plans of becoming an ally of Britain, and Emperor William I telegraphed his gratitude to Alexander: "Prussia will never forget that she owes it to you that the war has not assumed extreme dimension."[51] The European conference of 1871 in London solidified Russia's success.

Having achieved its key goal by practicing flexible coalition diplomacy, Russia again attempted to revive ties with France – partly to offset the growing power of a unified Germany. Although Russian-German ties were developing, Gorchakov sought to emphasize their purely defensive nature.[52] When France and Germany came close to a military confrontation in 1874 and 1875, Russia signaled its support for France, discouraging Germany from further upsetting the existing balance of power.[53] Russia also revived its ties with Austria in an attempt to restrain German policies toward the Habsburgs and to influence Vienna's Balkan policies.

The Recueillement, 1856–1871: Timeline

1856 May	Alexander Gorchakov succeeds Nesselrode as Russia's Foreign Minister
August	Alexander Gorchakov's note
1859 March	Treaty with France
1860	Balkan revolts; Russia calls Europe to pressure the Porte
1863	Polish revolt; Europe pressures Russia to grant Poland independence
1866	Austro-Prussian war; Russia does not interfere
1866–8	Balkan revolts and Russia offers restrained assistance
1868	Agreement with Prussia
1870	French-Prussian war; Russia repudiates the Paris conditions
1871	London conference cancels the Paris conditions on Russia

Explanation for the Policy of Recueillement

Intense Western diplomatic pressure and a low level of internal confidence were responsible for initiating and sustaining the policy of recueillement.

European Influences

The European powers sought to consolidate or even further to undermine Russia's post-Crimean position as a secondary power. The British government was the most hostile. Its hopes to rise to the position of European hegemon, as well as firmly entrenched Russophobia, shaped London's perception of Russia. Much of the European dislike of Russia originated in Britain soon after establishment of the Vienna Concert.[54]

Britain was the only power that opposed the end of the Crimean War on Austria-proposed conditions. London also labored to weaken Russia's influence in the Balkans and to prevent France and Prussia from becoming too close to Russia.[55] During the Polish revolt, Britain presented Alexander with the most strongly worded demands, with Palmerston characterizing Russia's actions as aiming to "exterminate the Poles."[56] British perceptions continued to harden in response to Russia's expansion in the Caucasus and Central Asia.[57]

The positions of other European powers toward Russia were not as hawkish, yet they too reflected the desire to prevent the rise of Russia as a great power competitor. The underlying reality was that the Europe-centered international system had entered the era of secular nationalist politics, with little room left for the traditional Christian values that had united the continent before the Crimean War. As Kalevi Holsti wrote, "the architects of the Paris and Vienna settlements ignored the principle of nationality,"[58] and the newly discovered approach of European states was to exploit national aspirations for the purpose of increasing their political and military power. That was especially true of Prussia, which aimed to unify the German lands around it and was interested in Russia only to the extent that the latter was able to offset potentially dangerous French and Austrian influences. That was also true of Austria, which sought to preserve its position in the Balkans and reached out to Russia only when Austria felt threatened by Prussia. Finally, that was true of France, which cared about the principle of nationality more than the other European powers, but was also eager to preserve the victorious status of the post-Crimean War system.

In that international context, Russia's vision of honor as morally driven cooperation with outside powers, which had underlined the Holy Alliance, could not be revived.

Domestic Conditions and Russia's Honor

Similarly Russia's weak economic and social conditions ruled out the possibility of acting under the assertive concept of state honor and defending cultural commitments outside the West. From an economic, technological, military, and administrative standpoint, Russia was lagging behind major European powers even before the Crimean War,[59] and the war only made it more difficult to pursue an activist foreign policy.

In addition to losing nearly a half-million people in the fighting,[60] Russia found itself in a dire financial situation. The postwar deficit was close to one billion rubles,[61] which some historians characterized as forcing Russia to the brink of bankruptcy.[62] Its foreign debt was almost

500 million rubles.[63] Western banks were reluctant to lend money under these conditions, and Russia had to rely on reviving private initiative in the economy.[64] Alexander, who reviewed the situation in 1862, assessed it as "indeed critical."[65]

The Russian military was both technologically backward and overly centralized. An enormous landmass, Russia nevertheless lacked railroads and often had to rely on horses or even moving the troops by foot.[66] The army was also poorly trained and underequipped. For example, in the Crimean War, Russian soldiers used flintlock muskets with a range of 200 yards, compared to the rifles used by the British and French that could reach a target 1,000 yards away.[67] No less important were the military's administrative deficiencies. Russia needed an improved system of military recruitment on a par with European practices of specialized training and mass nationalist mobilization.[68] In addition, the army lacked command flexibility, because any modification in military campaigns had to be approved by the Tsar himself.[69]

The Russian leadership understood that, before it could return to a more active foreign policy, it had to strengthen its domestic institutions by reforming the system. In Gorchakov's words, "Russia cannot play an active role in its external policy when it is faced with internal poverty and mismanagement."[70] To the chancellor, the central problem was the unresolved issue of serfdom, which he called "the cradle of all our evils."[71] Thinking in the framework of state honor, Russian statesmen began moving in the direction of reforming the institutions of autocratic power. In addition to emphasizing the importance of peasant emancipation, Gorchakov noted some advantages in involving the public in the business of ruling: "When a Palmerston commits infamous political acts, he takes refuge behind public opinion, majorities. . . . But the country is not dishonored, because it shields its honor behind the rampart of minorities."[72] While serving under Nesselrode, Gorchakov was the first to introduce to diplomatic language the term "Russia" as a personification of the state, in addition to the traditional "the Emperor."[73] Others, like Grand Duke Konstantin, were also worried about the country's political, rather than material, conditions: "we are both weaker and poorer than the first-class powers . . . not only in material but also in mental resources, especially in matters of administration."[74]

Although they realized the need to reform the system decisively, Alexander and Gorchakov could not neglect the traditional aspects of state honor, which included concerns for the Straits and the well-being of Orthodox Christians in the Balkans. The Straits were essential for commercial reasons, because Russia exported about 80 percent of its grain via them.[75] Their control enhanced Russia's security and ability to preserve stability in the Caucasus. For example, in February 1857 Polish and Hungarian troops arrived in the region via the Black Sea to challenge Russia's rule.[76] Not sympathetic to extreme pan-Slavist ideas, both Alexander and Gorchakov nonetheless remained faithful to Russia's traditional obligations in the Balkans. As Gorchakov wrote to the Russian ambassador in Constantinople in 1856, "It is an interest of the first order for us to have in our immediate neighborhood populations that are attached to us by the ties of the faith."[77]

The Recueillement's Internal Support and Opposition

Immediately after the Crimean War, few people opposed the new policy of flexible alliances and a concentration on domestic affairs. Supporters of the principles underlying the Holy Alliance, including Nesselrode, hoped that the recueillement was a temporary necessity driven by considerations of postwar recovery and that Russia would eventually revive its previously strong ties with Prussia and Austria.[78] Russia's pro-Western liberals too refrained from opposing Gorchakov's ideas and were encouraged by the government's initial rapprochement with France, which they viewed as a turn away from autocracy and toward liberal Europe. Finally, advocates of Russia's strong ties with the Balkan Slavs, the pan-Slavists, favored the government's objective of reversing the Treaty of Paris, particularly the clauses about the Black Sea and southern Bessarabia. Indeed, one pan-Slavist sympathizer, the great poet Fyodor Tyutchev, was a diplomat and Gorchakov's close friend who praised the official policy in his poetry.[79]

Further developments, however, divided the coalition of supporters. The advocates for ties with a conservative Europe were disappointed by the government's closer relationship with France. Russia's pro-Western liberals opposed the government's suppression of the Polish revolt and became alarmed by the prospects of a new European war in response to Russia's repudiation of the Paris conditions.[80] In general, Russia's progressive circles opposed the government's rapprochement with Prussia, and during the Franco-Prussian war of 1870 the Russian press were overwhelmingly on France's side.[81] Finally, the pan-Slavist groups increasingly viewed Alexander and Gorchakov as excessively pro-German and insufficiently decisive in developing Russian ties with the Balkan Slavs.

After the military defeat, pan-Slavism emerged as especially influential in response to the sense of national humiliation,[82] which ultimately led to strong domestic support for another war with Turkey in 1876. Successors to the Slavophiles, the pan-Slavists formulated an ambitious international program that sought the removal of the Balkan Slavs from the control of Turkey and the European powers, as well as the organization of the

Slavs into a federation under Russia's patronage.[83] They hoped that national affiliations of Slavs, including the Poles, would be superseded by a transnational identity.[84] To pan-Slavists such as Ivan Aksakov, Nikolai Danilevski, Vladimir Lamanski, Mikhail Katkov, and Mikhail Pogodin, the entirety of Europe, not just France or Germany, was the enemy because it did not accept Russia's "natural" Greco-Slavic way of living. Responding to the strengthening European discourse in Russia, Tyutchev warned in 1864,

Between Russia and the West there can be no alliance, either on the basis of interest or for the sake of any principle . . . the *only* policy for Russia with respect to the Western states is not an alliance with this or that state, but disunion, a divorce from them.[85]

The most serious threat to Russia in the West, according to the pan-Slavists, came from Germany and the Romano-Germanic type it represented.[86] Wrote Ivan Aksakov in 1867, if Slavs wished to remain Slavs, they had to choose "either the road to the West or the road to the East, the road to Latinity or the road of Orthodoxy, union either with the destinies of the Western European world or the destinies of the Greco-Slavic world."[87] From this ideological position, pan-Slavists advocated a forceful policy of liberating the Balkan Slavs.

The ability of pan-Slavists to influence Russia's official course was considerable – partly because of their ability to exploit the new openness, or *glasnost*, encouraged by the Great Reforms. The number of periodicals and their circulation increased fourfold from 1855–75.[88] Although the government continued to intervene where it felt necessary, censorship was not as strict as under Nicholas I. For example, when Ivan Aksakov's *Parus* was closed in 1859 on the grounds of interfering with official foreign policy, Gorchakov and others objected to the ban and helped revive the newspaper, albeit under a different name.[89] Ivan Aksakov later credited the new, more open conditions for promoting a war with Turkey: "public opinion conducted a war apart from the government and without any state organization."[90]

Another reason for the growing pan-Slavist influence was the presence of their sympathizers within the government. The most prominent home for pan-Slavists was the Asiatic department of the Foreign Ministry headed by E. Kovalevski and, during 1861–4, by Count Nicholas Ignatyev.[91] The latter advocated an assertive policy to strengthen Russia's position in the Balkans by providing extensive assistance to Serbia and other Slavic nations. Whenever an opportunity presented itself, Ignatyev argued, Russia had to assert control over the Slav lands, rather than merely expect Slavs to rise up against their masters. On that basis, he opposed Austria taking control of Bosnia and Herzegovina from the Ottoman Empire, insisting that Russia's interests would be harmed as a result. Especially hostile toward Austria, Ignatyev saw its war with Prussia as an opportunity for Russia.[92] Gorchakov and others within the government did not favor such an assertive stance,[93] but Alexander valued diverse voices and even appointed Ignatyev ambassador to Constantinople.[94]

Although the government was not united, the positions of Alexander and Gorchakov were very different from that of the pan-Slavists, and it would be a mistake to view Russia's foreign policy as driven solely by their ideas.[95] Despite being disappointed with the European powers' actions during the Crimean War, the government did not turn away from Europe, as the pan-Slavists had hoped. Fearful of internal unrest and external destabilization, Gorchakov was opposed to conducting "a revolutionary policy" of challenging Turkey's stability, hoping instead for "the natural decadence of Islam" to run its course.[96] His policy stance can be best described as moderate, state-centered Westernism. Although the government provided partial support for pan-Slavist organizations and sponsored some of their activities, such as the 1867 Panslav Congress in Moscow, such support did not rise to the level of association with pan-Slavist radicals. The chancellor was in fact contemptuous of the pan-Slavic program, and his views had broad support within the Council of Ministers.[97]

Alternative Explanations

According to defensive realism, states adopt a generally defensive stance in response to uncertainty within the international system. Under conditions of vulnerability, the weak state is expected to bandwagon with a more powerful state. Although Russia was most certainly a weak state after its military defeat, it refrained from pursuing a policy of bandwagoning with a powerful France or rising Germany. Instead, Russia's government decided to balance between the strong powers – partly because it was not satisfied with the conditions of the Paris peace treaty. Viewing the recueillement era as an example of a generally defensive and conciliatory foreign policy[98] is only partially correct, however, because Russia also had important revisionist objectives.[99] Presenting Gorchakov's policy as driven by irrational beliefs, rather than rational calculations of material weakness, is also problematic, because the overwhelming majority of the political class shared the "irrational" objective of revising the Paris conditions.

Defensive realism is therefore imprecise or even incorrect in characterizing Russia's post–Crimean war response. An honor-based account provides a more accurate interpretation of Russia's behavior by pointing to its government's obligations to Orthodox Christians and the importance of reviving the status of a great power. Limited by material conditions, St. Petersburg could not pursue the assertive policy favored by Ignatyev and the pan-Slavists. Nevertheless, Alexander and Gorchakov did not abandon their cultural obligations and used the opportunity to revise the post-Paris status quo when it presented itself. Although the Crimean War marked the transition of the European system to a period of greater anarchy,[100] cultural beliefs remained important, and Russia's statesmen should hardly be viewed as Western realist thinkers.[101] As one historian wrote, "'the primacy of domestic affairs imposed policies that clashed with the regime's conception of Russia's 'dignity' and 'honor.'"[102] Considerations of honor explain the durability of Russian nationalism and persistent expansion into Central Asia, despite the country's lack of financial, military, and technological resources.[103]

Offensive realist accounts may seem more compelling because they view the recueillement as an example of a back-passing in response to unfavorable conditions of the international system.[104] Yet this explanation too misses the honor component of the Russia's post–Crimean War policy, capturing only part of the government's motivation. Much of what offensive realists view as Russia's struggle for material power was in fact the politics of cultural honor and prestige. For example, although Bismarck advised St. Petersburg to build warships in the Black Sea after revising the Paris clauses, the Russians did not follow this advice and had no active fleet even by the time of their war with Turkey in 1877. As A. J. P. Taylor wrote, "the Russians wanted the other Powers to recognize their right to keep warships there, not actually to have them."[105]

Assessment

The policy of recueillement therefore expressed Russia's defensive concept of honor, which combined the nation's commitment to its cultural allies and domestic subjects with the pursuit of great power prestige.

The recueillement generally succeeded in meeting Russia's objectives – largely because those objectives were narrowly defined and because Gorchakov skillfully exploited a lack of unity among the Western powers. The empire could again keep its fleet in the Black Sea, which was critical for controlling the Straits and exercising cultural influence in the Balkans. The success was achieved by diplomatic means and not at the expense of Russia's domestic transformation. Indeed, while pursuing its foreign policy, the government made major progress in reforming the economy. The edict of March 1861 emancipated the serfs, an important precondition for the country's economic development. From 1860–77, Russia's industrial output increased severalfold,[106] and the nation's combined production of mining, textile, iron, and food from 1860–1900 outpaced not only the West but also the rest of the world.[107] By 1880, the government, in collaboration with the private sector, had linked 45 percent of European Russia by modern railroads.[108]

The foreign policy price of Alexander and Gorchakov's success was the emergence of a unified Germany on Russia's western border. Indeed, some have called Russia's inaction regarding the rise of the powerful revisionist state "the worst mistake that tsarist diplomacy ever made"[109] and a result of Gorchakov's "self-delusion."[110] Yet recovering the status of a Black Sea power while preventing the rise of Germany was hardly possible.[111] The chancellor was not a Germanophile – indeed he had initially favored an alliance with France and opposed German unification – but he turned to Bismarck as a way of revising the Paris treaty and counterbalancing French influences. Aware of the danger the unified German lands presented to Russia, Gorchakov returned to the policy of strengthening ties with France after its defeat by Germany. In addition, Russia's ties with Germany may have prevented a confrontation, because if William I and Bismarck had succeeded in their unification policy without Russia, Germany would have likely emerged as an enemy, and not merely a competitor. Russia's chancellor was certainly aware of his country's weakness – he once famously referred to it a "grande impuissance" (great powerless country)[112] – yet he believed that the way to strengthen it was through a domestic recovery.

Notes

1 Bushuyev, *A. M. Gorchakov*, p. 82.
2 According to Minister of Internal Affairs Pyotr Valuyev, Nesselrode characterized Gorchakov in the following manner, "He has served in my ministry for thirty years, and I have always thought that he is incapable of anything serious" (Valuyev, *Dnevnik Ministra vnutrennikh del*, p. 102).
3 *Kantsler A. M. Gorchakov*, p. 387. Echoing Nesselrode's position, some in the political circles were in fact advocating elimination of the diplomatic service altogether (Splidsboel-Hansen, "Past and Future Meet," 380).
4 Khitrova, "Rossiya sosredotachivayetsya," 50.
5 Jelavich, *Russia's Balkan Entanglements*, p. 146.
6 Taylor, *The Struggle for Mastery in Europe*, p. 91.

7 Vinogradov, "A. M. Gorchakov u rulya vneshnei politiki Rossiyi," 93.

8 Khitrova, "Rossiya sosredotachivayetsya," 53.

9 Ibid.; Mosse, *Alexander II and the Modernization of Russia*, p. 49.

10 Tarle, "Napoleon III i Yevropa," 471; Splidsboel-Hansen, "Past and Future Meet."

11 Bushuyev, *A. M. Gorchakov*, p. 82.

12 "Russia is not angry – it gathers its will" Tarle, "Napoleon III."

13 See, for example, Fuller, *Strategy and Power in Russia*, p. 266; Splidsboel-Hansen, "Past and Future Meet," 381; Geyer, *Russian Imperialism*, p. 31.

14 MacKenzie, "Russia's Balkan Policies under Alexander II," 223.

15 Ibid., 224–5.

16 Dmytryshyn, ed. *Imperial Russia*, p. 255.

17 Khitrova, "Rossiya sosredotachivayetsya," 58.

18 Tarle, "Napoleon," 485.

19 Taylor, *The Struggle for Mastery*, p. 106.

20 Ibid.

21 Khitrova, "Rossiya sosredotachivayetsya," 62–4.

22 Fuller, *Strategy and Power in Russia*, p. 270.

23 Taylor, *The Struggle for Mastery*, p. 138.

24 Ibid., p. 139.

25 Tarle, "Napoleon," 486.

26 Lincoln, *Nicholas I*, p. 168. Some Russian liberal and revolutionary circles supported Poland, but were marginalized.

27 Seton-Watson, *The Russian Empire*, p. 376.

28 Tarle, "Napoleon," 486.

29 Seton-Watson, *The Russian Empire*, p. 434.

30 Tarle, "Napoleon," 485.

31 Ibid., 483.

32 Seton-Watson, *The Russian Empire*, p. 435.

33 Jelavich, *Russia's Balkan Entanglements*, p. 148.

34 Ibid., 153. In their efforts to weaken Turkey, Serbs also worked with Austria. MacKenzie, "Russia's Balkan Policies," 226.

35 Rieber, "The Politics of Imperialism," 89.

36 Mosse, *Alexander II and the Modernization of Russia*, p. 93.

37 Tarle, "Napoleon," 486.

38 Khitrova, "Rossiya sosredotachivayetsya," 70.

39 Ibid.; Rieber, "The Politics of Imperialism," 89.

40 Radzinski, *Aleksandr II*, p. 179.

41 Seton-Watson, *The Russian Empire*, p. 435.

42 Tarle, "Napoleon," 484. The Russia-Prussian agreement to this effect is available in Dmytryshyn, ed. *Imperial Russia*, p. 289.

43 Baumgart, *The Peace of Paris 1856*, p. 203.

44 Potemkin, ed., *Istoriya diplomatiyi*, p. 512.

45 Khitrova, "Rossiya sosredotachivayetsya," 71.

46 Ibid., 76.

47 Ibid.

48 Ibid., 77.

49 Andreyev, *Posledniy kantsler rossiyskoi imperiyi Aleksandr Mikhailovich Gor-chakov*, pp. 10–11; Nol'de, *Vneshnyaya politika*, p. 91.

50 Taylor, *The Struggle for Mastery*, pp. 215–16.

51 Jelavich, *Russia's Balkan Entanglements*, p. 155.

52 Khitrova, "Rossiya sosredotachivayetsya," 81.

53 Ibid., 82–3.

54 For details, see Gleason, *The Genesis of Russophobia in Great Britain*; Malia, *Russia under Western Eyes*. Chapter 11 returns to this point.

55 Tarle, "Napoleon," 488; Goldfrank, *The Origins of the Crimean War*, p. 157.

56 Almedingen, *The Emperor Alexander II*, p. 198.

57 Ibid., p. 128.

58 Holsti, *Peace and War*, p. 169.

59 See, for example, cross-national comparisons in Goldfrank, *The Origins of the Crimean War*, pp. 22, 37; Kennedy, *The Rise and Fall of Great Powers*, pp. 170–7; and Mearsheimer, *The Tragedy of Great Powers*, p. 71. Chapter 11 returns to this point.

60 Kennedy, *The Rise and Fall of Great Powers*, p. 177.

61 Khevrolina, "Preobrazovaniya v Rossiyi i vneshnyaya politika," 23.

62 Geyer, *Russian Imperialism*, p. 33.

63 Ibid.

64 Khevrolina, "Preobrazovaniya v Rossiyi," 23.

65 Ibid.

66 Hosking, *Russia*, p. 194; Fuller, *Strategy and Power in Russia*, p. 278.

67 Hosking, *Russia*, p. 190.

68 Fuller, *Strategy and Power*, p. 274.

69 Ibid., p. 273.

70 Bushuyev, *A. M. Gorchakov*, p. 78.

71 Almedingen, *The Emperor Alexander II*, p. 111.

72 Fuller, *Strategy and Power*, p. 269.

73 Count Nesselrode reportedly replied to this: "we only know the Tsar. We don't care about Russia" (Akhtamzyan, "Gorchakov i Bismark – shkola yevropeyskoi diplomatiyi XIX veka," 147–8).

74 Kennedy, *The Rise and Fall*, p. 177.

75 N. I. Khitrova, "A. M. Gorchakov i otmena neytralizatsiyi Chernogo morya," 126.

76 Khitrova, "Rossiya sosredotachivayetsya," 66.

77 Jelavich, *Russia's Balkan Entanglements*, p. 147.

78 Khitrova, "Rossiya sosredotachivayetsya," 50.

79 Tyutchev praised Gorchakov's initial policy, and after the successful renunciation of the Paris conditions, the poet devoted a special verse to the Chancellor, "да вы сдержали ваше слово: /не двинув пушки, ни рубля,/ в свои права вступает снова/ Родная русская земля./ и нам завещанное море/ опять свободною волной,/ о кратком позабыв позоре,/ лабзает берег свой родной./ счастлив в наш век, кому победа / далась не кровью, а умом./ счастлив, кто точку Архимеда умел сыскать в себе самом" (Andreyev, *Posledniy kantsler rossiyskoi imperiyi*, p. 79).

80 Khitrova, "A. M. Gorchakov i otmena neytralizatsiyi," 135.

81 Seton-Watson, *The Russian Empire*, p. 437.

82 Some of the future pan-Slavists, such as Mikhail Pogodin, were actively encouraging the Tsar to liberate the Balkan Slavs even before and during the Crimean War. See Chapter 11 for details.

83 Jelavich, *Russia's Balkan Entanglements*, p. 157.

84 Petrovich, *The Emergence of Russian Panslavism*, pp. 285. For additional research on pan-Slavism, see especially Riasanovsky, *Russia and the West in the Teaching of the Slavophiles*; Kohn, *Panslavism*; Walicki, *A History of Russian Thought from Enlightenment to Marxism*; Duncan, *Russian Messianism*; Tuminez, *Russian Nationalism since 1856*; Khevrolina, "Problemy vneshnei politiki Rossiyi v obshchestvennoy mysli strany."

85 Petrovich, *The Emergence of Russian Panslavism*, p. 68.

86 For Russia's debate on Europe in the second half of the nineteenth century, see also Neumann, *Russia and the Idea of Europe*; Tsygankov, "Self and Other in International Relations Theory"; Utkin, *Vyzov Zapada i otvet Rossiyi*.

87 Petrovich, *The Emergence of Russian Panslavism*, p. 90.

88 Tuminez, *Russian Nationalism since 1856*, p. 79.

89 Petrovich, *The Emergence*, pp. 117–20.

90 Mosse, *Alexander II and the Modernization of Russia*, p. 129.

91 Tuminez, *Russian Nationalism*, p. 83.

92 Petrovich, *The Emergence*, pp. 261–2. Among pan-Slavists, the author of an influential work, *Opinion of the Eastern Question*, Rostislav Fadeyev also advocated an attack on Austro-Hungary as a way of conquering Constantinople and solving the Slav issue (Mosse, *Alexander II*, pp. 125–6).

93 Geyer, *Russian Imperialism*, p. 67.

94 Tuminez, *Russian Nationalism*, pp. 87–8. On Ignatyev's views and activities, see also Petrovich, *The Emergence*, pp. 259–63.

95 For statements supportive of such views, see Kissinger, *Diplomacy*, pp. 140–4; Geyer, *Russian Imperialism*, p. 65; MacKenzie, "Russia's Balkan Policies," 220.

96 Fuller, *Strategy and Power in Russia*, p. 271.

97 Petrovich, *The Emergence*, p. 121.

98 For examples of such perceptions, see Nol'de, *Vneshnyaya politika*, p. 91; Fuller, *Strategy and Power in Russia*, p. 267; Tuminez, *Russian Nationalism*, p. 87.

99 Splidsboel-Hansen, "Past and Future Meet."

100 Schroeder, *Austria, Great Britain, and the Crimean War*.

101 See, for example, Petrovich, *The Emergence*, p. 121.

102 Geyer, *Russian Imperialism*, p. 32.

103 Ibid., pp. 48, 53–4.

104 For a description of back-passing, see Mearsheimer, *The Tragedy of Great Powers*, p. 139.

105 Taylor, *The Struggle for Mastery in Europe*, p. 215.

106 Geyer, *Russian Imperialism*, p. 43.

107 Khromov, *Ekonomicheskoye razvitiye Rossiyi*, p. 284.

108 Khevrolina, "Preobrazovaniya v Rossiyi i vneshnyaya politika," 26.

109 Riasanovsky, *A History of Russia*, p. 385.

110 Fuller, *Strategy and Power*, p. 272.
111 Nol'de thinks Gorchakov was too careful and could have achieved his objective at a cheaper price. Nol'de, *Vneshnyaya politika*, pp. 91–2.
112 Valuyev, *Dnevnik Ministra vnutrennikh del*, p. 326.

"Victory of a revolution in a separate country was once thought impossible . . . now we need to assume such victory is possible given the unequal and uneven development of capitalist countries under the imperialism."

Joseph Stalin[1]

The Policy of Peaceful Coexistence

The policy of peaceful coexistence with Western capitalism was born out of the recognition that the Bolsheviks' theory of world revolution could no longer be sustained under harsh international and domestic conditions. Peaceful coexistence did not imply any serious commitment to cooperation with the West – rather, it was a limited cooperation balanced by a focus on domestic needs to win what Vladimir Lenin called "breathing space" in the struggle with capitalism. Despite important changes within and outside the country, peaceful coexistence lasted until World War II.[2] Overall, this period was more reminiscent of Gorchakov's era of domestic focus and flexible external alliances than of the times of robust cooperation with the West during the Holy Alliance or the Triple Entente.

The End of the World Revolution

The doctrine of world revolution rested on key foreign and domestic policies. Externally, it implied the need for a chain reaction of other socialist revolutions in Europe, without which the revolution in Russia would not be secure amid fierce opposition from capitalist nations.[3] In 1919, the Bolsheviks established the Communist International (Comintern) to promote such revolutions by spreading communist ideas and setting up new communist parties abroad. Internally, they established a system of military communism in which everything was to be decided from the top and executed with the help of an army of state bureaucrats. A product of the civil war, the system also had its roots in the Marxist critique of private property and "bourgeois" parliamentarism. For example, the Bolsheviks' dissolution of the Constitutional Assembly in January 1918 resulted not only from their frustration with the results of the elections but also from their belief that their system of soviets "as revolutionary organs of the entire people" was "incomparably superior to all parliaments anywhere in the world."[4]

By 1921, however, it had become clear that Bolshevik expectations of world revolution could no longer be matched by reality and that, without introducing a new policy, the Soviet regime was headed toward collapse. Externally, the Soviet Union was increasingly isolated. No revolutions had taken place in Europe. The new Soviet state had lost the war to Germany, and in March 1918 the Bolsheviks agreed to extremely harsh conditions of peace in Brest-Litovsk: Poland, Finland, the Baltic states, and Ukraine were ceded to Germany and Austria, with some territories in the Caucasus going to Turkey. The lost territories were a core of Russian industry, population, and fertile agricultural land.[5] The civil war was long, violent, and devastating[6] and took a formidable material toll. Industry was disorganized and agricultural production devastated. In addition to the violence, the horrific Volga famine, which was partly the result of the state requisition of grain from the peasantry, took the lives of an additional four million people.[7] As the revolt at the Kronstadt naval base of March 1921 demonstrated, the army was no longer prepared to follow the Bolsheviks' orders without changes in economic and political conditions.

In response, Lenin insisted on the New Economic Policy (NEP), presenting it to his comrades as a necessary compromise, a temporary "breathing space" in the struggle for world revolution. At the Tenth Party Congress in March 1921, the Bolshevik leader called on his followers to "learn from capitalism" in economics while preserving strict control of the "commanding heights" in politics. The peasantry was to obtain greater freedom in selling its products, yet the party would tolerate no factions, let alone dissent, within its ranks or outside. The NEP's foreign policy equivalent was what Lenin called "peaceful coexistence" with the capitalism world until "the capitalist states of Western Europe have completed their development to socialism."[8] Lenin sought to justify the new policy in terms of a temporary retreat from the original honorable objectives of the Soviet state. The assertive policy of seeking world revolution had to be replaced by the defensive nature of the NEP until the USSR was back on its feet and able to influence socialist transformations abroad.

Arguing against what he called "infantile leftism," Lenin visualized peaceful coexistence as "a new and lengthy period of development." During this period, Soviet leaders had to restore diplomatic ties with advanced capitalist nations of the West and learn how to obtain their "means of production (locomotives, machines, and electrical equipment)."[9] If they failed to do so, he argued, "we cannot more or less seriously rehabilitate our industry" or close the gap between the USSR and the advanced capitalist world.[10] Supported by other Bolsheviks, including Leonid Krasin, Aleksei Rykov, and Grigori Sokol'nikov, Lenin hoped to engage the West through trade and concessions to Russia's natural resources.[11] Although his policy remained ideologically antagonistic to the capitalist world, he envisioned mutual economic benefits from growing interactions with it.[12] At the same time the Comintern would continue to engage in propaganda and subversive activities abroad.[13]

Lenin's version of peaceful coexistence differed from that later adopted by Joseph Stalin in 1928. Stalin had initially supported Lenin in his argument with the left wing of Bolshevism, yet his interpretation of Lenin's policy was inflexible and isolationist. Only the "commanding heights" element of it survived, whereas the thinking about greater economic integration with the capitalist world was transformed beyond recognition. The key test came in 1929, when Stalin refused to ask for assistance and aid from other countries to address a severe grain shortage, choosing instead to return to a forced requisition of bread from the peasantry akin to the policy of military communism.

Peaceful Coexistence: Achievements and Promises

Several of Lenin's expectations were fulfilled: the Soviets were able to secure important gains in Western loans, trade, and diplomatic recognition.

The first Western nation to fully recognize the Bolsheviks was Germany. The rapprochement with Germany grew out of the Genoa Economic Conference in 1922, during which Britain and France sought to press the Soviet Union on the issue of tsarist debt and to pressure Germany on reparations. Thanks to the brilliant diplomacy of Soviet foreign commissar Georgi Chicherin, the two outcast nations soon agreed to cooperate with each other by signing the Treaty of Rappalo. The treaty renounced Russia's territorial claims on Germany in exchange for its diplomatic recognition of the USSR,[14] building on the already established trade relations between the two nations.[15] To the Soviets, the relationship became critical in organizing their ties with the West because it encouraged the Bolsheviks to accentuate divisions within the imperialist camp and think along the lines of *realpolitik*.[16] When in August 1924 Germany moved toward reconciliation with Britain and France by accepting the Dawes Plan on reparations in exchange for Western credit, Chicherin's first reaction was to play balance-of-power politics. In an attempt to weaken German rapprochement with the West, the Soviet minister traveled to Paris and even made a stop in Warsaw, the capital of Germany's enemy. To some historians, this meant Russia's attempts to revive the Franco-Russian alliance of the end of the nineteenth century.[17] Despite these diplomatic efforts, Germany's closer relationship with Britain and France survived and was reaffirmed in the Treaty of Berlin of April 1926.

Peaceful coexistence was bearing fruits in relations with Britain and France as well. Britain was the first to formally accept the Bolsheviks' offer of trade in March 1921, after which similar agreements were signed the same year with Germany, Norway, Austria, Italy, Denmark, and Czechoslovakia.[18] The British prime minister, David Lloyd George, became a vocal advocate for improving economic and political ties with Lenin's Russia even before the Genoa Conference.[19] The Soviet government exploited the opportunity by signing a de jure recognition treaty with the Labor government in 1924, although the more skeptical government of Ramsay MacDonald prevented further improvement of relations and made it difficult to ratify the treaty.[20] During the same year, France's new left government also recognized the new Russia because "the Soviet power was recognized by the Russian people."[21] However, Franco-Soviet relations remained tense because of the issue of tsarist debt and the special agreements signed by France with Poland and Romania that made it difficult for Soviet Russia to return Bessarabia.[22]

In addition to improving bilateral ties with the European nations, the Bolsheviks sought to reduce their international isolation by joining multilateral agreements. In 1928, with Maxim Litvinov as foreign commissar, the Soviet Union expressed interest in joining the Kellogg-Briand Pact. This pact obligated its signatories, including France and the United States, to renounce war as a means of settling international disputes and commit to policies of disarmament. The Bolshevik leaders viewed joining the pact as a means to obtain an additional platform for improving ties with the West, especially in light of Franco-German rapprochement as expressed in the 1925 Locarno pact; this pact affirmed France's recognition of the new border with Germany in exchange for the latter's acceptance of the Versailles Treaty.

The Isolationist Turn

Around 1928, soon after Russia declared interest in joining the Kellogg-Briand Pact, peaceful coexistence begun to move in a more isolationist and nationalist direction. The Soviet regime did not have much faith in the pact's objective and merely wanted to signal its desire to be a part of a

joint effort and avoid diplomatic marginalization. Responding partly to
the British decision to break off diplomatic relations in May 1927, the
Soviet Union began to pursue policies of domestic consolidation and
preparation for a possible war. Intimidated by prospects of military confrontation, Stalin even stated at the Fifteenth Party Congress in December 1927 that "the period of 'peaceful coexistence' is receding into the
past."[23] The new leader of the Soviet state was preparing the ground for
a turning inward that would fundamentally transform Russia's domestic
institutions.

In the agricultural area, Stalin moved away from the NEP's market-
based relationships with the peasantry. Because of a poor harvest and
inefficient state procurement policies, the country was experiencing a
severe shortage of grain. In January 1928, it purchased only 300 million
pounds relative to 428 million the year before.[24] The shortage meant
that the government had problems supplying the cities with bread, as
well as financing industrialization through the export of grain.[25] Under
these conditions, Stalin chose to implement a forced requisition of bread
and a "full-scale collectivization" in the rural sector, rather than raising
procurement prices or temporarily importing bread from abroad. The
justification he provided was the need to "save the hard currency for
importing industrial equipment."[26]

Simultaneously, the war-scare atmosphere prompted Stalin to adopt
contingency plans for war and favor a militaristic blueprint for economic development. The first five-year plan reflected his threat perception by connecting the issue of military power to that of economic
industrialization.[27] Although Soviet top commanders, such as Mikhail
Tukhachevski, advocated a rapid and thorough modernization of the
military during the first five-year plan, Stalin chose to build the entire
economy around mobilization for "the needs of total war."[28] The militarization of the economy, although also being undertaken by other
nations, including Italy, France, and Germany,[29] put additional strains
on the system. For example, from 1933–6, Soviet state procurement of
aviation equipment increased about fourfold, that of tanks threefold, and
that of naval construction and artillery fourfold.[30] The overall defense
budget also increased by several factors.[31]

Stalin's isolationism was reflected in media policies and relations with
the Comintern as well. Beginning in the early 1930s, the media increasingly promoted the notion of "Motherland" by connecting Soviet policies
to those of the tsarist state. In relation to the West, the Soviet propaganda
presented Stalin not only as a Leninist but also as a state builder in the
manner of Ivan Kalita, Ivan III, Ivan IV, and particularly Peter the Great,
who was forced to develop the capabilities of a great power in face of

growing threats from abroad.[32] The Comintern too was transformed to serve the needs of the Soviet state. As early as August 1927, Stalin proclaimed "an *internationalist*" anyone "who, unreservedly, without wavering, without conditions is ready to defend the USSR, because the USSR is the base of the world revolutionary movement."[33]

Despite the decidedly more isolationist turn, the Soviet state remained interested in engaging Western nations. By signaling its intent to participate in international disarmament efforts, initiating nonaggression pacts with its neighbors, and promoting the idea of an "Eastern Locarno" to define Germany's eastern border,[34] Stalin's Russia was hoping to preserve the accomplishments of peaceful coexistence with the West. New threats from Japan in the Far East only served to reinforce this thinking.[35] Indeed, subsequent efforts by Maxim Litvinov to promote collective security in Europe indicate that in its foreign policy the state saw no alternative to the overall framework of coexistence with the West.

From Collective Security to the Pact with Germany

The initial Soviet reaction to Fascism was hardly critical. For example, the leading party newspaper *Pravda* interpreted the electoral victory of the Nazis over the Social Democrats in September 1930 in terms of the Nazis' potential to restrain France's hegemonic ambitions. According to the newspaper, the results of elections "promise great difficulties for French imperialism . . . the appearance in the European arena of a powerful imperialist competitor in the form of German neo-imperialism does not fit into its plans."[36] As late as 1934 Stalin publicly expressed his hopes for "the most excellent relations" with Germany.[37]

With time, however, the rising threat from Hitler's Germany was turning the Soviet Union more decisively toward the Western nations. Beginning as early as 1933, the Soviet authorities worked hard to undermine Hitler by establishing an alliance with France and other Western states. The Soviet Union joined the League of Nations and began to sharply differentiate between revisionist and status quo states. Litvinov emerged as a vocal critic of the League's inability to punish aggressive actions, such as Italy's invasion of Ethiopia in 1935 and Germany's occupation of the Rhineland in 1936. The Soviet state also used the Comintern to serve the collective security agenda. The Kremlin signed nonaggression treaties, including those pledging military support in case of attack by a third power. From 1933–9 – after the Munich Conference and until August 1939 – Soviet diplomacy worked to secure bilateral military agreements with France and Britain.

The decision by Moscow to sign the nonaggression pact with Germany demonstrated the end of collective security diplomacy as practiced by both Litvinov and Stalin. Yet even that decision, although it opened the way to World War II, did not fundamentally contradict peaceful coexistence, with its emphasis on preserving its honorable ideological objectives and achieving a break from the struggle with capitalism.

The Peaceful Coexistence, 1921–1939: Timeline

1921	The New Economic Policy introduced at the Tenth Party Congress
1922	Treaty with Germany at Rapallo
1923	Diplomatic recognition by France
1924	Stalin's doctrine of "socialism in one country"
	Diplomatic recognition by Britain
1927	The "war scare"
	Britain breaks diplomatic ties with the Soviet Union
1928	Russia supports the Kellogg-Briand pact
1933	Diplomatic recognition by the United States
1934	Russia joins the League of Nations
1935	Mutual assistance pacts with France and Czechoslovakia
1938	France, Britain, Germany, and Italy meet at Munich
1939	USSR proposes triple alliance to Britain and France
	Soviet-British-French military negotiations in Moscow
	Soviet-German pact signed in Moscow
	World War II begins

Explaining the Soviet Defensiveness

Peaceful coexistence was a version of a defensive strategy with the West. Somewhat reminiscent of Gorchakov's recueillement, it reflected both dependence on and mistrust of the West.

Western Influences

Although they reflected a general mistrust, Soviet perceptions of the West varied over time. Stalin and his entourage viewed intentions of the "advanced capitalist countries" as either greatly or moderately threatening or even allowing the possibility of cooperation, depending on the Western nations' internal strength, degree of unity, and actions toward the USSR. From 1921–39, Soviet perceptions of the West went through three stages. Before 1927, the dominant view was that capitalism had become stable and "well-entrenched"; in response Russia sought to gain some attributes of and recognition as a normal state, while continuing to exploit capitalist divisions and weaknesses. Around 1927 and especially with the beginning of the Great Depression, the Soviet perception of the West shifted to that of an especially acute threat. In the Soviet mind, the danger was that imperial powers could attack the East in a desperate search for new markets. This perception also served Stalin's agenda of concentrating power and eliminating internal opposition to his rule. Finally, the appointment of Hitler as Germany's chancellor created a new divide in Europe between the increasingly powerful and revisionist Germany and the weak and status-quo-oriented liberal Western nations. In this third stage, Stalin's Russia worked hard to build a collective security regime to restrain Hitler, but in the end returned to balance-of-power policies. All three stages were faces of peaceful coexistence with capitalism.

The NEP's foreign policy extension survived until 1927, partly because the West reciprocated the Soviet diplomatic and trade advancements. The "stabilization of capitalism" became the main line within the Bolshevik circles of both Stalin and Bukharin. Even Trotski, whom Stalin presented as the main opposition to his theory of "socialism in one country," did not substantially oppose the stabilization thesis and the projected need for the USSR to maneuver among Western powers.[38] The USSR had to work hard not to be pushed into further isolation, especially after its seemingly special relations with Germany began to deteriorate after Germany signed the Locarno treaty. Stabilization, if it meant the emergence of Germany's alliance with France and Britain, was Moscow's worst nightmare. Taking a page from older tsarist diplomacy, Chicherin proposed to build an equivalent to the "grand alliance," but failed to convince either Germany or France to act in concert with the Soviet Union and against Britain.[39] The wave of recognitions of the USSR by European nations and some openness to developing ties with the East, combined with the relatively low degree of practical cooperation and remaining Western mistrust toward the Soviet Union, served to consolidate Moscow's policy of peaceful coexistence.

Around 1927, Soviet perception changed in response to a series of setbacks in relations with European powers. Germany was showing signs of a Western orientation, and the USSR's relationship with it had not produced the expected results of military cooperation. In 1926, a coup in Poland brought Marshal Pilsudski, Russia's enemy, back to power. In May 1927, the British Conservative government broke off diplomatic ties with Moscow, accusing it of promoting interference in the internal affairs of the United Kingdom.[40] In June of the same year, Pyort Voikov, the Soviet ambassador in Poland, was assassinated. In September, Soviet-French economic negotiations ended with no results, and Khristian Rakovski, the ambassador to France, was declared persona non grata.[41] Despite Chicherin's urges not to overreact to the setbacks in relations with European powers, Stalin took them extremely seriously, ordering the execution of twenty Russian nobles and arresting many German engineers in the coal industry.[42] In his mind, all these developments were related, reflecting a concerted effort by neighboring states to isolate and dominate the Soviet Union. On July 28, 1927, Stalin wrote,

It is hardly open to doubt that the chief contemporary question is that of the threat of a new imperialist war. It is a matter of a real and material *threat* of a new war in general, and a war against the USSR in particular.[43]

What shifted Soviet perceptions yet again was the economic crisis in the West and the subsequent rise of Germany in the mid-1930s. In response Communist theoreticians, led by Jeno Varga, again predicted "waves" of instability with potentially revolutionary consequences.[44] To Stalin, who had already decided to pursue collectivization of the peasantry and militarization of the economy, the new capitalist instability spelled dangers for his plans for domestic transformation. It also implied new geopolitical threats, particularly coming from the increasingly Western-influenced Eastern Europe. In September 1930, Stalin wrote to Molotov that Poland was working to draw the Baltic states into an alliance for a war against the USSR: "as soon as they've put this bloc together, they'll start to fight."[45]

With the ascendance of Hitler to power, the Soviets gradually focused their diplomatic efforts on deterring him by assembling an alliance with the West. France came back into the picture as a potential partner. Even Britain, which had restored its diplomatic ties with the Soviet Union in October 1929, now had to be engaged in an anti-German coalition. Initially viewing Germany's growing power[46] as a useful check on French ambitions in Europe, Moscow had now readjusted its attitude.

Domestic Conditions and Soviet Honor

Although the climate of mistrust between Soviet Russia and the West prevented efforts at serious cooperation, the overall fragility of the Soviet system precluded its leaders from developing assertive policies against the Western nations. This created conditions for the rise of a defensive discourse among state officials. From 1921–39, the Soviet discourse included various aspects of defensive honor – from the honor of building socialism with limited cooperation from the West, to the honor of defiance and reduced dependence on capitalist credit, to the honor of new socialist achievements in the late 1930s.

The NEP's discourse, despite the shift from the assertive stance of world revolution, reflected a degree of internal confidence. In Lenin's view, even while being surrounded by capitalist countries, the Soviet Union had obtained a degree of security after winning a devastating civil war and thwarting Western ambitions to topple the Bolshevik regime. As a result it was entering into a new period of development during which "our basic international existence in the context of capitalist states is secure."[47] Lenin emphasized the gradual process of building new socialist institutions, contrasting military communism's "revolutionary approach" to economic development with the cautious "reformist approach" under the NEP.[48] He believed that it was in the greedy nature of capitalism to do business with the Soviet Union, which the new Russian state must be able to exploit to its advantage: "the capitalists themselves will be happy to sell us the rope which we will use to hang them."[49] Some, like Chicherin, also proposed to establish a new collaborative organization devoted to global economic reconstruction and disarmament.[50]

At the time, Stalin seemed fully supportive of Lenin's ideas. Even before the NEP, during the debate on peace with Germany in 1918, Stalin had argued against continuous military confrontation, pointing to the absence of revolutionary movements in the West.[51] During the NEP, he championed the idea of "socialism in one country," justifying it by "the unequal and uneven development of capitalist countries at the stage of imperialism."[52] He argued against the views of some leaders, such as Grigory Zinovyev, head of the Comintern, and Lev Trotski, former Commissar for Foreign Affairs, who still saw Soviet success as dependent on mass revolutionary uprising abroad. In contrast, Stalin argued that it was "a fact that the Russian Revolution, which did not win the support of the Western proletariat and which has remained surrounded by hostile capitalist regimes, continues to exist."[53] At the time, his idea of socialism in one country, although having a nationalist overtone, was generally in line with views of the party's leading intellectual Nikolai Bukharin.[54]

In the late 1920s, in response to fears of the increasingly more hostile international environment, Stalin's perception changed. As the Western economies began to suffer from the Great Depression, the nationalist/isolationist component of socialism in one country became fully revealed. The idea of limited cooperation with capitalism was replaced with that of self-sufficiency and a minimized reliance on the outside world. In 1929, Stalin justified the forced requisition of grain from the peasantry by the need "to demonstrate to our enemies that we stand firmly on our feet and have no intention to be dependent on pity promises of [foreign] help."[55]

That Stalin was more nationalist-minded that many of his comrades was clear from his earlier activities within the party. Long before his argument with Lenin over conditions of integrating the non-Russian nationalities,[56] Stalin, a native Georgian then named Djugashvili, had predicated his decision to join the Bolsheviks on an ethnic basis. Referring to the Mensheviks as the "Jewish faction," he opted for the "true-Russian faction" and even had suggested the idea of conducting "a pogrom in the party."[57] Internationally, he hardly ever concerned himself with Russia's European roots and identity. In E. H. Carr's words, "Unlike Lenin and Trotsky, or even Zinoviev and Bukharin, Stalin cared nothing for what happened in western Europe except in so far as it affected the destinies of his own country."[58]

The notion of nationalist-isolationist honor shaped Stalin's autarchic policies of industrialization and collectivization and soon put him at odds with Bukharin and other advocates of continuing with the NEP. Stalin's thesis about the intensification of the internal "class war" under the "socialist offensive," although reflecting his own nationalist beliefs, also helped him discredit Bukharin within the party. Painting Bukharin and his supporters as soft on capitalism at home and abroad, Stalin was able to isolate his opposition, in part because Bukharin never developed the NEP's international corollary under the Great Depression.[59] Having defeated his opposition, Stalin finally had the power to launch his revolutionary policies. The appeal to nationalist honor also resonated within the party because it reflected a culturally accepted pattern of state-imposed modernization earlier practiced by the tsars. As Robert C. Tucker wrote, the Stalinist rural revolution from above and introduction of the *kolkhoz* bore a strong resemblance to serfdom and were "in essence an accelerated repetition of this tsarist developmental pattern."[60]

From the mid-1930s, Stalin was citing domestic achievements to justify his choices and provide a rationale for continuing with the policy of peaceful coexistence.[61] In his mind, the fact that the Soviet Union "oriented itself in past and present to the USSR and only the USSR" strengthened it internally, adding confidence to its foreign policy.[62]

Domestic Support and Opposition

Between 1921 and 1939, domestic debates focused on various versions of peaceful coexistence, rather than opposition to its key principles. Trotski and his supporters – in a paradoxical shift from their earlier theory of permanent revolution – advocated a version of integration with Europe, mainly through economic intercourse. They made it clear, however, that the purpose of such integration was to rebuild the economic foundations of Soviet Russia and ultimately liberate the "false" Europe of its capitalist vestiges in a new revolution.[63] Bukharin advocated a similar approach. An early supporter of "socialism in one country," he spoke in favor of "the internationalist revolution" and warned against an ideology of "national Bolshevism" that would only lead to a "backward socialism."[64] In the late 1920s, when Western capitalism could not be perceived as stable, both Trotski and Bukharin still insisted on a sustained engagement with the West, differing from Stalin, who now shifted to viewing the West as ready to launch a war on the USSR. Throughout the 1930s and until his arrest in February 1937, Bukharin also supported a coalition against Nazi Germany.

As did many within the party, Stalin did not support either assertiveness or strong cooperation with the Western nations. He shared the view that the main priority was for the country to rebuild its domestic foundations, and therefore it was necessary to avoid a confrontation with the outside world and to win diplomatic recognition by the Western states. For example, in the early 1930s, Stalin cautioned against a strong engagement on the anti-German side: "we shall have to come out, but we ought to be the last to come out. And we should come out in order to throw the decisive weight on the scales, the weight that should tilt the scales."[65]

However, Stalin generally favored a more isolationist version of peaceful coexistence than did Trotski, Bukharin, or Litvinov. Stalin's beliefs became obvious not just from his preferences for self-sufficient domestic modernization but also from his distinctly paranoid perception of the Western nations. Indeed, it was the latter that had precipitated the former. Like his tsarist predecessors, he thought in terms of overcoming Russia's backwardness in relation to the West, which he viewed as a potential threat to his country's survival.[66] While Bukharin and others were worried about balancing the budget,[67] Stalin was getting ready for a rapidly approaching war with capitalism, viewing collectivization and industrialization as essential prerequisites.

Stalin's views found support within the party because they reflected the dominant fear of capitalism at home and abroad. The NEP's long coexistence with the private sector required a certain sophistication on the part of the Bolshevik masses, and its rationale was never clearly articulated.[68] In addition, Trotski and Bukharin failed to develop a strong alternative to Stalin's international perspective, which emphasized the gathering external threats.[69]

Alternative Explanations

One common approach to peaceful coexistence interprets it as a version of an ideologically driven assertive policy or as a preparation for launching an offensive war on the West. A classic statement of this position can be found in George Kennan's condemnation of "a regime, the attitude of which towards Western governments, psychologically and politically, was equivalent to that which would prevail toward an enemy in time of war."[70] In this formulation, ideology is the principal source of Bolshevik antipathy vis-à-vis its hostile Western counterparts. To Kennan, Western nations came to hate the Soviet leaders "for what they *did*," whereas the Bolsheviks hated the Western states "for what they *were*, regardless of what they did."[71] This distinction has become common in Western scholarship on Soviet foreign policy since the Cold War. More recently, David R. Stone attributed the Bolshevik's domestic and foreign policies from October 1917 to the post–Great Depression years to the Soviet leaders' belief in the imminent war with capitalism.[72]

This perspective correctly identifies the central role of ideology in Soviet foreign policy formulation. It is indeed communist ideology that provided the Bolshevik state with a new sense of honor and international obligations. However, the problem with this perspective is that it lacks nuance and proportion. By dismissing considerations of security, it loses the ability to account for important differences in Russia's policy across time after the revolution. The USSR soon abandoned its initial commitment to world revolution – a version of a genuinely assertive strategy – in favor of a search for accommodation with capitalism. The Bolsheviks differed in their perception of outside threats, and the outside world too provided them with differing environments to which to respond. As result, Soviet policies included such widely varying options as the world revolution, the NEP's limited cooperation with capitalism, militant isolationism, collective security, and balance of power. Although a confrontation with capitalism was never off the table, Stalin viewed it as something that must be delayed, rather than welcomed.

Yet the view that attributes Soviet actions primarily to security motivations is also insufficient.[73] The ideological sense of honor gave an ostensibly security-driven foreign policy an overall motivation and purpose. It was the ideological difference between the West and the Soviet Union that ultimately made it impossible for the two sides to develop genuine cooperation, save during the exceptional circumstances of World War II. Just like Russia under Alexander II, after being defeated in the Crimean War, did not abandon its perceived obligation to serve as the protector of

Orthodox Christians in the Balkans, Stalin's Russia remained confident in its ability to ultimately convert Europeans to communist beliefs.

Assessment

The policy of peaceful coexistence served to defend and consolidate the Soviets' ideologically derived notion of honor. Stalin's theory of socialism in one country became the embodiment of this period, providing a purpose for foreign policy actions. In its various versions – including the NEP's limited cooperation with capitalism, isolationism, and the pact with Germany – peaceful coexistence reflected the combination of a deep mistrust of the West and a lack of confidence in aggressively promoting socialism abroad. That lack of confidence was expressed in Stalin's decision to quietly dismantle the Comintern and turn to more accepted tools of diplomacy.

The overall movement from the course of world revolution and toward peaceful coexistence helped the Soviet state win time for domestic transformation and recovery after the harsh years of military communism and civil war. Although political groups within the party differed in their assessment of internal and external policies of defending socialism, they agreed to rule out a confrontation with the capitalist world. Thus Bukharin and Stalin defended different versions of socialism in one country and advocated different foreign policies, but they each sought to exploit economic and political ties with the West to the Soviet advantage.

Over the long run, Stalin's isolationist approach to peaceful coexistence, combined with his decision to abruptly end the NEP's policies at home, came at a great price to the country. The rapid industrialization and collectivization that he imposed on Soviet society undermined trust of the peasantry in the state for several generations to come. Accompanied by Stalin's paranoid purges within the party, the military, and the intelligentsia, his transformation severely weakened, not strengthened, the country's preparedness to withstand an attack from the outside. It is hard to determine whether Bukharin's plan of borrowing from abroad for the sake of preserving relations with the peasant class would have worked well,[74] but it is clear that it would have saved the lives of millions of people. Externally, Stalin's purges greatly contributed to the image of an unreliable country with which to partner against Hitler. Although the suspicious attitudes of France and Britain toward the Soviet Union added to the failure of collective security, Stalin's own contribution to such failure stands in its own right.

Notes

1 Stalin, "O pobede sotializma v odnoi strane i mirovoi revolutsiyi," 103–4.
2 See Chapter 7 in this book.
3 Jacobson, *When the Soviet Union Entered World Politics*, p. 13.
4 Vladimir Lenin's remarks at the All-Russian Central Executive Committee of Soviets, in Suny, ed. *The Structure of the Soviet History*, p. 70. Bosheviks received 25% of the vote and seats compared to a more impressive performance by the Left Socialist Revolutionary Party that got 40%.
5 Donaldson and Nogee, *The Foreign Policy of Russia*, p. 37.
6 Alexander Yakovlev's Commission of the Glasnost' era estimated that about 8 million people were victims of the civil war and terror during 1918–22. Kennedy-Pipe, *Russia and the World*, p. 24.
7 Jacobson, *When the Soviet Union Entered World Politics*, p. 21.
8 Nation, *Black Earth, Red Star*, pp. 38–9.
9 Jacobson, *When the Soviet Union Entered*, p. 19.
10 Ibid.
11 Ibid., p. 24.
12 For Soviet analyses of Lenin's thinking about peaceful coexistence, see Zagladin, *Istoriya uspekhov i neudach sovetskoi diplomatiyi*, pp. 49–62 and Bovin, *Mirnoye sosushchestvovaniye*.
13 Vert, *Istoriya sovetskogo gosudarstva*, pp. 238–9.
14 Donaldson and Nogee, *The Foreign Policy of Russia*, p. 41.
15 Nation, *Black Earth*, p. 42.
16 Ibid., p. 43.
17 Ulam, *Expansion and Coexistence*, p. 158.
18 Nation, *Black Earth*, p. 40.
19 Fink, "The NEP in Foreign Policy," 13–14.
20 Gorodetsky, "The Formulation of Soviet Foreign Policy," 33; Vert, *Istoriya sovetskogo gosudarstva*, p. 243.
21 Vert, *Istoriya sovetskogo gosudarstva*, p. 243.
22 Ibid., p. 244.
23 Neumann, *Russia and the Idea of Europe*, p. 122.
24 Nove, *An Economic History of the USSR*, p. 150.
25 Ibid., p. 151; Ragsdale, *The Russian Tragedy*, p. 213.
26 Zagladin, *Istoriya uspekhov i neudach sovetskoi diplomatiyi*, p. 88; Kagarlitski, *Periferiynaya imperiya*, p. 424.
27 Wohlforth, *The Elusive Balance*, p. 48.
28 Samuelson, *Plans for Stalin's War Machine*, p. 202.
29 Ibid.
30 Ibid., p. 180. See also Stone, *Hammer and Rifle*, p. 214.
31 For a summary of statistics, see Stone, *Hammer and Rifle*, p. 217.
32 Tucker, *Stalin in Power*, p. 481.
33 Nation, *Black Earth*, p. 37.
34 Donaldson and Nogee, *The Foreign Policy of Russia*, p. 46.
35 Ibid.
36 Haslam, *Soviet Foreign Policy, 1930–1933*, p. 61.

37 Such was the tone of his speech at the Seventeenth Party Congress in January 1934. Shapiro, "Soviet Foreign Policy – 1928–1939," 221.

38 Wohlforth, *The Elusive Balance*, p. 40. For Trotski's views during this period, see also Kolakowski, *Main Currents of Marxism*, pp. 4–37; Deutscher, *The Prophet Unarmed*.

39 Suny, *The Soviet Experiment*, p. 162.

40 Samuelson, *Plans for Stalin's War Machine*, p. 35.

41 Gorodetsky, "The Formulation of Soviet Foreign Policy," 41.

42 Suny and Kennedy, *The Soviet Experiment*, p. 165; Mlechin, *Ministry inostrannykh del*, p. 111.

43 Ulam, *Expansion and Coexistence*, p. 165.

44 Nation, *Black Earth*, p. 62; Kagarlitski, *Periferiynaya imperiya*, p. 428.

45 Stone, *Hammer and Rifle*, p. 5.

46 For statistics on Germany's rising economic power and military expenditures, see Kennedy, *The Rise and Fall of Great Powers*, pp. 296, 303–10, 330.

47 Zagladin, *Istoriya uspekhov i neudach*, p. 59.

48 In a series of his late articles, Lenin advocated the establishment of volunteer economic associations, or cooperatives, through persuasion and the spread of enlightenment, or "culturalizing" (*kul'turnichestvo*) among the peasants and other social strata. Tucker, *Stalin as a Revolutionary, 1879–1929*, pp. 371–2.

49 Nation, *Black Earth*, p. 39.

50 Zagladin, *Istoriya uspekhov*, pp. 70–1.

51 Haslam, "Litvinov, Stalin and the Road Not Taken," 56.

52 Stalin, "O pobede sotializma v odnoi strane i mirovoi revolutsiyi," 103.

53 Gorodetsky, "The Formulation of Soviet Foreign Policy," 32.

54 Cohen, *Rethinking the Soviet Experience*, p. 59.

55 Zagladin, *Istoriya uspekhov*, p. 88.

56 Lenin, who was contemptuous of nationalism as a "bourgeois trick," denounced Stalin, as well as other Russified natives Feliks Dzerzhinski and Sergo Ordzhonikidze, as great Russian chauvinists. Martin, *The Affirmative-Action Empire*; Lewin, *The Soviet Century*, pp. 22–7.

57 Tucker, *Stalin as a Revolutionary*, p. 140.

58 Carr, *Socialism in One Country, 1924–1926*, pp. 179.

59 Wohlforth, *Elusive Balance*, p. 50.

60 Tucker, *Political Culture and Leadership in Soviet Russia*, p. 89. For a similar argument, see Lewin, *The Soviet Century*, pp. 70, 143–9.

61 See especially his reports to the Seventeenth and Eighteenth Party Congresses in 1934 and 1939, respectively (Stalin, *Voprosy leninizma*, pp. 423, 435–6, 565).

62 Stalin, *Voprosy leninizma*, p. 435.

63 Neumann, *Russia and the Idea of Europe*, pp. 117–19.

64 Cohen, *Rethinking the Soviet Experience*, pp. 74–5.

65 Kennedy-Pipe, *Russia and the World*, p. 31.

66 For a classic example of his reasoning, see Stalin, "On the Tasks of Workers in the Economy," 294–5.

67 Stone, *Hammer and Rifle*, pp. 7–11.

68 Nove, *An Economic History of the USSR*, p. 132.

69 Bukharin's strongest articulation of the alternative was his response to Yevgeni Preobrazhenski's work of "the main law of socialist accumulation," which also assumed a stable capitalist environment and did not anticipate a strong threat to Soviet security. Bukharin, "K voprosu o zakonomernostiyakh perekhodnogo perioda," 209–53.

70 Kennan, *Russia and the West under Lenin and Stalin*, p. 179.

71 Ibid., p. 181.

72 Stone, *Hammer and Rifle*, pp. 3–4.

73 For arguments that the Bolsheviks proceeded mainly from security assumptions, see, for example, Jacobson, *When the Soviet Union Entered World Politics*; Gorodetsky, "The Formulation of Soviet Foreign Policy"; Donaldson and Nogee, *The Foreign Policy of Russia*.

74 For a sympathetic discussion of Bukharin's alternative to Stalin, see Cohen, *Bukharin and the Bolshevik Revolution* and Cohen, *Rethinking the Soviet Experience*.

"The assertion about the absence in NATO of plans for the accession of the countries of Eastern and Central Europe to the North Atlantic Treaty in one form or another were made in 1990–1991 by Secretary of State, J. Baker, Minister of Foreign Affairs of Great Britain, D. Hurd, and even by a number of leaders of member-states of this bloc. What has remained of these assertions today?"

Yevgeni Primakov[1]

Russia's Policy of Containing NATO

In late 1992 the pro-Western foreign policy course of Boris Yelstin and Foreign Minister Andrei Kozyrev began to backfire. The IMF-recommended "shock therapy" was introduced in January 1992 and led to severe economic hardship for many people. The Yeltsin-Kozyrev security policy, especially in the Balkans, also came under heavy criticism, and the opposition's pressures further intensified when NATO launched air strikes against the Bosnian Serbs in 1994.

The Arrival of Yevgeni Primakov

In this increasingly politicized context, NATO made a decision to expand eastward by incorporating members of the former Soviet bloc in Eastern Europe.[2] The decision provided domestic nationalist opposition with additional arguments and resources to mobilize against the Westernist course.

Yevgeni Primakov, then director of Russia's Foreign Intelligence Service, issued a sharp criticism of the expansion, referring to the historical memory of the Cold War hostilities and warning that it would result in Russia's increased isolation. Critics of Yeltsin's course – both nationalists and communists – did well in the 1993 and 1995 elections, compelling Yeltsin to modify the pro-Western agenda. The president's sacking of Kozyrev and appointment of Primakov as the new foreign minister were a response to his critics. As the *Financial Times* editorialized, of all the possible successors to Kozyrev, Primakov was "probably the least welcome in Washington. By selecting him, President Boris Yeltsin has signaled that he cares more about assuaging nationalism at home than soothing US fears."[3] Primakov served as foreign minister from January 1996 to September 1998; he then served as prime minister, continuing to exert a guiding influence on foreign policy until May 1999.

Primakov's worldview solidified during his long career as a Middle East specialist and policy maker. During the Soviet era, he worked in several Middle Eastern countries as a correspondent for the leading communist newspaper *Pravda*. He also served as director of the Institute of Oriental Studies and, later, of the prestigious Institute of World Economy and International Relations. According to Primakov, "Russia is both Europe and Asia," and that concept had "to play a tremendous role in formulation of its foreign policy."[4] Aware of Russia's weakness, the new minister was worried about becoming dependent on the strongest power in the international system, and he wanted to pursue "multi-vector" policies that would achieve more balanced relations with the West and preserve strong ties with China, India, and the Islamic world. Such thinking was reflected in official documents. The country's National Security Concept of 1997 identified Russia as an "influential European and Asian power." It recommended that Russia maintain equidistant relations to the "global European and Asian economic and political actors," and it presented a positive program for the integration of CIS efforts in the security sphere.[5]

The key focus of Primakov's policy was undoubtedly NATO's eastward expansion and Russia's adaptation to this new reality.[6] The decision to expand the alliance was made in January 1994 in response to several security crises in the Balkans and pressures from the East European states. By the time Primakov had assumed his responsibilities in 1996, it had become clear that NATO, rather than the Russia-preferred Organization for Security and Cooperation in Europe (OSCE), was becoming the cornerstone of European security. It was equally clear that, despite Russia's original hopes, it was not about to be considered for membership in the organization.

Diplomatic Efforts in Europe

Under these conditions, Primakov saw his task as limiting the potential damage of the NATO expansion. His very appointment served the purpose of ameliorating anti-NATO backlash because of his already established reputation as a tough defender of Russia's national interests.

Primakov soon recognized that the expansion of the alliance was inevitable and that Russia had to shift from the mode of resistance to adaptation. Although he was highly critical of the developments, he recognized that "the expansion of NATO is not a military problem; it is a psychological one."[7] To reduce the perception of the alliance as a threat, Russia had little choice but to work on establishing closer diplomatic and political ties with the alliance. The result was the negotiated document signed by the two sides in May 1997, the Founding Act on Mutual Relations, Cooperation and Security between Russia and NATO. Russia saw this document as a quasi-institutionalization of its relationships with the alliance. In December 1997, in his speech to the State Duma, Primakov referred to the Founding Act as a major accomplishment, evidence of the success of Russia's diplomacy in attaining its objectives. Russia was also given the opportunity to collaborate with NATO in establishing a special body, the Permanent Joint Council, to consult about and – when appropriate – even participate in decision making[8] and joint action.

Until the Western military intervention in the Balkans, Primakov followed the policy of pragmatic cooperation with NATO members. A few months before he took office, the Dayton Accords of November 1995 had been signed with minimal input from Russia. Although the new foreign minister saw the role of Belgrade in European security differently from NATO members, he refrained from setting Russia's policy unilaterally by working, instead, through the Contact Group – the framework for diplomatic coordination among Russia, the United States, France, Britain, and Germany created in February 1994 at Yeltsin's initiative. Although Russia opposed NATO's command of peacekeeping forces and in some cases objected to specific acts of force against the Bosnian Serbs, in general it did not interfere with UN-sanctioned actions in Bosnia.[9]

However, NATO's decision to begin air strikes against Belgrade in March 1999 changed the framework of the relationship. The military intervention came as a shock to Russia's foreign policy community. In response, Prime Minister Yevgeni Primakov decided to cancel the economic negotiations with the United States and the IMF in Washington on March 24, 1999; en route to the United States when he heard about the airstrikes, Primakov ordered the plane to return home. Russia's official reaction was harsh: it accused the alliance of violating UN jurisdiction and the Helsinki act on the preservation of sovereignty, suspended its participation in the Founding Act agreement, withdrew its military mission from Brussels, and ordered NATO representatives to leave Russia.

This strong reaction reflected the largely negative attitudes toward the alliance within Russia's society and foreign policy community. An overwhelming majority believed that the Western actions were driven by

power and hegemonic ambitions, rather than by concerns over Milosevic's actions against Kosovo's Albanians. Among the general public,
about 90 percent opposed NATO's bombing of Belgrade and felt threatened by its actions.[10]

Yet it was the expansion of NATO, rather than the ethnic war in
the Balkans, that shaped Russia's perception of the intervention in
Yugoslavia. By the time of the airstrikes, the Western alliance had already
invited the Czech Republic, Poland, and Hungary to apply for membership. At the Madrid summit in the summer of 1997, U.S. State Secretary
of State Madeleine Albright specifically promised to extend an invitation
to the Baltic states, which had been a part of the Soviet Union before
1991. Despite the Founding Act agreement of May 1997, the post-
Madrid atmosphere of Russia–West relations was tense, as Primakov's
foreign ministry insisted again on the unacceptability of the alliance's
expansion. The clash over Kosovo intensified Russian fears; it responded
with elements of political escalation and, at times, came close to a military
confrontation. For instance, by just two or three votes, Russia's Duma fell
short of passing a resolution to accept Yugoslavia into the Russia-Belarus
Union, which would have made Russia a participant in the war.

Primakov had no plans to throw his support behind Serbia, which
his nationalist opponents called on him to do. Instead, he got involved
in mediating the conflict. Playing on the West's interest in Russia's
involvement, he formulated tough conditions for ending the war, which
included guarantees for Serbia's preserved sovereignty, broad autonomy
for Kosovo, and the UN's assuming leadership in the postwar settlement. Yet the peace was reached more on Western than Russia's terms.
Out of fear of further Russia–West political escalation, Yeltsin dismissed
Primakov as the key negotiator and replaced him with former prime minister Victor Chernomyrdin, who was much too pro-Western and inexperienced in foreign affairs to negotiate the peace that Primakov had in
mind. In early June, under pressure from Chernomyrdin, Serbia finally
accepted the conditions for peace, which did not include Russia's initial conditions. As one Russian observer described the outcome of the
war, "Russia took part in Yugoslavia's acceptance of the same NATO
conditions that it had previously called unacceptable."[11]

Diplomatic Efforts outside the West

The active foreign policy sought by Primakov required the development
of geostrategic and economic ties to countries outside the West. An Ara-
bist by training, Primakov became active in the Middle East and considerably increased Russian arms sales in the region. Everywhere he traveled

the new minister spread his message about the necessity of building a multipolar world order, which he viewed as the ultimate guarantee against the expansion of NATO. Three states played especially important roles in his vision – China, Iran, and India.

In addition to being the main buyer of Russian weapons, China shared Primakov's concerns about America's global dominance and perceived NATO expansion, the U.S. plans to build a national missile defense system, and interventions in Iraq and Kosovo as threatening developments. The countries also faced similar internal threats to security: from the separatist activities of Chechnya in Russia and the Muslim Uighur minority in China's province of Xinjiang. All of these factors brought the two countries closer together. In April 1996, the sides affirmed that they were entering into a new stage of partnership, and a year later the countries' leaders signed the Joint Declaration on a Multipolar World and the Formation of a New International Order, which reflected Primakov's vision of multipolarity as a work in progress. Developments in 1998–9, such as U.S. military strikes against Iraq, plans for the creation of a U.S.-Japanese theater missile defense, NATO expansion, and the bombing of Yugoslavia, again brought the two together to actively coordinate their responses to what they saw as threatening developments in world affairs.

Another potential strategic partner in Primakov's calculus was Iran. Politically, he saw the country as a regional ally in containing the influences of the Taliban regime in Afghanistan and Turkey, particularly in the states of Central Asia and Azerbaijan. Geopolitically, Iran was yet another potential ally in resisting the U.S.-controlled unipolarity. Economically, Russia was building nuclear reactors in Iran, supplying industrial equipment, and planning on forming a joint policy in developing energy pipelines in the Caspian region. Despite objections from Washington that Iran was building a nuclear weapon in violation of the existing Non-Proliferation Regime, Russia continued to cooperate with Iran, denying all the allegations.

Finally, Primakov's diplomacy sought to engage India as a partner of strategic importance. In trying to revive Russia as India's key rearmament agent the foreign minister was capitalizing on old Soviet ties. In 1997, the Indian prime minister announced that his country had purchased $3 billion in arms from Russia over the previous two years and that the two sides had discussed potential contracts totaling another $7 billion – an amount that would move India ahead of China in the ranks of Moscow's arms customers.[12] Politically, Primakov was interested in building closer relations between Russia, India, and China to balance the power of the United States, which was a marked shift from the previous policy of balancing China's power through an alliance with India. In December

1998, Primakov spoke of the desirability of the three countries' alliance as a "new pole in world politics." The alliance, however, remained wishful thinking, as neither India nor China had a similar interest in working together.

Diplomacy in the Former Soviet World

Reintegration of the former Soviet states was another key pillar of Primakov's strategy of balancing Western power and resisting NATO expansion. In February 1995 – partly in response to nationalist pressures – in his state of the nation address, Yeltsin argued for a new integration of the CIS, unfavorably referring to some "forces abroad" who wanted to downgrade Russia's international role.[13] The concept of reintegration was first clearly articulated on September 14, 1995, when Yeltsin issued a wide-ranging decree, "The Establishment of the Strategic Course of the Russian Federation with Member States of the CIS." The eight-page document had been developed from one of the Primakov-led Foreign Intelligence Service reports, and it was transformed into the "CIS Concept of Economic Integrational Development" adopted in March 1997. The proclaimed goal was to create "an economically and politically integrated alliance of states capable of achieving a worthy place in world society," which was similar to Primakov's definition of integration as a Russia-led "policy aimed at bringing together the states formed on the territory of the former Soviet Union."[14]

Although Primakov and Yeltsin were concerned also with the economic and cultural aspects of reintegrating the region, political and security issues drove the effort. For the politically driven Yeltsin, raising the issue of reintegration was a way to neutralize his domestic opposition and restore the state's capacity to conduct foreign policy. For Primakov, the security context, particularly NATO expansion, prompted the need for reintegration. Russia was eager to establish itself as a center of power, as an alternative to NATO, yet it faced multiple regional threats, including the new conflicts in the Caucasus, Moldova, and Tajikistan; terrorism; illegal immigration; and narcotics trafficking, especially on the Sino-Russian and Tajik-Afghan borders. To preserve Russia's traditional, powerful influence, it therefore had to bring order and stability to the region.

In response to these threats Moscow applied to the United Nations for special peacekeeping powers in the region and began to see these powers as an area of "special responsibility and special interest." It also began to advocate for a CIS collective security force and joint activities among the states. Taking as a point of departure the 1992 Treaty on Collective

Security, the Russia-led CIS members developed a fairly ambitious vision of military and defense coordination, which the CIS summit adopted in February 1995 as the Collective Security Concept. The Concept, among other things, assumed the right to set up CIS peacekeeping forces. Yeltsin also declared his intention to set up thirty Russian military bases in the CIS states, especially in Central Asia and the Caucasus.[15] Finally, to neutralize influences of Iran, China, and Afghanistan, Russia strengthened the border security of Turkmenistan, Kyrgyzstan, and Tajikistan.

Russia's integration efforts in the western direction differed from those in Central Asia and the Caucasus. In the West, Moscow was especially eager to respond to the "threat" of NATO's expansion by normalizing and developing military ties with Belarus and Ukraine. Given its vital geostrategic location and pro-Russian orientation, Belarus emerged as particularly important. In April 1996 the two sides had signed the Treaty on Formation of the Russia-Belarus Community, committing themselves to far-reaching integration in political and military areas. They developed a common perception of security threats and a close coordination of foreign policies, and pledged the establishment of a defense alliance. Under Primakov, Russia also activated political ties with Ukraine, which the new foreign minister saw as another top priority. As a result of Primakov's efforts, in May 1997 the two sides signed the so-called Big Treaty, which settled the status of the Black Sea Fleet and legalized the borders between the two countries. In terms of the most pro-Western Baltic states, Russia sought to minimize the negative consequences of NATO's expansion by offering them security guarantees and by making explicit its position that Baltic membership in NATO would endanger Russia's good relations with NATO.

Containing NATO Expansion, 1995–1999: Timeline

1994 January	The decision to expand NATO is made
February	The Contact Group is created
1995 February	CIS members adopt the Collective Security Concept
September	The concept of reintegrating the former Soviet region is first articulated
November	The Dayton Accords are signed with minimal input of Russia
December	Primakov replaces Kozyrev as foreign minister
1996 April	Treaty on Formation of Russia-Belarus Community is signed
December	Primakov visits Teheran

1997 March	Yeltsin insists that NATO should not include former Soviet states
	The CIS Concept of Economic Integrational Development is adopted
April	Russia and China sign the "Joint Declaration on a Multipolar World"
May	Yeltsin signs NATO-Russia Founding Act at summit with NATO leaders
	Russia and Ukraine sign the "Big Treaty" that legalizes the borders
July	NATO invites Czech Republic, Poland, and Hungary to become members
December	Russia adopts new National Security Concept
1998 September	Primakov assumes the post of prime minister
December	Primakov speaks of desirability of alliance with China and India
1999 March	NATO's air strikes against Serbia begin
	Primakov cancels the upcoming negotiations with the United States and the IMF
April	Yeltsin appoints Victor Chernomyrdin as Russia's envoy on Yugoslavia
June	Milosevic signs agreement on NATO terms for ending war
July	Russia-NATO Permanent Council meets after NATO's air strikes

Explaining the Policy

As with other cases of defensive honor, an explanation of the NATO containment policy must incorporate both pressures from the West and Russia's internal weakness.

Western Influences

Although the revival of Russia's defensiveness as the official foreign policy philosophy would not have occurred without security threats from both inside and outside the country, no less important was the relatively lukewarm reaction from the West, its significant other. After the breakup of the Soviet Union, Russia's pro-Western leaders were hoping for massive assistance, delivered quickly, from the West. After all, Russia was decisively breaking with its Soviet past. In the words of Russia's first foreign minister Andrei Kozyrev, the country's very system of values was to be changed, and the expectation was that such change would assist Russia greatly in raising it to the status of the front-rank countries, such as France, Germany, and the United States, within ten to twelve years.

The implications of the new liberal thinking were fundamental. Russia was presented as a "naturally" pro-Western nation, and its success was predicated on support and recognition from the West. However, the West's reaction was often excessively cautious or insensitive.[16] The decision made by the Western nations to expand NATO eastward, excluding Russia from the process, came as a major blow to the reformers, dashing Moscow's hopes to transform the alliance into a nonmilitary one or one that would admit Russia as a full member.[17] It strengthened the sense that Russia was not being accepted by Western civilization, and it provided the nationalist coalition with ammunition required to construct an image of an external threat and thereby question the objectives of the new government.

The decision to expand NATO reflected a broader change in the West's perception of the world. From the rhetoric of victory in the Cold War and the "end of history" in the early 1990s, the Western political community was becoming increasingly anxious about its ability to preserve peace and stability throughout the globe. The new ethnic conflicts in Europe and the former USSR, the perceived threat from the still extant regime of Saddam Hussein, and environmental and demographic pressures from Asia and Africa seemed to pose great risks. Various intellectual projects emerged to reflect the rising pessimism among U.S. policy makers about the future of the world order. With the growing awareness of new dangers came fear and suspicion of the non-Western world, which were best summarized by Samuel Huntington's thesis of the "clash of civilizations." Just as Francis Fukuyama once expressed the West's optimism, even euphoria, about the future world order,[18] Huntington expressed the growing feelings of anxiety and frustration. He insisted that, instead of expanding globally, the West should go on the defensive and prepare to fight for its cultural values in coming clashes with non-Western civilizations.[19] In this new intellectual context, Russia, with its authoritarian past and politically unstable present, was often viewed as a source of threat rather than a strategic partner. The once reborn liberal ally was now increasingly perceived to be driven by traditional imperial aspirations or to be a failing state unable to govern itself.

Domestic Conditions and Russia's Honor

Primakov's foreign policy objectives fit the defensive honor vision: the policy of containing NATO was shaped by Russia's relative decline and desire to revive its capabilities as a great power. Primakov made it explicit that his strategy was reminiscent of that of State Chancellor Gorchakov. After Russia's defeat in the Crimean War, Gorchakov recommended to Alexander II that, in light of Russia's weakened state, it "will have to focus persistently on the realization of [its] internal development and the entire foreign policy will have to be subordinated to this main task."[20] However, such a defensive policy would only be temporary, and after rebuilding its domestic base, Russia would again be in a position to defend its cultural allies and press for changes appropriate to its great power status. By pursuing flexible alliances, Russia was able to partially achieve its goal: in 1870 it felt strong enough to act unilaterally and partially renounce the conditions of the Paris peace treaty. Primakov too was hoping that, after rebuilding the economy, Russia would "return" to world politics. He shared with other officials a sense of responsibility to preserve ties with historic allies in the Balkans and with those gravitating to the new Russia, but out of domestic weakness, Primakov felt the need to concentrate on recovering the internal capabilities of a great power.

Like Gorchakov, Primakov believed that to enable a period of recovery Russia needed flexibility in international alliances and a pragmatic – that is low-cost – involvement in world politics, except where Russia's most vital interests were concerned. Although Russia had limited resources to pursue a grand foreign policy, Primakov's thinking was, counterintuitively, that the country had to pursue an "active" foreign policy (*aktivnaya vneshnyaya politika*)[21] to compensate for its currently limited resources in reforming the economy and preserving its territorial integrity. He believed that Russia was in a geopolitically dangerous environment and simply could not afford to concentrate on purely domestic issues. In relations with the West, Primakov insisted that Russia had to engage in balancing tactics against the strongest, the United States, to facilitate the emergence of a multipolar world. He argued that the unipolar world was not going to be liberal or democratic, despite American promises, and that Russia should not succumb to the rhetoric of the strongest. Instead, it must use a combination of both cooperation and balancing policies for the purpose of undermining that unipolarity. In the minister's own words,

Russia is both Europe and Asia, and this geopolitical location continues to play a tremendous role in formulation of its foreign policy. Its [geopolitical interests] include China, India, and Japan, and not just the United States or Europe. They also include the Middle East and the "Third World." Without such geopolitical scope, Russia cannot continue to be a great power and to play the positive role it has been destined to play. In building relationships with all these countries, one

Table 11.1. *Russia and Ex-Republics: Ethnic and Linguistic Dependencies*

	Ethnic Russians (Percentage of Population in 1989)	Fluency in Russian by Titular Nationality (Percentage of Population in 1989)
Armenia	1.6	44.3
Azerbaijan	5.6	31.7
Belarus	13.2	60.4
Estonia	30.3	33.6
Georgia	6.3	31.8
Latvia	33.9	65.7
Lithuania	9.4	37.4
Moldova	12.9	53.3
Kazakhstan	37.8	62.9
Kyrgyzstan	21.5	36.9
Tajikistan	7.6	30.0
Turkmenistan	9.5	27.6
Ukraine	22.1	59.5
Uzbekistan	8.4	22.2

Sources: Smith, *Post-Soviet States*, 36.

must remember that geopolitical values are constant and cannot be abolished by historical developments.[22]

Primakov also believed that Russia could not afford culturally isolationist policies and had to respond to the identity void left after the Soviet disintegration. Some twenty-five million Russians found themselves outside the "homeland" with which they continued to identify. Many non-Russian nationalities too identified with Russia, and not the new nationalist regimes in the former Soviet states (Table 11.1 summarizes the linguistic and cultural dependencies between Russia and the other former republics). As early as in his 1994 Foreign Intelligence Report, Primakov directly linked the fate of the Russians in the former USSR to the survival and prosperity of Russia. Inside Russia, many also could not accept the country's new national identity and continued to favor the preservation of strong cultural ties across the post-Soviet world. Polls indicated that most Russians supported voluntary reunification of the ex-republics with Russia. For instance, in December 1997, 61 percent of Russian citizens were sorry that the USSR had collapsed – an increase from 33 percent in December 1992. At the same time, most respondents did not approve of military intervention to integrate the former Soviet

Table 11.2. *Russia's Government Revenue and Expenditure, 1992–8 (% of GDP)*

	1992	1993	1994	1995	1996	1997	1998
Revenue	15.6	13.7	11.8	12.2	13.0	11.9	10.2
Expenditure	26	20.2	23.2	17.6	22.0	18.9	16.1

Source: Gould-Davies and Woods, "Russia and the IMF," 15.

region and were convinced that the only way to recovery was through successful development of the Russian economy.[23]

Russia's domestic conditions were dismal because of territorial disintegration, civil war in the Caucasus, and economic breakdown. Russia was confronted with growing challenges of secessionism and instability in one of its key southern regions, Chechnya. Yeltsin's failure to respond to Chechnya's announcement of independence in 1991, as well as the largely political nature of his decision to intervene in late 1994, contributed to a long and bloody confrontation. For Yeltsin, the military intervention was an attempt to divert public attention from the failure to meet his promises to improve or, at least, sustain the living standards of ordinary Russians. Partly as a reaction to Yeltsin's opportunism, the public remained largely skeptical of his military intervention. With little support at home, the army was unable to resolve the conflict by force, and disorder and terrorism increasingly spread throughout Chechnya and beyond.

In the meantime, the real income of ordinary Russians, most of whom were wage earners and pensioners, fell drastically, and the economy shrank considerably (see Table 3.3). By the time Primakov assumed office, Russia's foreign debt and domestic budget deficit had greatly increased. Its largest foreign debt payment was due in 1999, when Russia had to pay $17.5 billion to the IMF; its total domestic budget at the time was around $20 billion.[24] The budget deficit – primarily the result of the government's inability to collect taxes – was consistently large from the beginning of Yeltsin's economic reforms (see Table 11.2).

The government was desperate to find non-inflationary ways to reduce the deficit and to restructure and reschedule its growing debt. Yet room for political maneuvering was severely limited, and the government continued the practice of borrowing from the IMF. In its turn, the IMF imposed restrictive conditions in an effort to secure a more politically compliant Russia. For all of IMF's talk about depoliticized relations with countries-recipients, the political side of the IMF–Russia relationship was always visible. For example, its 1995–6 loan was negotiated in the context of the approaching presidential elections, in which Yeltsin's victory was the number one priority for the West. The Western intervention in Yugoslavia – against which Russia objected vehemently – took place as the Russian government was in the process of negotiating the restructuring of the approaching $17.5 billion payment.[25]

After assuming the responsibilities of prime minister, Primakov realized ever more painfully the difficulties of maintaining a posture of independence; even with what was considered to be a "leftist government," he had to submit to the State Duma a tight budget and to fully comply with the IMF conditions.

Internal Supporters

An overwhelming majority of Russia's political class welcomed Primakov's vision and the change in policy that stemmed from it. Members of the new coalition of support included the military industries, army, and security services, which saw the largely ignored potential to generate revenue through the development of new technologies and the export of conventional weapons. In one of its documents, the influential nongovernmental organization Council on Foreign and Defense Policy expressed an attitude typical of these circles, when it described the military-industrial complex as "a key, possibly, the key factor of Russia's struggle for a dignified place in the twenty-first century."[26] Over time, the Russian large security class grew in strength and was able to challenge the emerging and still nascent commercial class that promoted the Westernist component of Russia's identity. In addition to the security class, those constituencies that opposed the expansion of NATO on culturally essentialist grounds supported Primakov's course. Some advocated a cultural unity of Slavs and Muslims, whereas Russian ethnonationalists promoted the primacy of the Russian language and religion in the region. The Congress of Russian Communities, for example, proclaimed Russia responsible for Russian speakers in the former Soviet republics – a view later adopted by Yeltsin himself.

In this context of growing security threats, the insistence on viewing Russia as first and foremost a great power resonated with elites and the larger society. Primakov and his supporters did not see the forces of international cooperation as shaping world politics. They appealed to the historical notion of Russia as a *Derzhava* – an especially common term in the defensive honor vocabulary – which can be loosely translated as an entity that can influence the international power equilibrium. A *Derzhava* is capable of defending itself by relying on its own individual strength, and its main goal should be preservation of that status. To cultural nationalists, the term *derzhava* implied the ability to protect the national unity of the state. Although many Primakov supporters were former Westernizers, they no longer agreed that Russia was becoming a part of the West and argued that the country had its own interests to defend.

That NATO expanded without including Russia was incomprehensible in the light of Russia's historical commitments, its new relationships with the Western countries, and the West's own promises not to expand the alliance. Many Russians felt deceived, because the expansion followed Gorbachev's military withdrawals from Eastern Europe, Kozyrev's restriction of some profitable arms sales to comply with Western rules, and Russia's commitment to develop a strategic partnership with the West. Overwhelmingly, the Russian foreign policy community perceived the expansion as a violation of the norm of reciprocity and the very spirit of the post–Cold War transformation. Eventually, even radical Westernizers, such as Kozyrev, expressed their disillusionment. The general public, too, expressed concerns, which only increased over time. As former U.S. Defense Secretary William Perry put it, Russian reactions to NATO expansion "ranged from being unhappy to being very unhappy . . . This is a very widely and very deeply held view in Russia."[27]

Historical parallels between the new course and the notion of Gorchakov's "concentration" were widely accepted in scholarly and political circles. In 1998, an annual conference for scholars and practitioners to debate current foreign policy, established at the Moscow Institute of International Relations, was named after Gorchakov. In 2001 Primakov was awarded the State Gorchakov Commemorative Medal for "outstanding service in strengthening peace and promoting international cooperation."

The new course's pragmatic nature found strong support. Although virtually all statists wanted Russia to become one of the five great powers in the world – along with Germany, France, Japan, and China – most elites warned against attempts to organize foreign policy around resistance to the global influence of the United States.[28] In fact, some questioned the notion of the multipolar world as the guiding vision of the international system.[29]

Alternative Explanations

Alternative accounts of Russia's attempts to contain NATO expansion are either insufficient or incorrect. Defensive realists would be wrong to expect Russia, as a weak state, to bandwagon with a more powerful state or alliance of states. "Defeated" in the Cold War, instead Russia pursued a policy of balancing – however successful – with the powerful Western alliance. Nor was Russia as a power satisfied with the results of the post–Cold War international bargain. Instead, just as Gorchakov's Russia meant to revise the conditions of the Paris treaty, Primakov's Russia had every intention of returning to world politics as a great power with its own sphere of influence.[30]

That expectation did not mean, however, as some Western observers argue, that Russia intended to use the West to restore its weakened power capabilities and to rebuild its empire.[31] To argue this is to confuse pragmatic great power ambitions with Soviet-like imperial grandeur. It is also to ascribe one's own hegemonic viewpoint to policy makers, who made sense of the world in largely defensive categories of reviving great power capabilities in a multipolar world. The earlier cited evidence of Russia's material weakness demonstrates its inability to resist the encroachment of the Western military alliance.

Both defensive realist and imperialist perspectives also do not sufficiently take seriously what Primakov defined as the "psychological" dimension of the expansion of NATO. The notions of dignity, fairness, and equality were critical to the discourse of the Kremlin in dealing with the West. Primakov insisted that the principle of absolute power equality must be honored in each instance of cooperation not because he believed that NATO was presenting a serious military threat to Russia, but because he worried that Russia's status would be otherwise downgraded and it would be unfit to deliver on its obligations in the future. Primakov's insistence on upholding the power of the United Nations as the key agency for defining and enforcing the rules of international conduct and his efforts to develop close ties with influential states outside the Western hemisphere, such as China and India, can also be understood in terms of preserving the principles of fairness and equality in world politics. The minister was careful not to isolate Russia from the mainstream international politics centered at the UN Security Council. As a permanent member of the Security Council, Russia planned to exercise its voting power as it saw fit, while at the same time contributing to world peace and stability as a member of the world "concert of great powers." Primakov and his supporters saw these elements as critical to establishing a multipolar world order and containing the power of the West, particularly the United States.

The issue was not merely one of external honor or prestige, as in the neoclassical realist vocabulary, because Primakov's policy had important domestic constituencies outside the state elites. Combined, the Russian-language-influenced community totaled about 30 percent of the population of the non-Russian post-Soviet states, which made Russia, as one scholar acknowledged, "not simply a marginal *national* European state, but a potential center of a revived, distinct *civilization*."[32] In attempting to assist ethnic Russians in their accommodation in new states, the Kremlin promoted the idea of dual citizenship in the former Soviet states, viewing it as an alternative to providing direct support for Russians abroad advocated by the hard-line opposition. However, the idea did not prove viable, and by 1995 all the post-Soviet states, with the exception of Turkmenistan and Tajikistan, had rejected dual citizenship.

Assessment

Despite its similarity to the policy of recueillement in the second half of the nineteenth century, the policy of containing NATO was more ambitious but not nearly as successful.

However, Primakov's policy did have some successes. In addition to brokering peace in Moldova and Tajikistan, negotiating the Big Treaty with Ukraine, and working hard to improve ties with the countries of Asia and the Asian Pacific region, the minister could also be credited for making progress in Russia's negotiations with NATO. Despite several setbacks in the relationship, Russia developed a mechanism of permanent consultations with the alliance and obtained a written commitment not to deploy nuclear weapons or substantial new forces in the territory of new member states.

Primakov also restored some attributes of foreign policy autonomy. Although Russia continued to be highly dependent on the West in economic affairs, it made Washington more attentive to its national interests in the area of security. On issues such as arms sales and security in Yugoslavia, Primakov took a much tougher line than his predecessor, who, in the words of one journalist, "had corrupted Americans" by his willingness to follow in Washington's footsteps.[33] Both the elites and the general public expressed their strong support for the new course, welcoming the greater independence.

As analysts have acknowledged, Primakov accomplished these positive changes despite Russia's continuous economic decline from 1992–7 and lack of balancing options. In the former Soviet region, one scholar noted, "Despite the sharp decline of its power, Russia has been far more successful and far less reticent in asserting its interests in the southern Near Abroad than is generally acknowledged."[34] Another realist scholar was surprised to note that the weak Russia showed "a capacity to extract concessions"[35] in relations with the West. Policy activism from a position of weakness suggests yet again the limitations of realism as an interpretive tool for understanding Primakov's foreign policy. Rather than being driven by material power alone, that policy was a response to a particular combination of political and cultural international and domestic factors.

At the same time, Primakov's vision – although shaped largely by the same defensive honor perspective – proved to be insufficiently specific and unnecessarily expensive. Although pro-Western critics of the NATO expansion policy challenged the relevance of Gorchakov to contemporary foreign policy,[36] Primakov's course was much more ambitious. The task of containing NATO and building a multipolar world did not merit the valuable material and political resources devoted to it. Such a preoccupation was not pragmatic and, despite Primakov's own convictions, bore only a superficial resemblance to Aleksandr Gorchakov's strategy. Rather than "concentrating" on domestic economic and social revival, as that earlier strategy had prescribed, Primakov's Russia occupied itself with balancing the West and integrating the periphery (also in the context of balancing the West). The central thrust of his view of Russia's national interest – as a contributor to balancing U.S. unipolar ambitions in the world – was misguided. It is important to note that Primakov acted under conditions of unipolarity – a major structural difference from the nineteenth-century multipolar structure of the European politics. If Russia would ever succeed in building a multipolar world – the role assigned to it by its second foreign minister – it would have to take place in a different era and under different circumstances.

Primakov's failures to assert his vision in Europe – as well as his uninspiring attempts to establish a strategic triangle of Russia, China, and India to contain U.S. global hegemony – are cases in point. The potential for developing bilateral ties with China, Iran, and India was there, but in a world of unipolarity and global economic interdependence, none of these countries was eager to enter into the balancing coalition Russia sought. In the end, Yeltsin and Primakov were not willing to go too far in testing the United States' patience.

No more successful was the project of reintegrating the former Soviet region, which proved to be driven too much by geopolitical concerns and not sufficiently by economic grounds. Most multilateral CIS-based economic agreements were not working properly, and the former Soviet states continued to drift apart. Most also rejected Russia's economic, political, and cultural initiatives.[37] Several regional initiatives emerged without Russia's participation. Faced with Primakov's vision of reintegration in the former Soviet region, the Russian private sector was not willing to invest accordingly in the former USSR. The energy companies, for example, had grown strong by the time the integration strategy was implemented. Although interested in expanding to the former Soviet space and maintaining its stability, the energy entrepreneurs did not want to subsidize the former republics or supply them energy at lower prices in exchange for political loyalty to the Russian state. Despite some serious efforts on Russia's part, the results of integration left much to be desired. Post-Soviet integration did not provide the Russian economy with new opportunities for growth, attract any foreign investment, or relieve the burden of foreign debt.[38]

Nor did the new foreign policy strategy make serious progress in improving Russia's cultural well-being. The fact that Russia was going through an identity crisis was obvious to policy makers and observers alike. Symptomatic of this crisis was the discussion about Russia's new "national idea" that Yeltsin initiated immediately following his 1996 reelection as president. Primakov addressed the crisis by proposing a Eurasianist foreign policy orientation of building strategic relations with China, Iraq, and India. His cooperation with the West was merely pragmatic, as opposed to strategic, and NATO's intervention in Yugoslavia further pushed Russia away from the West. Yet the Westernist component of Russia's cultural identity had been confirmed by Russia's post-Soviet developments, and many Russians continued to identify with the West. The strategy of Eurasia-oriented containment of the Western alliance was not successful in addressing this part of the Russian national psyche.

Notes

1 Primakov, "The World on the Eve of the 21st Century," 3.
2 For analysis of the decision to expand NATO and Russia's reaction to it, see Goldgeier, *Not Whether.*
3 "The Need for a New Ostpolitik," *Financial Times,* January 16, 1996.
4 Yevgeni Primakov's presentation at the conference "Preobrazhennaya Rossiya" held at Moscow Institute of International Relations in 1992 (*Mezhdunarodnaya zhizn'* 3–4, 1992, 104).
5 National Security Concepts and Foreign Policy Concepts are available in Shakleyina, ed., *Vneshnyaya politika i bezopasnost' sovremennoi Rossiyi,* pp. 51–90, 110–11. For analysis, see Kassianova, "Russia: Still Open to the West?"
6 For other analyses of Russia's perspective on NATO expansion, see Antonenko, "Russia, NATO and European Security after Kosovo"; Black, *Russia Faces NATO Expansion*; Smith, *Russia and NATO since 1991;* Braun, *NATO-Russia Relations in the Twenty-First Century.*
7 As cited in Mlechin, *Ministry inostrannykh del,* p. 620.
8 The decision-making point became a contentious one. Contrary to Russia's expectations, the Founding Act did not give Russia the veto power it sought, which the subsequent intervention in the Balkans demonstrated all too painfully.

9 Lynch, "Realism of Russian Foreign Policy," 15, 28.

10 Antonenko, "Russia, NATO and European Security," 143.

11 Pushkov, "Sindrom Chernomyrdina."

12 Donaldson and Nogee, *The Foreign Policy of Russia*, p. 316.

13 *Rossiyskaya gazeta*, February 17, 1995, 5. Yeltsin's change of perception toward a more hegemonic role of Russia can be traced to the early 1994 TV interview, in which he called Russia "the first among equals" in the post-Soviet region.

14 *Rossiyskaya gazeta*, September 23, 1995; Primakov, "Rossiya v mirovoi politike," 11.

15 Webber, *CIS Integration Trends*, pp. 13–14.

16 See, for example, Rutland, "Mission Impossible?"; Gould-Davies and Ngaire Woods, "Russia and the IMF"; Black, *Russia Faces NATO Expansion*.

17 In addition, some influential foreign policy experts in the West spoke of "the premature partnership" with Russia. See, for example, Brzezinski, "The Premature Partnership."

18 Fukuyama, "The End of History?"

19 Huntington, "The Clash of Civilizations?"

20 As cited in Primakov, "Rossiya v mirovoi politike." For a more extended analysis, see Splidsboel-Hansen, "Past and Future Meet."

21 Primakov, *Gody v bol'shoi politike*, pp. 213, 217–21.

22 Primakov, Presentation at the conference "Preobrazhennaya Rossiya," 104.

23 The poll data are from Simes, *After the Collapse*, p. 220 and Birgerson, *After the Breakup of a Multi-Ethnic Empire*, p. 88.

24 Sakwa, *Russian Politics and Society*, p. 294.

25 Some Statists linked the two events directly. See, for example, Pushkov, "Otrezvlyayuschaya yasnost."

26 "Strategiya Rossiyi v XXI veke."

27 As cited in MacFarlane, "Realism and Russian Strategy after the Collapse of the USSR," 242.

28 The critics were communists and Eurasianists who advocated a more radical anti-Western foreign policy course and dreamed of restoring Russia's super-power status. For instance, some in the Ministry of Defense, such as General Leonid Ivashev, harbored such ambitions; see his article "Rossiya mozhet snova stat' sverkhderzhavoi." This group complained about the lack of radicalism in Primakov's vision and argued for a politico-economic autarchy and establishment of an independent Eurasian power. Dugin, "Yevraziyski proyekt"; Zyuganov, *Geografiya pobedy*.

29 For instance, Aleksei Bogaturov proposed vieweing the post–Cold War international system as a "pluralistic unipolarity" in which the unipolar center is a group of responsible states, rather than one state (the United States). Bogaturov saw Russia as a member of the group and argued for consolidation of its position within the global center, as well as for discouraging the formation of one-state unipolarity in the world. Bogaturov, "Pluralisticheskaya odnopolyarnost' i interesy Rossiyi"; Bogaturov, "Amerika i Rossiya."

30 For similar arguments, see Splidsboel-Hansen, "Past and Future Meet"; Mac-Farlane, "Realism and Russian Strategy"; Lynch, "Realism of Russian Foreign Policy."

31 The earliest case with such an interpretation of Russia's early post–Soviet foreign policy was made by Brzezinski, "The Premature Partnership."

32 Zevelev, *Russia and Its New Diaspora*, p. 175.

33 *Izvestiya* correspondent Stanislav Kondrashev, as quoted in Mlechin, *Ministry inostrannykh del*, p. 607.

34 Menon, "After Empire: Russia and the Southern 'Near Abroad,'" 148.

35 MacFarlane, "Realism and Russian Strategy, 244.

36 Fedorov, "Krizis vneshnei politiki Rossiyi."

37 For details, see Zevelev, *Russia and Its New Diaspora* and Tsygankov, *Russia's Foreign Policy*.

38 At a later stage, some of Primakov's supporters acknowledged this and withdrew their support for the strategy of post-Soviet integration. For instance, Andranik Migranian, once a prominent critic of Kozyrev's isolationism and a promoter of Russia's "Monroe doctrine" in the former Soviet area, now saw the CIS-centered integration as too costly and argued against Russia's remaining a leader in such integration. Migranyan, "Rasstavaniye s illuziyami." A new consensus soon emerged that found Primakov's vision of a multipolar world to be outdated, financially expensive, and potentially confrontational. Instead, the authors proposed the concept of "selective engagement," which they – again – compared with Russia's nineteenth-century policy after its defeat in the war with Crimea and with China's policy since Deng Xiaoping. Regarding the former Soviet area, the authors recommended a "considerable revision" of policy, which would involve abandoning the "pseudo-integration at Russia's expense" and "tough defense of our national economic interests." *Strategiya dlya Rossiyi.*

Part IV

Honor and Assertiveness

12   The Crimean War, 1853–1856

"Nothing is left to me, but to fight, to win, or to perish with honor, *as a martyr of our holy faith.*"

Nicholas I[1]

The War

The Ottoman Decline

The Vienna system of international relations did not include the Ottoman Empire, and each member of the Concert of Europe had its own way of regulating relations with the Ottomans. Russia followed the route of fighting multiple wars with Turkey and gradually developing a range of complex treaties to satisfy its interests in the East. A Christian and a conservative power, Russia wanted to protect the rights of millions of Christians within the Ottoman Empire, but not at the expense of destabilizing Constantinople politically. On a number of occasions, both Alexander and Nicholas had opportunities to undermine the Ottomans, but refused to challenge them over the rights of Christians.[2]

Several of Russia's treaties with Turkey deserve mention. By defeating Turkey in 1739, Russia gained access to the Black Sea through the Treaty of Belgrade. The Peace of Kuchuk Kainardzhi of 1774 and the Treaty of Jassy of 1792 solidified Russia's control over Azov and the Crimea in the coastal area. The Treaty of Kuchuk Kainardzhi also provided Russia with special rights to protect Orthodox Christians within the Ottoman Empire. Although these rights were not clearly defined,[3] Article 7 obligated the Porte to "give the Christian faith and its churches protection," and it granted "the Ministries of the Russian Imperial Court [the right] to protect all interests of the church built in Constantinople." Article 8 further stipulated the rights of subjects of the Russian Empire to freely travel to the "holy city of Jerusalem and other solemn places" and not to be subject to any form of taxation or payment.[4] From 1828–9 Nicholas fought another war with Turkey; the resulting Treaty of Adrianople gave

Russia control over southern Bessarabia and thereby greater influence over the Balkans. A few years later the Tsar intervened on behalf of the Sultan in suppressing Mehemed Ali's rebellion in Egypt. In response, the grateful Sultan signed in 1833 the Treaty of Unkiar Skelessi, which made the two empires into allies. In recognition of Russia's interests, a secret article of this treaty closed the Straits of the Bosporus and the Dardanelles to foreign warships in exchange for freeing Turkey from the obligation to provide military assistance to Russia.[5]

Around the same time as it was engaging in these various wars and treaties with Turkey, Russia developed a general understanding with the European powers regarding the Ottoman Empire. St. Petersburg viewed its objectives in the East as fully consistent with the Holy Alliance's obligations, and Russian tsars worked to explain to the outside world that they did not have any revisionist designs. In 1841 Russia and other European powers signed the Straits Convention reaffirming their agreement with Turkey. Nicholas also worked with individual countries to achieve a common understanding of the Eastern question. For instance, he traveled to London in 1844 to discuss the issue with Lord Aberdeen, the British foreign secretary, assuring him that Russia was keenly interested in keeping the Ottoman Empire stable for as long as possible.[6] Nicholas made clear that he wanted not a single inch of Turkey, but that he would also not allow anyone else to have it.[7]

However, the Ottoman Empire was progressively weakening on its own. Since 1828, it had experienced three attempts to assert power by Mehemed Ali, and in 1839–40 the European powers had to undertake a concerted intervention against Ali to prevent the empire's further disintegration and guarantee its territorial integrity. From Russia's perspective, the fact that Turkey was the "sick man" of Europe – as Nicholas referred to it[8] – meant the need to prepare for an unpleasant future. Russia had to guarantee the rights of millions of Orthodox Christians, preserve the closure of the Straits, and secure its position as a great power under changing international conditions. On the issue of Orthodox Christians, St. Petersburg could hardly afford "inaction in the Balkans," despite its loyalty to the Holy Alliance's principles.[9] With Greece gaining independence in 1829, inaction would have meant the growing radicalization of nationalities inside both Turkey and Russia. In addition, the Tsar had to face the ideologically opposing impulses of pan-Slavic and pan-Orthodox pressures at home.[10] The Russians had legitimate security reasons to refer to the Straits as "the key to our own house,"[11] so keeping them closed was too vital an objective to be left to uncertainty.

In addition, the decline of Turkey had the strong potential to serve as a catalyst for a renewed rivalry among European states for power and resources in the Near East. Britain was never satisfied with the Concert of Europe and sought to play a hegemonic role in international relations by ousting Russia from its position in the East.[12] Britain's role was critical, and some scholars claim that, if it were not for the rivalry between Britain and Russia, "the [Crimean] war would have not taken place."[13] British elites and the general public also harbored a strong animosity toward Russia, stemming from the latter's suppression of Poland in 1830 and other European nationalities in 1848–9. France had experienced a change in power, and the new Emperor Napoleon III was looking to enhance his international prestige, possibly at the expense of Turkey and Russia.[14] Russia's relationship with France, which had been difficult since the establishment of the Vienna system, further worsened with Nicholas's refusal to recognize the elected Louis Napoleon as his equal.[15] Austria had its own reasons to resent Russia's position in the European international relations, which had to do with St. Petersburg's influence in the Balkans.[16]

Nicholas's Perception and Strategic Objectives

These cultural and geopolitical considerations shaped Nicholas's perception of the situation developing in the East. Managing Russia's double commitment to Orthodox Christians and the Holy Alliance was proving to be a challenge, and Nicholas's way of doing so was different from that of his brother Alexander.

When France insisted on its exclusive right to protect Christian holy places in Jerusalem and Palestine, Nicholas found himself in a difficult situation. This issue, as well as the status of Christians in the Ottoman Empire, was far more important to Russia than to France. More than a third of the empire's population was Orthodox Christians – approximately thirteen million people – compared to a much smaller share of Catholic population in the Ottoman Empire. In addition, a large number of Orthodox pilgrims from Russia and abroad visited the holy places in Palestine.[17] To Nicholas, a truly devout churchgoer and a genuine believer in Russia's religious authority, protecting the Orthodox pilgrims had enormous significance. The Tsar was convinced of the absolute moral superiority of his country and the ethical obligations it entailed. His entire system of ruling was based on the principle of "Orthodoxy," and he justified all his domestic and international actions in the name of religion.[18] Nicholas therefore had no choice but to respond to the Sultan's decision to grant the Catholic Church special privileges to the holy places. He could not ignore the revolts of the "Orthodox community at Jerusalem, Constantinople, and even Petrograd against the treachery of the Sultan, who appeared to have made the Tsar ridiculous."[19]

Yet few rulers in Europe saw themselves as committed to the Holy Alliance's principles as Nicholas. He proved his commitment by not hesitating to intervene in Europe and even Turkey in defense of the conservative autocratic order and in suppression of revolutionary nationalist movements. In the 1820s, he was infuriated by Greek claims of independence and supported the Sultan's legitimacy even though Turkey was never a member of the Holy Alliance.[20] He went to war with the Ottoman Empire in 1828 in an effort to uphold his special relations with the Balkan Christians and to strike a new balance between his commitments to Orthodox Christians and the Holy Alliance. To avoid stark choices between the two commitments – his brother Alexander faced such a choice in 1821 – Nicholas advocated a more activist role for Russia within the Alliance. To support the Balkan Christians, he believed in the occasional necessity to act unilaterally and dictate to Europe the policies that he thought "were in Europe's best interests."[21] In 1826, the Tsar stated his views on the issue as follows:

I will be happy to reach an agreement with all of my allies on this question... [But] if they cannot or will not act in concert with me and thus force me to it, then my behavior will be absolutely different from that of the Emperor Alexander and I will consider it my duty to put an end to the matter.... I want peace in the East. Indeed, I need peace.... But, let me repeat: if even one of my allies should betray me, then I will be obliged to act alone and you can be certain that this will not trouble me in the least.[22]

Therefore, Nicholas's synthesis between the two foreign policy commitments was in favor of the Holy Alliance, but on Russia's terms. Europe was to support Russia's Christian policies in the Ottoman Empire, so long as Russia had no intentions of politically undermining the Porte or conquering it. Nicholas was consistent in advocating this philosophy and never seriously considered grand plans of advancing to Constantinople or partitioning Turkey without Europe's support.[23]

By choosing to challenge the Sultan on the issue of the holy places, Nicholas sought to achieve a diplomatic, not military victory over Turkey. He expected the major powers in Europe to support him, because he believed he was acting to return the Ottoman principalities to the European Concert. The Tsar's objectives were that "all the Christian parts of Turkey must necessarily become independent, must become again what they [formerly] were, principalities, Christian states, as such reenter the family of the Christian states of Europe."[24] The statement captures all three dimensions of Russia's complex definition of honor – commitment to the Christian European order, to fellow Orthodox Christians, and to great power prestige.

In terms of practical policies, Nicholas first invoked the old Kuchuk Kainardzhi treaty to remind the Sultan of his obligations to the empire's Orthodox Christians. This was done partly in response to France's reference to the even older 1740 treaty that it had concluded with Turkey over the holy places.[25] In 1853, in addition to sending Prince Alexander Menshikov to deliver Russia's demands to the Sultan, Nicholas also designed a three-stage plan for pressuring the Ottomans: occupation of the Christian principalities, the Austrian occupation of Bosnia-Herzegovina and Serbia, and a Russian blockade of the Bosporus. If these actions were not effective, then the fourth stage would be Turkey's partition by way of joint Austro-Russian recognition of the independence of Moldavia, Wallachia, and Serbia.[26] Nicholas, however, did not believe the last stage would be necessary, and even when war seemed unavoidable, the Russian ambassador to Vienna, Alexander Gorchakov, stated Russia's objectives in April 1854 in the same nonrevisionist way: "to reaffirm on a solid basis the religious immunities of our brothers of the Orthodox Church."[27]

From the Near Eastern to the European War

Subsequent events demonstrated that Britain and Austria neither understood nor shared Nicholas's position. The Tsar's first attempt to clarify his stance to British officials in 1844 elicited a reserved, albeit not explicitly disapproving, reaction from London.[28] In early 1853, Nicholas resumed his diplomatic efforts by holding a series of conversations with the British ambassador to St. Petersburg, Sir George Hamilton Seymour, assuring him of Russia's commitment to maintain the Ottoman Empire. Seymour's reaction was favorable until Nicholas broached the possibility of the empire's disintegration and proposed a partition scheme should Russia and Britain's joint effort to save the "sick man" prove insufficient. When the Tsar spoke of extending Russia's protectorate to the Danubian principalities of Serbia and Bulgaria in exchange for British control over Egypt and Crete, Seymour became suspicious.[29] After Nicholas mentioned his belief that Austria fully supported his position, Seymour and others in Aberdeen's cabinet interpreted the Tsar's speculations as being his actual plans and spoke of the need to thwart Russia's ambitions.[30]

In February 1853 Nicholas, a believer in tough diplomacy, sent Menshikov to Turkey with the mandate to coerce the Sultan into accepting Russia's conditions: settling the Holy Land dispute in Russia's favor and explicitly recognizing the rights of Orthodox Christians to visit the holy places. The Tsar assumed that Britain would not interfere, and the

Sultan would have little choice but to accept Russia's conditions. Britain, however, was of two minds. Although the more moderate members of Aberdeen's cabinet advocated for no interference, the anti-Russian hawks, such as then-Home Secretary Lord Henry Temple Palmerston and the ambassador in Constantinople Stratford Canning, lobbied on the Sultan's behalf to characterize Russia's conditions as an infringement of Turkish sovereignty.[31] It was actually Canning, rather than a Turkish official, who responded first to Menshikov's ultimatum.[32] Canning also convinced the Grand Vizier to dismiss Mehemet Ali in favor of Rechid Pasha, who refused to accept Russia's references to the Kuchuk Kainardzhi treaty.[33] Indeed, so close was British involvement in Russian-Turkish negotiations that Menshikov later wrote to Nesselrode, "There, my dear Count, is what the British agents have the effrontery to call the independence of the Turkish government."[34]

After the failure of Menshikov's mission, events progressed to the course of war. Learning about the Sultan's refusal to comply with Russia's conditions, Nicholas described himself as having felt "the five fingers on the Sultan on his cheek."[35] In response, the Tsar moved to stage one of his plan by ordering the occupation of Moldavia and Wallachia. In the meantime, Britain and France moved their fleets to Besika Bay, preparing to pass through the Dardanelles and then the Bosporus. Austria, Russia's trusted ally, acted against Nicholas's expectations. Rather than siding with St. Petersburg, Vienna proclaimed a policy of armed neutrality and attempted to mediate between Russia and Turkey.[36] Soon after that policy failed to produce the desired results and Turkey declared war on Russia in October 1853, Austria could no longer hide its interests in the Balkans. In June 1854, the Austrian government concluded a convention with the Ottomans on the joint Austrian-Turkish occupation of Wallachia and Austria's sole occupation of Moldavia.[37]

The war therefore moved beyond being about Turkey or the Balkans. With other European powers involved, it quickly obtained the status of a general European war. As A. J. P. Taylor wrote, "the real stake in the Crimean war was not Turkey. . . . The Crimean war was fought to remake the European system."[38]

The Defeat of Russia

That Russia's military capabilities were sufficient for defeating Turkey was evident not only in Admiral Nakhimov's overwhelming victory over the Turkish Black Sea fleet in the harbor of Sinope in November 1853 but also in important victories in the Caucasus. On August 5, 1854, General Bebutov defeated the main Ottoman army of the Caucasus front, which suffered 8,000 casualties and 2,000 prisoners against Russia's 3,000 casualties. The victory impressed the Persian government enough for it to sign a neutrality treaty with Russia.[39] Even after the final defeat in Sevastopol in September 1855, Russians won an important battle against Turks in the Caucasus by seizing Kars in November 1855.

However, Nicholas could not fight the war alone against major European powers for very long. France and Britain entered the Black Sea in January 1854, and in February they called on Russia to evacuate the principalities by April 30. In March they established a triple alliance of Britain, France, and Turkey, declaring war on Russia. Although the most decisive military developments took place in the Crimea, Russia had to face the enemy on three additional fronts – the Caucasus, the Baltics, and the Balkans. Fighting in the Balkans proved especially distracting: during the time it took to move his regular troops from the central part of Russia to the Crimea, Nicholas could have only used the roughly 20,000 troops he kept in the principalities. In addition, despite the large size of the Russian army – 1.8 million regular troops – only about 100,000 could be deployed to defend Sevastopol, the most important battle in the war.[40] Other troops were deployed elsewhere to defend various regions of the vast empire. Sevastopol fought bravely, holding out for some eight months, but eventually fell because of insufficient supplies[41] and the heavy bombardment of the European armies. In the meantime, the anti-Russian coalition kept expanding, as Palmerston was opposing any peace with Nicholas and publicizing his plans for partitioning Russia with portions of its territories to go to Prussia, Sweden, Turkey, and Austria.[42] In January 1856, presented with the Austrian ultimatum to negotiate, Russia accepted it unconditionally.

Unable to continue with the war, Russia had to accept harsh conditions for peace at the Paris congress.[43] Russia lost its rights to have fortifications and a fleet in the Black Sea and to protect Orthodox Christians in the principalities and the rest of the Ottoman Empire.[44] Although Palmerston did not have his way and Russia faced no threat of political destruction, Britain succeeded in destroying the Concert of Europe and the role that Russia had played in it. The Paris congress delivered a crushing blow to Russia's reputation as a Christian protector in the Balkans and to its prestige as a great power. Nesselrode called the defeat a national humiliation of the first order.[45] Russia was no longer viewed as a major European power, because it now "carried less weight in European affairs than any time since the end of the Great Northern war in 1721."[46] In addition, as a Russian historian wrote, "the entire southern border Russia in the Black Sea area was revealed as defenseless."[47]

The Crimean War, 1853–1856: Timeline

1852 December	Sultan grants France special privileges to the Holy Places
1853 January	Nicholas's conversation with the English ambassador
March–May	Menshikov's mission to the Sultan
June	British and French fleets arrive at Besika Bay
July	Russia moves to occupy the Romanian principalities
August	Proposal of the Austrian foreign minister Count Buol
September	Britain rejects Buol's proposal
	British and French fleets pass through the Dardanelles
October	Sultan declares war on Russia and sends troops across the Danube
November	Nakhimov destroys Turkish fleet in Sinop
1854 January	Nicholas sends Count Orlov to Vienna
February	Britain and France give the Tsar an ultimatum to leave the principalities
March	Britain and France formally declare war on Russia
April	Austria and Prussia sign an alliance of neutrality
June	Austria negotiates with Turkey on the occupation of Wallachia and Moldavia
July	Russia defeats Turkey in the Caucasus
August	Russia withdraws from the principalities
September	Russia loses the Battle of Alma and begins fortification of Sevastopol
1855 March	Russia breaks off negotiations in Vienna
September	Russia orders destruction of ships and ammunition in Sevastopol
December	Austria gives Russia an ultimatum to stop fighting
1856 January	Russia accepts the Austrian ultimatum
February–April	Paris congress imposes conditions on Russia

Explaining the War

Europe's opposition to Russia's policies in the Balkans, combined with Nicholas's firm sense of moral confidence in his actions, produced the conditions for a political conflict that was ultimately resolved through the use of force.

Table 12.1. *Relative Economic Wealth of Britain and Other European Powers (%)*

	Britain	France	Russia	Austria	Prussia
1816	43	21	19	9	8
1820	48	18	18	9	7
1830	53	21	15	7	7
1840	64	16	9	6	5
1850	70	12	7	7	4

Source: Mearsheimer, *The Tragedy of Great Powers*, 71.

Europe's Opposition to Russia

Midcentury developments, especially the 1848–9 revolutions in Europe, revealed that the continent's powers were growing resentful of Russia. In 1849, as Palmerston noted, Russia and Britain were the only powers "standing upright,"[48] but it was Russia that emerged as politically dominant after suppressing the revolutions. However, Nicholas did not want to be viewed as the continent's hegemon, and after helping Austria and the Hapsburgs suppress revolts in Italy and Hungary, he quickly withdrew to Russia. Yet his assumption that there was sufficient support in Europe for the old Holy Alliance system and Russia's role in it was incorrect. As Evgeni Tarle wrote, Nicholas made three principal errors of judgment that put his country on the course to the Crimean war: he assumed that France was weakened by the 1848–9 events, he counted Austria as an ally, and he miscalculated the reaction of Britain.[49]

The most important opposition to Russia came from Britain. It stemmed from geopolitics, cultural suspicions, and the political makeup of the ruling establishment. Geopolitically, British elites struggled to dominate the continent and were never comfortable with the Concert of Europe developed under the leadership of Alexander I. Given its power, Britain's role in preserving the Concert was crucial, yet already in the 1830s Palmerston and others were devising schemes to strengthen their influence with the Ottoman Empire and to undermine Russia's position. "By 1853 there was little enthusiasm in Britain for Concert diplomacy."[50] In addition, the British economic presence in the Near East had been steadily growing since 1829, whereas Russia's was declining.[51] Table 12.1 summarizes the growth of British economic wealth relative to that of Russia and other European powers. Russia was a formidable military power and had a large regular army, but Britain had a clear advantage in the

Table 12.2. *Balance of Power before the Crimean War**

	Britain	France	Russia	Austria	Turkey
Steam power (1,000 HP)	1,290	270	20	20	
Pig iron (1,000 tons)	2,250	410	250	200	
Railways (miles)	6,635	1,994	410	1,008	
Export (mln. pounds)	71.3	49	14	11	
"Line" ships	81	29	42	0	6
Frigates	114	57	32	6	16
Naval "guns"	13,391	5,200	6,008		1,500
Soldiers	489**	450?	1,100	350?	220

* 1850 for economic and 1853 for military indicators.
** Includes British India.
Source: Goldfrank,[108] *The Origins of the Crimean War*, pp. 22, 37.

number of ships, frigates, and naval guns. Table 12.2 shows the European power balance before the Crimean War, illustrating the relationship between military performance and the health of the economy.[52]

British opposition to Russia also had its roots in cultural Russophobia that had begun to develop in the 1830s and had matured in the 1840s.[53] In the British public's mind, Nicholas's policies in the Near East and his suppression of the Polish revolt in the 1830s and of national revolutions in the 1840s were all indicators of Russia's naturally oppressive instincts. By 1848, the two nations' "ideological incompatibility" produced, in Martin Malia's expression, "a paroxysm of Russophobic rage as universal as the revolution itself."[54] Nicholas was widely hated as the "gendarme of Europe" and the leading oppressor of forces of liberty. Although official relations with Russia remained courteous, public opinion was increasingly galvanized by highly distorted coverage of Russia in the Britain media, which in turn began to influence official policy.[55] By the time that Nicholas demanded the Sultan's respect for Orthodox Christian rights in the Holy Lands, British public opinion had already turned against Russia. Incidents such as the battle of Sinop during the Crimean War caused new waves of anti-Russian and pro-Turkish feelings in British society.

These geopolitical and cultural factors caused shifts in the ruling elites' attitudes away from Russia, further complicating a search for cooperative solutions before and during the war. Palmerston and his supporters had had considerable influence on British policy since the 1830s, when they already began entertaining the idea of a decisive war with Russia. "The fact is that Russia is a great humbug," Palmerston wrote to his brother in 1835, "and that if England were fairly to go to work with her, we should throw her back half a century in one campaign."[56] The war faction within the British establishment also wanted to stir up nationalities within the Russian Empire to facilitate its dismemberment.[57] During the war, this faction opposed peace with Russia and insisted on fighting Nicholas until achieving the more ambitious objective of the dissolution of Russia. According to Palmerston's memorandum of September 1855, the true aims of the war required that Russia's territory be reduced or at least "hemmed in" by "a long line of circumvallation" – an equivalent of the containment policy.[58] Although Palmerston had moderate and non-interventionist opponents, such as Richard Cobden, Lord Aberdeen, and Lord Stanley,[59] the war polarized the British political spectrum, giving the advantage to the hawks. The already mentioned Sinop battle, for example, severely weakened the position of moderates in the British cabinet and strengthened the pro-war faction.[60]

The opposition of other European powers was also important, albeit less pronounced. Neither France nor Austria directly challenged the Concert, but they wanted a greater share of power and each in their own way was uncomfortable with the strong and assertive Russia. France sought to renegotiate its relations with Turkey and used the Holy Lands issue to increase its influence in the Near East. The newly elected French emperor Louis Napoleon also aimed to increase his popularity at home by posturing as a defender of the Roman Catholic faith. Austria too wanted greater influence, particularly in the Danubian principalities that had been largely controlled by Russia and were occupied by Nicholas in response to the failure of the Menshikov mission. Not uncomfortable with the Concert, Austria sought greater room for itself within the system. This explains why Vienna sided with the Porte on the issues of Wallachia and Moldavia, but also worked to develop peace proposals during the war and generated the ultimatum that ended the military conflict. Overall, as a historian wrote, "Russia's strength, or appearance of strength, proved to be a serious political liability, for it tended to make other countries even more fearful of Russia."[61]

Russia's Sense of Confidence

To Russia, Europe's opposition seemed to reflect a lack of recognition of its legitimate foreign policy objectives. The Tsar and many of his subjects inside Russia felt sufficiently confident to defend their country's values and interests, and it would have been offensive to them to be denied such an opportunity.

As someone who attended church services every day (and sung in the church choir), who shared the messianic vision of Orthodox Christianity, and saw his reign as an act of God's providence, ~~Nicholas was sincere in his religious convictions.~~[62] "The divine protection" was his "guiding light in all matters,"[63] ~~including diplomacy.~~ For example, the Tsar was criticized for selecting Menshikov, a professional soldier, to send on the mission to the Sultan about the holy places.[64] Arguing that he "was a great deal more insistent than Nesselrode would have been," some even viewed Menshikov as "an extremist of the Orthodox party."[65] For Nicholas, however, the choice of Menshikov made sense both because he held Christian Orthodox convictions and because he was expected to be forceful in his demands. On the margins of Menshikov's written request for instructions, the Tsar wrote that "without a crisis of coercion it may be difficult for the Imperial Mission to regain the degree of influence that it formerly exercised over the Divan [the Turkish government]."[66]

As an Orthodox Christian, Nicholas also enjoyed strong support at home from Orthodox adherents and intellectuals committed to promoting the Slavic/Orthodox worldview and policies. In 1843 the Ecclesiastical Academy of St. Petersburg persuaded the Tsar to send several hundred missionaries to Damascus and Beirut.[67] Around the same time, partly in response to liberal Europe's outrage over Russia's suppression of Poland, a strong Slavophile movement emerged in Russia that sought to amplify the Tsar's vision and push him in a more radical direction. The movement included prominent thinkers, publicists, and diplomats, such as Ivan Aksakov, Konstantin Aksakov, Aleksei Khomyakov, Mikhail Katkov, Ivan Kireyevski, Rostislav Fadeyev, Mikhail Pogodin, Yuri Samarin, and Fyodor Tyutchev. ~~In contrast to supporters of Russia's pro-Western path of development or Westernizers, the Slavophiles thought of Russia as a unique cultural and religious community, rather than merely as an off-spring of European civilization.~~[68] With regard to the East, Slavophiles' attitudes were deeply ethnocentric and not much different from those widely shared in Europe.[69]

~~Slavophiles soon proclaimed the Crimean War to be "holy" and supported it as an effective means to promote their moral ideals.~~[70] For example, the poet Khomyakov, who volunteered to fight the Turks in 1828, insisted that the war was first and foremost about the Christian mission, and not about power. He also saw the Russian mission as superior to that of the West and the Christian wars fought by Western nations:

The Russian people does not think of conquest at all, conquest has never seduced it. The Russian people gives no thought to glory, this feeling never moved its heart. It thinks of duty, it thinks of a ~~sacred war.~~ I shall not call it a crusade, I shall not dishonor it by that name.[71]

Soon after the beginning of the war, Mikhail Pogodin, a professor of Russian history at Moscow University, wrote to Nicholas urging him to provide strong support to all revolutionaries who were fighting against Turkey and Austria. In his view, Serbia and the Slavs were culturally and politically pro-Russian and therefore would fight Austria if it were to break with Russia.[72] Similarly, Konstantin Aksakov wrote in 1854 about a new path of Russia's greatness associated with the unity of all Slavs under the supreme patronage of the Russian Tsar.[73]

Nicholas was sympathetic with some of the Slavophiles' ideas, although they did not drive his actions toward the Ottoman Empire. The Slavophiles' emphasis on the cultural aspects of the war, as well as their juxtaposition of two separate projects of the Enlightenment – Russian and Western European[74] – resonated with the Tsar's vision of Russia as the only representative of "true" Europe. With Khomyakov, he felt that he was "waging war *neither for worldly advantage nor for conquests*, but for a solely Christian purpose."[75] Nicholas also positively responded to Pogodin's call to be more supportive of pro-Russian revolutionaries.[76] However, the Tsar never endorsed the Slavophiles' call to topple Constantinople, nor did he provide the full-fledged assistance for the Slav and Orthodox revolutionaries urged by the Slavophiles. Nicholas was also wary of his supporters' views on Russia's political system, which included the abolition of serfdom and the establishment of egalitarian unity between the Tsar and the people.[77] Domestic censorship of the Slavophiles remained tight, and the war objectives remained limited and oriented to the status quo. Disappointed in Nicholas and the course of the war, the Slavophiles soon began to withdraw their support.[78]

Although the Tsar rejected plans from his own court to attack Constantinople,[79] he also failed to support those who advocated a policy of greater restraint or of cooperation with Western powers. His advisors Count Nesselrode and Baron Brunnow favored a more cautious approach. The former advocated the preservation of a strong alliance with Austria and Prussia and wrote to the Tsar that "honor does not oblige us to hurl ourselves into a bottomless abyss."[80] Brunnow argued against taking a tough and assertive line with the Turks, warning that such a stance might backfire by either destroying the Sultan or rallying his supporters against Russia.[81] Nicholas favored preserving the Ottoman Empire, but he insisted on preserving it on Russia's terms, rather than on the terms decided by the European powers. He was not persuaded by Nesselrode's logic, partly because the advisor was neither Russian nor Orthodox.[82]

Alternative Explanations

It is difficult to understand Russia's decision to fight the Crimean War by staying within the framework of offensive realism, although its logic, according to which a strong Russia is likely to maximize its power or status, does initially apply to this case. However, one problem with offensive realist logic is that it sometimes defines strength by cumulative material capabilities, and Russia was anything but strong in that dimension. After the establishment of the European Concert, as Mearsheimer himself demonstrated[83] (see also Table 12.1), Russia was becoming progressively weaker relative to Britain and France. Given its declining capabilities, Russia should have refrained from engaging in the risky behavior and the coercive diplomacy that Nicholas demonstrated in occupying Wallachia and Moldavia in 1853. Other theories posit that risk-taking may be a rational strategy to shore up a declining power.[84] However, this argument does not apply because Russia, although objectively weak relative to other European powers, did not view itself as a declining power.

Neoclassical realism focuses on Russia's claims of a great power status. For example, William Wohlforth has argued that Russia's power calculations centered on the symbolic dimension of prestige. According to this argument, to St. Petersburg the issue of the Holy Lands came to "symbolize the relative rankings of the powers,"[85] whereas none of the conflict's protagonists truly cared "which monastic order controlled the dusty shrines in Jerusalem."[86] This logic of status competition captures an important aspect of Russia's honor – the prestige of a great power – yet it downplays cultural considerations. Orthodox Christian commitments played a special role in the Tsar's overall assessment of the dispute with the Ottoman Empire, as well as his choices of bargaining tactics with the Sultan and European powers. In addition, Nicholas viewed Russia as part of the larger Christian Europe, which he felt obligated to protect against the Turks. Indeed, the very legitimacy of Russia, both internal and external, rested on the notion of its being a Christian power, and it was through this cultural lens that Russia's rulers made sense of the international environment. The war might have never taken place had the European powers, especially Britain and France, given greater recognition to Russia's values and interests in the Near East. When challenged from the outside, Nicholas characteristically framed his response in terms of Russia's European duties: "Russia will do in 1854 what it did in 1812."[87]

Defensive realism also underestimates Russia's cultural commitments by concentrating instead on the structure of the international system and elites' strategic biases. Defensive realists recognize that international conditions before the Crimean War did not encourage revisionist behavior on Russia's part. Unlike their offensive counterparts, defensive realists identify no important power changes in mid-nineteenth-century Europe. "Whether one blames the Crimean War on Nicholas I's pigheadedness, British and French domestic politics or Turkish intriguing," wrote Matthew Rendall, "clearly no big shift had occurred in the balance of power. While this war is often depicted as tragedy, a strong case can be made that it was a crime."[88] Consistent with this logic, scholars have written about a defense-dominant arrangement before the war and emphasized elites' underestimation of the power of defense.[89] The logic of competition for security also leaves insufficient room for culturally framed interpretations of national interests. Nicholas's errors of judgment do not imply that his international assertiveness lacked domestic support. A poor tactician, the Tsar nevertheless acted consistently with his perceived historic obligations and had ample societal backing for his actions at home. The decision to launch the "most unnecessary of wars"[90] was culturally supported and reflected the dominant perception of an internally confident power.

Assessment

Evidence that before and during the Crimean War Russia acted on its sense of cultural honor is abundant. Rather than seeking to maximize power, Nicholas wanted to confirm Russia's traditional authority as a Christian power in Europe and the Near East by available diplomatic means. As a statesman, he aimed to satisfy three essential and equally important constituencies: Orthodox Christians residing in Russia and the Ottoman Empire, conservative European powers interested in upholding the principles of the Holy Alliance, and the domestic security class committed to preserving Russia's status as a great power. In trying to emphasize St. Petersburg's commitment to its European obligations and the preservation of the status quo, as Baron Alexandre Jomini wrote, "good or bad, the Russian Government remained immutably, loyally, chivalrously faithful to that policy even to the detriment of its own interests," and it subordinated "those interests to what it considered the great interests of Europe."[91]

This is not to say that Nicholas was successful in defending Russia's international objectives. On the contrary: the Crimean War had a disastrous outcome. In addition to the 480,000 deaths,[92] the war became the reason why Russia lost the hard-gained right to protect Orthodox Christians within the Ottoman Empire. It greatly contributed to the end of the European Concert and what had been left of the Holy Alliance among conservative powers. The sophisticated system, in which Austria and Prussia were Russia's close allies and Britain was involved in keeping France in check, was now entirely destroyed. Russia's reputation of a great power also suffered a major blow, and until the nation defeated the Sultan in the new war of 1877, its status was downgraded to that of Turkey.[93] Finally, no longer the generally confident and geopolitically self-sufficient power that it had became after obtaining control over the Black Sea in 1833,[94] Russia again was vulnerable to a possible attack from the South.

Russia's failure was partly due to structural causes and partly self-inflicted. Structurally, it was becoming increasingly more difficult to pre-serve the Vienna system given the growing opposition from Britain and France and their decision to cooperate in checking Russia in the Near East from 1815 on.[95] The material power balance was also not in Rus-sia's favor, as its economic and military capabilities were progressively declining relative to those of the other European powers. Analyses of Russia's internal situation further support the conclusion that it was weak and unprepared for a major war. This weakness was evident in growing revolts among peasants and in the army – partly the result of Russia's unresolved issue of serfdom.[96] Russia was also lagging behind in technology[97] and finance,[98] and its best minds widely accepted the defeat as the price for its internal weakness. As Grand Duke Konstantin stated, "We are both weaker and poorer than the first-class powers, and furthermore poorer not only in material but also in mental resources, especially in matters of administration."[99] Similarly, the Slavophile Yuri Samarin reflected the already strong perception by concluding that "we were defeated not by external forces of the Western alliance, but by our own internal weakness."[100] Indeed some leaders, such as chief of staff of the Sevastopol garrison Prince V. I. Vasil'chikov, went as far as to claim that the interests of the Russian people were better served by defeat than by victory in 1855.[101]

What exacerbated Russia's weakness was Nicholas's excessive self-confidence and inability to use Russia's influence to negotiate a reformed system of international relations. Even if the Concert of Europe was structurally doomed, Russia was still in a position to preserve its impor-tant influence in the Balkans and larger Europe. Scholars agree that, even with a relative decline in material capabilities, Russia was still viewed as a major power because of its consistent record of defeating Turkey, sup-pressing nationalist revolts, and preserving stability in Europe. In addi-tion to miscalculating his own resources, Nicholas erred in anticipating the reactions of important European powers and therefore selected the wrong methods to defend his objectives. The failure of the European revolutions of 1848–9 made the Tsar ever more confident that he could rely on coercive diplomacy in his dealings with the Sultan. Furthermore, Nicholas was prepared to exercise all options of diplomatic escalation, yet failed to design an exit strategy. His clumsy conversations with Seymour in early 1853, the decision to dispatch the hawkish and diplomatically unskilled Menshikov to negotiate with the Sultan, and the fatal occupation of the Danubian Principalities were all steps in a spiral of conflict escalation.[102]

In pursuing his tactics of coercive negotiations with Turkey, Nicholas acted against the warnings of his own advisors and strong signs of resentment on the part of outside powers. For instance, Nesselrode – as timid and misleading as his advice might have been before the war[103] – was skeptical of the chosen coercive tactics and opposed supporting the independence of the Christian peoples at the expense of preserving ties with Britain and France.[104] Despite the growing opposition from Europe, Nicholas continued to act as if the Ottoman Empire was the only object of Russia's policies. Although he expected no interference from Britain, the Tsar nevertheless asserted that such intervention "would not stop me. I shall march along my path, as Russia's dignity demands."[105] As a Russian scholar wrote, "The cardinal mistake" was to take Turkey "alone into account, whereas it was necessary to consider the powerful European rivals of Russia as well – Great Britain, France, and Austria – which entered the struggle wielding the weapon of .. the principle of the preservation of the inviolability of the dominions of the Porte."[106]

Finally, convinced of the superiority of his domestic system, Nicholas misjudged the level of support for the war at home.[107] His expectations of the war's potential to mobilize Russian patriotic feelings – in the manner of the War of 1812 – were probably based on initially sympathetic commentaries by Slavophiles, but even they began to withdraw their support once the war began to go badly.

Notes

1 Riasanovsky, *Nicholas I and Official Nationality in Russia*, p. 265.
2 See Chapter 4 for details.
3 Seton-Watson, *The Russian Empire*, p. 46.
4 For the text of the agreement, see Dmytryshyn, ed., *Imperial Russia*, pp. 97–107.
5 Wetzel, *The Crimean War*, p. 28 (For the text of the agreement, see *Imperial Russia*, pp. 207–9). The Strait agreement was then reinforced in 1841 in a special convention signed by Austria, Britain, France, Prussia, and Russia.
6 Riasanovsky, *A History of Russia*, p. 336.
7 Tarle, "Ot iyul'skoi revolutstiyi vo Frantsiyi do revolutsionnykh perevorotov v Yevrope 1848 g.," 424.
8 Ibid., 423.
9 A. J. P. Taylor wrote that "Russian inaction in the Balkans was the essential condition for the Holy Alliance." Taylor, *The Struggle for Mastery in Europe*, p. 59.

212 Honor and Assertiveness

10 The next section elaborates on this point.

11 Efimov and Tarle, "Ot sozdaniya svashchennogo soyuza do iyul'skoi revolut-stiyi (1815–1830 gg.)," 403.

12 Bourgeois, "Early Years of the Second Empire: Crimean War Origins," 47; Schroeder, *Austria, Great Britain, and the Crimean War*, p. 34; Baumgart, *The Peace of Paris 1856*, p. 13.

13 Goldfrank, *The Origins of the Crimean War*, p. 3.

14 Fuller, *Strategy and Power in Russia*, p. 261.

15 Nicholas addressed him as "friend," not "brother" as other European monarchs did. Curtiss, *Russia's Crimean War*, p. 53.

16 Schroeder, *Austria, Great Britain, and the Crimean War*, pp. 13–14.

17 Rich, *Why the Crimean War?*, p. 19.

18 Riasanovsky, *Nicholas I and Official Nationality*, p. 85. Nicholas said to Seymour, "I am the Head of a People of the Greek religion, our co-religionists of Turkey look up to me as their natural protector, and these are claims which it is impossible for me to disregard." Royle, *Crimea*, p. 52.

19 Bourgeois, "Early Years of the Second Empire," 44.

20 Riasanovsky, *Nicholas I*, p. 239.

21 Lincoln, *Nicholas I*, p. 70.

22 Ibid., p. 115.

23 For arguments that he did, see Kissinger, *Diplomacy*, p. 93; MacKenzie, "Russia's Balkan Policies under Alexander II, 1855–1881"; Goldfrank, "Policy Traditions and the Menshikov Mission of 1853," 156. Such claims are challenged by Russia's historical record. Although some in the Tsar's court harbored such ideas, he did not share them. Riasanovsky, *Nicholas I*, pp. 239–40; Rich, *Why the Crimean War?*, p. 16; Fuller, *Strategy and Power in Russia*, p. 235; Vinogradov, "The Personal Responsibility of Emperor Nicholas I for the Coming of the Crimean War."

24 Vinogradov, "The Personal Responsibility of Emperor Nicholas I," 170.

25 Gooch, "Introduction," xiii.

26 Schroeder, *Austria, Great Britain, and the Crimean War*, p. 41.

27 Rich, *Why the Crimean War?*, p. 110.

28 Vinogradov, "The Personal Responsibility," 160.

29 E. V. Tarle, "Ot revolutstiyi 1848 g. do nachala Krymskoi voiny (1848–1853 gg.)," 434.

30 Rich, *Why the Crimean War?*, pp. 31, 40.

31 Bourgeois, "Early Years of the Second Empire," 46–7; Seton-Watson, "The Origins of the Crimean War," 50–1, 61.

32 Rich, *Why the Crimean War?*, p. 50.

33 Bourgeois, "Early Years," 46. For a different view of Stratford, see Goldfrank, *The Origins of the Crimean War*, p. 277 and Alexander W. Kinglake, "Transactions Which Brought on the War."

34 Rich, *Why the Crimean War?*, p. 55. In his turn, Nesselrode, generally more cautious than Menshikov, agreed with his assessment and wrote to Baron Philip Brunnow, Russia's ambassador at London, that the Menshikov mission had failed because of "the vehement opposition . . . chiefly on the part of the English Ambassador Redcliffe." Curtiss, *Russia's Crimean War*, p. 143.

35 Bourgeois, "Early Years," 46.

36 Baumgart, *The Peace of Paris 1856*, pp. 17–18.

37 Seton-Watson, *The Russian Empire*, p. 322.

38 Taylor, *The Struggle for Mastery in Europe*, p. 61.

39 Seton-Watson, *The Russian Empire*, p. 324.

40 Geoffrey Hosking, *Russia*, p. 194.

41 Sevastopol was lacking both food and ammunition supplies. Fuller, *Strategy and Power in Russia*, p. 262.

42 Sweden, in particular, was growing hostile. Ibid., 263. On Palmerston's plans, see Baumgart, *The Peace of Paris*, p. 13 and Tarle, "Diplomatiya v godu Krymskoi voiny," 447.

43 For details of the decision-making process and debate inside Russia, see Baumgart, *The Peace of Paris*, pp. 70–80.

44 For the text of the agreement, see Dmytryshyn, ed., *Imperial Russia*, pp. 209–18.

45 Fuller, *Strategy and Power in Russia*, p. 249.

46 Taylor, *The Struggle for Mastery in Europe*, p. 82.

47 Kerenski, *Istoriya Rossiyi*, p. 137.

48 Kennedy, *The Rise and Fall of Great Powers*, p. 171.

49 Tarle, "Ot revolutsiyi 1848 g.," 435.

50 Schroeder, *Austria, Great Britain, and the Crimean War*, p. 34. For the British bid for hegemony, see also Snyder, *Myths of Empire*, pp. 156–83. For an account that emphasizes British suspicions regarding Russia's motives in Persia and India, see Royle, *Crimea*, p. 345.

51 Vinogradov, "The Personal Responsibility of Emperor Nicholas I," 161–2. For a more detailed description of Russian-English industrial competition for control of potential markets in Asia as a cause of the Crimean War, see Puryear, "New Light on the Origins of the Crimean War."

52 For development of this argument, see especially Kennedy's *The Rise and Fall of Great Powers*, especially the chapter, "The Crimean War and the Erosion of Russian Power," 170–94.

53 For the best development of this argument, see Gleason, *The Genesis of Russophobia in Great Britain*.

54 Malia, *Russia under Western Eyes*, p. 147.

55 Gleason, *The Genesis of Russophobia*, pp. 279–80.

56 Snyder, *Myths of Empire*, p. 160.

57 Kerenski, *Istoriya Rossiyi*, p. 136.

58 Baumgart, *The Peace of Paris*, p. 12.

59 For their views, see Snyder, *Myths of Empire*, pp. 183–8; Rich, *Why the Crimean War?*, pp. 91–3.

60 Thus the relatively moderate Clarendon joined forces with Palmerston. For details of the polarization within the cabinet, see Curtiss, *Russia's Crimean War*, pp. 207–8.

61 Rich, *Why the Crimean War?*, p. 3.

62 Wetzel, *The Crimean War*, pp. 26–7.

63 Ibid.

64 Rich, *Why the Crimean War?*, p. 34.

65 Temperley, "Responsibilities for the Crimean War," 59.

66 Rich, *Why the Crimean War?*, p. 47.

67 Wetzel, *The Crimean War*, p. 31.

68 For good overviews of the Russian Westernizers-Slavophiles' debates, see Neumann, *Russia and the Idea of Europe* and Tolz, *Russia*. For a selection of Russian original writings of Westernizers and Slavophiles, see Kohn, ed., *The Mind of Modern Russia*. For development of Slavophile and pan-Slavic discourse after the Crimean War, see Tuminez, *Russian Nationalism since 1856*.

69 In the second half of the nineteenth century, Vladimir Solovyev, the spiritual leader of Slavophiles who placed Christian religion at the center of his reflections about the role of Russia in Europe, referred to Islam as an "inhumane God." Duncan, *Russian Messianism*, 44. Viewing the East with a mixture of superiority and fear, Westernizers and Slavophiles shared an attitude of superiority and sparred over how Europe should be leading the rest of the world toward a better future. Whereas Westernizers put the emphasis on its "progressive" institutions, Slavophiles pointed to Europe's decline and argued that only Russia could offer genuine salvation for the world. However, both currents of thought viewed the non-Western nations as an object of modernization or a source of threat either because of their "primitive" political institutions or because of their inferior religion.

70 Riasanovsky, *Russia and the West in the Teaching of the Slavophiles*, p. 182; Duncan, *Russian Messianism*, p. 28.

71 Riasanovsky, *Russia and the West*, p. 123.

72 Curtiss, *Russia's Crimean War*, p. 37.

73 Neumann, *Russia and the Idea of Europe*, p. 44.

74 Unlike Westernizers, Slavophiles were convinced that the West was finished in its role as the world's leader and that Russia must now become the capital of world civilization. Lincoln, *Nicholas I*, p. 250.

75 Neumann, *Russia and the Idea of Europe*, p. 46.

76 Curtiss, *Russia's Crimean War*, p. 37.

77 Duncan, *Russian Messianism*, pp. 26–8.

78 Curtiss, *Russia's Crimean War*, pp. 557–60; Tarle, *Krymskaya voina*, pp. 15–17.

79 Nicholas's son, the Grand Duke Konstantin, advocated the plan, which was endorsed by Prince Paskevich. Fuller, *Strategy and Power in Russia*, pp. 235–6.

80 Fuller, *Strategy and Power*, p. 248. On Nesselrode's role during the war, see also Rich, *Why the Crimean War?*, pp. 94–5.

81 Ibid., p. 58.

82 Nesselrode was a Baltic German and the son of a Catholic and a Jewess who converted to Protestantism; he was baptized as an Anglican. He was educated in Berlin and made a career at Alexander's court. Presniakov, *Emperor Nicholas I of Russia*, p. 45.

83 John Mearsheimer, *The Tragedy of Great Powers*, p. 71.

84 Copeland, *Origins of Major War*.

85 Wohlforth, "Unipolarity, Status Competition, and Great Power War," 44.

86 Ibid.

87 Bourgeois, "Early Years of the Second Empire," 47.

88 Rendall, "Defensive Realism and the Concert of Europe," 539.
89 Van Evera, *Causes of War*, pp. 172, 187.
90 Nicholas's reference to the war. Malia, *Russia under Western Eyes*, p. 155.
91 Jomini, "Diplomatic Study of the Crimean War," 61.
92 Kennedy, *The Rise and Fall of Great Powers*, p. 177.
93 Wohlforth, "Honor as Interest in Russian Decisions for War," 35–6.
94 On Russia as a satisfied and self-restrained power, see Rendall, "Defensive Realism."
95 Goldfrank, *The Origins of the Crimean War*, p. 157.
96 The number of peasant revolts since 1830s more than doubled from 148 to 348 in the early 1850s. Bestuzhev, *Krymskaya voina*, pp. 11–13.
97 Kennedy, *The Rise and Fall of Great Powers*, pp. 170–7.
98 Tuminez, *Russian Nationalism since 1856*, p. 66.
99 Kennedy, *The Rise and Fall*, p. 177.
100 Hosking, *Russia*, p. 317. For similar self-critical reactions, see Bestuzhev, *Krymskaya voina*, p. 167; Fuller, *Strategy and Power*, p. 266; Tsimbayev, *Slavyanofil'stvo*, pp. 187–209.
101 Vasil'chikov wrote that the victory was not to be because "[f]rom on high it was decided otherwise; probably in order that we Russians should not become completely conceited, should look seriously at out internal disorders, and should take thought about curing our failings." Curtiss, *Russia's Crimean War*, p. 564.
102 Fuller, *Strategy and Power*, p. 250.
103 Russian scholars have been especially critical of Nesselrode's lack of honest reports to the Tsar. Tarle, *Krymskaya voina*, p. 77; Zaichonkovsky, *Vostochnaya voina, 1853–1856*, p. 29. Other scholars wrote that before the war, Nesselrode fed Nicholas illusions that Britain and Austria were united in their desire to curb French influences in the Ottoman Empire. Goldfrank, *The Origins of the Crimean War*, p. 138.
104 Rich, *Why the Crimean War?*, p. 94; Fuller, *Strategy and Power*, p. 248. In his letter to Brunnov on January 2, 1853, Nesselrode accurately predicted that Russia would "face the whole world alone and without allies, because Prussia will be of no account and indifferent to the question, and Austria will be more or less neutral, if not favorable to the Porte." Royle, *Crimea*, p. 23.
105 Wohlforth, "Unipolarity, Status Competition, and Great Power War," 46.
106 Vinogradov, "The Personal Responsibility of Emperor Nicholas I," 161.
107 Fuller, *Strategy and Power*, p. 252; Presniakov, *Emperor Nicholas I of Russia*, pp. 68–9.
108 Similar military fleet statistics are cited in Tarle, *Krymskaya voina*, p. 48.

13   The Early Cold War, 1946–1949

"Our victory means, first of all, that our Soviet social order has triumphed, that the Soviet *social order* successfully passed the ordeal in the fire of war and proved its unquestionable vitality."

Joseph Stalin[1]

From Allies to Enemies

Although allies during World War II, Russia and the West were unable to sustain their cooperation and soon after the war returned to the familiar pattern of mistrust and rivalry. Within a few years of the Yalta and Potsdam agreements, their relationship escalated into a full-blown political confrontation with detrimental consequences for both sides.

The Agreements at Yalta and Potsdam

After the Soviet army's decisive victory in the Kursk battle of July 1943 and keenly aware that Hitler's days were numbered, Great Britain, Russia, and the United States began to prepare for negotiations about the postwar international order. In late 1943, Franklin Roosevelt was torn between the idea of "four policemen" – the United States, Russia, Britain, and China – and of preserving global openness for American influences.[2] Winston Churchill hoped to secure a sphere of influence agreement in accord with British interests, and on October 9, 1944 he concluded a bilateral deal with Joseph Stalin over dividing the Balkans.[3] In the meantime, the Soviet army was everywhere in Eastern Europe, liberating it from the Nazis, but also serving to strengthen Stalin's bargaining position in the postwar negotiations.

When the three leaders met at Yalta in February 1945, the most contentious issues involved Germany and Poland. On Germany, the three powers agreed to preserve the country's economic and political unity, while dividing it into occupation zones controlled by American, British, French, and Soviet troops.[4] The conference's communiqué insisted on

216

the "complete disarmament, demilitarization, and dismemberment of Germany,"[5] which suited Soviet interests well. In the meantime, the United States and Britain were already thinking about strengthening Germany in order to balance Soviet power in Europe.[6] On Poland, it was agreed that the core government would be formed by the pro-Soviet Lublin's Poles, but émigré Poles residing in London would also be included and free elections would then complete the formation of the country's political system.[7] Stalin also insisted on the Curzon Line along the Oder and Neisse rivers as the new Polish-German border, thereby adding a significant part of German land to Poland but also preserving the Soviet-Polish border as established by the 1939 pact with Hitler. In the vague language of the conference's Declaration, the Allies agreed to "consult" about affairs in the Eastern European countries and to "jointly assist" them in exercising their sovereign rights.[8]

At the Potsdam conference in July–August 1945, negotiations proved to be far more difficult. By the time the conference took place, Soviet intentions to preserve its dominant influence over Poland and the Balkans had become clear. In addition, Roosevelt was replaced by the tough-minded Harry S. Truman, who planned to make few concessions to Stalin and pointedly informed the latter of the United States' possession of a new destructive weapon. As a result, the Soviets extracted only a portion of the desired reparations from Germany – mostly from its eastern part – while the United States parted with the "four policemen" idea in favor of establishing dominant influence over the Western areas of occupation. Long before the Berlin crisis, Germany had been on its way to becoming a divided state.[9] With Stalin's long list of demands – which included increased control of the Dardanelles Straits, a military base in the Bosporus, and a part of Italy's colonies – and Truman's determination to demonstrate loyalty to Wilsonian principles of self-determination, the conference quickly turned, in Henry Kissinger's expression, "into a dialogue of the deaf."[10]

Yet, during the next few months Stalin acted with restraint and generally in the spirit of the Yalta-Potsdam agreements as he interpreted them. He was willing to tolerate Poland's independence, although within the Soviet area of influence.[11] He also planned no communist takeovers in Europe and advised the leaders of communist parties in Italy, France, Hungary, and Bulgaria to cooperate with national governments and not expect to assume power within the foreseeable future[12] – partly because he wanted to prevent the strengthening of independent communist centers.[13] Stalin also favored the conceptions of national democracy and "national paths" to socialism,[14] arguing at the time that Poland, Yugoslavia, and Czechoslovakia "may not need establishment of dictatorship of [the] proletariat and the Soviet system."[15] In post-war Europe, communists emerged as influential partly because they called for social and democratic reforms, not a radical anticapitalist transformation.[16]

In addition – and consistent with the division of influence agreement he had devised with Churchill – Stalin refused to interfere in Greece. In early 1945, the Soviet Union did not grant Bulgaria's request to help it annex coastal Greek territories.[17] Even in 1946, when Greek communists organized an uprising and were hopeful for Soviet assistance, Stalin made no attempt to get involved.[18] He further abstained from interfering in Finland, which he viewed as maintaining a generally "friendly" international posture.[19] Outside Europe, Stalin advised Chinese communists to enter into a coalition with their enemies, the nationalists.[20] He also refused to defy the United States by intervening in Japan and landing in Hokkaido, as some of his advisors encouraged him to do after the United States dropped two nuclear bombs on Hiroshima and Nagasaki in August 1945.[21]

First Complications and the Stalin–Churchill Exchange

Soon, however, more serious complications followed the Allies' meetings in Yalta and Potsdam. The Polish issue, in particular, was never successfully resolved. Despite U.S. pressure, Stalin did not allow genuinely free elections, including only a few pro-Western Poles in the government, and he did not agree to open the country to American financial influence.[22] Another serious issue was the nuclear factor and growing Soviet suspiciousness that partly stemmed from U.S. secrecy regarding its plans for the use of atomic weapons. In fact, Truman had used the weapon in Japan without consulting Stalin.[23] The latter responded by complaining that "war is barbaric, but using the A-bomb is a super barbarity," and demanding that Soviet scientists restore the "destroyed" balance by building a nuclear weapon.[24] In September 1945, Truman also ignored Secretary of War Henry Stimson's advice to build trust with Russia by directly and openly negotiating limits for the further development of nuclear power except for "peaceful and humanitarian purposes."[25]

In February 1946, in his speech before elections to the Supreme Soviet, Stalin offered his analysis of victory in the war and revived prewar dogmas about the relationship between war and capitalism. He billed the war as "the inevitable result of the development of world economic and political forces on the basis of modern monopoly capitalism."[26] By monopoly capitalism, he meant "fascist" Germany, and Stalin even referred to the United States and Great Britain as "freedom-loving states" with which it became possible to build "the anti-fascist coalition."[27] Yet Churchill and others in the West interpreted Stalin's words to mean that the war "had been caused not by Hitler but by the workings of the capitalist system."[28] In addition, Stalin warned about "all possible accidents" against the Soviet Union and demanded "three more Five-Year Plans . . . if not more" to guarantee security of the homeland.[29]

Aimed primarily at a domestic audience, the speech nevertheless caused a storm of alarmist reactions in the Western world. The *New York Times* front-page story declared that Stalin believed "the stage is set" for another war.[30] Two weeks later, on February 22, George Kennan sent his "long telegram" warning about the Kremlin's "traditional and instinctive sense of insecurity" that caused it to adopt confrontational Marxist ideology.[31] In March, Churchill traveled to Fulton on Truman's invitation to deliver his Iron Curtain speech. There he argued that Eastern Europe was now fully controlled by Moscow and that communist "fifth columns" were working inside Western states – also on orders from the Soviet Union. Along with Kennan and others, the disillusioned former British statesman questioned the possibility of an alliance with Stalin's Russia and proposed to reorder the world on the principles of "Christian civilization."[32]

A few days later, Stalin responded to Churchill via an interview in *Pravda*. Accusing him of racism, Stalin also spoke of "Mr. Churchill and his friends" bearing "a striking resemblance to Hitler" and calling "for war on the USSR."[33] The Soviet leader concluded the interview by expressing confidence that, should a new military campaign against the Soviet system be organized, the organizers would "be trashed, just as they were trashed once before."[34]

Stalin's position regarding the Allies' efforts to reconstruct Eastern Europe also toughened. He no longer sought to obtain a loan from the United States and refused to join the Bretton Wood institutions, such as the World Bank and the International Monetary Fund. The new Soviet attitude was that its membership in such institutions might be interpreted by the Western powers as a sign of weakness and a readiness to make unilateral concessions.[35] In October 1946, Foreign Minister Vyacheslav Molotov argued in one of his speeches that American capital was in a position to buy up the local industries of Eastern European states, thereby depriving them "of sovereignty and independence."[36] Furthermore, the U.S. plan to control atomic energy was entirely unacceptable to the Soviet Union. Initiated by Bernard Baruch, the plan called for the establishment of an Atomic Development Authority that would operate free of the UN Security Council veto and that would be largely controlled by the United States.[37]

This looked like a Cold War, and a number of American scholars date its beginning to spring 1946.[38] However, Churchill's speech at Fulton was met with only a reserved reaction from Truman,[39] and the Truman Doctrine was not put in force until a year later. On the part of the Soviet Union – rhetoric notwithstanding – the point of no return in dealing with the West was not reached until the formulation of the Marshall Plan in June 1947.

Soviet Assertiveness in all Directions

Without directly challenging the West, Soviet Russia had begun to advance a most assertive foreign policy as early as the end of 1945. After Yalta, Stalin indicated to his foreign minister that he planned on interpreting the conference agreements to secure the Soviet position in the international system: "We can implement it in our own way later. The heart of the matter is the correlation of forces."[40] By the end of 1945, the Soviet leader decided to act. Even though Stalin was pushing in the direction of establishing a USSR-centered geopolitical bloc, he did not plan to develop a hostile one, which he viewed as threatening Soviet interests.[41] The strategy was to secure considerable territorial control outside Russia to the extent acceptable to the Western Allies.

Eastern Europe and the Balkans became critical in establishing the USSR-centered sphere of influence. In Poland, Stalin empowered the secret police and authorized the arrest of those opposing the communist government. To the Western leaders protesting his actions, he justified them by the need to "protect the rear behind the front-lines of the Red Army."[42] In Romania, he demanded that its king install the pro-Soviet Petru Grozu as prime minister, but – in anticipation of the harsh Western reaction – Stalin did not dismantle the opposing political parties.[43] He further relied on Yugoslavia's support in reconstituting the Balkans, while restraining Josip Broz Tito's own ambitions for a "greater Yugoslavia."[44] Moscow also pressured Turkey to give up control of the Straits, the old ambition of Russia, and to allow Soviet military bases there. The demands escalated to pose the threat of war with Turkey, which Stalin diffused in September 1946 after he discovered that the United States was prepared to defend Turkey in case of a military confrontation.[45]

The Soviet Union was equally assertive, yet not openly confrontational, in other directions. Seeking to prevent Germany's possible alignment with the West, Stalin established control over the Soviet zone of occupation there by moving in millions of refugees from Eastern Europe, dismantling German industries, and taking over 30 percent of all industrial production in eastern Germany.[46] In Japan, Stalin planned to establish an area of

Soviet control in northern Hokkaido, but reconsidered after the United States dropped nuclear bombs on Hiroshima and Nagasaki. In China, he gave strong support to the Manchurian communists, but soon retreated after U.S. marines landed there in September 1946 to aid the nationalist government.[47] In Iran, Stalin refused to withdraw Soviet troops, and he supported the separatist Azeri movement, demanding the Soviet right to drill oil in the northern part of the country. A serious crisis erupted, and Stalin again yielded, but only after he had tried all types of political pressure, including in the United Nations.[48]

The Point of No Return

The really radical turn in the Soviet attitude toward the West did not occur until the Marshall Plan was officially proclaimed in June 1947. "There is little evidence," wrote Vladislav Zubok and Constantine Pleshakov, "that before the Marshall Plan Stalin had any master plan for immediate expansion."[49] Even after Truman first proclaimed his new doctrine in March, Stalin was hoping to continue political ties and negotiations with the United States and Great Britain. In April, he told the visiting Republican Senator Harold Stassen,

The economic systems of Germany and the USA are the same but nevertheless there was war between them. The economic systems of the USA and the USSR are different but they fought side by side and collaborated during the war. If two different systems can collaborate in war, why can't they collaborate in peacetime?[50]

Also in April, during a long meeting with U.S. Secretary of State George Marshall, Stalin argued for a possible compromise on "all the main questions" and insisted that "it was necessary to have patience and not become pessimistic."[51] Marshall, however, was of a different opinion, and in his radio address on April 28 he indicated that the United States was no longer in a mood to deliberate and was planning to take decisive actions.[52] On June 5, he delivered his Marshall Plan speech, in which he pledged financial assistance for the postwar reconstruction of the European continent.

Soon after, Stalin and Molotov articulated their alternative to Western policy: creating a separate bloc with the Eastern European states and suppressing any opposition to Soviet policy within the region. At the Paris conference in July devoted to a common European response to Marshall's speech, Molotov denounced the American proposal as an attempt to divide Europe and undermine the sovereignty of the continent's states.[53] A few days later, the Soviet authorities established the

Communist Information Agency (Cominform) and brushed aside Polish
and Czech hopes to join the Marshall Plan. At the founding meeting of
Cominform in September 1947, Andrei Zhdanov, the Stalin-appointed
ideologue of the new course, defined U.S. objectives as similar to those of
Hitler's Germany – "to strengthen imperialism, to hatch a new imperialist war, to combat Socialism and democracy, and to support reactionary
and anti-democratic pro-fascist regimes and movements everywhere."[54]
In early 1948, Stalin sponsored the communist takeover in Czechoslovakia, at that point the last Eastern European state with a multiparty
government.[55] Only Finland and Yugoslavia managed to stay out of the
Cominform.

At home, the new course meant a return to the prewar system of
mass mobilization and repression. Despite a severe drought in 1946 and
shortages of food, the state cut social welfare expenditures. In addition
to increasing taxes on the peasants by 150 percent between 1946 and
1950, the state refused to pay back funds to people who had loaned the
government money to fight the war.[56] Zhdanov introduced the notion
of "cosmopolitan spies" to purge those insufficiently critical of the West
within political, intellectual, and cultural circles.[57]

Taken together, these developments soon paved the way for future
Cold War crises, such as the Berlin blockade and the Korean War.

The Early Cold War, 1946–1949: Timeline

1945 February	Yalta conference
April	Truman becomes U.S. president
May	Germany surrenders to the Soviet army
July	Potsdam conference
August	A-bombs dropped on Japan
1946 February	Stalin's election speech
	Soviet-Iranian conflict
	Kennan's "long telegram"
March	Churchill's Iron Curtain speech
August	USSR demands joint control of the Black Sea Straits with Turkey
1947 February	Soviet peace treaties with Bulgaria, Finland, Hungary, Italy, and Romania
March	Truman's speech to U.S. Congress
June	Marshall Plan speech
September	Founding conference of the Cominform
1948 February	Communist coup in Czechoslovakia
June	Beginning of Berlin blockade

1949 March	Vyshinski replaces Molotov as Foreign Minister
April	NATO treaty is signed
May	Establishment of West German state
August	Soviet Union tests A-bomb
October	Chinese People's Republic is established
	Establishment of East German state

Explaining Soviet Assertiveness

The Soviet assertiveness and, ultimately, its political confrontation with the West had roots in two related and mutually reinforcing developments: the Soviet concept of honor in the wake of World War II and Britain and the United States' growing unwillingness to recognize the Soviet worldview and great power claims. In combination these developments resulted in the Cold War that politically defined the international system for some forty years.

Soviet Concept of Honor

The Soviet concept of honor emphasized pride in the social system that the Kremlin viewed as critical in winning the war against Hitler's Germany. To the ruling class, victory in the war was due to the "unquestionable vitality" of the system's domestic foundations on which Stalin elaborated in his preelection speech by praising industrialization, collectivization, and the series of five-year plans.[58] Externally, pride in the social system was reflected in the ideological conviction that socialism would now expand across the world, particularly throughout the Balkans and Eastern Europe.

Related to ideology was the notion of power prestige. Immediately after the war, Moscow began to demand a greater share of control over the world's territory and resources. As Nikita Khrushchev recalled, "after the defeat of Hitler, Stalin believed he was in the same position as Alexander I after the defeat of Napoleon – that he could dictate the rules for all of Europe."[59] Molotov, who rarely saw things differently from his boss, emphasized that "the USSR now stands in the ranks of the most authoritative of world powers" and that "now it is impossible to resolve the important issues of international relations without the participation of the Soviet Union."[60] Stalin, however, planned to act differently from Alexander I, who withdrew from the territory of the defeated French and even proposed to disarm national armies.[61] The Soviet leader's view on the link between the Soviet social system and power was clearly expressed during his conversation with Milovan Djilas: "This war is not as in the past; whoever occupies a territory also imposes his own system as far as his army can reach. It cannot be otherwise."[62] In Stalin's mind, enormous sacrifices suffered by the Russian people made the Soviet case for recognizing its superpower claims even more compelling – he who sacrificed much in war should receive much after it.[63]

The last layer of the Soviet perception was about security. It also was linked to prestige and ideology, because security of the newly emerged great power could no longer be achieved or protected within its prewar boundaries. Stalin therefore expected the Allies to respect the territorial arrangement he had made with Hitler in August 1939, by which the USSR obtained the Baltic states and parts of Finland, Poland, and Romania.[64] In fact, after defeating Hitler, the Kremlin planned no return to the pre-1939 conditions, but argued instead for additional territorial expansion. In the new Soviet view, Russia's postwar security required the dismantlement of Germany and the control of the territory between Russia and the defeated power. Stalin was worried about the revival of German military capabilities within fifteen years.[65] In the Balkans and Eastern Europe, he counted on historically established Slavic ties to facilitate Soviet control; Stalin argued in private that "if the Slavs keep united and maintain solidarity, no one in the future will be able to move a finger. Not even a finger!"[66] Soviet insecurity was further reinforced by the nuclear factor. Not having a bomb, Stalin felt he had to rely on a non-nuclear response to a potential nuclear attack from the United States.[67]

This concept of honor guided the Soviet interpretation of the Yalta and Potsdam agreements. To Stalin, their essence was the division of influence between Russia and the West, and acceptance of free elections meant to him a one-sided concession to the United States. At Potsdam, for example, he reminded Truman that he recognized Italy, where no elections had been held, and he therefore rejected the U.S. proposal to have elections in Romania and Bulgaria.[68] Stalin also pressed the Western nations hard on Polish and German issues that he viewed as critical to the Soviet Union's honor and security. He insisted at Yalta that

[The question] was one of honor because Russia had many past grievances against Poland and desired to see them eliminated. It was a question of strategic security not only because Poland was a bordering country but because throughout history Poland had been the corridor for attacks on Russia. We have to mention that during the last thirty years Germany twice has passed through this corridor. The reasons for this was that Poland was weak. Russia wants a strong, independent and democratic Poland.[69]

Despite broad agreement within the ruling circles on the principles of Soviet honor, there was debate on methods of pursuing the assertive foreign policy. Diplomats, including the former foreign minister Maxim Litvinov, former ambassador to Great Britain Ivan Maiski, and the ambassador to the United States Andrei Gromyko, advocated a more cautious approach. They agreed with key premises of Soviet assertiveness, such as the need to expand borders, keep Poland weak, and prepare for a lengthy recovery from the war, but argued for more extensive consultations with the Allies and greater respect for domestic choices within the Soviet area of international influence. Litvinov and Maiski each headed special commissions on postwar reparations and postwar peace treaties and argued in their 1944–5 memos for working closely with London and Washington while playing a balance-of-power game between them.[70] Gromyko viewed the United States as a force for peace, and Litvinov thought that spheres of influence should not be "detrimental to the independence of the states included in them."[71] After mid-1946, Litvinov became even more critical of the official foreign policy.[72]

Stalin and Molotov listened to what the "liberals" had to say, yet continued to act unilaterally by challenging the independence of Eastern European states and failing to consult the Allies. Such unilateral assertiveness was reminiscent of early militant Soviet policy (1928–34),[73] contributing to the evolution of the Kremlin's relations with the West away from the Grand Alliance and toward the Cold War. The vision of irreconcilable contradictions between capitalism and socialism, as well as the inevitability of their future war, was becoming increasingly dominant in ruling circles. The Marshall Plan became the critical threshold in the Soviet relations with the United States. Even though some around Stalin advocated the idea of joining the Marshall Plan,[74] he categorically rejected this option as incompatible with the Soviet idea of honor as independence from the West. Just as Nicholas I once refused to withdraw from the Ottoman principalities and took Russia to war with the West, Stalin refused to let Eastern European states join the Marshall Plan, thereby completing the transition to the Cold War. Both rulers were motivated by the exclusive vision of national honor and therefore rejected more cooperative international arrangements.

Domestic Confidence

Another key reason why the Kremlin felt emboldened to act in such an assertive fashion was the domestic perception of the Soviet Union's strength in the wake of the war. Foreign Minister Molotov expressed the dominant feeling in late 1945 by stating that the war had "shown all how our country grew and strengthened in the military-political sense."[75] The new confidence partly resulted from the Red Army's position in Europe.

Table 13.1. *Share of World Power, Industrial Strength, and Military Strength, 1946–50 (%)*

Country	World Power*		Industrial Strength**		Military Strength***	
	1946	1950	1946	1950	1946	1950
United States	36	28	71	50	38	23
Soviet Union	16	18	13	15	38	35
Great Britain	11	6	12	9	17	4
France	3	3	3	4	6	4

* Military expenditures, military personnel, total population, urban population, steel production, and consumption of industrial fuels.
** Steel production and fuel consumption.
*** Military expenditures and military personnel.
Source: Wohlforth, *The Elusive Balance*, 60.

As the Russian ambassador to Washington Nikolai Novikov argued in his long telegram in September 1946,

[T]he USSR's international position is currently stronger than it was in the prewar period. Thanks to the historical victories of Soviet weapons, the Soviet armed forces are located on the territory of Germany and other formerly hostile countries, thus guaranteeing that these countries will not be used again for an attack on the USSR.[76]

The economic and social reality was much less encouraging, however. Russia emerged after the war economically devastated and technologically worse off than before. In 1945 its national income was 83 percent, industrial production 92 percent, and agricultural production 60 percent of its 1940 levels.[77] Even though by comparison to other Western nations, such as Great Britain and France, the Soviet Union looked strong, it was no match for the growing capabilities of the United States (see Table 13.1), especially after the latter acquired the nuclear weapon. The Soviet Army's morale in Europe was not high, and at home the army was fighting anticommunist rebels in Western Ukraine and the Baltic republics.[78] A U.S. intelligence report in November 1945 realistically estimated that the USSR would not be willing to "risk a major armed conflict" for at least fifteen years.[79]

Aware of these weaknesses, the Soviet Union insisted on war reparations, and it was especially hopeful that it could dismantle German industries and exploit German workers.[80] In addition, Stalin instructed Molotov to ask the U.S. government for a $6 billion loan for postwar reconstruction.[81] To dampen his people's postwar expectations of a better life and strengthen his political control, Stalin was also making preparations for a new round of economic mobilization and new repressions.

Western Mistrust

Western suspicion and mistrust of the Soviet Union served to strengthen its determination to act assertively. From expressing a relatively high degree of willingness to work with the USSR before and during the meeting at Yalta, Great Britain and the United States soon moved to engaging in unilateral and potentially confrontational behavior. Winston Churchill led the way by changing his posture from the sphere of influence agreement with Stalin in October 1944 to the Iron Curtain speech in March 1946. Within a year and a half, London's attitude had evolved from seeking to cooperate with Moscow to insisting on reordering the world along Christian principles and without Soviet involvement.

The United States' evolution was more gradual, yet it was ultimately the position of U.S. officials that determined the West's relations with Russia. Differences between Roosevelt and Truman played an important role. Roosevelt planned no future major involvement in European affairs and wanted to withdraw American troops from the continent within two years. He was in favor of concluding a mutually acceptable territorial agreement with the Soviets. He recognized the Soviet mistrust of the West, but was hoping to reduce it by refraining from public criticism of the Kremlin, continuing with generous lend-lease aid, and avoiding retaliatory actions.[82] Truman, however, did not share the cooperation-through-persuasion attitude of his predecessor. Instead, he planned to exercise power unilaterally for the purpose of rebuilding the postwar world along American principles, and he was convinced that Russia would have little choice but to yield to the United States' determination. In Truman's own words, the United States had to have its way 85 percent of the time.[83] In addition, he was deeply mistrustful of Russia and had not even wanted it to win the war.[84]

Because of his unilateralist and anti-Russian beliefs, Truman had a propensity to take a hard line in disputes with the Soviet Union. During his first meeting with Foreign Minister Molotov in April 1945, Truman shouted at him for not complying with the Yalta agreement on Poland.[85] Molotov was shocked at Truman's rudeness; in turn the president described the USSR's actions this way to his advisors: "They don't know how to behave. They are like bulls in a china shop. They are only twenty-five years old. We are over a hundred and the British are centuries older. We have to teach them how to behave."[86] On the advice of his ambassador to Moscow Averill W. Harriman, Truman later softened his stance and reached an understanding with Stalin on Poland,[87] but their differences were again revealed at Potsdam. In June 1945, U.S. observers such as Walter Lippmann and C. L. Sulzberger also warned against forming the impression of an Anglo-American front against Moscow that "could only serve to . . . convince the Soviet Union of the necessity of unilateral action and reliance upon its own strength."[88] Truman saw the use of nuclear weapons as a means to "teach" the Soviets by asserting the American right to lead the postwar reconstruction. After using the bomb in Japan, he secured exclusive control over that country and in September 1945 rejected the Soviet proposal to establish an Allied Control Commission on Japan, similar to that on Germany. Stalin reacted furiously by cabling to Molotov that he felt that Americans had "no elementary respect towards their ally."[89]

Although Truman did not initially endorse Churchill's Iron Curtain speech given in March 1946, by its actions the United States was moving in the direction of isolating the USSR. In addition to ignoring the advice of Stimson, Lippmann, and others to build trust with the Soviets, Truman dismissed his secretary of commerce Henry Wallace because of his perceived pro-Soviet position. Alarmed by Churchill's speech, Wallace challenged the prospect of an Anglo-American anti-Soviet consensus, insisting on meeting Russia "half way" and accepting its influence in Eastern Europe.[90] After the crisis in Iran and Kennan's "long telegram" in March 1946, the United States and Britain began acting in concert to undermine Soviet policies from Eastern Europe to China and Japan. Also in March 1946, the State Department announced that the Russian $6 billion loan request had been "lost" and that a new discussion of a loan would require an evaluation of the Soviet policies in Eastern Europe and elsewhere.[91] By that time, lend-lease aid had been terminated.[92] Nuclear developments, particularly the Baruch Plan, also demonstrated that the United States was not interested in the Soviet perspective, but was aiming to preserve an American monopoly over atomic energy.[93]

As had been predicted by the critics of Churchill and Truman, the policies of Britain and the United States fueled Russia's suspicions about Western motives. Soon after Truman made public his doctrine of globally containing communism on March 12, 1947,[94] and especially after the Marshall Plan was proclaimed in June of the same year, Stalin and his entourage abandoned their attempts to mend fences with the West.

Alternative Explanations

Offensive realism attributes the Cold War to Soviet expansionist ambitions in Europe and Asia that were met with the U.S. determination to balance them. As John Mearsheimer has written, "no great power or combination of great powers existed in either Europe or Northeast Asia that could prevent the Soviet army from overrunning those regions, and therefore the United States had no choice but check Soviet expansion."[95] Another offensive realist theory explains the assertive behavior of the Soviet Union and the West by their determination to secure additional power advantages and delay each other's relative decline. As Dale Copeland has argued, risky behavior under the condition of bipolarity comes from either the preponderance or near-equal distribution of power.[96]

These explanations suffer from two problems. First, they tend to overestimate Soviet capabilities. For instance, Mearsheimer relies on statistics of the gross national product in 1950, by which time it had increased considerably, especially relative to France and Britain. A more realistic baseline would have been 1945 or the end of the war, rather than 1950. For example, during this five years between 1945–50, Russian industrial production increased by 73 percent, and the overall national income grew by 64 percent.[97] Also, by 1950, the combined world power of Great Britain and France had declined from 14 to 9 percent, their industrial strength from 15 to 11 percent, and their military strength from 23 to 8 percent.[98] Second and more importantly, offensive realists pay limited attention to Soviet beliefs and perceptions of power. Objectively, Russia was weaker than realists assess, yet subjectively it felt strong. This explains why, in response to the West's postwar policies, Russia failed to exercise restraint in its claims for the "fruits of victory."

Defensive realism explains Soviet assertiveness as caused by the Kremlin's "irrational" beliefs, such as security through expansion and territorial gains.[99] The key question for defensive realists is, as it was for Winston Churchill, "Why have they deliberately acted for three long years so as to unite the free world against them?"[100] By taking beliefs and perceptions seriously, this explanation comes closer to understanding Soviet behavior, yet it falls short of accounting for how widely the expansionist beliefs were held within the political class in Moscow or for the West's own contribution to the hardening of the Kremlin's beliefs. Although some have emphasized the differences in views of Stalin and Litvinov in 1944–5,[101] historians have revealed their similarities as well. The two statesmen not only shared a Marxist outlook on international affairs but they also agreed on the necessity to expand borders and keep competitors weak. As Voitech Mastny wrote, "there is no quarrel between Litvinov and Stalin, both ardent devotees of power politics."[102]

Finally, classical and neoclassical realism concentrates on national ideology and competition for power and prestige as the key motives underlying Soviet behavior. George Kennan described ideological impatience,[103]

Henry Kissinger highlighted "Pan-Slavism reinforced by communist ideology,"[104] and Paul Kennedy postulated the ideological exclusiveness of two universal ideas, liberalism and communism.[105] Those closer to neoclassical realism emphasized considerations of external reputation and prestige, but they too argued that "Stalin and his circle talked and acted exactly as such realists as E. H. Carr, Ralph Hawtrey, Geoffrey Blainey, and Robert Gilpin would expect."[106]

As important as ideology and power were to the Soviet rulers, these explanations are not sufficient. Part of the problem is that, as John Lewis Gaddis put it, ideology "was not simply a justification for actions already decided upon," but the internal lens through which the state viewed the very legitimacy of its actions.[107] The Cold War is not merely a case of ideological distortion; it is, as Martin Malia wrote, "*the* great example in modern history of the power of 'irrational', cultural forces in international affairs."[108] From a realist perspective, the Kremlin should have been satisfied with "a reasonable security alliance of East European states with the Soviet Union" without demanding that these states adopt a communist "social system."[109] Yet, such was the definition of Soviet honor, which – along with the West's failure to recognize the Kremlin's foreign policy claims – determined Russia's decision to impose its system abroad. By insisting on the universality of its principles, the West pushed Stalin farther away from the initially "nonprovocative military posture" and toward confrontational behavior.[110]

Assessment

Contrary to dominant explanations, the Cold War on the Soviet side resulted from a sense of hurt honor, rather than merely a drive to maximize power. Much of what a prominent Western scholar has called "reckless bravado"[111] was in fact a product of the Kremlin's pride in the Soviet *social* system and insistence on defending Russia's legitimate security interests. Having sacrificed enormous human and material resources to secure victory over Nazi Germany, the Soviet state expected the Allies to treat it with respect and recognize its claims of increased great power status. Stalin did not have global expansionist ambitions, but wanted to exercise considerable control over the policies of peripheral states in Europe and Asia.

Even though Stalin never wanted a confrontation with the Western nations, his responsibility for such a confrontation is obvious. Immediately after the war, he proceeded cautiously to implement claims to the Soviet area of influence by tolerating the independence of Eastern European states and advising communist parties in Europe and Asia to work within the government, rather than trying to oust it. Stalin rejected as impractical the advice of his most impatient comrades to cross the Elba and occupy some parts of the Western European nations.[112] Instead, he worked with those advocating consultations with the Allies and a reasonable respect for the independence of the Eastern European and Balkan nations. However, after 1945, Stalin's policies grew increasingly unilateral and oppressive vis-à-vis the Soviet periphery and domestic society. He hoped that his new assertiveness would win the Soviet Union new security frontiers before it provoked a confrontational response from the West. Yet, by instructing Molotov to demand more from the West and ignore Western objections, Stalin ultimately overplayed his hand and destroyed the thin layer of trust established with the Allies during the war.

As a result, Soviet assertiveness brought the recognition of status at the expense of continued economic and political cooperation with Great Britain and the United States. Realists recognize Stalin and Molotov's ability to play their "cards ably and correctly,"[113] resulting in a "stunning achievement in building status" of a great power, "despite a comparatively small economy and many other disadvantages."[114] Yet the Soviet tactical successes failed to yield long-term stability in relations with the West. Indeed, if Stalin never wanted a Cold War, then he failed to do his part to prevent it.

Yet the Western powers also played a part in bringing about the Cold War. A historically sensitive account will recognize that both sides were thinking in terms of expanding their territorial space to protect their visions of honor and security. Whereas the Soviets wanted to expand the socialist system to create a buffer zone to prevent a future attack from Germany, the West suspected them of ambitions to dominate the world. The U.S. government's even-handed assessments of Soviet intentions and capabilities of 1945 were soon replaced by a paranoid fear of the Kremlin's preparedness to invade Western nations.[115] Yet the Americans also believed in reconstructing the European continent in accordance with their ideas of democracy and security. They never seriously considered devising cooperative nuclear energy arrangements and placed low priority on plans for the Soviet Union to serve as a natural resources base for Europe, were the Kremlin to ever join the Marshall Plan.[116]

Stalin's geopolitically limited "socialist imperialism" was therefore met with the West's global "democratic imperialism."[117] Mutual mistrust exacerbated the situation, making it ever more difficult to prevent a full-fledged political confrontation. Western leaders had reason to be suspicious of Stalin who, in turn, was driven by his perception of the West's greed and by its betrayals from the dubious Treaty of Versailles to the appeasement of Hitler in Munich. As Walter LaFeber acknowledged,

[If the] Soviets were suspicious of the West, they were realistic, not paranoid: the West had poured thousands of troops into Russia between 1917 and 1920, refused to cooperate with the Soviets during the 1930s, tried to turn Hitler against Stalin in 1938, reneged on promises about the second front, and in 1945 tried to penetrate areas Stalin deemed crucial to Soviet security.[118]

Arrangements for the post–World War II world made by Britain, USSR, and the United States in Yalta and Potsdam proved insufficient to address these deep-seated suspicions.

Notes

1 "Stalin's 'Two Camps' Speech, 9 February 1946," 292.
2 LaFeber, *America, Russia, and the Cold War, 1945–1996*, p. 12.
3 "Churchill and Stalin Dividing the Balkans on a Half-Sheet of Paper," 51–2.
4 Ulam, *Expansion and Coexistence*, p. 442.
5 Suny, *The Soviet Experiment*, p. 343.
6 Ibid. Roosevelt was less definitive considering both destruction of the nation (even once mentioning mass castration) and controlled revival of its economy. LaFeber, *America, Russia, and the Cold War*, p. 23.
7 Ulam, *Expansion and Coexistence*, p. 366.
8 "The Declaration on Liberated Europe," 53–4.
9 "The Potsdam Agreement on Germany," 124–5.
10 Kissinger, *Diplomacy*, p. 434.
11 Suny, *The Soviet Experiment*, p. 344.
12 Roberts, *The Soviet Union in World Politics*, p. 19; LaFeber, *America, Russia, and the Cold War*, p. 20.
13 Daniels, *Russia: The Roots of Confrontation*, p. 220.
14 Nation, *Black Earth, Red Star*, p. 177; Pikhoya, *Moskva. Kreml'. Vlast'*, pp. 132–3.
15 Pikhoya, *Moskva. Kreml'. Vlast'*, p. 132.
16 For example, in Czechoslovakia's elections of April 1946, the communists obtained 38% of the vote. Suny, *The Soviet Experiment*, p. 348.
17 Zubok, *A Failed Empire*, p. 20.
18 Pikhoya, *Moskva. Kreml'. Vlast'*, p. 146.
19 Alperovitz, "How Did the Cold War Begin?," 22.
20 Roberts, *The Soviet Union in World Politics*, p. 19.
21 Suny, *The Soviet Experiment*, p. 345.
22 LaFeber, *America, Russia, and the Cold War*, p. 16.
23 David Holloway, *Soviet Union and the Arms Race*, p. 20. For elaboration on the Soviet nuclear developments, see Holoway, *Stalin and the Bomb*.
24 Gaddis, *The Cold War*, pp. 25–6.
25 "The Secretary of War (Stimson) to President Truman, September 11, 1945," 68.

26 "Stalin's Analysis of Victory," 142.
27 Ibid.
28 Kissinger, *Diplomacy*, p. 440.
29 "Stalin's Analysis of Victory," 146.
30 LaFeber, *America, Russia, and the Cold War*, p. 39.
31 "The Kennan 'Long Telegram'," 20–1. Kennan's article in *Foreign Affairs* signed by X developed the points about ideology as the driving force behind Soviet behavior. Kennan [X], "The Sources of Soviet Conduct."
32 Churchill, "The Iron Curtain Speech," 138.
33 Stalin, "Churchill's Speech is a Call for War on Russia," 139–40.
34 Ibid, 141.
35 Zubok, *A Failed Empire*, p. 51.
36 Molotov, "A Russian View of 'Equal Opportunity'," 57.
37 LaFeber, *America, Russia, and the Cold War*, p. 43.
38 Ibid, 40; Larson, *Origins of Containment*, p. 250; Trachtenberg, *A Constructed Peace*, p. 41; Kissinger, *Diplomacy*, p. 441. For a different interpretation, see Roberts, *The Soviet Union in World Politics* and Roberts, *Stalin's Wars*.
39 Ulam, *Expansion and Coexistence*, p. 424.
40 Gaddis, *The Cold War*, p. 21.
41 Roberts, *The Soviet Union in World Politics*, p. 20.
42 Zubok, *A Failed Empire*, p. 23.
43 Ibid, p. 24. For details on the Soviet policy in Eastern Europe, see Naimark and Gibianski, eds., *The Establishment of Communist Regimes in Eastern Europe*; Wettig, *Stalin and the Cold War in Europe*.
44 Zubok, *A Failed Empire*, p. 24.
45 Kydd, *Trust and Mistrust in International Relations*, p. 108.
46 Zubok, *A Failed Empire*, pp. 64–9.
47 Ibid., p. 35.
48 Kydd, *Trust and Mistrust*, pp. 102–3; Vert, *Istoriya sovetskogo gosudarstva*, pp. 316–17.
49 Zubok and Pleshakov, *Inside the Kremlin's Cold War*, p. 130.
50 Roberts, *Stalin's Wars*, p. 24.
51 Kissinger, *Diplomacy*, p. 444.
52 Ibid., p. 445.
53 Roberts, *The Soviet Union in World Politics*, p. 24.
54 "Zhdanov on the Founding of the Cominform," 243.
55 Gaddis, *The Cold War*, p. 33; Vert, *Istoriya sovetskogo gosudarstva*, pp. 319–20.
56 Zubok, *A Failed Empire*, p. 55.
57 Vert, *Istoriya sovetskogo gosudarstva*, p. 308.
58 "Stalin's 'Two Camps' Speech," 292.
59 Zubok and Pleshakov, *Inside the Kremlin's Cold War*, pp. 27–8.
60 Wohlforth, *The Elusive Balance*, p. 103. For similar statements by other key officials, such as Lazar' Kaganovich, Grigori Malenkov, and Andrei Zhdanov, see Lazar' Kaganovich, *Pamyatnyye zapiski*, p. 538; Banerjee, "Reproduction of Subjects in Historical Structures," 25–33.
61 Riasanovsky, *A History of Russia*, p. 318.
62 Djilas, "Stalin in 1944–1945," 49.

63 Gaddis, *The Cold War*, p. 11. A member of Stalin's closest circle, Grigori Malenkov, saw things in terms of the spoils of war: "There have been cases in history where the fruits of victory escaped the victors. It is up to us so as to conduct matters and so to work as to secure these fruits." As quoted in Banerjee, "Reproduction of Subjects," 30.

64 Gaddis, *We Now Know*, p. 15.

65 Djilas, "Stalin in 1944–1945," 49.

66 Ibid. On Stalin's pan-Slavism and sympathy with the ideas of traditional nationalist honor, see also Duncan, *Russian Messianism*, pp. 56–7; Pikhoya, *Moskva. Kreml'. Vlast'*, pp. 115, 18–9; Zubok and Pleshakov, *Inside the Kremlin's Cold War*, pp. 16–17.

67 Zubok, *A Failed Empire*, p. 81.

68 Larson, *Origins of Containment*, p. 199.

69 "Churchill, Roosevelt, Stalin at Yalta: Caesar's Wife in Fact Had Her Sins," 89–90.

70 Zubok and Pleshakov, *Inside the Kremlin's Cold War*, pp. 29–30; Pikhoya, *Moskva. Kreml'. Vlast'*, pp. 106–8.

71 Kydd, *Trust and Mistrust*, p. 90; Roberts, *Stalin's Wars*, pp. 232–3. The "liberals" also developed a sophisticated perspective on the international system, which had its roots in Nikolai Bukharin's "organized capitalism" position. Wohlforth, *The Elusive Balance*, p. 81; Nation, *Black Earth, Red Star*, p. 127.

72 Haslam, "Litvinov, Stalin and the Road Not Taken."

73 For a similar assessment, see Shulman, *Stalin's Foreign Policy Reappraised*, p. 15.

74 For example, Foreign Trade Minister Anastas Mikoyan supported it. Suny, *The Soviet Experiment*, p. 354.The leading party economist and Stalin's confidant, Eugen Varga, was also among the supporters. Fursov, "Kholodnaya voina, sistemnyi kapitalizm i 'peresdacha kart Istoriyi'.

75 Wohlforth, *The Elusive Balance*, p. 102.

76 "The Novikov Telegram," 5.

77 Nove, *An Economic History of the U.S.S.R*, p. 293.

78 Suny, *The Soviet Experiment*, p. 347.

79 LaFeber, *America, Russia, and the Cold War*, p. 28.

80 Molotov later recalled that reparations "amounted to a pittance." Zubok and Pleshakov, *Inside the Kremlin's Cold War*, p. 31.

81 Ibid., p. 32.

82 Larson, *Origins of Containment*, p. 75.

83 Leffler, *A Preponderance of Power*, p. 15.

84 In June 1941, Truman, then the senator from Missouri, recommended that America play Germany and the Soviet Union against each other: "if we see that Germany is winning, we ought to help Russia, and if Russia is winning we ought to help Germany and that way let them kill as many as possible." Kissinger, *Diplomacy*, pp. 425–6.

85 Zubok and Pleshakov, *Inside the Kremlin's Cold War*, p. 95.

86 Kissinger, *Diplomacy*, p. 426.

87 Larson, *Origins of Containment*, p. 177.

88 Ibid., pp. 172–73.

89 Zubok, *A Failed Empire*, p. 32.
90 Wallace, "The Tougher We Get, the Tougher the Russians Will Get (September 12, 1946)," 146.
91 Suny, *The Soviet Experiment*, p. 351.
92 Truman terminated it the first day the war was officially over.
93 Leffler, *A Preponderance of Power*, pp. 115–16; Copeland, *Sources of Major War*, pp. 156–9. For the text of the Plan, see Baruch, "The United States' Plan for Controlling Atomic Energy (June 14, 1946)," 72–6.
94 Truman, "The Truman Doctrine (March 12, 1947)," 151–7.
95 Mearsheimer, *The Tragedy of Great Power Politics*, p. 327.
96 Copeland, *Sources of Major War*, p. 55.
97 Nove, *An Economic History of the U.S.S.R.*, p. 293.
98 Wohlforth, *The Elusive Balance*, p. 60.
99 Snyder, *Myths of Empire*, chap. 6; Kydd, *Trust and Mistrust*, chap. 4.
100 Snyder, *Myths of Empire*, p. 213.
101 Kydd, *Trust and Mistrust*, pp. 89–90.
102 Mastny, *Russia's Road to the Cold War*, p. 222.
103 Kennan (X), "The Sources of Soviet Conduct."
104 Kissinger, *Diplomacy*, p. 438.
105 Kennedy, *The Rise and Fall of the Great Powers*, pp. 371–2.
106 Wohlforth, *The Elusive Balance*, p. 131.
107 Gaddis, *We Now Know*, p. 290.
108 Malia, *Russia under Western Eyes*, p. 360.
109 Ibid.
110 Nation, *Black Earth, Red Star*, p. 171.
111 Kissinger, *Diplomacy*, p. 439.
112 For example, General Semyon Budennyi advocated such intervention. Stalin reportedly responded to Budennyi by posing the rhetorical questions, "How are we to feed them?" Akstyutin, "Pochemu Stalin dal'neyshemu sotrudnichestvu s soyuznikami predpochel konfrontatsiyu c nimi?"
113 Kennan, *Russia and the West under Lenin and Stalin*, p. 330.
114 Wohlforth, "Honor as Interest in Russian Decisions for War," 37.
115 See, for example, Threats to the Security of the United States, 4–7; United States Objectives With Respect to Russia, 1–2; U.S. Objectives With Respect to the USSR to Counter Soviet Threats to U.S. Security, 1; Soviet Capabilities and Intentions, 1. For analysis of the United States' inflated assessments of the Soviet threat after the war, see Matthew A. Evangelista, "Stalin's Postwar Army Reappraised."
116 Leffler, *A Preponderance of Power*, pp. 185–6.
117 The terms "socialist" and "democratic imperialism" come from Zubok and Gaddis, respectively. Zubok, *A Failed Empire*, chap. 2; Gaddis, *We Now Know*, pp. 284, 289. For development of the argument about the United States' democratic missionary ideas after the war, see especially David S. Foglesong, *The American Mission and the "Evil Empire,"* chap. 5.
118 LaFeber, *America, Russia, and the Cold War*, p. 20.

"One state and, of course, first and foremost the United States, has overstepped its national borders in every way. This is visible in the economic, political, cultural and educational policies it imposes on other nations. Well, who likes this? Who is happy about this?"

Vladimir Putin[1]

"[W]e will not tolerate any more humiliation, and we are not joking."

Dmitri Medvedev[2]

The Russia–Georgia War

Since the Rose Revolution of 2003 that swept Mikhail Saakashvili to power in Georgia, Russia's relationship with its Caucasian neighbor had evolved through several clearly delineated, increasingly unhappy stages. The first, more hopeful stage came during Saakashvili's first months in office, when elites of both nations seemed genuinely interested in cooperating to improve relations from their post-Soviet nadir reached toward the end of the Eduard Shevardnadze era. Because of persistent disagreements, including Russia's reluctance to reduce its military presence in Georgia, Georgia's increasingly Western leanings and apparent ingratitude for Russian assistance in solving the Adjara crisis, and ultimately Georgian bellicosity toward South Ossetia, the relationship moved in the second stage from cooperation to an atmosphere of "passive containment" by Russia. Continuing tensions combined with the spy scandal of 2007 moved the environment into the third stage of "active containment," in which Russia recalled its ambassador and cut off almost all links between the countries. Finally, in August 2008, the small-scale post-Soviet cold war escalated into a military confrontation that lasted for five days.

The Rose Revolution and the Stage of Nascent Cooperation

Despite Georgia's unequivocally Western orientation, the Rose Revolution of November 2003 provided the nation with an opportunity to mend fences with Russia. Although the two countries have deeply intertwined cultural and historical ties, before the Rose Revolution the Russian-Georgian relationship had deteriorated to its lowest ebb since the Soviet breakup. Russia routinely accused Georgia of providing haven to Chechen separatists in the remote Pankisi gorge and did not exclude military action as a potential response. Georgia was irritated with the Russians' reluctance to remove its military bases from Georgian soil, despite a 1999 agreement to do so. Russia's accelerated passport distribution to residents of Georgia's breakaway republics, Abkhazia and South Ossetia, further undermined Tbilisi's claims to sovereignty over these territories. Shevardnadze's stated intention to join NATO and Georgia's involvement in the Baku-Ceylon oil pipeline, which was to bypass Russia, further irritated Russia.

When in November 2003 the Shevardnadze administration was besieged, both countries recognized an opportunity to improve relations. The first sign of cooperation was when the Russian foreign minister Igor Ivanov played an important role in averting potential bloodshed by convincing Shevardnadze to resign – the dour Ivanov was even met with a crowd of Georgians chanting his name adoringly. Putin guardedly expressed hope that the forthcoming Georgian election would install an administration that would work "to restore the traditions of friendship between our two countries,"[3] but clearly indicated that the onus was on the Georgian side.

President-elect Mikhail Saakashvili made "closer, warmer and friendlier relations"[4] with Russia an immediate priority; one of his first actions was to attend a summit at the Kremlin in February 2004. Unlike Shevardnadze, who denied that Chechen separatists were present in Georgian territory, Saakashvili acknowledged their existence and vowed to help fight them. A series of crackdowns ensued, pleasing Russia but worrying human rights groups. Saakashvili also campaigned to impede the spread of Islamic fundamentalism ("We are for freedom of religion, but not that religion"),[5] a sop to Russia's treatment of the Chechen problem as a struggle against Taliban-style repression.

Economic links between the two countries were strengthened as well. A Russia–Georgia economic forum in May 2004 was the largest business gathering between the two countries to date. Russia worked to restructure Georgia's debt, provided it electrical supplies and energy subsidies, and stepped up investment in Georgia. Visa regimes – a sticking point between the two nations – were relaxed, and a more open labor market policy was adopted.

Perhaps the greatest indicator of Russo-Georgian cooperation during this period was Russia's assistance in defusing the Adjara uprising in May 2004 and bringing about a peaceful result. Rather than allow Georgia to endure the humiliation and possible bloodshed of another separatist quagmire, Russia intervened, removing the Moscow-backed Adjaran leader Aslan Abashidze by helicopter and paving the way for a triumphant and face-saving consolidation of sovereignty by Saakashvili.[6] This gesture provided a brief window of hope that Russia and Georgia would be able to work together on the separatist issues of Abkhazia and South Ossetia.

Yet despite all of this ostensible cooperation, there were several issues undermining the Russia–Georgia relationship during this period. Throughout this time, Russia and Georgia were at odds over the presence of Russia's military bases: Georgia wanted them out immediately and pushed this point strenuously, while Russia, in apparent foot-dragging, continued to provide variable but lengthy estimates for the time it would take to remove them. Georgia's westward course continued unabated – one need only contrast Saakashvili's sober Kremlin summit with his chummy visit to America later that month to judge the relative strengths of Georgia's respective alliances. The Georgian president announced in April 2004 that he wanted eventually to join the EU, the NATO-Georgian courtship continued, and the Baku-Ceyhan pipeline was proceeding according to plan. Abkhazia and South Ossetia were still intractable problems.

The cooperative period ended with Georgia's bellicose response to crises in South Ossetia in August 2004.[7] By August Russia too changed its tactics in relation to its southern neighbor.

"Passive" and "Active Containment"

When Georgia chose to use force against South Ossetia, Russia balked. In August 2004 Russia suspended talks with Georgia and stopped issuing visas to Georgians, an oft-repeated tactic throughout the relationship. The two candidates in Abkhazia's disputed election met in Moscow in November with Russia as mediator, highlighting Russia's de facto preeminence in a territory that theoretically belonged to Georgia. In February 2005 Russia reiterated that it reserved the right to wage preventive strikes into Georgian territory against potential terrorists[8] – a chilly regression to the rhetoric of the Shevardnadze era. It also announced its intention to raise the price of gas, just in time for winter.

Georgia, meanwhile, began to see a nefarious Russian hand behind most developments. The Georgians were quick to point out the "double standard" of Russia's behavior: opposing separatists at home yet evidently supporting separatism in Georgia.[9] When a mysterious pipeline explosion cut off gas delivery to Georgia in the winter of 2006, followed by delays to its repair, Georgia's instinct was to label it Russian sabotage, which it did so vociferously.[10] Georgia accused Russia of violating Georgian airspace and of complicity in a series of bombings, and Russian peacekeepers in the breakaway regions were characterized as threatening rather than neutral. To Russia's great annoyance, Georgia took several steps, including a parliamentary resolution in February 2006, to the effect that Russian peacekeepers were no longer welcome in the breakaway regions.[11]

Shortly after the February resolution Russia again stopped issuing visas. In March Russia banned Georgian wine, a national symbol, 90 percent of which was exported to Russia, and Georgian mineral water, ostensibly for health reasons. In July, Russia temporarily closed its only overland border with Georgia for "construction," disrupting Georgian exports amid cries of unfriendliness and provocation.

There were some moments of cooperation, however exceptional, during this period. In early 2005 a Russian-Georgian railway ferry link was opened. After much discussion, Russia agreed to pull out its two military bases in Batumi and Akhalkalaki on an accelerated time frame. In response Saakashvili claimed to be offering Russia a hand of friendship, though he lamented that his hand was "hanging in the air."[12]

What little hope there was of renewed cooperation was destroyed by Georgia's actions and Russia's response in the spy scandal of September 2006, which initiated the transition from Russia's passive to active containment. When Georgia arrested four Russian intelligence officers and prepared to put them on trial for spying, a tipping point was evidently reached. Even though international pressure persuaded Georgia to release the officers to the OSCE after only a few days, Russia did not temper its response. The troop pullout was temporarily suspended, all transport and postal links between the countries were severed, Georgian-run businesses inside Russia were scrutinized and harassed, and many Georgians in Russia were rounded up and deported. Gazprom discussed doubling the price of gas and threatened (at the onset of winter, of course) to shut off supplies if they were not paid for.

Georgia responded with accusations of Russian "blackmail" and characterized its policies as racist and xenophobic.[13] Appealing to the international community, it sued Russia at the European Court of Human Rights in April 2007 over the deportations. Saakashvili spun the standoff as an opportunity to wean Georgia from its dependence on Russia and to deepen economic and energy partnerships with other nations. The NATO membership process continued apace.

In October 2007 Georgia declared its intention to formally end Russia's peacekeeping mandate in Abkhazia after Russian soldiers allegedly apprehended and beat a group of Georgian police officers. Georgia also continued to accuse Russia of routine violations of its airspace. A bizarre mini-scandal surrounding a rocket that landed in August 2007 in a field near the Georgian-South Ossetian border – which Georgia, of course, insisted was of Russian provenance and Russia, of course, denied – was a typical incident.[14]

Georgia's elections in January 2008 presented a similar opportunity to that in 2003 to have another go at improved relations. Significantly weakened in his current political state, Saakashvili underscored the importance of improving relations with Russia, saying he wanted the two nations to start "with a clean slate."[15] Russia, however, was the leading voice questioning the legitimacy of his reelection. The head of Russia's diplomatic mission, Vyacheslav Kovalenko, echoing Putin's rhetoric after the Rose Revolution, expressed a desire for improved relations, but clearly indicated that it was Georgia's responsibility to pursue them: "Russia wants friendship [but] it expects from Georgia specific steps and actions that could be viewed as aiming at improving our relationship."[16] Movement toward renewed friendship was disrupted by Kosovo's declaration of independence on February 17, 2008, and Russia's lifting of sanctions on Abkhazia twenty days later in response. The latter action further dimmed hopes for reconciliation. From that point on the Kremlin's policies went beyond measures to contain Georgia, indicating that Russia was no longer confident in the diplomacy of containment and was preparing for a possible military confrontation.

Confrontation and the Five-Day War

Russia did not stop at lifting sanctions on Abkhazia. In April, the Kremlin reinforced its peacekeeping forces in the republic with 1,500 fresh troops without consulting or informing the Georgian side. In the meantime, ethnic Russians assumed the positions of prime minister, security minister, and defense minister in the South Ossetian government. Both South Ossetia and Abkhasia continued to oppose Georgia's membership in the Western alliance and to press for their own integration with Russia. The Kremlin was still not prepared to legally recognize Georgia's separatist territories, but in April, Russian President Putin issued a decree establishing direct relations between Moscow and both of Georgia's breakaway republics. In early June, Russia repaired the Abkhaz railroad, ending Georgia's blockade of the republic and enabling the transport of additional Russian forces into Abkhazia.[17] All of these policies took place in the context of growing provocations and military hostilities between Georgia and its breakaway republics that included abductions of civilians, attacks against the republics' officials,[18] intelligence activities, and gunfire in villages on both sides of the border.

Violence escalated in June and even more so in July, with intensification of ceasefire violations by both sides and mutual accusations of war preparations. In early July Georgian forces attacked homes in the South Ossetian capital Tskhinvali and in nearby villages with artillery fire.[19] Claiming that the South Ossetian side had attacked first, Tbilisi continued its offensive actions and stopped only when South Ossetia announced a general mobilization and appealed to Russia to come to its defense. The Russian foreign minister condemned Georgian attacks on South Ossetia as an "open act of aggression"[20] and insisted that all sides sign an agreement rejecting the use of force. Russia also presented a draft resolution on the situation in the conflict zones of South Ossetia and Abkhazia to the UN Security Council. Tbilisi responded by accusing Russia of de facto annexation of Georgian territory by establishing direct relations with the breakaway republics and violating Georgia's airspace by flying Russian military planes over South Ossetia. Georgia also refused to sign the non-use of force agreement and demanded that Russian peacekeeping forces be withdrawn from the region. Western officials issued several statements expressing concerns over the deteriorating situation in the Caucasus, and the German foreign minister Frank-Walter Steinmeier traveled to the region to facilitate resolution of the conflict. However, Georgia and its autonomous regions continued to be engaged in provocative actions, firing shots on each others' positions and surrounding villages[21]; in addition, Georgia continued to concentrate heavy weaponry on the border with South Ossetia.[22] According to Western observers,[23] by the morning of August 7 Georgia had amassed 12,000 troops on its border with South Ossetia and had positioned 75 tanks and armored personnel carriers near Gori.

On the night of August 8, 2008, Georgia attacked the South Ossetian capital Tskhinvali in an attempt to restore control over the rebellious province. Georgian troops killed ten Russian peacekeepers and, by attacking the city with heavy artillery, inflicted heavy civilian casualties on South Ossetia.[24] It did so despite a ceasefire agreement it had accepted on August 7. Within several hours, Russian forces responded by crossing the Georgian border into South Ossetia through the Roki Tunnel.[25] Its response was overwhelming and included several armored battalions, air power, and marines, defeating and destroying much of the Georgian military. Russia also recognized the independence of South Ossetia and Abkhazia and imposed areas of security control throughout Georgia. Despite Saakashvili's efforts to present his offensive as a response to Russia's aggression, and although it seems possible and even plausible that

Russia "set a trap" for Georgia's notoriously hot-headed leader, sources as diverse as intelligence agencies, human rights organizations, OSCE, the European Union's investigation, Georgian exiled leader Irakli Okruashvili, and various government analysts agreed that the initial aggression came from Tbilisi, not Moscow.[26]

The five-day war demonstrated the failure of Russia's active containment policies and the Kremlin's willingness to use force in the areas that it viewed of critical importance to its security. Its actions in the Caucasus demonstrated that Russia no longer viewed the old methods of preserving stability and security in the region as sufficient. Russia cemented its military presence in the Caucasus by defeating Georgia and recognizing its autonomous republics' independence.

The Russia–Georgia War, August 2008: Timeline

2003 November	Rose Revolution in Georgia
2004 February	First Russia–Georgia summit in the Kremlin
May	Russia formulated its proposals for a good neighbor treaty with Georgia
	Russia–Georgia economic forum
	Georgia secures control of Adjara
June	Russia and Georgia agree on withdrawal of Russia's military bases
August	Georgia attempts to use force in South Ossetia
2005 February	Russia claims the right to use preventive strikes into Georgian territory
March	A colored revolution in Kyrgyzstan
May	President George W. Bush visits Tbilisi
2006 January	Pipeline explosion cuts off gas delivery to Georgia
February	Georgia's parliament "outlaws" Russian peacekeepers in the region
March	Russia bans import of Georgia's wine
June	Russia declares opposition to Ukraine or Georgia joining NATO
September	Georgia arrests several Russian intelligence officers; Russia closes the border with Georgia and deports illegal Georgians
2008 January	Saakashvili is reelected as president
February	Kosovo declares independence
March	Russia ends its compliance with CIS sanctions on Abkhazia

April	NATO Bucharest Summit denies Georgia a Membership Action Plan
	U.S. President Bush continues to support Georgia in NATO
	Russia reinforces its peacekeeping forces in Abkhazia
	Russia shoots down a Georgian drone over the conflict zone
May	A car bomb explodes in South Ossetia on its independence day
June	Escalation of violence on the Georgia–South Ossetia border
	Russia sends unarmed railroad troops into Abkhazia
	NATO's general secretary travels to Georgia to discuss its membership
July	Russia proposes that all sides sign a non-use of force agreement
	U.S. Secretary of State Condoleezza Rice travels to Georgia
	German foreign minister travels to the region to reduce tensions
August	Georgia amasses 12,000 troops on the border with South Ossetia
	Georgia uses force in South Ossetia; Russia intervenes

Explaining Russia's Intervention

The honor perspective is helpful in explaining Russia's intervention. Russia viewed itself as an established honest broker and a guarantor of peace in the Caucasus, and that perception was widely supported by the public at home. Indeed, a number of the small nations in the region perceived Russia favorably.[27] These constituencies upheld and promoted Russia's more assertive actions toward Georgia, which they viewed as the bully in the region. They were largely supportive of Russia's decision to wage war and recognize Abkhazia and South Ossetia.[28] Yet Georgia too was motivated by honor considerations in its relationships with Russia. Just as Russia was frustrated by the lack of recognition by the United States and NATO, Tbilisi was angry with Moscow's unwillingness to honor Georgia's independence and right to determine its own foreign policy orientation. The Russia–Georgia relationship severely deteriorated as a result of the nations' *perceived* lack of recognition of each other's special interests and cultural obligations.

Honor and Humiliation in Russia

Russia's initial attempt to cooperate with Georgia was possible because the Kremlin's honor expectations were not at odds with those of Georgia and the United States. By assisting Tbilisi with the power transition after the Rose Revolution and not interfering with its efforts to restore control over Adjara, the Kremlin communicated its willingness to help Georgia strengthen its territorial integrity. In exchange Russia expected Georgia to honor Russian interests in the Caucasus by not pressuring for immediate military withdrawals, not using force in its dealings with South Ossetia and Abkhazia, and consulting Russia on vital security issues such as membership in NATO. In May 2004, after Saakashvili's meeting with Putin in Moscow, the Kremlin formulated its proposals for signing a good neighbor treaty and forwarded them to Tbilisi.[29]

In August 2004 the Kremlin's expectations of honor were violated, when Tbilisi used force against South Ossetia, possibly attempting to win control over the strategic Djava district,[30] and failed to consult Russia. Putin responded by calling for Georgia to show restrain and honor its pledge to resolve sovereignty disputes peacefully. "It is important," he said, "that the negotiation process continue with a view to creating an atmosphere of trust and preserving peace and stability. Russia will do its utmost to foster this process."[31] Russia therefore was trying to get Georgia to honor the initial expectation of cooperation. Instead of a partner in the region, Moscow felt it was confronted with an ungrateful and uncooperative neighbor that wanted to accelerate Russian withdrawal and integrate, even by the use of force, the separatist enclaves.

The Kremlin therefore changed its tactics by canceling Putin's official trip to Georgia, stopping the issuance of visas for Georgians, strengthening ties with Abkhazia and South Ossetia, and escalating its political rhetoric. Over time, Russia also adopted a more combative tone in relations with the United States. Most irritating and insulting to the Kremlin was Washington's newly revealed strategy of global regime change that was now being implemented in the former Soviet region, not just in Iraq. Russia was fearful that the so-called colored revolutions in Georgia, Ukraine, and Kyrgyzstan during 2003–5 would undermine Russia's stability and influence in the region. That postrevolutionary Georgia and Ukraine had expressed their desire to join NATO only added to Russia's sense of being vulnerable and politically isolated by the West. Georgia saw Russia's response as an indicator of Russia's imperial complex and unwillingness to recognize its neighbor's independence; Georgian officials engaged in inflammatory rhetoric and referred to the Kremlin as a "fascist regime."[32]

The escalation of Russia's efforts to contain Georgia demonstrated that the Kremlin was prepared to go far to make others recognize its honor and special status in the region. Although its decision after the spy scandal to impose tough sanctions against Georgia elicited almost universal condemnation in the West, that condemnation only served to validate Russia's already formed suspicions vis-à-vis Western, particularly American intentions in the Caucasus. By now, the Kremlin felt it had only one option left – the toughest possible response short of using force. As Western officials demonstrated their support for Georgia,[33] the Kremlin sought to send a strong warning to both Tbilisi and the West. A most important aspect of the warning was that Russia would no longer tolerate its disregard by Western countries, as demonstrated by the prospects of Georgia's membership in NATO. Although Western nations helped defuse the crisis in which Russia's officers were arrested and also sought to discourage Tbilisi from using force against its separatist territories, the Kremlin did not see such efforts as sufficient in recognizing Russia's vital role in the region. In June 2006, Russia's foreign minister warned that if Ukraine or Georgia joined NATO that could lead to a colossal shift in global geopolitics.[34] The Kremlin was determined to stop the alliance expansion, and the spat with Georgia seemed to be a crucial test of will for Moscow. The Russia–Georgia crisis therefore became an indicator of a bigger Russia–West crisis.

The Kremlin also acted on its perceived obligation to protect Russians and those gravitating to Russia in the former Soviet region.[35] Unable to offer such protection earlier because of its internal weakness, Russia was now determined to demonstrate that it had not forgotten those loyal to its values and interests in the Caucasus. On a number of occasions South Ossetia had expressed its desire to reintegrate with Russia, and neither Abkhazia nor South Ossetia recognized their membership in Georgia after the Soviet breakup. In addition, the overwhelming majority of Abkhasians and South Ossetians obtained Russian passports throughout the 1990s and 2000s. For example, according to the chairman of the Russia's Duma committee for the CIS and compatriot affairs, Andrei Kokoshin, "Russian citizens constitute a large share of population living on the territory of South Ossetia and Abkhazia," which meant that "Russia must protect their lives, health, property, honor and dignity by all available means, like the United States and other Western nations are doing."[36] Russia expected other powers to recognize its claims to special status as a guardian of cultural balance in the Caucasus and the larger Soviet region.

Finally, developments during 2006–7 provided ample reasons to view Russia as a power that was angry and frustrated by what it perceived as unfair treatment by the United States and NATO. President Putin's criticism of the U.S.-led "unipolarity" initiative, beginning with his speech at the Munich Conference on Security Policy in January 2007, as well as his threats to withdraw from already signed international treaties, such as the Intermediate Nuclear Missile Treaty, was meant to convey Russia's frustration with its inability to win recognition and develop more equitable relations with the United States. Although humiliation is a sensitive subject,[37] it is not difficult to see that Russians felt humiliated by the situation and were increasingly prepared to do anything to change it. The West's geopolitical advances into what Russia has traditionally viewed as its sphere of interests and the desire expressed by postrevolutionary Georgia and Ukraine to join NATO exacerbated Russia's sense of vulnerability and isolation. After the NATO summit in Bucharest in April 2008 Russia reiterated that it would do everything in its power to prevent expansion of the alliance and extension of its membership to Georgia.[38] The so-called frozen conflicts were merely leverage in the Kremlin's hands, and the Kremlin planned to keep them frozen until NATO scuttled its plans to continue its march to the East. However, in the aftermath of the Bucharest summit, some Russian analysts[39] began to argue that if membership in NATO was so important to Georgia, then Tbilisi was likely to obtain it at the cost of its territorial integrity.

The Kremlin's policy was largely supported by both elites and the general public at home. In response to Tbilisi's provocative and militarist behavior, many in Russia felt that tough reciprocal actions were fully justified – this sentiment was reinforced by irritation about the U.S. policy of promoting democracy and special relations with Georgia. The Russian public was also very critical of the United States in general and viewed the earlier bid to build a strategic partnership with the United States as a failure. In 2006, more than 60 percent of the general public believed that the U.S. role was mainly negative.[40] In September 2008, 67 percent of Russians felt negative feelings about the United States and 75 percent about Georgia, compared to 39 percent about the European Union.[41] In addition, support for the army increased considerably.[42] There was also strong support for a tough foreign policy. One poll indicated that about 61 percent viewed Russia's course to be "well-considered and well-balanced."[43]

Table 14.1. *Russia's Basic Economic Indicators, 1999–2007 (%, annual change)*

	1998	1999	2000	2001	2002	2003	2004	2005	2006	2007
Real GDP growth	−5.3	6.3	10.0	5.1	4.3	7.7	7.2	6.4	6.7	7.3
Real wages	−10	−22	18	20	16	11	11	13	13	16
Budget surplus (% of GDP)	−5.3	0.5	3.5	3.0	1.4	1.7	4.5	8.1	8.5	5.5
Urals oil prices ($/barrel)	12	17	27	23	24	27	34	50	61	69

Source: Rutland, "Putin's Economic Record," 1052.

Russia's Domestic Confidence

After years of economic depression after the Soviet breakup, Russia's domestic conditions had changed dramatically. From 1999–2007, the economy improved, enabling it to catch up with the 1990 level (see Table 14.1), and it thereafter continued to grow at the annual pace of about 7 percent. The overall size of the economy increased sixfold in current dollars – from $200 billion to $1.3 trillion. Russia's per capita GDP quadrupled to nearly $7,000, and about 20 million people were lifted out of poverty.[44] Russia's middle class now constitutes about 25 percent of the population.[45] From 2000–5, the average Russian experienced a 26 percent annual growth in income, compared to only a 10 percent rise in that of the average Chinese.[46] Direct foreign investments in the Russian economy skyrocketed, making it the first in the world among developing economies.[47] In early 2008, for example, industrial production rose an annual 9.2 percent.[48] Although much of the economic recovery was due to high oil prices, the government continued to work to reduce the economy's reliance on energy exports. The percentage of Russians who thought that the chosen development course in Russia was correct grew year by year.[49]

In response to Russia's perceived humiliation in the arena of international relations and its growing domestic strength, a consensus emerged in favor of an assertive foreign policy style for achieving the objectives of development, stability, and security. The Foreign Ministry report, *A Review of the Russian Federation's Foreign Policy*, commissioned by the Kremlin and released on March 27, 2007, elaborated on the new face of Russia's great power pragmatism. It indicated an important change in Russia's thinking since the 2000 Foreign Policy Concept. The report embraced the notion of multipolarity based on "a more equitable distribution of resources for influence and economic growth,"[50] which laid the ground for a more self-confident and assertive Russia. The document presented Russia as ready to actively shape international relations by challenging the actions of others, particularly the United States, if they were "unilateral" and disrespectful of international law. At the same time, the report was not anti-American and did not call for any concerted effort to undermine the U.S. global position. Instead, it defended the notion of collective leadership and multilateral diplomacy as the alternative to unilateralism and hegemony in international relations. Russia's new president Dmitri Medvedev amplified on the assertive vision that positioned Russia as a global player and a maker of new global rules. Speaking in Berlin in June 2008 he outlined a broad perspective on Europe "from Vancouver to Vladivostok" and proposed an all-European Treaty to establish a new security architecture by moving beyond NATO expansion and the conflict over Kosovo.[51]

The West and Georgia

Russia's desire to remain a great power and preserve its special interest and influence in the Caucasus led to foreign policy objectives that directly or indirectly contradicted Georgia's interpretation of its own sovereignty. Although Russia saw itself as a stabilizer and protector of small nationalities in a volatile region, Tbilisi viewed Russia as an overt barrier to Georgian territorial integrity because of its presence and policies in Abkhazia and South Ossetia.[52]

Initially Georgia and the United States did not seem prepared to oppose Russia in the region. During his summit with Putin, Saakashvili humbled himself by referring to Georgia as "a small country" and pledged to respect Russia's security interests in the region. Although he expected Russia to begin to dismantle its bases in Akhalkalaki and Batumi, he also promised not to have foreign troops on Georgia's territory after Russia's withdrawal. The United States – although it had already expressed its doubts about Russia's domestic centralization[53] – was still hoping to make the post-9/11 partnership with Moscow work. In turn the Kremlin was still expecting to be consulted by the White House on issues relating to security in the Caucasus.

Soon, however, Tbilisi adopted a different strategy to achieve its objectives. It aimed to resolve territorial disputes without assistance from Russia by relying on political support from the United States, which had emerged as Georgia's most important ally and patron in the region. Washington had provided $1.2 billion in aid to Georgia during the 1990s, and it had deployed military advisors in Georgia ostensibly to train and equip forces to eradicate terrorism from the lawless Pankisi Gorge. Yet a Georgian Defense Ministry official revealed the real reason for the military advisors: the U.S. military intended to "train our rapid reaction force, which is guarding strategic sites in Georgia – particularly oil pipelines."[54] The United States was determined to secure its access to the Caspian oil and strengthen its geostrategic presence in the Caucasus, which the Kremlin saw as evidence of America's bias and lack of recognition for Russia's role in the region. In contrast, Tbilisi felt emboldened by Washington's support. The Georgian Foreign Ministry did not respond to Russia's offer of a good neighbor treaty until October and then in an unsatisfactory manner.[55] Although the United States' official position regarding the violence in South Ossetia was for both sides to disengage militarily and work toward negotiations,[56] Georgian leaders felt compelled to continue trying to solve the territorial disputes by whatever means necessary.[57]

Russia's policy of active containment and its new attitude of frustration only further reinforced the already strong sense in Tbilisi that the Kremlin had no respect for Georgia's independence. Just as Russia was frustrated by the lack of recognition by the United States and NATO, Georgia demonstrated anger at what it saw as Russia's lack of respect for its own choice of foreign policy orientation. President Saakashvili and other officials were defiant and continued to condemn Russia's "imperialism" and unwillingness to honor Georgia's independence. The discourse of anger and frustration is expressed clearly in many policy statements, such as the following from President Saakashvili: "In my opinion, Russia is unable to reconcile itself with Georgia's independence. It wants to revert to the Soviet rule although this is impossible. Georgia is no longer a country that it was some four or five years ago, when we did not have either an army or police and corruption was rife in this country. Georgia is now able to protect its territorial integrity and sovereignty."[58]

Capitalizing on its special relationship with the United States and determined to benefit from the growing confrontation between Russia and the West, Tbilisi seemed, in Russian eyes, determined to humiliate Russia further. In Tbilisi there was no longer talk of Georgia's military neutrality after Russia's withdrawal; instead, a discussion was underway that a future Georgia might not object to possible future deployment by NATO of weapons of mass destruction on its territory.[59] The issue came full circle when Russia insisted that Georgia's foreign policy choice was not independent, but instead was formed by the United States, as Tbilisi's most important ally in the Caucasus.

The last stage in the Russia–Georgia escalation occurred in August 2008 when Georgia moved from anti-Russian actions and a refusal to sign a non-use of force agreement to concentrating heavy weaponry on

Abkhazia and South Ossetia's borders, while the United States and other Western nations provided an implicit legitimization for Georgia's actions. Although the United States was not directly responsible for the Russia–Georgia confrontation, by its actions, it emboldened both nations to act in a more assertive and unilateral fashion. On the one hand, support of Kosovo's independence by the United States and other Western powers encouraged Georgia's breakaway republics to secede, making it more difficult for Russia to resist recognizing their independence claims. It was after the recognition of Kosovo in February 2008 that Russia lifted sanctions on Abkhazia and established direct relations with both Abkhazia and South Ossetia.[60] On the other hand, the United States did little to restrain Georgia's militarization and ambitions to rein in its autonomous republics by force. American support of Georgia's NATO aspirations, economic assistance, and training of the Georgian military were crucial in heightening the sense of confidence in Tbilisi.

As developments were proceeding in the summer of 2008, it was becoming increasingly difficult to prevent military confrontation. With Georgia and South Ossetia engaged in constant provocations and exchanges of fire, some urgent and concerted actions were necessary on the part of the larger players – the United States, the European Union, and Russia. Yet that was not forthcoming because the European Union was only beginning to be aware of the need for mediation, and the United States and Russia were acting in a partisan manner by supporting opposite sides in Georgia's conflict with its breakaway republics. While Russia was increasing its support for Abkhasia and South Ossetia, NATO and the U.S. officials were backing Tbilisi, rarely criticizing Georgia's actions publicly. For example, on June 20, NATO's general secretary met with President Saakashvili to discuss the planned conclusion of a Membership Action Plan (MAP) for Georgia and scheduled a session of the North Atlantic Council to be held in Georgia in September. Less than a month before the war, U.S. Secretary of State Condoleezza Rice traveled to Europe. She found no time to visit Moscow, but on July 9, Rice went to Tbilisi to demonstrate support for Georgia's territorial integrity and the MAP.

Alternative Explanations

Offensive realism expects states to maximize power and, whenever possible, to achieve the status of a regional hegemon.[61] In this account, Russia then should be expected to pursue a policy of dominating Georgia by all means available. Strategic reasons that the Kremlin may view as compelling would include isolation of the external powers' ability to penetrate the Northern Caucasus, control over energy transportation from the Caspian Sea, and securing easy access to Armenia, Russia's ally. Providing support for Georgia's separatists in South Ossetia and Abkhazia would therefore serve as a way to destabilize Tbilisi's grip on power from inside the country.

Russian area studies scholars, consciously or not, have reasoned about the motives of Russia's foreign policy using the offensive realist logic. Moscow's ties with separatist leaders, as well as its eagerness to exchange energy assistance for control over some strategic assets in Armenia and Georgia, prompted some scholars to speculate that Russia sought to preserve its hegemonic power in the region – a view that was reinforced by Moscow's recent reluctance to dismantle its military bases in Georgia and occasional promises to "preventively" use force outside its own territory to respond to terrorist threats. Some speculated that Russia's talk of using preventive force was in fact a pretext for invading Georgia.[62] Others proposed that Russia was satisfied with the status quo, but would continue to seek instability and war in the region.[63] According to this group of scholars, what drove the Kremlin's increasingly assertive international policy was its perceived insecurity in response to the colored revolutions and the specter of Islamic radicalism.[64] Still others asserted that the war with Georgia was a part of a broader geopolitical plan to revive Russia's hegemony in the former Soviet region and strengthen Moscow's ability to challenge the West globally.[65] Many Georgian scholars and policy makers also viewed Russia's behavior in terms of expansionism and power domination.[66]

As logically compelling as it may seems, the power perspective is not supported by strong evidence. For example, it is plausible to assume that Russia's insistence on Georgia's non-use of force agreement was dictated by Russia's material weakness and inability to exercise force against Tbilisi. Yet the evidence for such intentions by the Kremlin is not available, and it is at least as plausible to interpret Russia's motives as driven by defense and security considerations. It is even more difficult to find support for the offensive realist expectation that Russia's military response was driven by power objectives. If it was, why then did the Kremlin wait as long as it did; even more importantly, why did it not try to remove Saakashvili from power to secure full control over Georgia's territory and resources[67]? Again, interests of Russia's security are at least as helpful in determining its behavior and explaining why it limited itself to recognizing Abkhazia and South Ossetia's independence, but abstained from pursuing more expansionist objectives. The power/domination perspective lacks nuance and a sense of proportion; by presenting Russia as inherently imperialist and anti-Western, this perspective is less inclined to seriously consider the impact of contemporary developments on Russia's actions.

Defensive realism seems a more plausible lens through which to interpret Russia–Georgia policy. Rather than emphasizing power accumulation, defensive realists focus on imperatives of security and survival, and they argue that states more commonly respond to security dilemmas with balancing or bandwagoning than with war or blackmail, as in offensive realism. In terms of primary motivating factors, defensive realists[68] delineate misperceptions and institutional biases that may stand in the way of a correct reading of signals coming from the anarchical international system.

Scholars influenced by defensive realism may see Russia's policies in the Caucasus as serving the objectives of security, such as preventing a major war on its borders or allowing NATO, a potentially competitive military alliance, to use Georgia as a proxy for securing additional geopolitical gains in the region. In this case, Russia is on defense, not offense, and it is the United States and NATO that want to maximize power at the expense of Russia, not the other way around. Because they may not intend to attack Russia, the United States and NATO may not present real threats, but they certainly are threats in the eyes of Russia's officials. This perspective is useful in understanding some of Russia's motivations, and there are ample statements by the country's officials and members of the political class framing their response to Georgia in terms of defending security objectives.[69] However, this perspective is insufficient because it fails to consider Russia's prestige and historical obligations to small nationalities in the Caucasus. This explains why, although defensive realism offers a plausible interpretation of Russia's limited objectives during the war and its insistence on Georgia's non-use of force agreement before the war, it does not predict Russia's recognition of Abkhazia and South Ossetia's independence.

Neoclassical realism[70] agrees with structural realists about the primary impact of the structure of the international system on state behavior, but focuses on considerations of external reputation and prestige. Russia's insistence on brokering Georgia's peace agreement with its breakaway republics can then be understood in terms of the Kremlin's desire to gain recognition by Western nations, which Russia historically viewed as its significant other. Similarly, Russia's limited objectives during the five-day war can be understood in terms of its fear of losing political standing in relations with the United States and Europe. Neoclassical realism seems less helpful, however, in explaining why Russia went to war and why it chose to officially recognize Georgia's breakaway republics. Although these steps made sense from the perspective of defending Russia's honor or prestige as a great power – especially when viewed in the larger context of Georgia's aspirations to join NATO – such steps may also be viewed as undermining the West's recognition of Russia as a democratic nation that is bound by international law.

Part of the problem with neoclassical realism is that it tends to view intangibles as determined by the structure of the international system, rather than by local historical factors. Considerations of honor and reputation then are merely endogenous to the international power balance, and not factors that may have a potentially significant independent effect. By overplaying the role of anarchy in determining state foreign policy, neoclassical realists cannot fully account for the perception of threat that is partly domestic. Their analysis therefore overlooks some aspects of honor and prestige that are domestically formed and defended on the basis of Russia's cultural perceptions of threats and challenges abroad.

Assessment

Overall, the honor/recognition perspective adds to our understanding of Russia's behavior in the Caucasus. Russia views itself as an established honest broker and a guarantor of peace in the region, and that perception is widely supported by the public at home and by small nationalities in the region, such as Abkhazia and South Ossetia. It is this dynamic of mutually exclusive honor claims by various actors, rather than the structure of the international system per se, that was largely responsible for the deterioration of Russian-Georgian relations. Combined with Russia's perceived internal strength, the sense of humiliation from external treatment provided the necessary conditions for the rise of an assertive honor vision in the Kremlin. Even if the international system is anarchic, focusing on everyday interactions provides an understanding of what anarchy means to various players and how social contexts of power are being formed and unformed. State behavior is shaped by emotions and power calculations, but can only be understood in contexts of everyday interactions and socio-historical development.

Through its military intervention, Russia managed to solve several important foreign policy tasks. It protected the South Ossetian people from Georgian troops, thereby confirming Russia's historically won authority as a pacifier in the region. Russia also cemented its military presence in the strategic area of the Southern Caucasus by defeating Georgia's attack on South Ossetia, thereby demonstrating to the world that Russia is capable of defending its prestige as a great power using available military means. From Europe to the Middle East and Asia, scholars and politicians are increasingly recognizing the prominent role of Russia in international affairs. Even those American pundits who can hardly be suspected of a pro-Russian bias, such as Stratford founder and CEO George Friedman, concede that the Kremlin conducted the war with Georgia "competently if not brilliantly," reestablishing the credibility of the Russian army.[71]

It remains to be seen whether the Kremlin's decision to go to war with Georgia will continue to assist Russia in achieving its international objectives. Russia did not start the military confrontation in the Caucasus, and the Kremlin had hardly any other way to prevent further violence in the region and defend Russia's historic reputation as guarantor of peace in the Caucasus. Concentrating Russian troops in the region[72] does not constitute evidence of Russia's intent to go to war – it was Mikhail Saakashvili who ordered the offensive.[73] At the same time, Russia's decision to go to war further weakened international institutions' ability to preserve peace. International law was silent in the Caucasus because it had been silent when Yugoslavia and Iraq were attacked by Western powers without UN approval.[74] Russia's recognition of South Ossetia and Abkhazia followed the West's recognition of Kosovo, establishing yet another dangerous precedent for redrawing the political map of the world.

Given the involvement of Western states, such as the United States, the conflict had a dimension of a Russia–West confrontation. The Russia–Georgia war seriously exacerbated Russia's already damaged relationships with the West. For example, if President George W. Bush had listened to Vice President Dick Cheney's advice to use force against Russia,[75] the two nations might have found themselves at war. Alternatively, if the Republican presidential nominee, Senator John McCain, had won the 2008 election in the United States, the two countries might have moved to the next level of confrontation – possibly of a military nature. Few people in the U.S. political class had been more ardent than McCain in advocating U.S. ties with the small Georgia at the expense of relations with Russia. Some of McCain's advisers were also known to have worked as paid lobbyists for Georgia's membership in NATO. Clearly they were not concerned that, had Georgia been a member of the alliance when the violence erupted in South Ossetia, the United States would be in a state of war with Russia.

The Russia–Georgia conflict is therefore reminiscent of competition among great powers in the nineteenth and twentieth centuries, which was about material power as well as honor and prestige. For example, the Crimean War also came about because Russia could not defend the rights of its co-religionists without being perceived as a revisionist power. The Cold War too had an unmistakable dimension of competing claims of prestige. After World War II, the United States wanted to secure Europe on its own terms, while Russia was insisting that it too deserved "fruits of victory." Having made a more considerable human and material effort to defeat Hitler than the Allies and having suffered much greater losses, Moscow felt vindicated in demanding recognition of its newly acquired great power status. Although post-Soviet Russia was weaker, the underlying causes of its conflict with the West were similar, and Russian leaders felt they had been humiliated by the Western powers for too long.

Notes

1 "Speech at the Munich Conference on Security Policy," Munich, February 10, 2007. www.kremlin.ru.
2 As quoted in Andrew Kuchins' notes from a meeting with Medvedev at the Valdai Discussion Club in September 2008. Geyer, "Russia First to Test New President."
3 Peuch, "Russia, US Redistribute Pawns on Caucasus Chessboard after a Year of Change."
4 Lambroschini, "Georgia: Russia Watches Warily as Saakashvili Comes to Power."
5 "Georgia: Saakashvili Sees in 'Wahhabism' a Threat to Secularism."
6 "The President of Georgia Wins His Standoff in Adjaria."
7 Chivers, "Georgia's New Leader Baffles U.S. and Russia Alike"; Peuch, "Georgia: Tensions Flare in Separatist Provinces"; Hahn, "The Making of Georgian-Russian Five-Day August War."
8 "Ivanov Surprised at Georgia's Reaction to Russia's Possible Anti-Terrorist Strikes."
9 "Georgia Accuses Russia of Abkhazia Double Standards."
10 Giragosian, "Georgia: Gas Cutoff Highlights National Security Flaws"; Saakashvili, "Ya ne schitayu, chto kogo-to ubivat' – eto metod."
11 "Gruzinskiy parlament prishel k vyvodu rossiyskikh mirotvortsev."
12 "Saakashvili: Georgia Now a 'Model' Country."
13 "Unprovoked Onslaught"; Tchourikova and Moore, "Georgia: Burdjanadze Seeks Support in Row with Moscow."
14 "Georgia Condemns Russian Raid."
15 "Tblisi-Moskva: Lyubov's Chistovo Litsa."
16 Ibid.
17 In describing this stage of Russia–Georgia relations, I rely on timetables produced by scholars Gordon Hahn and Nicholas Petro. Hahn, "The Making of Georgian-Russian Five-Day August War" and Petro, "Crisis in the Caucasus." In addition to being consistent with each other, these timetables incorporated, to the extent possible, accounts of events by Russia's and Georgia's governments.
18 For example, the head of the South Ossetian police was killed on July 3; South Ossetia Minister for Special Affairs Boris Chochiev attributed this assassination to the Georgian secret services.

19 Russian and European observers noted Georgia's active fortification of its positions in the closest proximity to the breakaway republics. For example, in mid-June military observers of the OSCE Mission sponsoring the Joint Control Commission for the Regulation of the Georgian-Ossetian Conflict (JCC) confirmed the Georgians were fortifying their position in the conflict zone in the village of Ergneti in violation of the Dagomys agreements and established a police post with a firing position illegally within the conflict zone. The commander of the peacekeeping forces called on the OSCE and the Joint Committee of the Combined Peacekeeping Force to acknowledge these violations. Commander of the peacekeeping forces Marat Kulakhmetov also noted the urgency of resuming negotiations under JCC auspices, which the Georgian side was "first of all" refusing to do. He also reported the continuing equipping and fortification of positions by Georgian forces in the conflict zone "aimed at unleashing aggression" (www.kavkaz-uzel.ru/newstext/news/id/1225132.html). Quoted in Hahn, "The Making of Georgian-Russian Five-Day August War." Georgia denied these accusations.

20 "Rossiya vyvela Gruziyu na sebya."

21 "Gruzinskiye voyennyye zaderzhalis' v Yuzhnoi Ossetiyi."

22 Minoborony Yuzhnoi Osetiyi."

23 Chivers and Barry, "Georgia Claims on Russia War Called into Question"; Ertel, Klussmann, Koelbl, Mayr, Schepp, Stark and Szandar, "Road to War in Georgia."

24 Human Rights Watch estimated that between 300 and 400 South Ossetian civilians were killed in the Georgian attack. Bush, "The Russia-Georgia War Revisited."

25 Hahn, "The Making of Georgian-Russian Five-Day August War."

26 For a sample of such analyses, see, for example, *A Month after the War*; Armstrong, "The War He Actually Got"; Rohan, "Saakashvili 'Planned, S. Ossetia Invasion"; *Independent International Fact-Finding Mission on the Conflict in Georgia*; "Did Saakashvili Lie?"; Chivers and Barry, "Georgia Claims on Russia War."

27 Tsygankov, "If Not by Tanks, then by Banks?"; Hewitt, "Abkhazia and Georgia."

28 In fact some of these constituencies expected an even harder liner from the Kremlin and were disappointed by its decision not to remove Saakashvili from power. See, for example, the article by Mezhuyev, "Vernite Shervadnadze!" and its discussion by *Russki zhurnal*, Russia's leading online publication.

29 Gurev, "Gruzinskaya tema."

30 Chivers, "Georgia's New Leader Baffles U.S. and Russia."

31 Peuch, "Russia Weighs in as Fighting Continues in South Ossetia." Russia's first Deputy Foreign Minister Valerii Loshchinin also indicated that Moscow held Tbilisi responsible for the increasing tensions in South Ossetia. "Foreign Minister Blames Tbilisi for Escalating Tensions."

32 "Echshe odin soratnik Saakashvili obvinil Rossiyu v fashizme."

33 Many Western officials insisted on immediate cessation of the sanctions, and the special representative of the NATO Secretary-General Robert Simmons extended his support for Tbilisi during his demonstrative trip to Georgia in the midst of the crisis.

34 "Georgia, Ukraine NATO Accession May Cause Geopolitical Shift – FM."
35 Allison, "Russia Resurgent?", 1166–8.
36 As quoted in Illarionov, "The Russian Leadership's Preparations for War," 229–30.
37 Most face-saving Russians prefer not to articulate their frustration with the United States in terms of pride, honor, and dignity in public. Still some do, as did leading Russian politician Vladimir Yakunin. Responding to the German magazine *Der Spiegel's* question "What should the West do?" Yakunin said, "It should not humiliate us. You can throw a bucket of cold water on Russians, and we can take it. But one shouldn't humiliate us! The political scientist Hans Morgenthau said that countries should not forget the national interests of other countries when defining their own. The current American government becomes irritated over every attempt on the part of a country to go its own way – especially when it is as big and wealthy as Russia. That's political arrogance." Yakunin, "The West Shouldn't Humiliate Us."
38 "Russia Again Vows to Block NATO Enlargement," *RFE/RL Newsline*, April 9, 2008.
39 Tsyganok, "On the Consequences of Georgia's NATO Entry."
40 "Russians Positive on China's Foreign Policy, Economic Model."
41 "Russians Negative about U.S., EU, Ukraine and Georgia."
42 The army is the third most trusted institution in Russia after the president and the Church. Goltz, "Bremya militarizma"; "Most Russians Certain Army Can Beat Back Any Aggressor – Poll."
43 "Polls Suggests Russians Favor Tough Foreign Policy."
44 "Russia's Economy under Vladimir Putin: Achievements and Failures"; "Russia Turns from Debtor into Creditor Country – Medvedev"; Chazan, "Lighting a Spark."
45 "Middle Class Grows Atop."
46 Crandall, "Invest in China? Invest in Russia."
47 "Russia Is Most Attractive Emerging Economy for Investors."
48 Abelsky, "Russia Industrial Output Rises 9.2%, Nine-Month High."
49 "Russians Think Chosen Development Course Correct – Poll."
50 "Obzor vneshnei politiki Rossiyskoi federatsiyi."
51 "Medvedev Doubts Effectiveness of OSCE/NATO-Based Security System." See also Medvedev, Speech at the Meeting with Russian Ambassadors and Permanent Representatives to International Organizations. Also see the article by Russia's Foreign Minister Sergei Lavrov, "A Strategic Relationship: From Rivalry to Partnership."
52 Nino Burjanadze's dismissal of the Russian position is revealing: "The move [to NATO] won't leave Russia any worse off – unless, of course, our NATO membership is seen as detrimental to Russian imperial interests. It certainly isn't detrimental to any other Russian interests." *Nezavisimaya gazeta*, January 15–17, 2007.
53 Slevin and Baker, "Bush Changing Views on Putin."
54 Georgian, "U.S. Eyes Caspian Oil in 'War on Terror.'"
55 Georgia did not respond to Russia's proposals to consult the Kremlin on security issues and pledge non-use of force in the region (Gurev, "Gruzinskaya tema.")

56 Chivers, "Georgia's New Leader Baffles U.S. and Russia."

57 According to the former Defense Minister Irakli Oruashvili, Georgia planned a military invasion of South Ossetia in 2006. "Irakli Okruashvili."

58 Saakashvili, "Georgian Leader Warns Russia against Recognition of Breakaway Regions."

59 "US Embassy Denies American Experts Probe Ground for NMD in Georgia."

60 Chivers, "Russia Expands Support for Breakaway Regions in Georgia."

61 Mearsheimer, *The Tragedy of Great Powers*, chap. 7.

62 Socor, "Georgia under Growing Russian Pressure Ahead of Bush-Putin Summit."

63 Baev, "Useful War."

64 Cohen, "Domestic Factors Driving Russia's Foreign Policy"; Lapidus, "Between Assertiveness and Insecurity."

65 Asmus, *A Little War That Shook the World*, pp. 9, 14, 217–18; Blank, "From Neglect to Duress," 104; Cornell and Starr, "Introduction," 8; Sherr, "The Implications of the Russia-Georgia War for European Security," 224.

66 Burjanadze, "Georgia's Acting President Says Country Will Survive Current Turmoil"; Gegeshidze, "Rossiya podderzhivayet ne oppozitsiyu, a destabilizatsiyu."

67 Some sources indicate that the Kremlin considered the decision to remove Saakashvili. Prime Minister Vladimir Putin and Russian Foreign Minister Sergei Lavrov both indicated that they wanted Georgia's president "to go" and at first considered this a condition for a ceasefire. Asmus, *A Little War That Shook the World*, pp. 199, 220. According to Gleb Pavlovski, one faction within the Kremlin wanted to march on Tbilisi in order to challenge the West and fully revive Russia's domination in the Caucasus. Felgenhauer, "After August 7," 178–9. For the argument that the war was important to the Kremlin for internal legitimacy reasons, see Allison, "Russia Resurgent?", 1169; Filippov, "Diversionary Role of the Russia-Georgia Conflict."

68 Waltz, *Theory of International Politics*; Snyder, *Myths of Empire*; Jervis, "Cooperation under Security Dilemma."

69 Lavrov, "America Must Choose between Georgia and Russia"; Medvedev, "Why I Had to Recognize Georgia's Breakaway Regions."

70 Rose, "Neoclassical Realism and Theories of Foreign Policy"; Wohlforth, "Honor as Interest."

71 Friedman, "Georgia and the Balance of Power."

72 Cornell and Starr, "Introduction"; Felgenhauer, "After August 7"; Illarionov, "The Russian Leadership's Preparations for War."

73 See the sources cited in fn. 27.

74 On different analyses of the West's role in the Russia-Georgia conflict, see Cooley, "How the West Failed Georgia"; English and Svyatets, "A Presumption of Guilt?"; Asmus, *A Little War*, pp. 215–34.

75 Cheney reportedly proposed the possibility of bombardment and sealing of the Roki Tunnel and other strikes to stop Russia's military advancement. Asmus, *A Little War*, p. 186.

15   Conclusion

"All healthy human action...must establish a balance between utopia and reality, between free will and determinism."

E. H. Carr[1]

The Book's Findings

Russia's Western Choices and Its Domestic Opponents

Since its emergence as an independent centralized state, Russia has followed three distinct trajectories in relations with the West. Its identity as a Christian power encouraged the Russian rulers to work on strengthening ties with the Holy Roman Empire by opening a permanent mission in Rome and seeking the West's support in a war against Lithuania in the early seventeenth century. Throughout the two following centuries, Russia frequently sided with a coalition of Western states against those that it viewed as challenging Christian unity from inside or outside of Europe. The pattern of Russia-West cooperation survived even after the European nations entered the era of interstate relations and ceased to define their ties in religious categories. This pattern of cooperation had its opponents inside Russia, but the official commitment proved strong enough to defeat the opposition.

The Holy Alliance is the last case of Russia's religion-driven cooperation with Europe. Having defeated Napoleonic France, Alexander I sponsored the Europe-wide arrangement that committed key states to suppressing all revisionist and revolutionary movements on the continent. This official course elicited opposition from several directions. Supporters of balance-of-power politics, such as the war strategist Marshal Kutuzov, insisted on not destroying the French army in order to preserve a counterbalance against British ambitions to dominate the continent. Others advocated the idea of becoming Europe's hegemonic power and expanding the fight to conquer Constantinople as well. Still others, especially within the Church, took issue with Alexander's universal and European interpretation of Christianity, arguing for turning away from ambitious external commitments and reviving Christian principles at home.

Almost a century later, Russia formed a different alliance with Western states. Threatened by the rapid rise of German power, Nicholas II accepted the French assessment that the defeat of Germany was the key objective in a European war, and in 1907 Russia also concluded a military convention with Britain. The Triple Entente emerged despite various critiques at home. Supporters of the traditional school of Russian diplomacy, beginning with Alexander Gorchakov and Nikolai de Giers, believed in the virtue of preserving even-handed relations with both France and Germany while keeping distance from Britain. Alternative courses of action also included the proposal from the conservative right to build an autocratic values-based alliance with Germany and the Bolsheviks' secret cooperation with the Germans to deprive the Tsar of his support at home. Initially strong, the Triple Entente collapsed within ten years under the pressures of World War I and the Russian revolution.

Barely fifteen years after the revolution, the Soviet government was pressed to adopt yet another course of cooperation with Western powers. The ascendance of the Nazi Party to power in Germany and the rising threat from Japan prompted the Bolsheviks to forget about their recent confrontation with France and Britain over the nature of the Soviet system. The new foreign minister, Maxim Litvinov, became an ardent proponent of a new rapprochement with the West and a collective security system in Europe. Soviet Russia joined the League of Nations and became a vocal critic of the organization's weak enforcement capabilities, particularly in response to Italy's invasion of Ethiopia and Germany's occupation of the Rhineland. At home Litvinov's pro-Western policy was increasingly opposed by those who advocated a pro-German course of action and those who favored the tactics of flexible alliances between Germany and the West. Stalin had appointed Livinov to see what might come out of his efforts to establish a lasting institutional arrangement with European nations, but Stalin himself preferred a more defensive and restrained version of cooperation against Hitler.

The case of the war against terrorism concludes my analysis of Russia's efforts to cooperate with the Western nations. After the terrorist attack on the United States on September 11, 2001, Russia pledged important resources to help America and European nations in fighting a global war with terrorism. This course indicated the Kremlin's break with the more traditional line of balancing between the West and non-Western nations

Table 15.1. *Domestic Opposition to Russia's Cooperation with the West*

The Official View	Opposing Views
Holy Alliance	Balance of Power
	European Hegemony
	Orthodox Distinctiveness
Triple Entente	Balance between France and Germany
	Alliance with Germany
	Defeat of the Government
Collective Security	Balance between France and Germany
	Pact with Germany
War with Terrorism	Balance between West and Non-Western States
	Alliance with Non-Western States

advocated by the majority of the Russian political class. Within the political class, there were also some who, like the Communist Party leader Gennadi Zyuganov, wanted higher priority to be given to Russia's relations with China and the old Soviet allies in Asia, the Muslim world, and Latin America (Table 15.1 summarizes the official and opposing views on Russia's cooperation with the Western nations).

The second trajectory of Russia's relations with the West is that of defensiveness, or balancing through domestic revival and flexible international alliances. Domestic opposition to the official course came from those favoring closer ties with the Western nations and those wanting to actively challenge the West by insisting on Russia's cultural exceptionalism.

When Alexander Gorchakov proclaimed the course of recueillment after defeat in the Crimean War, his most important opposition inside the political class came from those who, like his old boss Nesselrode, failed to see the change in the nature of world politics and favored a revival of ties with Austria and Germany within the Holy Alliance framework. Gorchakov, however, wanted "a full freedom of action," and not because of bitterness over the betrayal of Austria, but because he understood that Austrian interests in the Balkans had changed and Russia could no longer fully cooperate with others to restore its positions in the region and outside. The other course of action might have been an alliance-like relationship with France, which was strongly backed by Russia's liberal Westernizers. The chancellor and the Tsar initially sought to improve their ties with France, but only to the extent necessary for weakening

British and Austrian influences. Finally, some factions in Russia pressured the government to devise an openly pro-Serbian and pro-Balkan pan-Slavist policy for organizing the Slavs into a federation free of "hostile" European influences.

Stalin's course of peaceful coexistence with the Western nations is yet another example of Russia's defensive foreign policy. Like recueillment, peaceful coexistence was premised on the importance of Russia's economic revival after years of instability and limited cooperation with the "capitalist" world. Within the government, Stalin sided with Lenin on the New Economic Policy against those whom the latter referred to as "infantile leftists" who supported the doctrine of world revolution on the international scene. Although instinctively favoring a more isolationist version of coexistence with the West than the one advocated by his predecessor, in the early 1930s Stalin authorized the policy of collective security to counter the rising threat from Germany. Isolationism did not prove to be a viable option, and until August 1939, the Kremlin was engaged in politics of balancing between France and Germany. The Soviet policy of rebuilding the domestic economy, while balancing between key European states, was reminiscent of Gorchakov's great power maneuvering in the nineteenth century. Francophone and Germanophile voices within the government never received full official backing.

After the end of the Cold War, in yet another effort to revive the principles of Gorchakov's foreign policy, Yevgeni Primakov devised a course of containing the military expansion of NATO. Russia sought to preserve and develop relations with the Western alliance while increasing ties with non-Western powers, such as China, India, and Iran, and consolidating the former Soviet area. Primakov did not accept the premises of liberal Western thinking that remained influential in liberal circles and considered ties with NATO as the way to address Russia's security concerns. Nor did Primakov favor the position of Russia's anti-Western politicians who advocated breaking relations with the Western military alliance (Table 15.2 summarizes the official and opposing views on Russia's defensiveness).

Finally, Russia has historically resorted to assertiveness in relations with the West, as exemplified by the cases of the Crimean War, Cold War, and the Russia–Georgia war in August 2008. In each of those cases, domestic opposition to the official policy of assertiveness came from advocates both for a more restrained policy and for a more extreme expansion. In the Crimean War, some of Nicholas's advisors, such as Count Nesselrode and Baron Brunnow, urged him to be cautious in negotiations with the Ottomans and in consultations with Austria and Prussia. In turn, the Slavophiles pressured the Tsar to extend military

Table 15.2. *Domestic Opposition to Russia's Defensiveness*

The Official View	Opposing Views
Recueillement	Revival of Ties with Austria and Germany
	Rapprochment with France
	Pan-slavism
Peaceful Coexistence	Export of Revolution
	Cooperation with Germany
	Cooperation with the West
Containment of NATO	Rapprochment with NATO and the West
	Break of Ties with NATO

support to the Balkan Slavs and soon proclaimed that the Crimean War served the "holy" purpose of reviving Russia's Christian mission.

Similar policy choices existed in Soviet Russia after World War II. Until the beginning of the Cold War, former foreign minister Maxim Litvinov and the ambassador to the United States Andrei Gromyko defended the approach that included more respect for the choices of Eastern European states and more extensive negotiations with the Western nations. Although the military expansion option had no strong support within the political establishment, some upper rank military, like Semyon Budennyi, did favor it.

The moderate and expansionist options were also available to the Kremlin before and during the war with Georgia. Those Russians who had earlier argued for priority relations with NATO and the West were skeptical of the use of force against Georgia. Others, however, defended an even more hawkish version of military engagement that included occupation of Tbilisi and removal of Mikhail Saakashvili from power (Table 15.3 summarizes the official and opposing views on Russia's assertiveness).

Table 15.3. *Domestic Opposition to Russia's Assertiveness*

The Official View	Opposing Views
Crimean War	Restraint and Negotiations
	Slav Expansion
Cold War	Restraint and Consultations
	Military Expansion
Russia–Georgia War	Restraint and Negotiations
	Advancement to Tbilisi

Explaining Russia's Choices

Realism is insufficient for explaining the trajectories of Russia's relations with the West. Throughout the book, I have argued that focusing on power, security, and prestige – as realists do – only partially explains why Russia acted in the ways that it has. Even though Russia's policy makers frequently invoked those objectives to justify state actions, the broader context for their behavior is best described by the concept of honor. The Russian idea of honor captures both external and internal attributes of state, such as special relations with the West, great power prestige, and pride in domestic institutions. Diverse historical experiences have taught Russia's rulers the value of simultaneously relating to several relevant communities – Western nations, the domestic population, and cultural allies. Doing so required an elaborate system of justifying its actions, which included explanations of state origins, legitimacy, institutional structure, and potential allies.

In different eras the state acted on different ideologies of honor. Each ideology provided the state with the sense of purpose, ethical principles, and meaningful context in which to act. Throughout the nineteenth and early twentieth centuries, the dominant ideology was that of a Christian autocracy. Russians justified their actions abroad, including military ones, by the duty to defend "the faith, the Tsar and the fatherland" (*za veru, tsarya i otechestvo*). Soviet ideology fundamentally transformed the myth of state honor, replacing Christianity and autocracy with beliefs in communism and single-party rule. In addition to attaining international prestige and security, the Soviet state sought to uphold and promote this new system of values. The new post-Soviet ideology is still in the process of being formed and currently includes values of Russianness (*Rossiyane*) and a strong state (*derzhava*).

Russians have usually not defined their system of values as anti-Western and, indeed, have viewed the West's recognition as a critical component of such a value system. That explains the multiple cases of Russia's cooperation with Western nations, including the Holy Alliance, the Triple Entente, collective security, and the war against terrorism. In each case, Russia acted jointly with Western nations by defending its cultural beliefs, international stability, and peace. When the West recognizes the validity of Russia's foreign policy claims and the values behind those claims, a meaningful international cooperation can emerge and endure.

However, when Russia's significant other challenges its actions and values, Russia is likely to turn away from cooperative behavior. In such cases, it feels the need to relate to its non-Western constituencies and is compelled to act on non-Western components of its state honor. Whether Russia turns to a defensive or an assertive foreign policy to sustain its

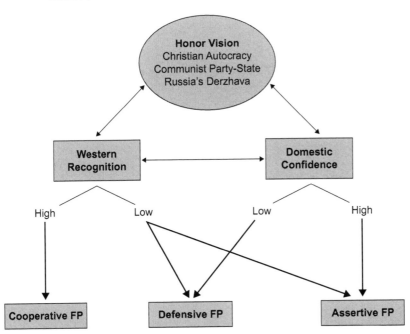

Figure 15.1. Explanation of Russia's Relations with the West

values depends on its perceived level of domestic confidence. In situations of perceived weakness Russian rulers are cautious in their international behavior and abstain from actions that they view as necessary but impossible to sustain; the state typically concentrates on defending the prestige of great power and abstains from acting on other components of its honor. During the periods of recueillment, peaceful coexistence, and NATO containment, Russia's rulers felt the need to defend their cultural and ideological allies abroad – the Orthodox Christians, communists, and those gravitating to Russia after the breakup of the USSR – yet in each of these cases Russia lacked the confidence to act assertively.

During periods of growing confidence, Russia may turn to a more assertive promotion of its values. Then the West's failure to accept such values is likely to encourage Russia to act alone, as it did in the Crimean War, Cold War, and the war with Georgia. In these cases, power prestige and security were not the only stakes. Each time the state also acted on its culturally and ideologically defined sense of duty to protect those who defined their own values in terms of a strong affinity with Russia.

Figure 15.1 summarizes the role of honor in Russia's relations with the West.

The Record of Russia-West Relations

Russia's foreign policy has enjoyed a mixed record of success. Russia has generally been successful in achieving its objectives when it acts in concert with the West and when such cooperation does not infringe on Russia's non-Western cultural obligations. For example, the Holy Alliance system, before it outlived its usefulness, had provided Russia with a long-lasting peace and stability on its European borders. However, even during that golden period of cooperation with the West, Russia defaulted on some of its cultural obligations, such as protecting the Balkan Christians in Greece from oppression by the Turkish Sultan. The war against terrorism was successful during its first years, until Russia and the West's definition of values begun to diverge around 2004. Responding to the colored revolutions in Georgia and Ukraine, the United States pushed the former Soviet regions toward transforming their political institutions, which Russia viewed as a threat to its own stability and a deviation from the U.S. global war against terror. Similarly, cooperation in the era of collective security cooperation fell short because neither the Soviet Union nor the West had sufficient trust in each other's intentions and values.

Russia has also been relatively successful when it acts defensively on a realistic assessment of its foreign policy resources. Thus recueillement may be judged to have been more successful than containing NATO, which was based on an incorrect assumption that Russia had sufficient confidence and ability to build alternative alliances. In contrast, the recueillement defined foreign policy objectives more narrowly – as improvement of domestic capabilities and return to the Black Sea – and Russia had the ability to maneuver among great powers under conditions of multipolarity. The policy of peaceful coexistence too helped Soviet Russia win time for domestic recovery and mobilization. Alas, Stalin squandered much of this opportunity by initiating domestic repression of the peasants, the party, the military, and the intelligentsia.

Russia has been only partly successful in its assertive policy, even when it calculates its resources accurately and achieves a desired victory. For instance, Russia secured much of the territory it wanted to control during the Cold War, but the price of alienating the West turned out to be excessively high: it delayed Russia's integration into the global economy for some forty years. In confronting Georgia's use of force against one of its provinces in August 2008, Russia again acted in defiance of Europe and the United States. Even though Russia had no option but to intervene and even though it had defeated Georgia decisively, the Western reaction was largely negative. So long as gradual integration into the West's economies remains critical for Russia's development, the Kremlin will have to calibrate its decisions against reactions from the West.

Russia has been the least successful when it acts assertively and without a careful calculation of available resources. A case in point is the Crimean War, which resulted from Nicholas's misjudgment of reactions from the Sultan and key European states, as well as Russia's own military capabilities. No less successful have been attempts to act in concert with Western allies, yet without appropriate regard for Russia's domestic constraints and obligations. The words of caution by Count Nesselrode to Nicholas I before the Crimean War – "honor does not oblige us to hurl ourselves into a bottomless abyss"[2] – may also apply to Nicholas II before entering World War I.[3] Were Russia to continue with the course of domestic reforms and flexible alliances, it might have prevented the war or at least helped decide on a prudent and limited form of military involvement. A "bottomless abyss" in the form of revolution and state collapse might have then been avoided.

Both Russia and the West have contributed to these successes and failures. The obvious lesson for Russia is that, while remaining faithful to its other honorable obligations, it should seek Western engagement and recognition. If, in the absence of such recognition, Russia turns away from attempting to establish strong cooperation with Western nations, then it should at least be conservative in assessing its resources and set narrow, specific foreign policy objectives. For the West, the lesson is that pressuring or enticing Russia into submission at the price of its obligations to domestic constituencies and cultural allies may be ultimately counterproductive. The West will hardly ever possess the power to fully determine the shape and direction of Russian developments and therefore must seek reciprocal forms of engaging Russia. Anything short of reciprocity is likely to result in Russia resorting to defensive or assertive policy responses.

The Promise of Honor-Based Constructivism

Honor-Based Constructivism and the Theory of Foreign Policy

A practically relevant theory of foreign policy ought to successfully address several important tasks. First, it has to clearly establish a meaningful context in which a policy maker acts and seeks to achieve his or her goals. In the world of human interactions, beliefs and emotions often influence what ostensibly are rationally calculated decisions. Therefore, rather than assuming what an action means to those initiating it, scholarly responsibility demands that we establish this meaning by studying the relevant social and political contexts. Second, a practically relevant theory of foreign policy must formulate a cause–effect relationship by identifying the most prominent social forces or variables that drive an international decision. Furthermore, and related to causality, it is necessary to delineate the process through which a causal relationship takes effect. As advocates of process tracing have argued, this technique is important for getting closer to identifying the causal agency and making sure that the identified correlation is really causal, and not spurious.[4] Finally, a good theory of foreign policy ought to have some predictive power. Although no theory can claim the ability to predict the exact time and shape of change, a good theory identifies powerful factors that point to the direction of change.

Key factors of the theory proposed in this book are honor, confidence, and recognition. The notion of honor characterizes the system of commitments assumed by policy makers. Honor provides the state with answers to questions of its actions' purpose, legitimacy, and scope. Grasping the system of honor is difficult yet critical. Without studying it, the scholar has no adequate knowledge of how the state defines its vision and the social and emotional contexts in which it acts. Confidence provides the state with the required internal platform for action, and it incorporates power capabilities, institutional capacity, and the leadership's perceptions of actions necessary for implementing the vision. As to recognition, it serves the purpose of external legitimization of state behavior on the international scene. By providing moral, diplomatic, financial, and institutional support for the state, the outside world encourages it to stay on the chosen path and not deviate to revisionist behavior.

The proposed honor-based theory of foreign policy combines insights from both constructivism and realism and fits with the recently introduced realist-constructivist approach. The approach retains the constructivist commitment to viewing the world as a social interaction, not a natural necessity, but it also argues against transcending power in international politics.[5] It takes the constructivist sensitivity to local systems of perceiving the outside world and the appreciation for studying origins of such perceptions. From realism, it takes the attention to power and the structure of the international system. Whereas realism is agnostic about domestic and cultural factors, constructivism lacks focus in its own way. Because of its intense focus on social interactions it does not pay sufficient attention to factors outside the cultural sphere. The role of constructivism in theories of foreign policy may therefore be to serve as a point of departure, rather than a final destination. Along with other factors of critical importance, constructivism may assist scholars in sketching a road map for analysis, but constructivist scholars are hardly in a position to conduct such analysis in its entirety. In order to fully illuminate the process of foreign policy making, a broad range of factors other than culture and identity must be utilized.

A more expansive approach to foreign policy incorporates both ideas and power. The logic of realist-constructivism requires that we take seriously material factors of power, but to do so within the framework of a socially interactive approach. Following such logic, we should not view systemic factors, such as the anarchical environment or the absence of a strong international authority, as ultimate or decisive in determining the nature of foreign policy. Rather, we should expect that both domestic ideas of honorable international behavior and material capabilities will figure prominently in shaping a state's foreign policy. Material power may have the especially dangerous effect of playing into an assertive policy mood, but it does not have an independent causal effect and does not set off the causal process. Rather, the local system of perceptions does.

In addition to the already considered elements of honor, confidence, and recognition, factors of domestic politics and perceptions of individual leaders may be integrated to specify the overall causal process. Leaders' interpretations of structural factors may become responsible for their unexpected effects. For example, Nicholas's excessive self-confidence and inability to use Russia's influence to negotiate a reformed system of international relationships greatly contributed to the outbreak of the Crimean War. Even if the Concert of Europe was structurally doomed, Russia was still in a position to preserve its important influence in the Balkans and larger Europe. Although its material capabilities were declining, Russia was still viewed as a major power because of its consistent record in defeating Turkey, suppressing nationalist revolts. and preserving stability in Europe. In addition to miscalculating his own resources, Nicholas erred in anticipating the reactions of important European powers and therefore selected the wrong methods to defend his objectives. The Tsar was prepared to exercise all options of diplomatic escalation, yet failed to develop an exit option. Were he to be more prudent, Russia's assertiveness might have stayed on the diplomatic level, not escalating to a military confrontation.

Honor-Based Constructivism and the Twenty-First-Century
Great Powers

The theory of honor-based constructivism offers its own assessments of the twenty-first-century world order and great powers' behavior that differ from those viewing such behavior through lens of the power transition theory. Among the latter, John Mearsheimer has argued that the post–Cold War system with its increasingly "unbalanced multipolarity" is likely to yield intense security competition among great powers by 2020.[6] In his assessment, such competition will result in the rise of China as the most dangerous threat to the United States, a revisionist Russia, and a greater likelihood of war in Europe. A more nuanced approach will need to go beyond analysis of power capabilities and incorporate the states' vision, degree of confidence, and external recognition.

At least three groups of states can be identified within the current international system that have the potential to shape its structure – established, rising, and recovering great powers. Whereas the United States and the European Union remain *established* powers, China, India, and Brazil are frequently classified as *rising* powers.[7] Russia is a *recovering* power that will continue to aspire to the status of an established one. Although considering these states' power position is important, it would be simplistic to ignore their ideas of honor and degree of recognition by the outside world.

The United States envisions itself as the leader of liberal democratic states across the world. However, it is unlikely to continue to be the assertive great power it has been throughout much of the post–World War II era. Military overstretch and an undermined economy – the latter revealed by the global financial crisis – limit the country's ability to promote its values abroad the way it has been accustomed to. In addition, in response to the United States' tendency to act unilaterally, the non-Western countries have grown considerably more skeptical of its positive role in the world. The idea of Western-style democracy, although still attractive, no longer commands the same attention.

Provided that the U.S. leadership follows these changes in the world correctly, American foreign policy is likely to evolve in either a cooperative or defensive direction. If it evolves cooperatively, President Barack Obama's emphasis on greater multilateralism, bilateral negotiations, economic globalization, and gradual military retreat will be sustained until the country recovers its confidence and recognition. If it takes a defensive direction, the United States will increasingly scale down its international commitments and turn inward to rebuild its power capabilities and other aspects of domestic confidence.

The European Union's vision of self is also democratic, albeit with a stronger emphasis on social programs and nonmilitary engagement abroad. Relative to the rise of non-Western powers, such as China and India, the EU's confidence has suffered considerably. The global financial crisis has exacerbated the problem of slow, sometimes stagnant, economic growth since the early 1990s. In addition, the enlarged union has not become more cohesive or capable of exercising coherent policies at home and abroad. While recognizing the economic power and potential influence of the EU, the outside world often views it as lacking political will and the military capabilities to purse a course of active global involvement.

Given these predicaments, the European leaders will likely to continue seeking multilateral cooperation with the world, as evident in much of their behavior throughout the post–Cold War era. However, one cannot exclude the defensive course of relative isolation. For example, surveys of the European elites and public reveal the organization's enlargement fatigue, which may encourage a turn inward. In the foreseeable future, the EU is unlikely to embark on a course of assertive promotion of its social values in the world.

China sees itself differently from the Western nations. Although Beijing presents its grand vision as consistent with the ideas of democracy and the free market, its emphasis is on the ability to resist the global spread of the West's values. The Chinese discourse is that of political control at home and democracy in international relations. The latter is expressed in its Five Principles of Peaceful Coexistence: mutual respect for territorial integrity and sovereignty, mutual nonaggression, mutual noninterference in internal affairs, equality and mutual benefits, and peaceful coexistence.[8] Chinese concepts of a "socialist spiritual civilization" and a multipolar world fit more comfortably with values of nationalism and a strong state than those of Western-style democracy. Beginning with Chairman Deng Xiaoping, Chinese policy makers have viewed nationalism and globalization as not incompatible, but as existing in a virtuous relationship. Beijing anticipates new violent conflicts and expects that the developed states will continue to bully the developing states and encourage conflict between them.[9]

Although recognition of China as a rising global power is rather mixed – many in Africa, Latin America, and the Middle East welcome it, whereas policy makers in the West and Asia frequently express their reservations – Beijing is increasingly confident and comfortable with its growing international status. It is therefore not very likely that China will continue to follow a defensive foreign policy, which was once recommended by Deng as "hide brightness and foster obscurity." This does not mean, however, that China will necessarily become a rule challenger to the existing and largely West-centered international order or that Beijing's aspiration to a greater status would necessarily lead to a unilateral effort to revise the existing rules.[10] The fact that the Chinese rise is based on an authentic cultural vision should not be viewed as an indicator of an approaching conflict with the West. Whether the unprecedented growth of Chinese power will translate into an assertive and potentially dangerous policy partly depends on the world's ability to recognize the legitimacy of Beijing's interests and engage it as a full-fledged participant in the international system.

India and Brazil's self-images are distinct yet similar in terms of their emphasis on domestic democracy and general willingness to work within the existing international rules. Over the last decade, both countries have demonstrated considerable growth in economic and military capabilities and have indicated their desires to transform the structure of international institutions, such as the United Nations Security Council and the G-8. In addition to democratic institutions and growing material power, India and Brazil's increased internal confidence has been reinforced by their stable performance during the global financial crisis. Both are increasingly global powers and are unlikely to adopt a defensive foreign policy. Nor is it likely that the two countries will turn in an assertive direction. Although they have disagreed with the United States and other Western nations on multiple issues, India and Brazil are also beneficiaries of a growing international recognition of their rising status. Within the next ten to twenty years, they will likely work on resolving their issues with the outside world by adopting a largely cooperative foreign policy.

Russia's vision of its values is more similar to China than to the West, India, and Brazil. The concepts of sovereign democracy, energy self-sufficiency, and a multipolar world sound like nationalist, rather than Western liberal, themes. Russia is also similar to China in the sense that the Kremlin demonstrates growing internal confidence, but is only partly successful in gaining the international recognition it seeks. Although Russia's economy has been growing since 1999, many in the West see the growth as too dependent on high oil prices and are in no hurry to recognize the Kremlin's aspiration to a greater independence in defining the rules of military security in Europe and Eurasia. In response, Russia has been notably more assertive in its policy since 2005, which has prompted some scholars to speculate that the Kremlin has become the leading challenger of the existing international order and the West.[11] Russia may indeed remain assertive, especially if the Western nations fail to recognize the legitimacy of its security interests. However, this assertiveness is unlikely to openly and unilaterally challenge the existing international system for two reasons: Russia is a recovering, not a rising, power and does not possesses the capabilities of China, and because the West remains an important cultural signifier of Russia's own identity.

Another possibility is that Russia will develop a cooperative approach in relations with the West, thereby continuing with the policies of Dmitri Medvedev. Around the fall of 2009, Russia's foreign policy began to depart from the assertive course that had culminated in the war with

Table 15.4. *The Honor-Based Constructivism and the Twenty-First-Century Great Powers*

	Vision	Confidence	Recognition	Foreign Policy
Established Powers				
United States	Democracy	Decline	Mixed	Cooperative or Defensive
European Union	Democracy	Decline	Mixed	Cooperative or Defensive
Rising Powers				
China	Statism	Rise	Mixed	Cooperative or Assertive
India	Democracy	Rise	Rising	Cooperative
Brazil	Democracy	Rise	Rising	Cooperative
Recovering Powers				
Russia	Statism	Rise	Mixed	Cooperative or Assertive

Georgia in August 2008. In response to the global financial crisis and U.S. attempts to "reset" relations with Russia the Kremlin revived its emphasis on cooperation. Under Medvedev's presidency, the country adopted a more nuanced approach to the outside world – one that emphasized the soft, rather than hard, dimension of power, and was dictated by the need to modernize the domestic economy. The new approach stressed the importance of building "modernization alliances" across the world, especially with those nations that could offer investments and technologies for economic development.[12] Having reestablished itself as a major power, Russia was now turning to domestic modernization and inviting the outside world to contribute to it.[13] This approach may or may not survive depending on Russia's internal changes and the West's willingness to recognize Russia as a partner.

Table 15.4 summarizes expectations of great powers' behavior from the honor-based constructivist perspective.

This analysis suggests that within the next ten to twenty years, the existing international order has a good chance of surviving, especially if the United States stays engaged with it and does not turn inward. In such a case, China and Russia will be further encouraged to pursue a cooperative, rather than an assertive or even openly revisionist foreign policy. In the less likely event that the United States actively withdraws from its central position within the international system, the world order is likely to evolve in one of two directions. A new institutional structure may emerge that successfully accommodates rising and recovering powers, or there may be created a dangerous multipolarity in which China and Russia increasingly challenge the existing rules without being able to impose new ones. Exactly which of these scenarios materializes – the old

West-centered status quo, the new institutional order, or the conflictual world – only time can tell.

A Final Word

The cases of Russia's relations with the West demonstrate the promise of a dialogue between realism and constructivism for developing a practically relevant foreign policy theory. These theoretical paradigms can and should cooperate in exploring pressing questions of international relations. Both vision and realistic assessment of foreign policy resources are critical here – vision for a locally sensitive strategy formulation, and realism for its implementation. Or, if we are to follow Carr's formula, both utopia and reality, free will and determinism, are essential in successful foreign policy making. Russia confirms the old wisdom that foreign policy is as much a science of revealing some patterns of behavior as it is an art of following them, by creatively synthesizing national and global imperatives. Although both art and science are necessary for developing a coherent interpretation of foreign policy, our analytical ability to understand state international behavior can go a long way.

Notes

1 Carr, *The Twenty Years' Crisis, 1919–1939*, p. 11.
2 Fuller, *Strategy and Power in Russia*, p. 248.
3 The list of Russia's unsuccessful attempts to develop a strategic cooperation with the West may be continued and includes Mikhail Gorbachev's New Thinking and Boris Yelstin's Liberal Westernism, both of which came at an excessively high domestic price. For details, see my *Russia's Foreign Policy*, chaps. 2–3.
4 For process-tracing, see especially McKeown, "Case Studies and the Statistical Worldview"; George and Bennett, *Case Studies and Theory Development in the Social Sciences*.
5 Jackson, "Bridging the Gap: Toward a Realist-Constructivist Dialogue."
6 Mearsheimer, *The Tragedy of Great Power Politics*, p. 385.
7 See, for example, the project by Young, "Perspectives on the Changing Global Distribution of Power."
8 These principles were first enunciated in the 1950s and have been continuously reemphasized by Deng Xiaoping and other Chinese officials since 1988. As the late Deng stated, "National sovereignty and national security should be the top priority.. national rights are more important than human rights" (Deng, "Conception of National Interests," 51).
9 For analyses of China's vision, see Hughes, "Globalization and Nationalism"; Deng, "Conception of National Interests"; Callahan, "Chinese Visions of World Order."

10 Deng, *China's Struggle for Status*; Johnston, *Social States*.
11 Lucas, *The New Cold War*.
12 Medvedev, Speech at meeting with Russian ambassadors, July 12, 2010.
13 For analyses of Medvedev's foreign policy, see Mankoff, "Changing Course in Moscow," and Petro, *Russian Foreign Policy, 2000–2011*.

Bibliography

Abelsky, Paul, "Russia Industrial Output Rises 9.2%, Nine-Month High," *Bloomberg*, May 20, 2008.

Akhiyezer, A. S., *Rossiya: kritika istoricheskogo opyta*. 3 vols. (Moscow, 1991).

Akhtamzyan, A. A., "Gorchakov i Bismark – shkola yevropeyskoi diplomatiyi XIX veka," in: *Kantsler A. M. Gorchakov. K 200-letiyu so dnya rozhdeniya*, edited by Ye. M. Primakov, I. S. Ivanov, et al. (Moscow: Mezhdunarodnyye otnosheniya, 1998).

Akstyutin, Yuri, "Alexander's Vision of the Future," in: *Russia and the West from Peter to Khrushchev*, edited by L. Jay Oliva. (Boston: D. C. Heath, 1965).

"Alexander's Proclamation to the Nation, July 18, 1812," in: *Imperial Russia: A Source Book, 1700–1917*, edited by Basil Dmytryshyn. (Hinsdale, IL: Harcourt, 1974).

"Pochemu Stalin dal'neyshemu sotrudnichestvu s soyuznikami predpochel konfrontatsiyu c nimi?" in: *Kholodnaya voina: novyye podkhody, novyye dokumenty*, edited by M. M. Narinski. (Moscow: Russian Academy of Sciences, 1995).

Ali, Tariq, *The Clash of Fundamentalisms: Crusades, Jihads and Modernity*. (London: Verso, 2002).

Alker, Hayward R., Tahir Amin, Thomas Biersteker, and Takachi Inoguchi, "How Should We Theorize Contemporary Macro-Encounters: In Terms of Superstates, World Orders, or Civilizations?" (Unpublished ms., 1998).

Almedingen, E. M., *The Emperor Alexander II*. (London: Bodley Head, 1962).

Allison, Roy, "Russia Resurgent? Moscow's Campaign to 'Coerce Georgia to Peace,'" *International Affairs*, **84**, 6 (2008).

Alperovitz, Gar, "How Did the Cold War Begin?" in: *The Origins of the Cold War, 1941–1947: A Historical Problem with Interpretations and Documents*, edited by Walter LaFeber. (New York: John Wiley & Sons, 1971).

Ambrosio, Thomas, *America's Image Further Erodes, Europeans Want Weaker Ties*. Washington, DC: Pew Research Center for the People and the Press, March 18, 2003, www.people-press.org

Challenging America's Global Preeminence: Russia's Quest for Multipolarity. (London: Ashgate, 2005).

Andreyev, A. P., *Posledniy kantsler rossiyskoi imperiyi Aleksandr Mikhailovich Gorchakov*. (Moscow: Belyi volk, 1999).

Antonenko, Oksana, "Russia, NATO and European Security after Kosovo," *Survival*, **41**, 4 (1999/2000).

Armstrong, Nicholas, "The War He Actually Got," *Johnson's Russia List*, September 17, 2008.

Aron, Leon, "Russian Oil and U.S. Security," *New York Times*, May 5, 2002.

Aron, Raymond, *Peace and War: A Theory of International Relations*. (New York: Doubleday, 1966).

Asmus, Ronald D., *A Little War That Shook the World: Georgia, Russia, and the Future of the West*. (New York: Palgrave Macmillan, 2010).

Averintsev, S. S., *Krescheniye Rusi i put' russkoi kul'tury*. (Moscow: Nauka, 1990).

Baev, Pavel, "Useful War," *Russian and Eurasia Review*, September 17, 2002, www.jamestown.org

Banerjee, Sanjoy, "Reproduction of Subjects in Historical Structures: Attribution, Identity, and Emotion in the Early Cold War," *International Studies Quarterly*, **35**, 1 (1991).

Barkin, Samuel, "Realist Constructivism," *International Studies Review*, 5 (2003).

Barma, Naazneen, Ely Ratner, and Steven Weber, "The World without West," *National Interest*, **90**, 4 (2007).

Baruch, Bernard, "The United States' Plan for Controlling Atomic Energy (June 14, 1946)," in: *The Origins of the Cold War, 1941–1947: A Historical Problem with Interpretations and Documents*, edited by Walter LaFeber. (New York: John Wiley & Sons, 1971).

Bassin, Mark, *Imperial Visions: Nationalist Imagination and Geographical Expansion in the Russian Far East, 1840–1865*. (Cambridge: Cambridge University Press, 1999).

Bassin, Mark and Konstantin E. Aksenov, "Mackinder and the Heartland Theory in Post-Soviet Geopolitical Discourse," *Geopolitics*, **11**, 1 (Spring 2006).

Baumgart, Winfried, *The Peace of Paris 1856: Studies in War, Diplomacy and Peacemaking*. (Santa Barbara, CA, 1981).

Berdyayev, Nicholai, *Istoki i smysl russkogo kommunizma*. (Paris: IMCA Press, 1937).

    Russkaya ideya. in: *O Rossiy i russkoi filosofskoi kul'ture*, edited by Mikhail Maslov. (Moscow: Nauka, 1990).

Best, Geoffrey, *Honor among Men and Nations: Transformation of an Idea*. (Toronto: University of Toronto Press, 1982).

Bestuzhev, I. V., *Krymskaya voina*. (Moscow: Nauka, 1956).

Billington, James H., *The Icon and the Axe: An Interpretive History of Russian Culture* (New York, 1970).

Birgerson, Susan, *After the Breakup of a Multi-Ethnic Empire*. (New York: Praeger, 2002).

Black, Cyril E., "The Pattern of Russian Objectives," in: *Russian Foreign Policy: Essays in Historical Perspective*, edited by Ivo J. Lederer. (New Haven, CT: Yale University Press, 1967).

Black, J. L., *Russia Faces NATO Expansion: Bearing Gifts or Bearing Arms?* (Lanham, MD: Rowman & Littlefield, 2000).

Blank, Stephen, "From Neglect to Duress: The West and the Georgian Crisis before the 2008 War," in: *The Guns of August 2008: Russia's War in Georgia*, edited by Svante E. Cornell and Frederick Starr. (New York: M. E. Sharpe, 2009).

Bogaturov, Aleksei, "Pluralisticheskaya odnopolyarnost' i interesy Rossiyi," *Svobodnaya mysl'*, **2** (1996).

"Amerika i Rossiya: ot izbiratel'nogo partnerstva k izbiratel'nomu soprotivleniyu," *Mezhdunarodnaya zhizn'*, **6** (1998).

Boot, Max, "The Case for American Empire: The Most Realistic Response to Terrorism Is for America to Embrace Its Imperial Role," *Weekly Standard*, October 15, 2001.

Booth, Ken and Nicholas J. Wheeler, *The Security Dilemma: Fear, Cooperation and Trust in World Politics*. (New York: Palgrave Macmillan, 2008).

Bourgeois, Emile, "Early Years of the Second Empire: Crimean War Origins," in: *Origins of the Crimean War*, edited by Brison D. Gooch. (Lexington, MA: Heath and Co, 1969).

Bovin, A. Ye, *Mirnoye sosushchestvovaniye: istoriya, teiriya, politika*. (Moscow: Progress, 1988).

Bovykin, V. I., *Ocherki istoriyi vneshnei politiki Rossiyi. Konets XIX veka-1917 god*. (Moscow: Uchebno-pedagogicheskoye izdaniye ministerstva prosvescheniya RSFSR, 1960).

Bowker, Mark, *Russia, America and the Islamic World*. (London: Ashgate, 2007).

Bowman, James, *Honor: A History*. (New York: Encounter Books, 2006).

Braun, Aurel, *NATO-Russia Relations in the Twenty-First Century*. (London: Routledge, 2008).

Brooks, Jeffrey, *Thank You, Comrade Stalin! Soviet Public Culture from Revolution to Cold War*. (Princeton: Princeton University Press, 2000).

Brooks, Stephen G. and William C. Wohlforth, "Power, Globalization and the End of the Cold War: Reevaluating a Landmark Case for Ideas," *International Security*, **26**, 4 (Spring 2002).

"American Primacy in Perspective," *Foreign Affairs* (July–August 2002).

World out of Balance: International Relations and the Challenge of American Primacy. (Princeton: Princeton University Press, 2008).

Browley, Mark R., "Neoclassical Realism and Strategic Calculations: Explaining Divergent British, French, and Soviet Strategies toward Germany between the World Wars (1919–1939)," in: *Neoclassical Realism, the State, and Foreign Policy*, edited by Steven E. Lobell, Norrin M. Ripsman, and Jeffrey W. Taliaferro. (Cambridge: Cambridge University Press, 2009).

Brzezinski, Zbigniew, "The Premature Partnership," *Foreign Affairs*, **73**, 1, 1994.

The Grand Chessboard: American Primacy and Its Geostrategic Imperatives. (New York: Basic Books, 1998).

Bugajski, Janusz, *Expanding Russia: Russia's European Ambitions*. (Washington, DC: Center for Strategic and International Studies, 2008).

Burjanadze, Nino, "Georgia's Acting President Says Country Will Survive Current Turmoil," *RFE/RL*, November 27, 2007, http://www.rferl.org

Bush, George W., "Graduation Speech at West Point," United States Military Academy West Point, New York, June 1, 2002, http://www.whitehouse.gov/news/releases/2002/06/20020601-3.html

Bush, Jason, "The Russia-Georgia War Revisited," *Business Week*, November 10, 2008.

"Bush's Russian Romance," *Economist*, May 22, 2002.

Bushkovitch, Paul, *Religion and Society in Russia. The Sixteenth and Seventeenth Centuries*. (Oxford: Oxford University Press, 1992).

Bushuyev, S. K., *A. M. Gorchakov*. (Moscow: Izdatel'stvo Instituta Mezhdunarodnykh Otnosheni, 1961).

Callahan, Patrick, *Logics of American Foreign Policy: Theories of America's World Role*. (New York: Pearson Longman, 2004).

Callahan, William A., "Chinese Visions of World Order: Post-Hegemonic or a New Hegemony?" *International Studies Review* **10**, 4 (2008).

Carr, Edward Hallett, *Socialism in One Country, 1924–1926*. Vol. 1. (New York: Macmillan, 1958).

The Twenty Years' Crisis, 1919–1939. (New York: Harper & Row, 1964).

Chadayev, Aleksei, *Putin i yego ideologiya*. (Moscow: Yevropa, 2006).

Chakrabarty, Dipesh, *Provincializing Europe: Postcolonial Thought and Historical Difference*. (Princeton, NJ: Princeton University Press, 2000).

Chazan, Guy, "Lighting a Spark. Fueled by Oil Money, Russian Economy Soars," *Wall Street Journal*, March 13, 2007.

Chernaya, Lyudmila, "Ot ideyi 'sluzheniya gosudaryu' k ideye 'sluzheniya otechestvu' v russkoi obschestvennoi mysli," in: *Obschestvennaya mysl': issledovaniya i publikatsiyi. Vypusk I.*, edited by A. L. Andreyev and K. Kh. Delokarov. (Moscow: Nauka, 1989).

Chivers, C. J., "Georgia's New Leader Baffles U.S. and Russia Alike," *New York Times*, August 17, 2004.

"Russia Expands Support for Breakaway Regions in Georgia," *New York Times*, April 17, 2008.

Chivers, C. J. and Ellen Barry, "Georgia Claims on Russia War Called into Question," *New York Times*, November 7, 2008.

"Churchill and Stalin Dividing the Balkans on a Half-Sheet of Paper," in: *The Origins of the Cold War, 1941–1947: A Historical Problem with Interpretations and Documents*, edited by Walter LaFeber. (New York: John Wiley & Sons, 1971).

"Churchill, Roosevelt, Stalin at Yalta: Caesar's Wife in Fact Had Her Sins," in: *The Origins of the Cold War, 1941–1947: A Historical Problem with Interpretations and Documents*, edited by Walter LaFeber. (New York: John Wiley & Sons, 1971).

Churchill, Winston, "The Iron Curtain Speech," in: *The Origins of the Cold War, 1941–1947: A Historical Problem with Interpretations and Documents*, edited by Walter LaFeber. (New York: John Wiley & Sons, 1971).

Clunan, Anne L., *The Social Construction of Russia's Resurgence: Aspirations, Identity, and Security Interests*. (Baltimore: John Hopkins University Press, 2009).

Cohen, Ariel, "Domestic Factors Driving Russia's Foreign Policy," *Heritage Foundation*, Memo # 2084, November 9, 2007.

Cohen, Stephen F., *Bukharin and the Bolshevik Revolution: A Political Biography, 1888–1938*. (New York: Oxford University Press, 1980).

Rethinking the Soviet Experience: Politics and History since 1917. (New York: Oxford University Press, 1985).

Cooley, Alexander, "How the West Failed Georgia," *Current History* (October 2008).

Copeland, Dale C., *The Origins of Major War.* (Ithaca, NY: Cornell University Press, 2000).

Cornell, Svante E. and Frederick Starr, "Introduction," in: *The Guns of August 2008: Russia's War in Georgia,* edited by Svante E. Cornell and Frederick Starr. (New York: M. E. Sharpe, 2009).

Crandall, Andrea, "Invest in China? Invest in Russia," *Johnson's Russia List,* no. 22, April 19, 2006, at http://www.cdi.org/russia/johnson

Crawford, Netta, "The Passion of World Politics: Proposition on Emotion and Emotional Relationships," *International Security,* 24, 4 (2000), 116–56.

Crews, Robert D., "Czartoryski on the Education of Alexander I," in: *Russia and the West from Peter to Khrushchev,* edited by L. Jay Oliva. (Boston: D. C. Heath, 1965).

For Prophet and Tsar: Islam and Empire in Russia and Central Asia. (Cambridge, MA: Harvard University Press, 2006).

Cox, Robert W., "Civilizations: Encounters and Transformations," *Studies in Political Economy,* 47 (1995).

Curtiss, John Sheldon, *Russia's Crimean War.* (Durham, NC: Duke University Press, 1979).

Daniels, Robert V., "The Declaration on Liberated Europe," in: *The Origins of the Cold War, 1941–1947: A Historical Problem with Interpretations and Documents,* edited by Walter LaFeber. (New York: John Wiley & Sons, 1971).

Russia: The Roots of Confrontation. (Cambridge, MA: Harvard University Press, 1985).

Deng, Xiaoping, "Conception of National Interests: Realpolitik, Liberal Dilemma, and the Possibility of Change," in: *In the Eyes of the Dragon. China Views the World,* edited by Xiaoping Deng and Fei-Ling Wang. (Lanham, MD: Rowman & Littlefield Publishers, 1999).

China's Struggle for Status: The Realignment of International Relations. (Cambridge: Cambridge University Press, 2008).

Deutscher, Isaac, *The Prophet Unarmed: Trotsky 1921–1929.* (London: Verso, 2003).

"Did Saakashvili Lie?" *Der Spiegel,* September 15, 2008.

Djilas, Milovan, "Stalin in 1944–1945," in: *The Origins of the Cold War, 1941–1947: A Historical Problem with Interpretations and Documents,* edited by Walter LaFeber. (New York: John Wiley & Sons, 1971).

Dmytryshyn, Basil, ed., *Imperial Russia: A Source Book, 1700–1917.* (Hinsdale, IL: Harcourt, 1974).

Donaldson, Robert H. and Joseph L. Nogee, *The Foreign Policy of Russia.* (Armonk, NY: M. E. Sharpe, 1998).

Donelan, Michael, *Honor in Foreign Policy: A History and Discussion.* (London: Palgrave, 2007).

Donnelly, Jack, *Realism and International Relations.* (Cambridge: Cambridge University Press, 2000).

Doyle, Michael W., "Draft Declaration Regarding a Definition of Aggression," in: *Russia and the West from Peter to Khrushchev*, edited by Jay Oliva. (Boston: D. C. Heath, 1965).

Ways of War and Peace: Realism, Liberalism and Socialism. (New York: W. W. Norton, 1997).

Dugin, Aleksandr, "Yevraziyski proyekt," *Zavtra*, August, 1996.

"Terakty 11 Sentyabrya: economicheski smysl," in: *Geopolitika terrora.* (Moscow: Arktogeya tsentr, 2002).

Duncan, P. J. S., *Russian Messianism: Third Rome, Revolution, Communism and After.* (London: Routledge, 2000).

Durkheim, Emile, *Professional Ethics and Civic Morals.* (London: Routledge, 1992).

Efimov, A. V. and E. V. Tarle, "Ot sozdaniya svashchennogo soyuza do iyul'skoi revolutstiyi (1815–1830 gg.)," in: *Istoriya diplomatiyi*, edited by V. P. Potemkin, vol. 1. (Moscow: OGIZ, 1945).

Eidel'man, Natan, *"Revolutsiya sverkhu" v Rossiyi.* (Moscow: Moskovski rabochi, 1989).

English, Robert R., *Russia and the Idea of the West. Gorbachev, Intellectuals, and the End of the Cold War.* (New York: Columbia University Press, 2000).

"Power, Ideas, and New Evidence on the Cold War's End," *International Security*, **26**, 4 (2002).

English, Robert and Ekaterina Svyatets, "A Presumption of Guilt? Western Media Coverage of the 2008 Russia-Georgia War," paper presented at the annual convention of International Studies Association, New York, February 20, 2010.

Ertel, Manfred, Uwe Klussmann, Susanne Koelbl, Walter Mayr, Matthias Schepp, Holger Stark and Alexander Szandar, "Echshe odin soratnik Saakashvili obvinil Rossiyu v fashizme," *Izvestia*, April 18, 2006.

"Road to War in Georgia," *Der Spiegel*, August 25, 2008, posted on Johnson's Russia List, #162, www.cdi.org/russia/johnson, accessed August 31, 2008.

Evangelista, Matthew A., "Stalin's Postwar Army Reappraised," *International Security* 7, 1 (Winter 1982–3).

Evans, Alfred B., *Power and Ideology: Vladimir Putin and the Russian Political System.* (Pittsburgh: University of Pittsburgh Center for Russian and East European Studies, 2008).

Fattah, Khaled and K. M. Fierke, "A Clash of Emotions: The Politics of Humiliation and Political Violence in the Middle East," *European Journal of International Relations*, **15**, 1 (2009), 67–93.

Feklunina, Valentina, "Battle for Perceptions: Projecting Russia in the West," *Europe-Asia Studies*, **60**, 4 (2008).

Felgenhauer, Pavel, "After August 7: The Escalation of the Russia-Georgia War," in: *The Guns of August 2008: Russia's War in Georgia*, edited by Svante E. Cornell and Frederick Starr. (New York: M.E. Sharpe, 2009).

Ferguson, Niall, *The Pity of War: Explaining World War I.* (New York: Basic Books, 2000).

"Our Imperial Imperative," *Atlantic Monthly*, May 25, 2004.

Filippov, Mikhail, "Diversionary Role of the Georgia-Russia Conflict: International Constraints and Domestic Appeal," *Europe-Asia Studies*, **61**, 10 (2009).

Fink, Carole, "The NEP in Foreign Policy: The Genoa Conference and the Treaty of Rappalo," in: *Soviet Foreign Policy, 1917–1991: A Retrospective*, edited by Gabriel Gorodetsky. (London: Frank Cass, 1994).

Florovski, Georgi, *Puti russkogo bogosloviya*. (Paris: IMCA Press, 1983).

Foglesong, David S. "Foreign Minister Blames Tbilisi for Escalating Tensions," *RFE/RL Newsline*, August 19, 2004.

The American Mission and the "Evil Empire": The Crusade for a "Free Russia" since 1881. (Cambridge: Cambridge University Press, 2007).

Freyberg-Inan, Annette, *What Moves Man: The Realist Theory of International Relations and Its Judgment of Human Nature*. (New York: State University of New York Press, 2004).

Friedman, George, "Georgia and the Balance of Power," *New York Review of Books*, **55**, 14, accessed September 25, 2008, http://www.nybooks.com/articles/21772

Fukuyama, Francis, "The End of History?" *National Interest*, **16** (Summer 1989).

Fuller, William C., Jr., *Strategy and Power in Russia, 1600–1914*. (New York: Free Press, 1992).

Fursov, Andrei, "Kholodnaya voina, sistemnyi kapitalizm i 'peresdacha kart Istoriyi'," *Politicheski klass*, **8** (2009).

Fyodorov, Yuri, "Krizis vneshnei politiki Rossiyi," *Pro et Contra*, **6**, 1–2 (2001).

Gaddis, John Lewis, *We Now Know: Rethinking Cold War History*. (Oxford: Clarendon Press, 1997).

The Cold War: A New History. (New York: The Penguin Press, 2005).

Gadzhiyev, Kamaludin S., *Geopolitika Kavkaza*. (Moscow: Mezhdunarodnyie otnosheniya, 2001).

Gartell, Peter, *The Tsarist Economy, 1850–1917*. (New York: St. Martin's Press, 1986).

Gegeshidze, Archil, "Georgia: Saakashvili Sees in 'Wahhabism' a Threat to Secularism," *RFE/RL*, February 18, 2004.

"Georgia Accuses Russia of Abkhazia Double Standards," *RFE/RL*, November 1, 2004.

"Rossiya podderzhivayet ne oppozitsiyu, a destabilizatsiyu," *Pankisi.info*, November 11, 2007, http://www.pankisi.info/analitic/?page=ge&id=206

"Georgia, Ukraine NATO Accession May Cause Geopolitical Shift – FM," *RIA Novosti*, June 7, 2006.

"Georgia Condemns Russian Raid," *BBC News*, August 7, 2007.

Georgian, Armen, "U.S. Eyes Caspian Oil in 'War on Terror,'" *Foreign Policy in Focus*, April 30, 2002, www.fpif.org

Geyer, Dietrich, *Russian Imperialism: The Interaction of Domestic and Foreign Policy 1860–1914*. (New York, Hamburg: Berg Publishers, 1987).

Geyer, Georgie Anne, "Russia First to Test New President," *Chicago Tribune*, November 14, 2008, www.chicagotribune.com/news/nationworld/chi-oped1114geyernov14,0,7013815.story

Giragosian, Richard, "Georgia: Gas Cutoff Highlights National Security Flaws," *RFE/RL*, February 2, 2006.

Gleason, John Howard, *The Genesis of Russophobia in Great Britain: A Study of the Interaction of Policy and Opinion*. (Cambridge: Cambridge University Press, 1950).

Goldfrank, David M., "Policy Traditions and the Menshikov Mission of 1853," in: *Imperial Russian Foreign Policy*, edited by Hugh Ragsdale. (Cambridge: Cambridge University Press, 1993).

The Origins of the Crimean War. (London: Longman, 1994).

Goldgeier, James, *Not Whether, but When: The US Decision to Enlarge NATO*. (Washington, DC: Brookings Institution Press, 1999).

Goltz, Aleksandr, "Bremya militarizma, " *Otechestvennyye zapiski*, **26**, 5 (2005).

Gooch, Brison D., "Introduction," in: *Origins of the Crimean War*, edited by Brison D. Gooch. (Lexington, MA: Heath and Co, 1969).

Gorodetsky, Gabriel, "The Formulation of Soviet Foreign Policy: Ideology and *Realpolitik*," in: *Soviet Foreign Policy, 1917–1991: A Retrospective*, edited by Gabriel Gorodetsky. (London: Frank Cass, 1994).

Grand Delusion: Stalin and the German Invasion of Russia. (New Haven: Yale University Press, 1999).

Gould-Davies, N. and N. Woods, "Russia and the IMF," *International Affairs*, **75**, 1 (1999).

"Gruzinskiy parlament prishel k vyvodu rossiyskikh mirotvortsev," *Kommersant*, July 9, 2006.

"Gruzinskiye voyennyye zaderzhalis' v Yuzhnoi Ossetiyi," *Kommersant*, July 9, 2008.

Gurev, Vladimir, "Gruzinskaya tema," *Mezhdunarodnaya zhizn'*, 1 (2005).

Guzzini, Stefano, *Realism in International Relations and International Political Economy: The Continuing Story of a Death Foretold*. (London: Routledge, 1998).

Haas, Mark L., *The Ideological Origins of Great Power Politics*. (Ithaca, NY: Cornell University Press, 2005).

Habermas, Jurgen, *Theory and Practice*. (Boston: Beacon Press, 1973).

Hagan, Joe, "Domestic Political Sources of Stable Peace: The Great Powers, 1815–1854," in: *Stable Peace among Nations*, edited by Arie M. Kacowicz, Yaacov Bar-Smiman-Tov, Ole Elgstrom, and Magnus Jerneck. (Lanham, MD: Rowman & Littlefield, 2000).

Hahn, Gordon M., "The Making of Georgian-Russian Five-Day August War: A Chronology, June-August 8, 2008," http://www.russiaotherpointsofview.com/gordon-hahns-underground-.html

Hanson, Philip, "Joining but Not Signing Up? Russia's Economic 'Integration' into Europe," *Russian and Eurasia Review*, March 18, 2003, www.jamestown.org

Harkavy, Robert E., "Defeat, National Humiliation, and the Revenge Motif in International Politics," *International Politics*, **37** (2000), 345–68.

Haslam, Jonathan, *Soviet Foreign Policy, 1930–1933: The Impact of Depression*. (London: Macmillan, 1983).

The Soviet Union and the Struggle for Collective Security in Europe, 1933–1939. (London: Macmillan, 1984).

"Litvinov, Stalin and the Road Not Taken," in: *Soviet Foreign Policy, 1917–1991: A Retrospective*, edited by Gabriel Gorodetsky. (London: Frank Cass, 1994).

No Virtue like Necessity: Realist Thought in International Relations since Machiavelli. (New Haven: Yale University Press, 2002).

Hauner, Milan, *What Is Asia to Us? Russia's Asian Heartland Yesterday and Today* (Boston: Allen & Urwin, 1990).

Headley, James, *Russia and the Balkans: Foreign Policy from Yeltsin to Putin.* (New York: Columbia University Press, 2008).

Helleiner, E. and A. Pickel, eds., *Economic Nationalism in a Globalizing World.* (Ithaca, NY: Cornell University Press, 2005).

Herspring, Dale R. and Peter Rutland, "Putin and Russian Foreign Policy," in: *Putin's Russia: Past Imperfect, Future Uncertain.* (Lanham, MD: Rowman & Littlefield, 2004).

Hewitt, George, "Abkhazia and Georgia: Time for Reassessment," *Brown Journal of World Affairs*, Spring/Summer (2009).

Hirschmann, Albert O., *The Passions and the Interests: Political Arguments for Capitalism before Its Triumph.* (Princeton: Princeton University Press, 1977).

Hochman, Jiri, *The Soviet Union and the Failure of Collective Security, 1934–1938.* (Ithaca, NY: Cornell University Press, 1984).

Holborn, Hajo, "Russia and the European Political System," in: *Russian Foreign Policy*, edited by Ivo J. Lederer. (New Haven, CT: Yale University Press, 1967).

Holloway, David, *Soviet Union and the Arms Race.* (New Haven, CT: Yale University Press, 1984).

Stalin and the Bomb: The Soviet Union and Atomic Energy, 1939–1956. (New Haven, CT: Yale University Press, 1994).

Holsti, Kalevi J., "The Holy Alliance," in: *Russia and the West from Peter to Khrushchev*, edited by L. Jay Oliva. (Boston: D. C. Heath, 1965).

Peace and War: Armed Conflicts and International Order, 1648–1989. (Cambridge: Cambridge University Press, 1991).

Hopf, Ted, *Social Construction of International Politics: Identities and Foreign Policies, Moscow, 1955 and 1999.* (Ithaca, NY: Cornell University Press, 2002).

Hosking, Geoffrey, *Russia: People and Empire, 1552–1917.* (Cambridge, MA: Harvard University Press, 1997).

Hughes, Christopher, "Globalization and Nationalism: Squaring the Circle in Chinese International Relations Theory." *Millennium* **26**, 1 (1997).

Huntington, Samuel, "The Clash of Civilizations?" *Foreign Affairs*, 72, 4 (1993).

The Clash of Civilizations and the Remaking of World Order. (New York: Simon & Schuster, 1996).

Illarionov, Andrei, "Ivanov Surprised At Georgia's Reaction To Russia's Possible Anti-Terrorist Strikes," *RIA Novosti*, March 4, 2005.

"Irakli Okruashvili: President khotel ubrat' Badri," *Izvestia*, September 28, 2007.

"The Russian Leadership's Preparations for War, 1999–2008," in: *The Guns of August 2008: Russia's War in Georgia*, edited by Svante E. Cornell and Frederick Starr. (New York: M. E. Sharpe, 2009).

Independent International Fact-Finding Mission on the Conflict in Georgia. Report, September 2009, www.ceiig.ch

Inayatullah, Naeem and David L. Blaney, *International Relations and the Problem of Difference.* (London: Routledge, 2004).

Ivanov, Igor, *Vneshnyaya politika Rossiyi v epokhu globalizatsiyi.* (Moscow: Mezhdunarodnyye otnosheniya, 2001).

Ivashev, Leonid, "Rossiya mozhet snova stat' sverkhderzhavoi," *Nezavisimaya gazeta,* March 7, 1995.

"Iz predlozheni Soyuza SSR po sozdaniyu v Yevrope sistemy kollektivnoi bezopasnosti, odobrennykh TsK VKP(b) 19 dekabrya 1933 g." in: *Sistemnaya istoriya mezhdunarodnykh otnosheniy, 1918–2000,* edited by A. D. Bogaturov, vol. 2. (Moscow: Moskovski rabochi, 2000).

Jackson, Patrick Thaddeus, "Bridging the Gap: Toward a Realist-Constructivist Dialogue," *International Studies Review,* **6** (2004).

"Constructivist Realism or Realist Constructivism? A Forum," *International Studies Review,* **6** (2004).

"Paradigmatic Faults in International Relations Theory," *International Studies Quarterly,* **53,** 4 (2009).

Jacobson, Jon, *When the Soviet Union Entered World Politics.* (Berkeley: University of California Press, 1994).

Jelavich, Barbara, *A Century of Russian Foreign Policy, 1814–1914.* (New York: J.B. Lippincott Company, 1964).

Russia's Balkan Entenglements, 1806–1914. (Cambridge: Cambridge University Press, 1991).

Jervis, Robert, "Cooperation under Security Dilemma," *World Politics,* **30** (1978).

Jervis, Robert and Jack Snyder, eds., *Dominous and Bandwagoning: Strategic Beliefs and Great Power Competition in the Eurasian Rimland.* (New York: Columbia University Press, 1991).

Johnston, Alastair Iain, *Social States: China in International Institutions, 1980–2000.* (Princeton: Princeton University Press, 2008).

Jomini, Alexandre, "Diplomatic Study of the Crimean War," in: *Origins of the Crimean War,* edited by Brison D. Gooch. (Lexington, MA: Heath and Co, 1969).

Jones, Branwen Gruffydd, ed. *Decolonizing International Relations.* (Lanham, MD: Rowman & Littlefield, 2006).

Joshi, Shashank, *Honor in International Relations.* Harvard University, Weatherhead Center for International Affairs, Working Paper Series, Paper No. 2008–0146, December 2008.

Kaarbo, Juliet, "Foreign Policy Analysis in the Twenty-First Century: Back to Comparison, Forward to Identity and Ideas," *International Studies Review,* **5** (2003).

Kagan, Donald, *On the Origins of War and the Preservation of Peace.* (New York: Doubleday, 1995).

Kagan, Robert, *Of Paradise and Power: America and Europe in the New World Order.* (New York: Public Affairs, 2004).

Kanet, Roger E, ed., *A Resurgent Russia and the West: The European Union, NATO and Beyond.* (Republic of Letters Publishing, 2009).

Kaganovich, Lazar', *Pamyatnyye zapiski.* (Moscow: Vagrius, 2003).

Kaplan, Robert D., "The Hard Edge of American Values," *Atlantic Monthly,* June 18, 2003.

Kassianova, Alla, "Russia: Still Open to the West?" *Europe-Asia Studies,* **53,** 6 (2001).

Katzenstein, Peter J., "The Kennan 'Long Telegram,'" in: *Origins of the Cold War: The Novikov, Kennan, and Roberts "Long Telegrams" of 1946,* edited by Kenneth M. Jensen. (Washington, DC: United States Institute of Peace Press, 1993).

Cultural Norms and National Security: Police and Military in Postwar Japan. (Ithaca, NY: Cornell University Press, 1996).

Kennan, George F. (X), "The Sources of Soviet Conduct," *Foreign Affairs,* **25,** (1947).

Russia and the West under Lenin and Stalin. (New York: Mentor Book, 1961).

The Fateful Alliance: France, Russia, and the Coming of the First World War. (New York: Pantheon Books, 1984).

Kennedy, Paul, *The Rise and Fall of Great Powers: Economic Change and Military Conflict from 1500 to 2000.* (New York: Vintage, 1986).

Kennedy-Pipe, Caroline, *Russia and the World, 1917–1991.* (London: Arnold, 1998).

Kerenskiy, Aleksei, *Istoriya Rossiyi.* (Irkutsk: "Zhurnalist," 1996).

Khevrolina, V. M., "Problemy vneshnei politiki Rossiyi v obshchestvennoy mysli strany," in: *Istoriya vneshnei politiki Rossiyi. Vtoraya polovina XIX veka,* edited by A. N. Sakharov. (Moscow: Mezhdunarodnyye otnosheniya, 1997).

"Preobrazovaniya v Rossiyi i vneshnyaya politika: vzaimosvyaz' i vzaimovliyaniye," in: *Istoriya vneshnei politiki Rossiyi. Vtoraya polovina XIX veka,* edited by A. N. Sakharov. (Moscow: Mezhdunarodnyye otnosheniya, 1997).

Khitrova, N. I., "Rossiya sosredotachivayetsya," in: *Istoriya vneshnei politiki Rossiyi. Vtoraya polovina XIX veka,* edited by A. N. Sakharov. (Moscow: Mezhdunarodnyye otnosheniya, 1997).

"A. M. Gorchakov i otmena neytralizatsiyi Chernogo morya, 1856–1871," in: *Kantsler A. M. Gorchakov. K 200-letiyu so dnya rozhdeniya,* edited by Ye. M. Primakov, I. S. Ivanov at el. (Moscow: Mezhdunarodnyye otnosheniya, 1998).

Khromov, Pavel A., *Economicheskoye razvitiye Rossiyi.* (Moscow: Nauka, 1967).

Khvostov, V. M., "Bor'ba Antanty i Avstro-germanskogo bloka," in: *Vseobschaya istoriya diplomatiyi,* edited by M. Priz. (Moscow: Eksmo, 2009).

Kinglake, Alexander W., "Transactions Which Brought on the War," in: *Origins of the Crimean War,* edited by Brison D. Gooch. (Lexington, MA: Heath and Co, 1969).

Kissinger, Henry, *Diplomacy.* (New York: Simon & Schuster, 1994).

Klein, Donald C., "The Humiliation Dynamic: An Overview," *Journal of Primary Prevention,* **12,** 2 (1991), 93–121.

Kohn, Hans, *Panslavism: Its History and Ideology.* (Notre Dame: University of Notre Dame Press, 1953).

Kohn, Hans, ed., *The Mind of Modern Russia. Historical and Political Thought of Russia's Great Age*. (New York: Harper & Row, 1955).

Kokovtsev, Vladimir, *Iz moyego proshlogo. Vospominaniya 1903–1919*, Vol. 2. (Moscow: Nauka, 1992).

Kolakowski, Leszek, *Main Currents of Marxism: Its Origins, Growth and Dissolution. Vol. 3: The Breakdown*. (New York: Oxford University Press, 1978).

Kollmann, Nancy Shields, *By Honor Bound: State and Society in Early Modern Russia*. (Ithaca, NY: Cornell University Press, 1999).

Kolossov, Vladimir A. and Natalya A. Borodullina, "Rossiya i Zapad: mneniye rossiyan," *Russia in Global Affairs*, 1 (2003).

Koritski, Eduard B., ed., *Puti razvitiya: diskussiyi 20-kh godov*. (Leningrad: Lenizdat, 1990).

Kortunov, Sergei, "Rossiysko-Amerikanskoye partnerstvo?" *Mezhdunarodnaya zhizn'*, 4 (2002).

Kovalevskii, Maksim, "The Growth of Serfdom," in: *Readings in Russian History*, edited by Warren B. Walsh. (Syracuse, NY: Syracuse University Press, 1948).

Kozyrev, Andrei, "Rossiya v novom mire," *Mezhdunarodnaya zhizn'*, 3–4 (1992). "Russia and Human Rights," *Slavic Review*, 51, 2 (1992).

Krauthammer, Charles, "The Unipolar Moment, *Foreign Affairs*, 70, 1 (1990–1). "The Unipolar Moment Revisited – United States World Dominance," *National Interest* (2002).

"Why Only in Ukraine?" *Washington Post*, December 3, 2004.

Kupchan, Charles A. and Clifford A. Kupchan, "Concerts, Collective Security, and the Future of Europe," *International Security*, 16, 1 (1991). "The Promise of Collective Security," *International Security*, 20, 1 (1995).

Kydd, Andrew H., *Trust and Mistrust in International Relations*. (Princeton: Princeton University Press, 2005).

LaFeber, Walter, *America, Russia, and the Cold War, 1945–1996*, 8th ed. (New York: McGraw-Hill, 1997).

Lambroschini, Sophie, "Georgia: Russia Watches Warily as Saakashvili Comes to Power," *RFE/RL*, January 6, 2004.

Lamsdorff, V. N., *Dnevnik. 1891–1892*. (Moscow: Academia, 1934).

Lapidus, Gail W., "Between Assertiveness and Insecurity: Russian Elite Attitudes and the Russia-Georgia Crisis," *Post-Soviet Affairs*, 23, 2 (2007).

Larson, Deborah Welsh, *Origins of Containment: A Psychological Explanation*. (Princeton: Princeton University Press, 1985).

Larson, Deborah Welsh and Alexei Shevchenko, "Status Seekers: Chinese and Russian Responses to U.S. Primacy," *International Security*, 34, 4 (2010).

Laruelle, Marlene, *Russian Eurasianism: An Ideology of Empire*. (Baltimore: John Hopkins University Press, 2008).
In the Name of a Nation: Nationalism and Politics in Contemporary Russia. (London: Palgrave, 2009).

Lavrov, Sergei, "A Strategic Relationship: From Rivalry to Partnership," *Russia Beyond the Headlines*, May, 28 2008, http://www.rbth.rg.ru
"America Must Choose between Georgia and Russia," *Wall Street Journal*, August 20, 2008.

Lebow, Richard Ned, *The Tragic Vision of Politics: Ethics, Interests and Orders.* (Cambridge: Cambridge University Press, 2003).

LeDonne, John P., *The Russian Empire and the World, 1700–1917: The Geopolitics of Expansion and Containment.* (New York: Oxford University Press, 1997).

The Grand Strategy of the Russian Empire, 1650–1830. (New York: Oxford University Press, 2004).

Leffler, Melvin P., *A Preponderance of Power: National Security, the Truman Administration, and the Cold War.* (Stanford: Stanford University Press, 1992).

Legro, Jeffrey, *Rethinking the World: Great Power Strategies and International Orders.* (Ithaca, NY: Cornell University Press, 2005).

Legvold, Robert, "Russian Foreign Policy during State Transformation," in: *Russian Foreign Policy in the Twenty-First Century and the Shadow of the Past,* edited by Robert Legvold. (New York: Columbia University Press, 2007).

Legvold, Robert, ed., *Russian Foreign Policy in the Twenty-First Century and the Shadow of the Past.* (New York: Columbia University Press, 2007).

Lenin, Vladimir, "Imperialism, the Highest Stage of Capitalism," in: V. I. Lenin, *Selected Works,* vol. 1. (Moscow: Progress, 1967).

Lewin, Moshe, *The Soviet Century.* (London: Verso, 2005).

Lieven, Anatol, *Chechnya. Tombstone of Russian Power.* (New Haven, CT: Yale University Press, 1998).

America Right or Wrong: Anatomy of American Nationalism. (New York: Oxford University Press, 2004).

Lieven, Anatol and John Hulsman, *Ethical Realism: A Vision for America's Role in the World.* (New York: Pantheon, 2006).

Lieven, D. C. B., *Russia and the Origins of the First World War.* (New York: St. Martin's Press, 1983).

Lieven, Dominic, *Empire: The Russian Empire and Its Rivals.* (New Haven, CT: Yale University Press, 2000).

Russia against Napoleon: The True Story of the Campaigns of 'War and Peace.' (New York: Viking, 2010).

Lincoln, Bruce W., *Nicholas I: Emperor and Autocrat of All the Russians.* (DeKalb, IL: University of Illinois Press, 1978).

Litvinov, Maxim, *Against Aggression: Speeches.* (New York: International Publisher, 1939).

Lobell, Steven E., Norrin Ripsman and Jeffrey Taliaferro, eds., *Neoclassical Realism, the State, and Foreign Policy.* (Cambridge: Cambridge University Press, 2009).

Löwenheim, Oded and Gadi Heimann, "Revenge in International Politics," *Security Studies,* **17**, (2008), 685–724.

Lucas, Edward, *The New Cold War: The Future of Russia and the Threat to the West.* (London: Palgrave, 2009).

Luttwack, Edward N., *The Grand Strategy of the Soviet Union.* (New York: St. Martin's Press, 1983).

Lynch, Allen, "Realism of Russian Foreign Policy," *Europe-Asia Studies,* **53**, 1 (2001).

Lynch, Allen C., *How Russia Is Not Ruled: Reflections on Russian Political Development.* (Cambridge: Cambridge University Press, 2005).

MacFarlane, Neil, "Realism and Russian Strategy after the Collapse of the USSR," in: *Unipolar Politics*, edited by Ethan B. Kapstein and Michael Mastanduno. (New York: Columbia University Press, 1999).

MacFarlane, S. Neil, "Russian Perspectives on Order and Justice," in: *Order and Justice in International Relations*, edited by Rosemary Foot, John Gaddis, and Andrew Hurrell. (Oxford: Oxford University Press, 2003.)

MacIntyre, Alastair, *After Virtue: A Study in Moral Theory*. (Notre Dame: University of Notre Dame Press, 1984).

MacKenzie, David, "Russia's Balkan Policies under Alexander II, 1855–1881" in: *Imperial Russian Foreign Policy*, edited by Hugh Ragsdale. (Cambridge: Cambridge University Press, 1993).

MacKinnon, Mark, *The New Cold War: Revolutions, Rigged Elections and Pipeline Politics in the Former Soviet Union*. (New York: Random House, 2007).

Madsen, Deborah L., *American Exceptionalism*. (Jackson: University Press of Mississippi, 1998).

Malia, Martin, *Russia under Western Eyes: From the Bronze Horseman to the Lenin Mausoleum*. (Cambridge, MA: Cambridge University Press, 1999).

Mandelbaum, Michael, *The Ideas That Conquered the World: Peace, Democracy, and Free Markets in Twenty-First Century*. (New York: Public Affairs, 2002).

Mankoff, Jeffrey, *Russian Foreign Policy: The Return of Great Power Politics*. (Boulder, CO: Rowman & Littlefield, 2009).

"Changing Course in Moscow," *Foreign Policy*, September 7, 2010.

Mannheim, Karl, *Ideology and Utopia: An Introduction to the Sociology of Knowledge*. (New York: Harvest-HBJ Book, 1968).

Markey, Daniel Seth, "Prestige and the Origins of War: Returning to Realism's Roots," *Security Studies*, **8**, 4 (1999).

The Prestige Motive in International Relations. PhD Diss. (Princeton University, 2000).

Martin, Terry, *The Affirmative Action Empire: Nations and Nationalism in the Soviet Union, 1923–1939*. (Ithaca, NY: Cornell University Press, 2001).

Mastny, Vojtech. *Russia's Road to the Cold War: Diplomacy, Warfare, and the Politics of Communism, 1941–1945*. (New York: Columbia University Press, 1979).

McDaniel, Tim, *The Agony of the Russian Idea*. (Princeton, NJ: Princeton University Press, 1996).

McDonald, David MacLaren. *United Government and Foreign Policy in Russia, 1900–1914*. (Cambridge, MD: Harvard University Press, 1992).

Mead, Walter Russell, *Special Providence: American Foreign Policy and How It Changed the World*. (London: Routledge, 2002).

Mearsheimer, John, *The Tragedy of Great Power Politics*. (New York: W. W. Norton, 2001).

Medvedev, Dmitriy, *Speech at the Meeting with Russian Ambassadors and Permanent Representatives to International Organizations, Russian Foreign Ministry*, Moscow, July 15, 2008.

Speech at World Policy Conference, Evian, France, October 8, 2008.

"Why I Had to Recognize Georgia's Breakaway Regions," *Financial Times*, August 26, 2008.

Speech at the Meeting with Russian Ambassadors and Permanent Representatives to International Organizations, July 12, 2010.

Menon, Rajan, "After Empire: Russia and the Southern 'Near Abroad,'" in: *The New Russian Foreign Policy*, edited by Michael Mandelbaum. (New York: Council on Foreign Relations, 1998).

Mercer, Jonathan, *Reputation and International Politics*. (Ithaca, NY: Cornell University Press, 1996).

"Emotional Beliefs," *International Organization*, **64**, (2010), 1–31.

Mezhuyev, Boris, "Vernite Shervadnadze!" *Russki zhurnal*, August 12, 2008, http://www.russ.ru/lyudi/vernite_shevardnadze

"Minoborony Yuzhnoi Osetiyi: Gruziya kontsentriruyet voiska na granitse," August 3, 2008, www.kavkaz-uzel.ru/newstext/news/id/1226450.html, accessed on November 11, 2008.

Mickethwait, John and Adrian Wooldridge, *The Right Nation: Conservative Power in America*. (New York: Penguin, 2004).

Migranyan, Andranik, "Rasstavaniye s illuziyami," *Nezavisimaya gazeta*, October 27, 1999.

Mikoyan, A. I., "Diplomat leninskoi shkoly," in: *Maksim Maksimovich Litvinov: revolutsioner, diplomat, chelovek*, edited by Z. Sheinis. (Moscow: Politizdat, 1989).

Mlechin, Leonid, *Ministry inostrannykh del: romantiki i tsiniki*. (Moscow: Mezhdunarodnyye otnosheniya, 2001).

Mohanty, Chandra T., "Under Western Eyes: Feminist Scholarship and Colonial Discourses," in: *Comparative Political Culture in the Age of Globalization*, edited by Hwa Yol Jung. (Lanham, MD: Lexington Books, 2002).

Molotov, V. M., "A Russian View of 'Equal Opportunity,'" in: *The Origins of the Cold War, 1941–1947: A Historical Problem with Interpretations and Documents*, edited by Walter LaFeber. (New York: John Wiley & Sons, 1971).

A Month after the War: Violations of Human Rights and Norms of Humanitarian law in the Conflict Zone in South Ossetia. Special press release by the Memorial Human Rights Center, September 16, 2008.

Morgenthau, Hans J., *Politics among Nations: The Struggle for Power and Peace*, 5th Edition, revised. (New York: Alfred A. Knopf, 1978).

Mosse, W. E., *Alexander II and the Modernization of Russia*. (New York: Macmillan, 1962).

"Most Russians Certain Army Can Beat Back Any Aggressor – Poll," *ITAR-TASS*, February 20, 2007.

Nadzhafov, D. G., "Bor'ba za ukrepleniye Versal'skogo perioda i vosstanovleniye yevropeiskogo ravnovesiya (1921–1926)," in: *Sistemnaya istoriya mezhdunarodnykh otnosheniy, 1918–2000*, edited by A. D. Bogaturov, vol. 2. (Moscow: Moskovski rabochi, 2000).

Naimark, Norman and Leonid Gibianski, eds., *The Establishment of Communist Regimes in Eastern Europe, 1944–1949*. (Boulder, CO: Westview Press, 1997).

Nation, R. Craig, *Black Earth, Red Star: A History of Soviet Security Policy, 1917–1991*. (Ithaca, NY: Cornell University Press, 1992).

Neilson, Keith, *Britain, Soviet Russia and the Collapse of the Versailles Order, 1919–1939.* (Cambridge: Cambridge University Press, 2006).

Nekrich, Alexandr M., *Pariahs, Partners, Predators: German-Soviet Relations, 1922–1941.* (New York: Columbia University Press, 1997).

Neumann, Iver B., *Russia and the Idea of Europe. A Study in Identity and International Relations.* (London: Routledge, 1996).

 Uses of the Other. (Minneapolis: University of Minnesota Press, 1998).

 "Russia's Standing as a Great Power, 1494–1815," in: *Russia's European Choice,* edited by Ted Hopf. (London: Palgrave, 2008).

Nol'de, B. E., *Vneshnyaya politika. Istoricheskiye ocherki.* (Petrograd: "Pravo", 1915).

Nove, Alec. *An Economic History of the USSR.* (New York: Penguin Books, 1982).

 "The Novikov Telegram," in: *Origins of the Cold War: The Novikov, Kennan, and Roberts "Long Telegrams" of 1946,* edited by Kenneth M. Jensen. (Washington, DC: United States Institute of Peace, 1993).

Offer, Avner, "Going to War in 1914: A Matter of Honor?" *Politics and Society,* **23,** 2 (1995), 213–41.

Oslon, A., ed., *Amerika: vzglyad iz Rossiyi.* (Moscow: Institut Fonda "Obschestvennoye mneniye, 2001).

O'Hagan, Jacinta, *Conceptualizing the West in International Relations: From Spengler to Said.* (London: Palgrave, 2002).

O'Neill, Barry, *Honor, Symbols, and War.* (Ann Arbor: University of Michigan Press, 1999).

Oren, Ido, "Is Culture Independent of National Security? How America's National Security Concerns Shaped 'Political Culture' Research," *European Journal of International Relations,* **6,** 4 (2000).

 Our Enemy and US: America's Rivalries and the Making of Political Science. (Ithaca, NY: Cornell University Press, 2002).

Orlik, Ol'ga V., *Rossiya v mezhdunarodnykh otnosheniyakh: Ot Venskogo kongressa do Adrianopol'skogo mira.* (Moskva: Mezhdunarodnyye otnosheniya, 1998).

Overy, Richard/ *War and Economy in the Third Reich.* (New York: Oxford University Press, 1994).

Ozhegov, S. I., *Slovar' russkogo yazyka.* (Moscow: Nauka, 1990).

Oyewumi, Naumi. *The Invention of Women.* (Minneapolis: University of Minnesota Press, 1997).

Pangle, Thomas L. and Peter J. Ahrensdorf, *Justice among Nations: On the Moral Basis of Power and Peace.* (Lawrence: University Press of Kansas, 1999).

Perez-Rivas, Manuel, "U.S. Quits ABM Treaty," *CNN.com,* December 14, 2001, http://archives.cnn.com/2001/ALLPOLITICS/12/13/rec.bush.abm

Petro, Nicolai N., *The Rebirth of Russian Democracy: An Interpretation of Political Culture.* (Cambridge, MA: Harvard University Press, 1995).

 "Crisis in the Caucasus: A Unified Timeline," August 7–16, 2008, http://www.npetro.net/7.html

 Russian Foreign Policy, 2000–2011: From Nation-State to Global Risk Sharing. Bologna, PECOB's Papers Series, June 2011, #12.

Petrov, Nikolai, "The War in Iraq and the Myth of Putin," *Russia and Eurasia Review*, April 15, 2003, www.jamestown.org

Petrovich, Michael Boro, *The Emergence of Russian Panslavism, 1856–1870*. (New York: Columbia University Press, 1956).

Peuch, Jean-Christophe, "Russia, US Redistribute Pawns on Caucasus Chessboard after a Year of Change," *RFE/RL*, December 29, 2003.

"Georgia: Tensions Flare In Separatist Provinces," *RFE/RL*, August 5, 2004.

"Russia Weighs in as Fighting Continues in South Ossetia," *RFE/RL*, August 19, 2004.

Phillips, Hugh D., *Between the Revolution and the West: A Political Biography of Maxim M. Litvinov*. (Boulder: Westview Press, 1992).

Pikhoya, Rudol'f, *Moskva. Kreml'. Vlast'. Sorok let posle voyny*. (Moscow: Rus'-Olimp, 2007).

Pipes, Richard, "Is Russia Still an Enemy?" *Foreign Affairs*, September-October (1997).

Platonov, S. F., *Polnyi kurs lektsii po russkoi istoriyi*. (Petrozavodsk: Petrozavodski universitet, 1996).

Poe, Marshall T., *"A People Born to Slavery": Russia in Early Modern European Ethnography, 1476–1748*. (Ithaca, NY: Cornell University Press, 2000).

The Russian Moment in World History. (Princeton: Princeton University Press, 2003).

"Polls Suggests Russians Favor Tough Foreign Policy," *RFE/RL Newsline*, March 14, 2007.

Potemkin, V. P., ed., *Istoriya diplomatiyi*, vol. 1. (Moscow: OGIZ, 1945).

"The Potsdam Agreement on Germany," in: *The Origins of the Cold War, 1941–1947: A Historical Problem with Interpretations and Documents*, edited by Walter LaFeber. (New York: John Wiley & Sons, 1971).

"The President of Georgia Wins His Standoff in Adjaria," *The Economist*, May 6, 2004.

Presniakov, A. E., *Emperor Nicholas I of Russia: The Apogee of Autocracy, 1825–1855*. (Gulf Breeze, FL: Academic International Press, 1974).

Primakov, Yevgeni, Presentation at the Conference "Preobrazhennaya Rossiya," *Mezhdunarodnaya zhizn'* 3–4 (1992).

"The World on the Eve of the 21st Century," *International Affairs*, **42**, 5–6 (1996).

"Rossiya v mirovoi politike," *Mezhdunarodnaya zhizn'*, **5** (1998).

Gody v bol'shoi politike. (Moscow: Sovershenno sekretno, 1999).

Primakov, Ye. M., I. S. Ivanov, et al., eds., *Kantsler A. M. Gorchakov. K 200-letiyu so dnya rozhdeniya*. (Moscow: Mezhdunarodnyye otnosheniya, 1998).

Prokhanov, Aleksandr, "Ameriku potseloval angel smerti," *Zavtra*, September 18, 2001.

Puryear, Vernon J., "New Light on the Origins of the Crimean War," in: *Origins of the Crimean War*, edited by Brison D. Gooch. (Lexington, MA: Heath and Co, 1969).

Pushkarev, S. G., *Obzor russkoi istoriyi*. (Moscow: Knizhnaya palata, 1991).

Pushkov, Aleksei, "Otrezvlyayuschaya yasnost,' *Nezavisimaya gazeta*, March 1999.

"Sindrom Chernomyrdina," *Nezavisimaya gazeta*, June 11, 1999.

Putin, Vladimir, "Rossiya na rubezhe tysyacheletiy," *Nezavisimaya gazeta*, December 31, 1999.

"Vystupleniye na soveschaniyi 'O perspektivakh razvitiya Dal'nego Vostoka i Zabaikalya'," Blagoveschensk, July 21, 2000, www.kremlin.ru

"Vystupleniye na rasshirennom soveschaniyi s uchastiyem poslov Rossiyskoi Federatsiyi v MID Rosiyi," July 12, 2002, www.kremlin.ru

"*Poslaniye Federal'nomu Sobraniyu Rossiyskoy Federatsiyi*," May 16, 2003, www.kremlin.ru

"*Poslaniye Federal'nomu Sobraniyu Rossiyskoy Federatsiyi*," April 25, 2005, www.kremlin.ru

"Poslaniye Federal'nomu Sobraniyu Rossiyskoy Federatsiyi," May 10, 2006, www.kremlin.ru

Speech at the Munich Conference on Security Policy, Munich, February 10, 2007, www.kremlin.ru

"*Poslaniye Federal'nomu Sobraniyu Rossiyskoy Federatsiyi*," April 26, 2007, www.kremlin.ru

"Putin Policy Shift Is Bold but Risky," *Financial Times Survey*, April 15, 2002.

Putnam, Robert D., "Diplomacy and Domestic Politics: The Logic of Two-Level Games." *International Organization*, 42, 2 (1988).

Raack, Richard C., *Stalin's Drive to the West, 1938–1945: The Origins of the Cold War*. (Stanford: Stanford University Press, 1995).

Radzinski, Edward, *Aleksandr II: Zhizn' i smert'*. (Moscow: AST, 2007).

Ragsdale, Hugh, "Introduction: The Traditions of Imperial Russian Foreign Policy – Problems of the Present, Agenda for the Future," in: *Imperial Russian Foreign Policy*, edited by Hugh Ragsdale. (Cambridge: Cambridge University Press, 1993).

"Russian Projects of Conquest in the Eighteenth Century," in *Imperial Russian Foreign Policy*, edited by Hugh Ragsdale. (Cambridge: Cambridge University Press, 1993).

The Russian Tragedy: The Burden of History. (Armonk, NY: M. E. Sharpe, 1996).

"Russian Foreign Policy, 1763–1815," in: *The Transformation of European Politics, 1763–1815: Episode or Model in Modern History?* edited by Peter Kruger and Paul W. Schroeder. (Munster, Germany, 2002).

The Soviets, the Munich Crisis, and the Coming of World War II. (Cambridge: Cambridge University Press, 2004).

Remarks by the President and Russian President Putin, The White House, Office of the Press-Secretary, September 27, 2003, http://www.whitehouse.gov/news/releases/2003/09/20030927-2.html

Rendall, Matthew, "Russia, the Concert of Europe, and Greece, 1821–1829: A Test of Hypotheses about the Vienna System," *Security Studies*, 9 (2000).

"Defensive Realism and the Concert of Europe," *Review of International Studies*, 32 (2006).

Reus-Smit, Christian, *The Moral Purpose of the State: Culture, Social Identity, and Institutional Rationality in International Relations*. (Princeton: Princeton University Press, 1999).

Riasanovsky, Nicholas V., *Russia and the West in the Teaching of the Slavophiles: A Study of Romantic Ideology*. (Cambridge: Cambridge University Press, 1952).

Nicholas I and Official Nationality in Russia, 1825–1855. (Berkeley, CA: University of California Press, 1959).

A History of Russia, 4th ed. (New York: Oxford University Press, 1984).

The Image of Peter the Great in Russian History and Thought. (New York: Oxford University Press, 1985).

Rich, Norman, *Why the Crimean War? A Cautionary Tale*. (Hanover, NH: Dartmouth University Press, 1985).

Richter, James, *Khrushchev's Double Bind: International Pressures and Domestic Coalition Politics*. (Baltimore: John Hopkins University Press, 1994).

Rieber, Alfred J., "The Politics of Imperialism," in: *The Politics of Autocracy: Letters of Alexander II to Prince A. I. Bariatinskii, 1857–1864*, edited by Alfred J. Rieber. (Paris: Mouton, 1966).

"Persistent Factors in Russian Foreign Policy," in: *Imperial Russian Foreign Policy*, edited by Hugh Ragsdale. (Cambridge: Cambridge University Press, 1993).

Ringman, Eric, "The Recognition Game: Soviet Russia against the West," *Cooperation and Conflict*, **37**, 2 (2002).

Roberts, Geoffrey, *The Unholy Alliance: Stalin's Pact with Hitler*. (Blumington: Indiana University Press, 1989).

The Soviet Union and the Origins of the Second World War: Russo-German Relations and the Road to War, 1933–1941. (New York: St. Martin's Press, 1995).

The Soviet Union in World Politics: Coexistence, Revolution and Cold War, 1945–1991. (London: Routledge, 1999).

Stalin's Wars: From World War to Cold War, 1939–1953. (New Haven, CT: Yale University Press, 2006).

Roberts, J. M., *A History of Europe, 1880–1945*. (New York: Longman, 1997).

Rohan, Brian, "Saakashvili 'Planned S. Ossetia Invasion': Ex-Minister." *Reuters*, September 15, 2008.

Rose, Gideon, "Neoclassical Realism and Theories of Foreign Policy," *World Politics*, **51**, 1 (1998).

Rose, Richard, "How Floating Parties Frustrate Democratic Accountability," in: *Contemporary Russian Politics*, edited by Archie Brown. (Oxford: Oxford University Press, 2001).

"Rossiyani podderzhivayut sozdaniye soyuza RF i SshA v bor'be s mezhdunarodnym terrorizmom," *Nega-Set*, November 18, 2001.

"Rossiya vyvela Gruziyu na sebya," *Kommersant*, September 8, 2008.

Royle, Trevor, *Crimea: The Great Crimean War, 1854–1856*. (New York: St. Martin's Press, 2000).

"Russians Positive on China's Foreign Policy, Economic Model, Negative on US Policies, Bush But Russians Give American Democracy High Marks," *World Public Opinion.org*, May 30, 2006, at <http://www.worldpublicopinion.org>

"Russia Turns from Debtor into Creditor Country- Medvedev," *Itar-Tass*, January 27, 2007.

"Russia Is Most Attractive Emerging Economy for Investors," *Kommersant*, February 14, 2008.

"Russia's Economy under Vladimir Putin: Achievements and Failures," *RIA Novosti*, March 1, 2008.

"Russia Again Vows to Block NATO Enlargement," *RFE/RL Newsline*, April 9, 2008.

"Russians Negative About U.S., EU, Ukraine And Georgia As Never Before – Poll," *Interfax*, September 25, 2008.

Russia's Wrong Direction: What the United States Can and Should Do. (New York: Council on Foreign Relations, 2006).

Rutland, Peter, "Mission Impossible? The IMF and the Failure of the Narket Transition in Russia," *Review of International Studies*, **25**, (1999).

"Putin's Economic Record: Is the Oil Boom Sustainable?", *Europe-Asia Studies*, **60**, 6 (2008).

Saakashvili, Mikhail, "Saakashvili: Georgia Now A 'Model' Country," *Eurasianet.org*, February 11, 2005.

"Ya ne schitayu, chto kogo-to ubivat' – eto metod," *Kommersant*, February 27, 2006.

"Georgian Leader Warns Russia against Recognition of Breakaway Regions. Excerpt from report by Georgian TV station Rustavi-2," *BBC Monitoring*, October 10, 2007.

Said, Edward W., *Culture and Imperialism*. (New York: Alfred A. Knopf, 1993).

Sakwa, Richard, *The Rise and Fall of the Soviet Union, 1917–1991*. (London: Routledge, 1999).

Russian Politics and Society, 3d ed. (London: Routledge, 2002).

Sakwa, Richard, ed. *Chechnya: From Past to Future*. (London: Pluto, 2005).

Samuelson, Lennart, *Plans for Stalin's War Machine: Tukhachevskii and Military-Economic Planning, 1925–1941*. (London: Macmillan Press, 2000).

Saurette, Paul, "You Dissin Me? Humiliation and Post 9/11 Global Politics," *Review of International Studies*, **32** (2006), 495–522.

Sazonov, Sergei D., *Vospominaniya*. (Minsk: Kharvest, 2002).

Schimmelpenninck Van Der Oye, David, *Toward the Rising Sun: Russian Ideologies of Empire and the Path to War with Japan*. (DeKalb, IL: Northern University of Illinois Press, 2001).

Schroeder, Paul W., "The Secretary of War (Stimson) to President Truman, September 11, 1945," in: *The Origins of the Cold War, 1941–1947: A Historical Problem with Interpretations and Documents*, edited by Walter LaFeber. (New York: John Wiley & Sons, 1971).

Austria, Great Britain, and the Crimean War: The Destruction of the European Concert. (Ithaca, NY: Cornell University Press, 1972).

The Transformation of European Politics, 1763–1848. (Oxford: Oxford University Press, 1994).

Shakleyina, Tatyana, ed., *Vneshnyaya politika i bezopasnost' sovremennoi Rossiyi*, vol. 4. (Moscow: ROSSPEN, 2002).

Shapiro, Leonard, "Soviet Foreign Policy – 1928–1939," in: *Russia and the West from Peter to Khrushchev*, edited by L. Jay Oliva. (Boston: D. C. Heath, 1965).

Sheinis, Z., *Maksim Maksimovich Litvinov: revolutsioner, diplomat, chelovek*. (Moscow: Politizdat, 1989).

Sherr, James, "The Implications of the Russia-Georgia War for European Security," in: *The Guns of August 2008: Russia's War in Georgia*, edited by Svante E. Cornell and Frederick Starr. (New York: M. E. Sharpe, 2009).

Shulman, Marshall D., *Stalin's Foreign Policy Reappraised*. (Cambridge, MD: Harvard University Press, 1963).

Seton-Watson, Hugh, *The Decline of Imperial Russia, 1855–1914*. (New York: Frederick A. Praeger, 1956).

The Russian Empire, 1801–1917. (Oxford: Oxford University Press, 1967).

Seton-Watson, R. W., "The Origins of the Crimean War," in: *Origins of the Crimean War*, edited by Brison D. Gooch. (Lexington, MA: Heath and Co, 1969).

Simes, Dimitri K., *After the Collapse: Russia Seeks Its Place as a Great Power*. (New York: Simon & Schuster, 1999).

Sipols, V. Ya, *Sovetski Soyuz v bor'be za mir i bezopasnost', 1933–1939*. Moscow: Mysl', 1974.

Slantchev, Branislav L., "Territory and Commitment: The Concert of Europe as Self-Enforcing Equilibrium," *Security Studies*, **14**, (2005).

Slevin, Peter and Peter Baker, "Bush Changing Views on Putin," *Washington Post*, December 14, 2003.

Smith, Graham, *Post-Soviet States: Mapping the Politics of Transition*. (London: Arnold, 1999).

Smith, Martin A., *Russia and NATO since 1991: From Cold War through Cold Peace to Partnership?* (London: Routledge, 2006).

Snyder, Jack, *The Ideology of the Offensive: Military Decision Making and the Disaster of 1914*. (Ithaca, NY: Cornell University Press, 1984).

"Science and Sovietology: Bridging the Methods Gap in Soviet Foreign Policy Studies," *World Politics*, **40**, 2 (1988).

"International Leverage on Soviet Domestic Change," *World Politics*, **42**, 1 (1989).

Myths of Empire: Domestic Politics and International Ambition. (Ithaca, NY: Cornell University Press, 1991).

Socor, Vladimir, "Georgia under Growing Russian Pressure ahead of Bush-Putin Summit," *Russian and Eurasia Review*, February 15, 2005, www.jamestown.org

Solonevich, I. L., *Narodnaya monarkhiya*. (Moscow: Feniks, 2003).

Sorensen, Georg, "The Case for Combining Material Forces and Ideas in the Study of IR," *European Journal of International Relations*, **14**, 1 (2008).

"Soviet Capabilities and Intentions," *National Intelligence Estimate*, November 15, 1950.

Sperling, J., S. Kay, and S. V. Papacosma, eds., *Limiting Institutions? The Challenge of Eurasian Security Governance*. (Manchester: Manchester University Press, 2003).

Splidsboel-Hansen, Flemming, "Past and Future Meet: Aleksandr Gorchakov and Russian Foreign Policy," *Europe-Asia Studies*, **54**, 3 (2002).

Spruyt, Hendrik, "Stalin's Analysis of Victory," in: *A Documentary History of Communism*, edited by Robert V. Daniels, vol. 2 (New York, Vintage Books, 1960), 142.

Sovereign State and Its Competitors. (Princeton, NJ: Princeton University Press, 1994).

"Stalin's 'Two Camps' Speech, 9 February 1946," in: *The Rise and Fall of the Soviet Union, 1917–1991*, edited by Richard Sakwa (London: Routledge, 1999).

Stalin, I. V., *Voprosy leninizma*, 11th ed. (Moscow: OGIZ, 1947).

"O pobede sotializma v odnoi strane i mirovoi revolutsiyi," in: *Sistemnaya istoriya mezhdunarodnykh otnosheniy, 1918–2000*, edited by A. D. Bogaturov, vol. 2. (Moscow: Moskovski rabochi, 2000).

"On the Tasks of Workers in the Economy," in: *The Structure of the Soviet History: Essays and Documents*, edited by Ronald Grigor Suny. (New York: Oxford University Press, 2003).

Stalin, Josef, "Churchill's Speech Is a Call for War on Russia," in: *The Origins of the Cold War, 1941–1947: A Historical Problem with Interpretations and Documents*, edited by Walter LaFeber. (New York: John Wiley & Sons, 1971).

Steinberg, Blema S., "Shame and Humiliation in the Cuban Missile Crisis," *Political Psychology*, **12**, 4 (1991), 653–90.

Stewart, Frank Henderson, *Honor.* (Chicago: University of Chicago Press, 1994).

Stockdale, Melissa Kirschke, *Paul Miliukov and the Quest for a Liberal Russia, 1880–1918.* (Ithaca, NY: Cornell University Press, 1996).

Stone, David R., *Hammer and Rifle: The Militarization of the Soviet Union, 1926–1933.* (Lawrence: University Press of Kansas, 2000).

Strategiya dlia Rossiyi: Povestka dlya prezidenta – 2000. (Moscow: Sovet po vneshney i oboronnoi politike, 2000).

Suny, Ronald Grigor, *The Soviet Experiment: Russia, the USSR, and the Successor States.* (New York: Oxford University Press, 1998).

Why We Hate You: The Passions of National Identity and Ethnic Violence. (Berkeley: University of California, Program in Soviet and Post-Soviet Studies, 2004).

Suny, Ronald and Michael Kennedy, eds., *Intellectuals and the Articulation of the Nation.* (Ann Arbor: University of Michigan Press, 1999).

Suvorov, Victor, *Icebreaker: Who Started the Second World War.* (London: Viking, 1990).

Tarle, E. V., "Diplomatiya v godu Krymskoi voiny i Parizhski kongress (1853–1856 gg.)," in: *Istoriya diplomatiyi*, edited by V. P. Potemkin, vol. 1. (Moscow: OGIZ, 1945).

"Napoleon III i Yevropa," in: *Istoriya diplomatiyi*, edited by V. P. Potemkin, vol. 1. (Moscow: OGIZ, 1945).

"Ot revolutstiyi 1848 g. do nachala Krymskoi voiny (1848–1853 gg.)," in: *Istoriya diplomatiyi*, edited by V. P. Potemkin, vol. 1. (Moscow: OGIZ, 1945).

"Ot iyul'skoi revolutstiyi vo Frantsiyi do revolutsionnykh perevorotov v Yevrope 1848 g.," in: *Istoriya diplomatiyi*, edited by V. P. Potemkin, vol. 1. (Moscow: OGIZ, 1945).

Krymskaya voina, 2nd ed., vol. 1. (Moscow: Nauka, 1950).

1812 god. (Moscow: Izdatel'stvo akademiyi nauk, 1961).

"Tblisi-Moskva: Lyubov' S Chistovo Litsa," *BBC Russian* January 11, 2008.

Taylor, A. J. P., *The Struggle for Mastery in Europe, 1848-1918.* (Oxford: Oxford University Press, 1954).

The Origins of the Second World War. (New York, Simon & Schuster, 1996).

Tchourikova, Natalia and Kathleen Moore, "Georgia: Burdjanadze Seeks Support In Row with Moscow," *RFE/RL*, October 10, 2006.

"Threats to the Security of the United States," *Central Intelligence Agency*, September 28, 1948.

Temperley, H.W.V., "Responsibilities for the Crimean War," in: *Origins of the Crimean War*, edited by Brison D. Gooch. (Lexington, MA: Heath and Co, 1969).

Text of Joint Declaration, The White House, Office of the Press Secretary, May 24, 2002, http://www.whitehouse.gov/news/releases/2002/05/20020524-2. html

Timasheff, Nicholas S., "World Revolution or Russia," in: *The Structure of the Soviet History: Essays and Documents*, edited by Ronald Grigor Suny. (New York: Oxford University Press, 2003).

Tolz, Vera. *Russia.* (London: Arnold, 2001).

Trachtenberg, Marc, *History and Strategy.* (Princeton: Princeton University Press, 1991).

A Constructed Peace: The Making of the European Settlement, 1945-1963. (Princeton: Princeton University Press, 1999).

Trenin, Dmitri, *Getting Russia Right.* (Washington, DC: Carnegie Endowment for International Peace, 2007).

Post-Imperium: A Eurasian Story. (Washington, DC: Carnegie Endowment for International Peace, 2011).

Troitskiy, Nikolai, *Aleksandr I protiv Napoleona.* (Moscow: Eksmo, 2007).

Trubetskoi, Yevgeni, *Iz proshlogo. Vospominaniya. Iz putevykh zametok bezhentsa.* (Tomsk: Vodolei, 2000).

Truman, Harry S., "The Truman Doctrine (March 12, 1947)," in: *The Origins of the Cold War, 1941-1947: A Historical Problem with Interpretations and Documents*, edited by Walter LaFeber. (New York: John Wiley & Sons, 1971).

Tsimbayev, N. I., *Slavyanofil'stvo: Iz istoriyi russkoi obschestvenno-politicheskoi mysli XIX veka.* (Moscow: MGU, 1986).

Tsygankov, Andrei P., *Whose World Order: Russia's Perception of American Ideas after the Cold War.* (South Bend, IN: University of Notre Dame Press, 2004).

"Vladimir Putin's Vision of Russia as a Normal Great Power," *Post-Soviet Affairs* **21**, 2 (2005).

"If Not by Tanks, then by Banks? The Role of Soft Power in Putin's Foreign Policy," *Europe-Asia Studies*, **58**, 7 (2006).

"Finding a Civilizational Idea: 'West', "Eurasia' and 'Euro-East' in Russia's Foreign Policy," *Geopolitics*, **12** (2007).

"Russia's International Assertiveness: What Does It Mean for the West?" *Problems of Post-Communism*, **55**, 1 (2008).

"Self and Other in International Relations Theory: Learning from Russian Civilizational Debates," *International Studies Review*, **10**, 4 (2008).

Russophobia: Anti-Russian Lobby and American Foreign Policy. (New York: Palgrave, 2009).

"Russia in the Post-Western World: The End of the Normalization Paradigm?" *Post-Soviet Affairs* **25**, 4 (2009).

Russia's Foreign Policy: Change and Continuity in National Identity. Second edition. (Lanham, MD: Rowman & Littlefield, 2010).

Tsygankov, Andrei P. and Matthew Tarver-Wahlquist, "Dueling Honors: Power, Identity and the Russia-Georgia Divide," *Foreign Policy Analysis*, **5**, 4 (2009).

Tsyganok, Anatoly, "On the Consequences of Georgia's NATO Entry," *Fondsk.ru*, January 2, 2008, http://www.fondsk.ru/article.php?id=1148

Tucker, Robert C., *Stalin as a Revolutionary, 1879–1929: A Study in History and Personality.* (New York: W. W. Norton & Company, 1973).

"The Emergence of Stalin's Foreign Policy," *Slavic Review*, **36** (1977).

Political Culture and Leadership in Soviet Russia: From Lenin to Gorbachev. (Brighton: Wheatsheaf Books, 1987).

Stalin in Power: The Revolution from Above, 1928–1941. (New York: W. W. Norton & Company, 1992).

Tuminez, Astrid S., *Russian Nationalism since 1856: Ideology and the Making of Foreign Policy.* (Lanham, MD: Rowman & Littlefield, 2000).

Ulam, Adam B., *Expansion and Coexistence: Soviet Foreign Policy, 1917–1973*, 2nd ed. (New York: Praeger, 1974).

Uldricks, Teddy J., "Debating the Role of Russia in the Origins of the Second World War," in: *The Origins of the Second World War Reconsidered: A. J. P. Taylor and the Historians*, edited by Gordon Martel, 2nd ed. (London: Routledge, 2006).

"Unprovoked Onslaught," *Wall Street Journal*, October 12, 2006.

Uribes-Sanches, E., "Rossiyskoiye obschestvo i vneshnyaya politika," in: *Istoriya vneshnei politiki Rossiyi. Konets XIX – nachalo XX veka*, edited by A. V. Ignatyev. (Moscow: Mezhdunarodnyye otnosheniya, 1999).

"US Embassy Denies American Experts Probe Ground for NMD in Georgia," *Itar-Tass*. September 26, 2007.

"United States Objectives with Respect to Russia," *National Security Council Report*, August 18, 1948.

"U.S. Objectives with Respect to the USSR to Counter Soviet Threats to U.S. Security," *National Security Council Report*, November 2, 1948.

Utkin, Anatoli, *Zabytaya tragediya: Rossiya v pervoi mirovoi voine.* (Smolensk: Rusich, 2000).

Vyzov Zapada i otvet Rossiyi. (Moscow: Logos, 2002).

Valuyev, P. A., *Dnevnik Ministra vnutrennikh del.* (Moscow: Nauka, 1961).

Van Evera, Stephen, *Causes of War: Power and the Roots of Conflict.* (Ithaca, NY: Cornell University Press, 1999).

Vasquez, John A., "The Vienna System: Why It Worked and Why It Broke Down," in: *The Transformation of European Politics, 1763–1815": Episode or Model in Modern History?* edited by Peter Kruger and Paul W. Shroeder. (Munster, Germany: Lit Verlag, 2002).

Vekhi: Sbornik statei. (Moscow: Molodaya gvardiya, 1991).

Vercuil, Julien, "Opening Russia? Contemporary Foreign Trade," *Russian and Eurasia Review*, **2**, 4 (February 18, 2003, www.jamestown.org)

Vernadsky, George, *A History of Russia.* (New Haven, CT: Yale University Press, 1930).

Vert, Nikola, *Istoriya sovetskogo gosudarstva, 1900–1991.* (Moscow: Progress, 1992).

Vinogradov, V. N., "The Personal Responsibility of Emperor Nicholas I for the Coming of the Crimean War: An Episode in the Diplomatic Struggle in the Eastern Question," in: *Imperial Russian Foreign Policy*, edited by Hugh Ragsdale. (Cambridge: Cambridge University Press, 1993).

"Gorchakov u rulya vneshnei politiki Rossiyi," in: *Kantsler A. M. Gorchakov. K 200-letiyu so dnya rozhdeniya*, edited by Ye. M. Primakov, I. S. Ivanov, et al. (Moscow: Mezhdunarodnyye otnosheniya, 1998).

Vitalis, Robert, "The Graceful and Generous Liberal Gesture: Making Racism Invisible in American International Relations," *Millennium*, **29** (2000).

Walicki, Andrzej, *A History of Russian Thought from Enlightenment to Marxism.* (Stanford: Stanford University Press, 1979).

Wallace, Henry, "The Tougher We Get, the Tougher the Russians Will Get (September 12, 1946)," in: *The Origins of the Cold War, 1941–1947: A Historical Problem with Interpretations and Documents*, edited by Walter LaFeber. (New York: John Wiley & Sons, 1971).

Walt, Stephen, *Origins of Alliances.* (Ithaca, NY: Cornell University Press, 1987).

Waltz, Kenneth, *Theory of International Politics.* (Reading, MA: Addison-Wesley, 1979).

Webber, Mark. *CIS Integration Trends: Russia and the Former Soviet South.* (London: Royal Institute of International Affairs, 1997).

Wendt, Alexander, *Social Theory of International Politics.* (Cambridge: Cambridge University Press, 1999).

Wettig, Gerhard. *Stalin and the Cold War in Europe: The Emergence and Development of East-West Conflict, 1939–1953.* (Lanham, MD: Rowman & Littlefield, 2007).

Wetzel, David. *The Crimean War: A Diplomatic History.* (New York: Columbia University Press, 1985).

What the World Thinks in 2002. Washington, DC: Pew Research Center for the People and the Press, December 4, 2002.

Wiarda, Howard J., "The Ethnocentrism of the Social Science. Implications for Research and Policy," *Review of Politics*, **43** (1981).

Wight, Martin, *International Theory: The Three Traditions.* (New York: Holmes & Meier, 1992).

Williams, Michael C., *The Realist Tradition and the Limits of International Relations.* (Cambridge: Cambridge University Press, 2005).

Wines, Michael, "NATO Plan Offers Russia Equal Voice on Some Policies," *New York Times*, November 23, 2001.

Witte, Sergei Yu, *Izbrannyye vospominaniya 1849–1911*. (Moscow: Mysl', 1991).

Wohlforth, William C., "The Perception of Power: Russia in the Pre-1914 Balance," *World Politics*, **34**, 3 (1987).

   The Elusive Balance: Power and Perception during the Cold War. (Ithaca, NY: Cornell University Press, 1993).

   "Honor as Interest in Russian Decisions for War, 1600–1995," in: *Honor among Nations: Intangible Interests and Foreign Policy*, edited by Elliot Abrams. (Washington, DC: Ethics and Public Policy Center, 1998).

   "Honor as Interest and "A Test of Neorealism," *Review of International Studies*, **27** (2001).

   "Russia," in: *Strategic Asia 2002–03: Asian Aftershocks*, edited by Richard J. Ellings and Aaron L. Friedberg. (Washington, DC: The National Bureau of Asian Research, 2003).

   "Heartland Dreams: Russian Geopolitics and Foreign Policy, in: *Perspectives on the Russian State in Transition*, edited by Wolfgang Danspeckgruber. (Princeton: Liechtenstein Institute on Self-Determination at Princeton University, 2006).

   "Unipolarity, Status Competition, and Great Power War," *World Politics*, **61**, 1 (2009).

Wolfe, Alan, *Whose Keeper? Social Science and Moral Obligation*. (Berkeley: University of California Press, 1989).

Wolfers, Arnold, *Discord and Collaboration: Essays on International Politics*. (Washington, DC: Johns Hopkins University Press, 1965).

Yakunin, Vladimir, "The West Shouldn't Humiliate Us," *Der Spiegel Online*, October 10, 2007, available at *Johnson Russia List* 2007–214, October 11, 2007.

Yanov, Alexander, *The Russian Challenge and the Year 2000*. (Oxford: Oxford University Press, 1987).

Yemelyanova, Galina, "Islam in Russia: An Historical Perspective," in: *Islam in Post-Soviet Russia*, edited by Hilary Pilkington and Galina Yemelyanova. (London: Routledge, 2003).

Young, Alasdair, "Perspectives on the Changing Global Distribution of Power: Concepts and Context, in: *Perspectives on the Changing Global Balance of Power*, edited by Alasdair Young, Jane Duckett, and Paul Graham, *Politics*, 30, 4 (2010).

Zagladin, N. V., *Istoriya uspekhov i neudach sovetskoi diplomatiyi*. (Moscow: Mezhdunarodnyye otnosheniya, 1990).

Zaichonkovsky, A. M., *Vostochnaya voina, 1853–1856*, vol. 2, part 1. (St. Petersburg: Poligon, 2002).

Zakaria, Fareed, *The Post-American World*. (New York: Norton, 2008).

Zenkovsky, Serge, "The Russian Church Shism," in: *Readings in Russian Civilization, Volume I, Russia before Peter the Great, 900–1700*, 2nd ed., edited by Thomas Riha. (Chicago: Chicago University Press, 1969).

Zevelev, Igor. "Zhdanov on the Founding of the Cominform," in: *Russia and the West from Peter to Khrushchev*, edited by L. Jay Oliva. (Boston: D.C. Heath, 1965).

Russia and Its New Diaspora. (Washington, DC: United States Institute of Peace, 2001).

Zimmerman, William. *The Russian People and Foreign Policy: Russian Elite and Mass Perspectives, 1993–2000.* (Princeton: Princeton University Press, 2002).

Zubok, Vladislav M., *A Failed Empire: The Soviet Union in the Cold War from Stalin to Gorbachev.* (Chapel Hill: University of North Carolina, 2009).

Zubok, Vladislav M. and Constantine Pleshakov, *Inside the Kremlin's Cold War: From Stalin to Khrushchev.* (Cambridge, MA: Harvard University Press, 1996).

Zyuganov, Gennadi, *Geografiya pobedy.* (Moscow, 1998).

Index

Abashidze, Aslan, 238
Abkhazia, 35, 37–45, 248, 250–4
absolutism, 29, 36
Abyssinia, 100, 103, 108
the Adjara crisis, 236
Afghanistan, 1, 4, 34, 48, 50, 118–21, 123,
    126, 176, 178
    See also Taliban
Africa, 180, 271
agreement with France, (1891), 78–9, 82,
    84
agreement with France, (1892), 78, 80,
    82
Aksakov, Ivan, 147, 206
Aksakov, Konstantin, 206–7
Al Qaida, 121–2
Ali, Mehemed, 196, 200
alliance with France, (1894), 79–80, 82
Alexander I, 42, 68, 203, 223, 259
    and European liberals, 68–9
    internal reforms, 69–70
    and support for conservative Europe, 42,
        67, 70–1
    vision of Holy Alliance, 68–9
    See also Holy Alliance
Alexander II, v, 42, 137, 167, 181
    and the Great Reforms, 145–6, 148
    See also Recueillement
Alexander III, 43, 79
Alliance in Vienna, (1815), 69
alliance of oligarchs and *chekists*, 132n20
Alsace and Lorraine, 142
antiballistic missile (ABM) treaty, 119–20,
    122–3, 127, 130
Archduke Francis Ferdinand, 81, 83
Aristotle, 21
Armenia, 182, 251
arms control, 43
    See nuclear weapons
Aron, Raymond, 16, 19, 25n30
Asia, 1, 32–3, 47, 80, 92, 173, 180–1, 187,
    213n51, 228–30, 253, 261, 271

assertiveness, i, vii, x, 3, 6, 9, 40–1, 44,
    46–50, 52–5, 195–211, 216–32,
    236–55, 260, 262–3, 269, 272
    growing domestic strength, 4–6, 46,
        52–3, 57, 205–7, 225–7, 247–8,
        265
    and national interest, 7–8, 49, 55, 248
    and security, 5–7, 48, 54, 196, 209, 219,
        224, 229, 230–2, 241–2, 244, 247–8,
        251–2, 265–6
    record of, 6, 49–50, 209–11, 230–2,
        253–5, 266
    worldview, 3–4, 46–9, 197–9, 223–5,
        244–6, 262–63
    See also Crimean War; Cold War;
        revisionism; revisionist behavior;
        Russia-Georgia War; Russia's
        cooperation with the West
Astrakhan, 46
Athenians, 14
Austerlitz, 63
Austria, 41–2, 50, 63, 65, 67, 69, 74,
    81–4, 87, 89–92, 102–3, 110, 137–44,
    146, 148, 156, 158, 197, 199–201,
    205, 207, 209, 211, 261–3
Austria's occupation of Bosnia and
    Herzegovina, 78, 81–2, 148
Austro-Hungary, 2, 42
autocracy, 30, 32–3, 36, 37, 71, 74, 84,
    146, 264–5
autonomy, 22, 31, 35, 49, 53, 68, 86, 175,
    187
Azerbaijan, 176, 182
Azov, 47, 195

backwardness of Russia, 33, 42, 45, 107,
    129, 166
Baku-Ceyhan oil pipeline, 238
the Balkans, 4, 6, 42, 44, 46–7, 56, 69,
    72–3, 78, 81–3, 85, 90–2, 119, 138–9,
    144–7, 149, 168, 172–5, 181, 196–7,
    200–2, 216–7, 220, 223–4, 261, 269

305

316   Index

Truman, Harry S., 217–8, 220–2, 224, 227–8, 234n84, 235n92
Tskhinvali, 241
Tucker, Robert C., 165
Tukhachevski, Mikhail, 101, 103, 107–8, 159
Turkey, 3, 34, 45, 47, 50, 65–8, 81, 89, 91, 109, 122, 139, 146–7, 149, 156, 176, 195–202, 204–5, 207, 210–1, 222, 269
Turkmenistan, 178, 182, 187
21st century great powers, 269–74
    established powers, 270–1
    recovering power, 270, 272–3
    rising powers, 270, 271–2
    See also great power; power
Tyutchev, Fyodor, 146–7, 152n79, 206

Ukraine, 3, 45–6, 123–4, 130, 133, 140, 156, 178–9, 182, 187, 226, 242, 244–6, 266
    annexed by Russia, 3, 45
    See also Orange Revolution; NATO and Ukraine
unipolarity, 128, 132n32, 176, 181, 188, 190n29, 246
United Nations (UN), 1, 48, 121–2, 177, 186, 221, 272
United Nations Security Council (UNSC), 1, 121, 186, 219, 241, 272
United States, ix, 1, 4, 18, 43–4, 46, 48, 53, 56, 109, 118–23, 125–31, 158, 161, 174, 176, 179–81, 185–6, 188, 190, 216–21, 223–9, 231, 236, 243–6, 248–50, 252, 254, 257n37, 260, 263, 266, 270, 272–3
    See also early Cold War; unipolarity; NATO; Russia-Georgia War; September 11, 2001; war on terror
Uvarov, Sergei, 71
Uzbekistan, 182

values:
    autocratic values, 42, 130, 260
    change of, 53, 264
    communist values, 104
    core values, 4–5, 7
    democratic values, 35, 46–7
    European values, 65, 68, 124
    distinctive values, 36, 44, 266
    defense and promotion of, 45, 205, 245, 265, 270–1
    dynastic values, 29
    geopolitical values, 182
    moral values, 28

shared values, 72, 74, 77n77
values of free economy and society, 23
values of sovereignty, 131n15
Western values, 180
See also Christian values; honor
Varga, Yevgeni, 163, 234n74
velvet revolutions
Versailles Treaty, (1918), 97, 101, 158, 232
the Vienna Concert, 143
the Vienna Congress, 63, 66, 68
the Vienna system, 63–4, 73–4, 195, 197, 210
Vietnam, 27n66
Vladivostok, 10, 248
Voikov, Pyort, 163

The Wall Street Journal, 119
Wallace, Henry, 228
War Minister Sukhomlinov, 85, 88, 92
war with Japan, 50, 56, 78, 80, 85, 87–8, 95n73
war on terror, (2001–2005), vii, 3, 8, 50, 57, 118–31, 132n26
    assessment of, 129–31
    domestic support of, 125–7
    and Chechnya, 121, 126
    key events of, 123
    and offensive realism, 128
    and opposition to the Iraq war, 120–2
    and partnership with the U.S., 118–23
    vision of, 124–5
    See Putin
war with Turkey, (1828–1829), 50, 66
Warsaw Pact, 50
Weber, Max, 20, 131
West
    See European Union; international recognition; Russia's relations with the West; United States; Western civilization
Western civilization, 35, 51, 53, 129, 180
Western distrust, 109
Westernizers, 70, 185, 206, 214n68, 214n69, 214n74, 261
Wight, Martin, 16
William, Frederick, 69
William I of Austria, 139
William II, 82, 93
Witte, Sergei, 47, 85, 88, 91–2, 94n26, 95n73
Wohlforth, William, v, 17, 25n40, 116n89, 208, 226
the world revolution, 4, 43, 47, 50, 97, 104, 155–6, 164, 167–8, 262

73069948R00180

Made in the USA
Columbia, SC
02 September 2019